Simplicius

On Aristotle Physics 1.1–2

Ancient Commentators on Aristotle

GENERAL EDITORS: Richard Sorabji, Honorary Fellow, Wolfson College, University of Oxford, and Emeritus Professor, King's College London, UK; and Michael Griffin, Associate Professor, Departments of Philosophy and Classics, University of British Columbia, Canada.

This prestigious series translates the extant ancient Greek philosophical commentaries on Aristotle. Written mostly between 200 and 600 AD, the works represent the classroom teaching of the Aristotelian and Neoplatonic schools in a crucial period during which pagan and Christian thought were reacting to each other. The translation in each volume is accompanied by an introduction, comprehensive commentary notes, bibliography, glossary of translated terms and a subject index. Making these key philosophical works accessible to the modern scholar, this series fills an important gap in the history of European thought.

A webpage for the Ancient Commentators Project is maintained at ancientcommentators.org.uk and readers are encouraged to consult the site for details about the series as well as for addenda and corrigenda to published volumes.

Simplicius

On Aristotle Physics 1.1–2

Translated by
Stephen Menn

BLOOMSBURY ACADEMIC
LONDON • NEW YORK • OXFORD • NEW DELHI • SYDNEY

BLOOMSBURY ACADEMIC
Bloomsbury Publishing Plc
50 Bedford Square, London, WC1B 3DP, UK
1385 Broadway, New York, NY 10018, USA
29 Earlsfort Terrace, Dublin 2, Ireland

BLOOMSBURY, BLOOMSBURY ACADEMIC and the Diana logo are trademarks of
Bloomsbury Publishing Plc

First published in Great Britain 2022
This paperback edition published 2024

Copyright © Stephen Menn, 2022

Stephen Menn has asserted his right under the Copyright, Designs and Patents Act, 1988,
to be identified as Author of this work.

For legal purposes the Acknowledgements on p. viii constitute
an extension of this copyright page.

Cover design: Terry Woodley

All rights reserved. No part of this publication may be reproduced or transmitted
in any form or by any means, electronic or mechanical, including photocopying,
recording, or any information storage or retrieval system, without prior permission
in writing from the publishers.

Bloomsbury Publishing Plc does not have any control over, or responsibility for,
any third-party websites referred to or in this book. All internet addresses given
in this book were correct at the time of going to press. The author and publisher
regret any inconvenience caused if addresses have changed or sites have ceased
to exist, but can accept no responsibility for any such changes.

A catalogue record for this book is available from the British Library.

Library of Congress Cataloging-in-Publication Data

Names: Simplicius, of Cilicia, author. | Menn, Stephen Philip, 1964-translator.
Title: On Aristotle Physics 1.1-2 / Simplicius; translated by Stephen Menn.
Other titles: Commentarii in octo Aristotelis Physicae auscultationis
libros. 1.1-2. English | Simplicius on Aristotle Physics 1.1-2
Description: New York: Bloomsbury Academic, 2022. | Series: Ancient
commentators on Aristotle | Includes bibliographical references and index.
Identifiers: LCCN 2021052139 | ISBN 9781350285682 (hardback) |
ISBN 9781350285729 (paperback) | ISBN 9781350285699 (ebook) |
ISBN 9781350285705 (epub) | ISBN 9781350285712
Subjects: LCSH: Aristotle. Physics. | Aristotle. Physics. Book 1. |
Physics–Early works to 1800. | Nature–Early works to 1800.
Classification: LCC Q151.A8 S51713 2022 | DDC 530–dc23/eng/20211223
LC record available at https://lccn.loc.gov/2021052139

ISBN: HB: 978-1-3502-8568-2
PB: 978-1-3502-8572-9
ePDF: 978-1-3502-8569-9
eBook: 978-1-3502-8570-5

Series: Ancient Commentators on Aristotle

Typeset by RefineCatch Limited, Bungay, Suffolk

To find out more about our authors and books visit www.bloomsbury.com
and sign up for our newsletters.

Acknowledgements

The present translations have been made possible by generous and imaginative funding from the following sources: the National Endowment for the Humanities, Divison of Research Programs, an independent federal agency of the USA; the Leverhulme Trust; the British Academy; the Jowett Copyright Trustees; the Royal Society (UK); Centro Internazionale A. Beltrame di Storia dello Spazio e del Tempo (Padua); Mario Mignucci; Liverpool University; the Leventis Foundation; the Arts and Humanities Research Council; Gresham College; the Esmée Fairbairn Charitable Trust; the Henry Brown Trust; Mr and Mrs N. Egon; the Netherlands Organisation for Scientific Research (NOW/GW); the Ashdown Trust; the Lorne Thyssen Research Fund for Ancient World Topics at Wolfson College, Oxford; Dr Victoria Solomonides, the Cultural Attaché of the Greek Embassy in London; and the Social Sciences and Humanities Research Council of Canada. The editors wish to thank Fabio Acerbi, Christoph Helmig, Henry Mendell, the late Ian Mueller, and Robert Wardy for their comments; Dawn Sellars for preparing the volume for press; and Alice Wright, Commissioning Editor at Bloomsbury Academic, for her diligence in seeing each volume of the series to press.

Contents

Conventions	vi
Abbreviations	vii
Acknowledgements	viii
Principal Philosophers and Mathematicians Discussed	1
Editors' Preface	5
Note on Text and Translation	25
Translation	37
Notes	153
Bibliography	207
English–Greek Glossary	211
Greek–English Index	227
Index of Names	249
Index of Subjects	255

Conventions

[...]   Square brackets enclose words or phrases that have been added to the translation for purposes of clarity. The only exception to this is where square brackets appear at the start of a paragraph. Here, the words or phrases enclosed and printed in italics are a summary by the translators of what follows in Simplicius' text.

(...)   Round brackets, besides being used for ordinary parentheses, contain transliterated Greek words.

<...>   Angle brackets enclose conjectures relating to the Greek text, i.e. additions to the transmitted text deriving from parallel sources and editorial conjecture, and transposition of words or phrases. Accompanying notes provide further details.

†   An obelus marks a corrupt text for which no convincing solution has been found.

Abbreviations

References beginning with 'A' or 'B' (e.g. A15, B12) are to texts in the relevant chapter of DK.

Bekker	Immanuel Bekker, *Aristoteles Graece*, 2 vols (Berlin: Reimer, 1831)
CAG	*Commentaria in Aristotelem Graeca*
DG	*Doxographi Graeci*, ed. Hermann Diels (Berlin: Reimer, 1879)
Diels	Hermann Diels, ed., *Simplicii in Aristotelis Physicorum Libros Quattuor Priores Commentaria*, *CAG* 9 (Berlin: Reimer, 1882)
DK	Hermann Diels and Walther Kranz, eds, *Die Fragmente der Vorsokratiker*, 6th edn, 3 vols (Berlin: Weidmann, 1952)
FHS&G	W. W. Fortenbaugh, Pamela Huby, Robert Sharples, and Dimitri Gutas, eds, *Theophrastus of Eresus: Sources for his Life, Writings, Thought, and Influence*, 2 vols (Leiden: Brill, 1992–3)
LSJ	H. G. Liddell, R. Scott, and H. S. Jones, *Greek–English Lexicon*, 9th edn (Oxford: Oxford University Press, 1940)
MXG	*On Melissus, Xenophanes, Gorgias* (Ps.-Aristotle)
OCT	Oxford Classical Text
Phys. Dox.	*Physicorum opiniones* (Theophrastus), in *DG*, 475–95
Ross	W. D. Ross, *Aristotle's Physics: A Revised Text with Introduction and Commentary* (Oxford: Clarendon Press, 1936)
SVF	*Stoicorum Veterum Fragmenta*, ed. H. von Arnim, 3 vols (Leipzig: Teubner, 1903–5)

Acknowledgements

This translation of Simplicius' commentary on Aristotle's *Physics* 1.1-2 was originally planned, and begun, as joint work with Rachel Barney. Rachel unfortunately had to withdraw from the project, and I finished it on my own and take full responsibility for the final product, but it would never have happened without Rachel, and I thank her first and foremost, for her work and initiative and for many hours of puzzling through the text of Simplicius together, trying to reconstruct his meaning and argument and to think of an English approximation. I produced the initial draft of each section of the translation, and then Rachel and I revised it together, except in the mathematical section, which is entirely my work; I then revised the entire draft. The endnotes to the translation are joint work; Rachel composed the paragraph-summaries at the head of each paragraph of Simplicius, some of which we later jointly revised. The reports of manuscript Mo are mine.

Roberto Granieri prepared the extremely helpful first draft of the Greek–English Index, which allowed me to see inconsistencies in the translation, and he also gave me a series of notes on translation issues arising from the Index. Henry Mendell generously supplied the diagrams in the mathematical section, as well as giving detailed comments on the translation of that section.

For comments on parts or all of the translation Rachel and I would like to thank our vetters (Fabio Acerbi, Christoph Helmig, Henry Mendell, the late Ian Mueller, Tim Wagner [in an unofficial role], and Robert Wardy), and Pantelis Golitsis, Roberto Granieri, the graduate student participants (Nicholas Aubin, Argyro Lithari, Robert Roreitner) in a workshop in Berlin in July 2017 on commentaries from the school of Ammonius, and Richard Sorabji. I thank Pantelis also for advice about the manuscripts of Simplicius, and for an early draft of his edition of roughly the first third of Simplicius' commentary on *Physics* 1.1-2, although unfortunately I saw it too late to make systematic use of it.

I thank the Aristoteles-Archiv of the Freie Universität Berlin for giving me access to microfilms of the manuscripts, and the Berlin Graduiertenkolleg 'Philosophy, Science and the Sciences', based at the Humboldt-Universität Berlin, for supporting the workshop in July 2017. Support from the Alexander-von-

Acknowledgements ix

Humboldt Stiftung, the Graduiertenkolleg 'Philosophy, Science and the Sciences', and a James McGill Professorship at McGill University, gave me some time free from teaching and the opportunity to work in an ideal research environment in Berlin. Thanks to support from Brad Inwood's and then Rachel Barney's Canada Research Chairs at the University of Toronto, Rachel and I were able to work together for short periods of time in Toronto, Montreal and Berlin, and to employ Roberto Granieri to prepare the first draft of the Greek–English Index.

Finally, I thank Michael Griffin and Dawn Sellars for their help in preparing the manuscript and advising on editorial issues, and Cristalle Watson for providing the line-numbering and the English–Greek Glossary.

Principal Philosophers and Mathematicians Discussed

Early Greek philosophers

Thales of Miletus, 6th century BCE

Anaximander of Miletus, 6th century BCE

Anaximenes of Miletus, 6th century BCE

Xenophanes of Colophon, 6th century BCE

Hippasus of Metapontum, 6th–5th century BCE Pythagorean

Heraclitus of Ephesus, 6th–5th century BCE

Parmenides of Elea, 6th–5th century BCE

Melissus of Samos, 5th century BCE

Zeno of Elea, 5th century BCE student of Parmenides

Anaxagoras of Clazomenae, 5th century BCE

Empedocles of Acragas, 5th century BCE

Leucippus of Abdera, 5th century BCE

Democritus of Abdera, 5th century BCE, student of Leucippus

Diogenes of Apollonia, 5th century BCE

Hippo, 5th century BCE

Archelaus of Athens, 5th century BCE, student of Anaxagoras and teacher of Socrates

Antiphon of Athens, 5th century BCE

Gorgias of Leontini, 5th–early-4th century BCE

Lycophron, 5th–4th century BCE

Socrates of Athens, 5th century BCE

Menedemus of Eretria, 5th–4th century BCE, student of Socrates

Archytas of Tarentum, 5th–4th century BCE, Pythagorean (some genuine, some spurious texts)

Timaeus of Locri, fictional 5th century BCE Pythagorean

Plato of Athens, 5th–4th century BCE, student of Socrates, founder of Academy in Athens

2   *Principal Philosophers and Mathematicians Discussed*

Speusippus of Athens, 4th century BCE, nephew, student, and successor of Plato

Xenocrates of Chalcedon, 4th century BCE, successor of Speusippus as head of the Academy

Aristotle of Stagira, 4th century BCE, student of Plato, founder of Peripatetic School in Athens

Theophrastus of Eresus, 4th–3rd century BCE, Peripatetic, student and successor of Aristotle

Eudemus of Rhodes, 4th–3rd century BCE, Peripatetic, student of Aristotle

Mathematicians

Hippocrates of Chios, late-5th century BCE

Euclid, early-3rd century BCE

Archimedes of Syracuse, 3rd century BCE

Nicomedes, 3rd century BCE

Apollonius of Perga, late-3rd century BCE

Nicomachus of Gerasa, 1st–2nd century CE, mathematician and neo-Pythagorean philosopher

Eutocius, 6th century CE, commentator on mathematical texts, active in Alexandria

Later Greek philosophers and commentators

Andronicus of Rhodes, 1st century BCE, Peripatetic

Nicolaus of Damascus, 1st century BCE, Peripatetic

Plutarch of Chaironeia, 1st–2nd century CE, Platonist

Atticus, 2nd century CE, Platonist

Adrastus of Aphrodisias, 1st–2nd century CE, Peripatetic

Aspasius, 2nd century CE, Peripatetic

Alexander of Aphrodisias, 2nd–3rd century CE, Peripatetic, chairholder in Athens

Ammonius Saccas, early-3rd century CE, Platonist, teacher of Plotinus in Alexandria

Plotinus of Lycopolis, mid-3rd century CE, Platonist, taught in Rome

Longinus, mid-3rd century CE, Platonist, taught in Athens, adviser to Zenobia of Palmyra

Porphyry of Tyre, late-3rd century CE, Platonist, student of Longinus and then of Plotinus

Iamblichus of Chalcis, 3rd–4th century CE, Platonist, rebellious student of Porphyry

Themistius, 4th century CE, Peripatetic, active in Constantinople

The Athenian and Alexandrian Platonist schools of the 5th-6th centuries CE

Syrianus, 4th–5th century CE, Platonist, chairholder in Athens

Proclus of Lycia, 5th century CE, Platonist, student of Syrianus, chairholder in Athens

Hermias, 5th century CE, Platonist, student of Syrianus, taught in Alexandria

Ammonius, 5th–6th century CE, Platonist, son of Hermias, student of Proclus, chairholder in Alexandria

Olympiodorus, 6th century CE, Platonist, student and second successor of Ammonius

Damascius, 6th century CE, Platonist, last chairholder in Athens

Simplicius of Cilicia, 6th century CE, Platonist, student of Ammonius and Damascius

Priscian of Lydia, 6th century CE, Platonist, active in Athens

John Philoponus, 6th century CE, Christian, active in Alexandria

Editors' Preface

Michael Griffin and Richard Sorabji

With Stephen Menn's translation of *Simplicius On Aristotle Physics 1.1-2*, the Ancient Commentators on Aristotle series has published a complete English version of Simplicius' commentary on Aristotle's *Physics* in twelve volumes.[1] We do not know how long Simplicius took to write his commentary, which occupies more than half a million words in Greek; but its English counterpart has involved more than fifteen translators working across three decades, with the international collaboration of dozens of scholars and students. We want to take this opportunity to reiterate our gratitude to every colleague who has contributed to this enterprise. We are also grateful to our generous funders, listed in the Acknowledgements to this volume, who have made the project possible, and to our publishers, first at Duckworth and now at Bloomsbury, who have seen each translation to press with diligence and patience.

Simplicius' comments on the first two chapters of Aristotle's *Physics* are the last to be rendered into English. They are also among the most complex, because they lay the methodological and philosophical foundations for the entire work. In introducing them, Professor Menn has surveyed the complete translation by many hands. He explains Simplicius' interpretation of Aristotelian natural science, his motives and methods for writing Aristotelian commentaries, and his reasons for copying extensive verbal quotations from otherwise lost sources, like the Presocratic philosophers. Menn also engages in a novel way with the commentary's many exegetical, philosophical, and mathematical difficulties, and offers new textual readings, based on an autopsy of manuscripts, including a witness unknown to Diels, the editor of the currently standard text.

Menn's book-length introduction amounts to a significant new monograph on Simplicius' commentary as a whole, including a close study of 1.1-2 in particular. In light of its length and scope, we have agreed with Bloomsbury's proposal to print this text separately as a *General Introduction*, preceding the final instalment of the translation itself. In addition, we offer here a shorter overview of the work and Menn's central conclusions.

6 *Editors' Preface*

We note to the reader that § 4 of Menn's *Introduction* (and our summary) focus specifically on the content of this translation, Simplicius' discussion of *Physics* 1.1-2. The mathematical stretch of the translation (53,30-69,34) is annotated to support the reader, who is especially encouraged to consult the endnotes in this section. Consultation of Menn's detailed discussion in the *Introduction* (§ 4.5) will be helpful for deeper study (see below, pp. 20–1).

The following remarks briefly introduce *Simplicius On Physics 1.1-2*. We also aim to survey the main conclusions of Stephen Menn's *Introduction*, printed separately. Any errors, however, are our own. Our section headings correspond to those in Menn, and the reader is encouraged to consult the *Introduction* for further discussion and supporting arguments; references to 'Menn' followed by a number are to page numbers in that volume.

1. Simplicius' life and work

Simplicius was a philosopher from Cilicia, located in what is now southern Turkey, who lived from *c.* 480–560 CE. This was a period of social and political transformation in the eastern Mediterranean world, dominated by Justinian I's attempt to renovate the Roman Empire.[2] Modern convention would designate Simplicius a pagan and a Neoplatonist, although he would not likely endorse either label.[3] Early in his life, Simplicius studied under Ammonius, who taught philosophy from the public chair at Alexandria. Later, Simplicius became a junior colleague of Damascius, the last Platonic scholarch in Athens. Damascius was a brilliant and inventive metaphysician, and Simplicius' extant works display evidence of his efforts to balance the views and methods of both his mentors. As Menn emphasizes in his *Introduction*, Simplicius passionately defends aspects of his teachers' pagan philosophy against John Philoponus (*c.* 490–570 CE), a committed Christian who also became Aristotle's most sophisticated late antique critic. This defence, as we shall see, also guided Simplicius' approach to interpreting Aristotle's *On the Heaven* and *Physics*.

In 529 CE, Justinian I issued an edict that is broadly construed as a ban on pagan teaching. The Platonist school in Athens closed, and Damascius guided a community of seven philosophers, including Simplicius, to the court of the Persian king Chosroes I (according to Agathias, *Hist.* 2.30-31). Here they took refuge until Chosroes arranged for their safety in the 'Perpetual Peace' treaty of 532. It is unclear where they went next and how they lived, although the conventional reading of Agathias' testimony is that the philosophers were blocked from teaching publicly. Alan Cameron has argued that they returned to Athens and did teach; Michel Tardieu and Ilsetraut Hadot that they went to Harran; Pantelis Golitsis that they returned each to their home cities (see Menn 122).

At different stages during his eventful life, Simplicius found time to write voluminously. We have three substantial Aristotelian commentaries by him, in addition to his treatment of the *Handbook of Epictetus* by Arrian,[4] and several misattributed works. As Menn explains (2–3), it is possible to date the Aristotelian commentaries relative to one another. The commentary *On the Physics* refers to the commentary on *On the Heaven* (e.g., 1117,15-1118,11), while the commentary *On the Categories* refers to the commentary *On the Physics* (435,20-24): so the sequence of composition was presumably *On the Heaven – Physics – Categories*. Philippe Hoffmann has proposed that Simplicius began the commentary on *On the Heaven* under Damascius' mentorship, and composed the *Physics* commentary after Damascius' life.[5]

'The last great pagan-Christian polemic of Greek antiquity' looms large over the first two commentaries (Menn 1). John Philoponus had brilliantly denied the Aristotelian doctrines of the eternity of the world and the incorruptibility of the heavenly bodies, citing Plato as his ally. In response, Simplicius carefully elucidated and defended Aristotle, and displayed the 'harmony' of the ancients. There is considerable debate about Simplicius' intended audience: these commentaries are not, at least directly, intended for oral lectures. Pantelis Golitsis has suggested that Simplicius writes for Alexandrian teachers who could draw on his commentaries in their lectures, much as Olympiodorus and Philoponus draw on Damascius' commentaries.[6]

2. Simplicius' philosophical aims in his commentaries on Aristotle's *Physics* and *On the Heaven*

Simplicius' commentary on the *Physics* contains a great deal of value to historians and philosophers. Famously, it is a pivotal witness for otherwise lost material: Simplicius verbally quotes many Presocratics, like Parmenides, at length, and is the sole or fullest source for many of their fragments. In addition, he gives us essential reports about philosophers like Alexander, Porphyry, Eudemus and Theophrastus, and the early mathematician Hippocrates of Chios. Simplicius' extended quotations are no accident, but part of his positive project, as Menn underscores: he aims to rehabilitate earlier thinkers, or correct misinterpretations of them, by showing what they actually said.

To understand Simplicius' motives in commenting on Aristotle's *Physics*, as Menn shows, we have first to understand his motives in commenting on Aristotle's *On the Heaven*. Simplicius wrote this earlier commentary in order to defend the harmony of Aristotle with Plato, and specifically the implicit agreement of *On the Heaven* with Plato's *Timaeus*. To a modern reader, this may seem like a strange and even quixotic enterprise. But proving the compatibility of Aristotle with Plato was an important project for late ancient Platonist philosophers,[7] and in this case, it has a specific target. Simplicius sometimes refers obliquely to those who 'are accustomed to take pride in the apparent contradictions (*hai dokousai . . . enantiologiai*) of the ancients (*hoi palaioi*)' (e.g. *in Phys.* 640,12-18), a familiar characterization by Christian critics of pagan philosophers who appear to disagree among themselves. John Philoponus was such a critic, specifically of Aristotelian physics. Simplicius wants to demonstrate that Philoponus is not only wrong to attack Aristotle's view, but also wrong to suppose that Plato is his ally against Aristotle (Menn 6).

Which philosophical issues were most at stake in Simplicius' attempt to 'harmonize' Aristotelian natural science with Plato? Centrally, Plato's *Timaeus* appears to describe a creation of the cosmos at a definite temporal point in the past, whereas Aristotle argues in *On the Heaven* that the cosmos has always existed. Moreover, the *Timaeus* posts four elementary bodies (earth, water, air, and fire) where Aristotle posits a fifth body (aether). And Aristotle appears to reject – or at least offers no explicit support for – the sort of entity that the Demiurge of Plato's *Timaeus* was often taken to be: an incorporeal Reason that is also an efficient cause. Throughout antiquity, philosophers who defended Plato, Aristotle, or both, were obliged to offer some account of these differences.

In the second section of his *Introduction*, Menn develops a helpful map of the exegetical terrain that evolved between two extreme poles of this debate. The boundary cases were 'extreme Platonists', like Atticus, who assert that Plato is correct about these issues against Aristotle; and 'extreme Aristotelians', like Alexander, who maintain that Aristotle is correct about these issues against Plato. Between them is the ground held by 'moderate Platonists' who are also 'moderate Aristotelians' (Menn 5–7). One of these is Simplicius. Simplicius maintains that the *Timaeus* and *On the Heaven* are right about their respective theses. He argues that Aristotle is reacting, not against Plato *rightly understood*, but against a superficial and 'extremist' interpretation of Plato. On this 'extremist' view, Plato's Demiurge is an efficient cause that begins to act at a certain moment in time. In addition, the heavens are made from the same burning, destructive fire that we encounter in the sublunary world, so that a soul must constrain them against their nature to move in perfect circles. Earlier Neoplatonists, like Proclus, had been chiefly concerned to save Plato *rightly understood* against Aristotle. Simplicius is also concerned to save Aristotle, and to deny Philoponus' 'extremist' interpretation of Plato. For on Simplicius' view, only a superficially read *Timaeus* could lend support to Christian cosmogony, particularly to the thesis that the cosmos is temporally created and corruptible.

Simplicius maintains that Aristotle does not deny Plato's real doctrine, but only Plato's 'apparent' meaning (*to phainomenon*; compare Syrianus, *in Metaph.* 171,9-20, with Menn 6–7). Plato is prepared to use the *language* of temporal creation, but he *means* to describe an eternal process. And as Simplicius puts it elsewhere, the good interpreter should 'not convict the philosophers of discord by looking only to the letter (*lexis*) of what Aristotle says against Plato ... but must look toward the spirit (*nous*), and track down (*ankhineuein*) the harmony that reigns between them on the majority of points' (*in Cat.* 7,23-9, tr. after Chase 2003). As a second example, Plato is more willing than Aristotle to deploy names drawn from ordinary experience, like 'fire', to describe transcendent things, like aether; but Aristotle knows that 'most people's imaginations are easily carried away by names', so Aristotle uses a different name, 'fifth substance', 'in order that we should put forth conceptions of it as of something entirely transcending the things here' (*in Cael.* 87,1-17; see Menn 7). Throughout, Simplicius wants to show that Aristotle tells the truth, and that his criticism of 'Plato' is directed against a mistaken interpretation of Plato.

This strategy governs Simplicius' 'harmonization' of Aristotle and Plato throughout his commentary on *On the Heaven*. As Menn argues (8), it was a natural next step for Simplicius to turn to the underlying framework of Aristotle's *Physics*, where Aristotle sets out more fundamental reasons to believe that motion has no origin in time but has an eternally unmoved cause, now relying not on empirical cosmological assumptions but (as Simplicius maintains) on explicit analysis of natural principles (*archai*), like form and matter, and their concomitants, like place and time. In fact, as Menn emphasizes (9), Simplicius thinks that Aristotle actually surpasses Plato in one respect, by treating physics in distinction from first philosophy (metaphysics or theology), and by addressing natural body itself and in its own right (*in Phys.* 7,27-34). So Aristotle addresses 'the fundamental concepts presupposed by cosmology rather than treating them incidentally as they come up in cosmology itself' (Menn 36). Simplicius even

10   *Editors' Preface*

calls Aristotle 'divine' (*theios*, e.g. *in Phys.* 611,8; *in Cael.* 87,26-28), and is the only
Neoplatonist to do so.[8]

3. Simplicius' methods of commentary and use of earlier commentators

Why should we attend closely to *how* Simplicius practises commentary? First,
Simplicius' conception of philosophy is deeply intertwined with his exegetical
practices: for example, he believes that investigating and resolving problems
arising from philosophical texts can give rise to 'beautiful theorems' for
philosophical contemplation (*in Cat.* 2,1-2). Second, the modern philosopher's
interpretation of Simplicius' quotations from lost texts hinges on our sensitivity
to how he engages with his sources. The third section of Menn's *Introduction*
offers an invaluable treatment of the anatomy of Simplicius' treatment of his
predecessors, the sequence of his sources, precedents in earlier genres, and how
he positions his own views. We attempt to summarize several of Menn's central
conclusions here.

First, it is possible to track a reasonably consistent pattern in Simplicius'
commentary on a lemma (stretch of Aristotelian text), with room for variation
in individual cases (Menn 10). Typically, (a) Simplicius summarizes the general
thought of the lemma; (b) he reviews problems or puzzles that arise from it
(frequently objections to its prima facie meaning); (c) he offers solutions to these
puzzles, which draw extensively on earlier commentators and authors; and (d)
he offers observations (*epistaseis*), pointing out features of the text not adequately
explained by earlier interpretations, and then states his own preferred solution,
frequently introduced by the word *mêpote*, which can be translated 'perhaps', in
order to do justice to these observations (Menn 26–32). In stages (b) and (c)
especially, we can observe how Simplicius 'wraps' his commentary around
earlier commentators; in the case of the *Physics* commentary, these predecessors
are typically Alexander and Porphyry, and Simplicius' summary of the issues
usually follows Alexander. Simplicius' detailed quotation of other authors,
including the Presocratics, is often motivated in stage (c) by his project of solving
problems and objections.

The following subsections outline (1) Simplicius' use of earlier commentators,
(2) his relationship to the earlier philosophical genres of commentary, problems,
and monograph treatise, (3) his sequence of sources and sequential procedure
for consulting his library, and (4) his introduction of original material.

3.1 Simplicius' use of earlier commentators

On the *Physics*, Simplicius consults three earlier commentators regularly: Alexander of Aphrodisias (late 2nd–early 3rd centuries CE); Porphyry of Tyre (*c.* 234–*c.* 305 CE); and the paraphrase by the philosopher and orator Themistius (317–*c.* 388 CE) (Menn 11–14). He also relies on the oral lectures of his own teacher Ammonius (cf. 59,23-31), and cites others like Syrianus.[9] Alexander is Simplicius' usual point of departure, or 'default' interpretation; he considers Alexander 'the most genuine of Aristotle's interpreters' (80,15-16; 258,16-17), and sometimes prefers Alexander to Porphyry, even though Simplicius himself is closer ideologically to Porphyry. In particular, he criticizes Alexander's representation of Aristotle as *really* disagreeing with Plato, which motivates a number of Simplicius' detailed investigations.

Since Diels, interesting arguments have been offered that Simplicius' commentary is really an 'expurgated' version of Alexander's: in other words, he mainly follows Alexander, but deletes or explains away cases where Alexander supports the disagreement of Aristotle with Plato. In favour of these arguments, we might cite Simplicius' apparent suppression of Alexander's name in a view that he offers in his own voice (13,16-21; 14,13-19). Menn discusses this issue in detail, and proposes that the reality is more complex, partly on the grounds that Simplicius' commentary is likely much longer than Alexander's, and not all of his interventions 'against' Alexander are motivated by defending Plato or another precursor (14). Menn proposes to see Simplicius' commentary not as an expurgated version of Alexander's, but as a metacommentary on Alexander's commentary, raising problems against the text as Alexander interprets it, and solving them by proposing new interpretations of the text. Although Alexander's commentary on the *Physics* is lost, Marwan Rashed has edited significant scholia to the *Physics* that he argues are extracted directly from Alexander, and Menn supports Rashed's conclusions (11, n. 24); compared carefully, these scholia can also help us to understand Simplicius' procedure in using Alexander's commentary.

3.2 Commentaries, problems and monographs

As Menn shows, Simplicius' procedures can be explained in light of the origins of the genres he adopts, including commentaries, problems and monographic treatises that go back to the Hellenistic grammarians and Homeric scholarship; some of the relevant scholarly procedures are already illustrated in Plato

12 *Editors' Preface*

(*Protagoras* 338E-347B), and by Hellenistic grammarians' projects of rescuing Homer from the appearance of internal inconsistency. Philosophical treatises that investigate and resolve 'problems' are common in late antiquity, and Menn helpfully compares Plotinus' treatises, viewed as extended monographs motivated by problems that arise from reading, particularly from reading Plato or Aristotle. A 'commentary' might contain many monographs along these lines; Simplicius' 'Corollaries' on Place and Time, included in his commentary on *Physics* 4, are good examples, alongside various minor essays on issues like matter, nature, and chance (Menn 17).[10] In this context, we can read Simplicius' response to Philoponus' critique of *Physics* 8 within a long philosophical tradition of raising and solving problems. Specifically, a 'problem' arises for Simplicius when Aristotle seems to contradict Plato directly or implicitly; Alexander's interpretation often introduces or emphasizes such contradictions.

3.3 Simplicius' sequence of sources

What can we say about how Simplicius actually consulted his sources? Menn draws a threefold distinction between (a) earlier texts to which Simplicius has direct access, and which he always consults (in the *Physics*, this includes Alexander, Porphyry on Books 1–4, Themistius, and the *Physics* of Eudemus of Rhodes except on Book 7); (b) earlier texts to which Simplicius has direct access, and which he consults only when there is a particular reason in a particular passage that leads him to look them up (in the *Physics*, this includes at least Theophrastus, many of the Presocratics, Plotinus, Damascius, and Philoponus); and (c) texts to which Simplicius has only indirect access (including, for example, Andronicus, Aspasius, Nicolaus of Damascus, Hippocrates of Chios, and Democritus) (Menn 19–26).

In this section of the *Introduction*, Menn describes a plausible procedure. (1) When a problem arises and Alexander's interpretation seems dissatisfying, Simplicius turns next to Porphyry and Themistius, and explores their differences as a source of new puzzles. (2) Next, he turns to early Peripatetic texts (that is, to Aristotle's near successors): in particular to Eudemus, whom Simplicius frequently prefers to Alexander, and to Aristotle's successor Theophrastus (*c.* 371–*c.* 287 BCE). (3) Third, Simplicius turns to pre-Peripatetic sources, mainly those cited but (on Simplicius' view) often *misinterpreted* by the Peripatetics; these mainly include Plato and the Presocratic philosophers. In this latter project, Simplicius is especially motivated to 'save' the Eleatics, Anaxagoras, and Empedocles; but more broadly, he wants to show that all the best earlier

Editors' Preface

philosophers can be harmonized. The ancients may be saying different things, but not *contrary* things (Menn 25–6): and we can discover this by comparing their views as shedding light on different aspects of their topic (see *in Phys.* 36,15-20; and compare Aristotle's own position at *Metaph.* 2.1).

3.4 Simplicius' introduction of original material

After he has outlined earlier commentators' positions, Simplicius often uses the Greek word *epistasis* and its cognates[11] to signpost his own remarks, calling our attention (*prosekhein*) to a place where we, the text's readers, ought to 'pause' and take notice. Simplicius thinks that attending to these features of the text, which earlier commentators have rushed by too quickly, will give us the basis for a more adequate interpretation and allow us to resolve the difficulties.

Most characteristically, as Diels already recognized, Simplicius introduces his own view (typically based on his observations or *epistaseis*, but going beyond them in conjecturing a solution) by the Greek word *mêpote*, loosely translatable as 'perhaps'. This will usually follow Simplicius' *epistaseis* and his rejection of earlier solutions to the problems that he has identified. Menn stresses that the 'epistemic modesty' implicit in *mêpote* is genuine (29). It is likely elliptical for a construction like *ei mê pote*, as if to say: 'all of the solutions offered so far are open to objections, *unless perhaps* . . .' (cf. *in Phys.* 59,16). Sometimes this usage introduces Simplicius' climactic solution to a major problem, or sometimes there are many 'small *mêpotes*'. Attending to Simplicius' usage in this way illustrates his commitment to problem-solving as philosophizing: again, discussing problems can give rise to 'beautiful theorems' for contemplation (cf. *in Cat.* 2,1-2).

In concluding this section, Menn observes with a summary of Simplicius' understanding of his own project in these commentaries (32):

> [Simplicius'] main concerns in the commentaries on the *Physics* and *On the Heaven* are to show how Aristotelian scientific arguments work, to defend the 'pious conception of the universe' (and thus the right conception of the relations between the demiurgic *nous*, the heavens and the sublunar world), and to harmonize Aristotle with Plato (and with the Eleatics and Pythagoreans and Anaxagoras and Empedocles, and everyone else while he is at it). But he also wants to take every occasion for investigation (*zêtêsis*), and to show how thinking through problems and objections to the text can lead us to glimpses of higher theorems, so that someone who turns to Simplicius' commentaries to help him understand Aristotle (and perhaps as an aid in teaching) might be inspired with a love for the higher Platonic mysteries.

14   *Editors' Preface*

4. Themes of Simplicius' commentary on *Physics* 1.1–2

Menn turns next to the contents of Simplicius' commentary on the opening two chapters of Aristotle's *Physics*, and to the present volume of translation. Although the spotlight of Simplicius' textual focus is now on *Physics* 1.1-2, his remarks involve a study of the project of the entire *Physics*, requiring 102 *CAG* pages to treat about one and a half Bekker pages of Aristotle.

As Menn explains (32–3), Simplicius reads our *Physics* 1.1 as Aristotle's proem outlining the programme for the entire *Physics*. The target of the work is to study the principles of natural things, and Book 1 especially addresses the *elements* of natural things. Next, *Physics* 1.2 introduces a critical survey of Presocratic accounts of such principles, focusing on a critical examination of the Eleatics Parmenides and Melissus. In this latter portion of the commentary, Simplicius' main concerns are to save the Eleatics from criticism, to prove that Aristotle is not criticizing Plato, and to prove that Aristotle follows Plato in his critical examination of the Eleatics (Menn 33).

4.1 Simplicius' Proem (1,3–8,30)

Before he addresses Aristotle's text, Simplicius' commentary opens with his own proem to the *Physics*. Following the standard protocol of late antique philosophical commentaries, he examines the object or target (*skopos*) of the work, its title, usefulness, order in the reading sequence, authenticity, and its division into parts. He also considers less standard topics, like the history of natural philosophy up to Aristotle, and the reason why a difficult and technically precise 'acroamatic'[12] work like the *Physics* demands a commentary. His overarching goal is to praise the text, motivate the reader, and show that, while the material is challenging, a commentary can help the reader to reap its rewards (see Menn 39).

The commentarial category of the 'target' or 'object' (*skopos*) of the book is a metaphor drawn from archery, which was already used by Aristotle in different contexts (*EE* 1.2, *EN* 1.2). It picks out 'what anything aims at'. The *skopos* of the *Physics*, according to Simplicius, is 'to teach concerning the things which belong in general to all natural things inasmuch as they are natural': and these general properties are *principles* (*arkhai*), like matter and form, and their *concomitants*, like place and time (*in Phys.* 3,13-18).

Menn helpfully sets out two core distinctions that Simplicius relies on in the ensuing discussion (36–7): (1) between principles and concomitants, and (2)

Editors' Preface   15

between principles that are *auxiliary causes* (*sunaitia*), including matter and immanent form, and principles that are *causes proper*, including efficient, final, and – omitted by Aristotle – paradigmatic causation. Through this latter division, Simplicius aims to vindicate Aristotle's physics against Proclus' worry that Aristotle studies only *auxiliary* causes and not true causes. Much of what Simplicius says here is drawn from Aristotle's own programmatic remarks at the outset of *Physics* 3, and applies in particular to *Physics* 1-4, four books that sometimes carried the label *On Principles* in antiquity.

As Menn shows, Simplicius makes a genuine effort to motivate the student to pursue natural science (4,25-5,26):

> Simplicius gives a surprisingly eloquent encomium of natural science: the knowledge of nature is useful for more practical sciences (medicine and mechanics), and it theoretically perfects the part of the rational soul that is not elevated enough to grasp divine things, but, beyond this, understanding the greatness of the cosmos and the smallness of our body and lifespan will lead us to higher, rationally perfected versions of all the moral virtues, courage and temperance and so on. (Menn 38–9)

4.2 Simplicius on Aristotle's proem, *Physics* 1.1

Next, Simplicius turns to a textual discussion of Aristotle's own 'proem' (8,32; 17,32), the stretch of text that we number *Physics* 1.1. Simplicius divides it into two subsections for commentary, aiming to show:

> (i) That we should determine the principles of natural things first in studying natural science (184a10-16).
> (ii) How we should go about determining these principles (184a16-b14).

(i) The first subsection or lemma is relatively unproblematic for Simplicius. But it invites a puzzle, already studied by Eudemus and Porphyry: in an Aristotelian framework, can any science discover and judge its own principles? Porphyry answered that natural philosophers take their principles from a 'higher' science, namely, first philosophy. But Simplicius' nuanced reply gives more agency to natural philosophers. They can demonstrate the principles of natural things, as the doctor can demonstrate that the human body is composed from four elements (but it is the natural philosopher's taxonomically 'higher' work to characterize the power of those elements). This sort of demonstration is not scientifically rigorous, but amounts to the 'recognition' (*gnôrizein*, a verb also used by Aristotle in this part of the text) that natural things have principles, and

16   *Editors' Preface*

what they are. Menn discusses many further points of interest in this section (40–52). Again, Simplicius stresses that Aristotle, in arguing against the Eleatics, is arguing against a superficial *interpretation* of their view (21,15-20). He also examines Aristotle's relative clause at 184a11, which seems to imply that some disciplines may *not* have principles *and* causes *and* elements. To avoid difficulties identified by earlier commentators, Simplicius offers a revisionary construal: 'of which the principles are either causes or elements', where he takes the elements of natural things, namely their matter and immanent form, to be auxiliary causes rather than true causes. And when Aristotle says that we know each thing 'when we recognize its first causes and first principles and as far as the elements', Simplicius takes this to mean not 'when we recognize its first causes and first principles, i.e. as far as the elements' but 'when we go both as far up as the highest causes and principles, and also as far down as the lowest, most proximate principles, namely the elements'.

(ii) The second subsection or lemma introduces a more significant worry. At 184a16-b14, Aristotle appears to imply that wholes (or universals) are better known to us and particulars are better known by nature, contradicting what he says elsewhere (*An. Post.* 1.2, *Metaph.* 1.2). This has troubled both ancient and modern commentators. Alexander proposed that Aristotle means that we should start from universals when we study natural science, and he points out that Aristotle seems to follow this procedure in practice (*Phys.* 1.7, 189b30-32); in particular, Alexander thinks Aristotle wants us to start from 'topic-neutral axioms' like the principles of non-contradiction and the excluded middle (Simplicius, *in Phys.* 17,25-31).

Simplicius' own solution to the conundrum is different, as Menn explains (48). Simplicius maintains that Aristotle must be talking about different *kinds* of universals in *Physics* 1.1 and *An. Post.* 1.2. In *Physics* 1.1, Aristotle wants us to start from a universal that causally depends on the principles, and can be compared to a whole compounded from the principles – not from a truth *about* the principles (19,33-20,2). This means that Aristotle wants us to reason from perceptible *effects* back to their *causes*. The background for Simplicius' solution is a Neoplatonic division, with roots in earlier commentators, of the universal or 'common' item (*to koinon*) into three kinds: (1) a one F before the many Fs, causing them in common (like the paradigmatic 'animal-itself' of Plato, *Timaeus* 30C2-31A1); (2) a one F in the many Fs, that is, the effect of the common cause, present in the many F things; and (3) a one F after the many Fs, a concept of F present in the rational soul, which has abstracted it from observing the many F things (see Simplicius, *in Cat.* 82,35-83,16). Simplicius' models for reasoning

Editors' Preface 17

from effects to principles are provided both by abstracted concepts in sense (3) above, which are better known to us but omit differences in the objects, and by confusedly perceived wholes. In either case we start from a crude overall grasp of an object, 'divide' it to discern its particulars or its constituent parts, and attain thereby a more precise grasp of the universal or the whole.

4.3 Simplicius on *Physics* 1.2: Views about the principles, division, and harmonization

Simplicius turns next to 1.2 (184b15-25), an analysis of opinions about the principles of natural things. Commentators differed about the procedure that Aristotle adopted here.[13] For Simplicius, Aristotle is not trying to provide an exhaustive taxonomy; he passes over some divisions that are theoretically possible (22,16-18), because, as Menn puts it, 'he is not interested in sections that no one has inhabited'. For Simplicius, this division is intended to help us *understand* the principles. As Menn explains (53–4):

> Simplicius adds a deeper investigation of these people's meanings, in order to show 'how the ancients, although appearing to disagree in their doctrines about the principles, nonetheless come together in harmony' (29,4-5). Simplicius thinks that this deeper investigation is important, not merely in order to do historical justice to past thinkers or to block Christian arguments from the disagreement of ancient authorities, but in order to assist the enquiry into the principles.

Aristotle and Simplicius will devote considerable time in this and following chapters to a study of the Eleatics. Unlike Alexander (see also § 4.4, below), Simplicius holds that Aristotle is always examining *real people*'s claims throughout this section – sometimes in their apparent meaning, but consistently with a view to clarifying their real intention. Thus Simplicius is not willing to accept that Aristotle's targets think something that is self-evidently ridiculous. Parmenides might well maintain that the *principle* of things is one and motionless, but he could never have maintained the absurd view that there is only one *thing*. Perhaps only one thing is *strictly* a being, but this is a principle of the many that come-to-be, and are objects of sensation and opinion.

More broadly, for Simplicius, when philosophers like Parmenides, Melissus, or Empedocles say that 'being(s) are F', they really mean to say that 'the principle(s) of beings are F'. But this is already a claim belonging to first philosophy (theology or metaphysics), not physics or natural philosophy. Unsurprisingly, Simplicius

18   *Editors' Preface*

thinks that Parmenides and Melissus are doing first philosophy. Perhaps more surprisingly, he thinks that many more Presocratic philosophers – including the Pythagoreans, Xenophanes, Empedocles, and Anaxagoras – draw some kind of distinction between first philosophy and natural philosophy, although many people miss this distinction because of its obscurity (21,14-19).

What should we make of Aristotle's refutation of the *apparent* absurdities, then, that there is only one thing, or that the cosmos is motionless? These arguments, for Simplicius, are directed against a common misunderstanding of the 'Parmenidean' position, not against the actual text of Parmenides himself (on which, see below). Beneficially, Aristotle forces us to make explicit the distinctions just mentioned, including the distinction between first philosophy and natural philosophy. And for Simplicius, this amounts to drawing a line between two different targets of discussion: roughly, distinguishing objects that are *intelligible* from objects that are *sensible*. Intelligible objects are available to Reason (*nous*), while sensible objects are available to sense-perception.

The intelligible–sensible distinction is a familiar commonplace of ancient Platonist metaphysics and epistemology. Its role as an exegetical instrument in addressing Aristotle's treatment of the Presocratics may be unexpected, but perhaps it is not entirely intrusive. Menn shows how it motivates Simplicius' extensive quotations from Parmenides (58–9). In particular, Simplicius claims that Parmenides' text, read carefully and verbally, illustrates Parmenides' recognition of what Platonists call the 'intelligible' (that is, Parmenides' Truth) and the 'sensible' (that is, Parmenides' Mortal Opinion) (30,14–16). Simplicius thinks his contemporaries take Aristotle to criticize Parmenides *himself* because of 'the current widespread ignorance of ancient writings' and uncritical reliance on doxography (39,20-21; Menn 59). He applies a similar model to Empedocles (31,18-32,1) and Anaxagoras (34), and for all these reasons, it is important to Simplicius to cite what they actually say.

4.4 Arguing against the Eleatics, the whole and parts puzzle, and 'later ancients'

In this section, Menn studies Simplicius' sustained engagement with Alexander, Porphyry, and Eudemus throughout his treatment of *Physics* 1.2 (and 1.3). Where Alexander thinks the Eleatics maintain that only one thing exists, Simplicius, as we have seen, insists that the Eleatics mean that one *principle* really exists. Aristotle is right (184b25-185a1) that the Eleatic claim belongs to first philosophy, but it introduces a puzzle about nature along the way, and the physicist or natural philosopher is obliged to reply (70,3-71,10). But how can the physicist respond to someone who denies the principles of physics? Not by scientific demonstration, but by relying on the *principles* of demonstration itself (49,23–50,4). Simplicius agrees with Alexander that the physicist's response can rely on 'topic-neutral axioms' like the Principle of Non-Contradiction, but Simplicius also thinks that the physicist's response can rely on sensation and induction. Aristotle, as Menn points out (66–7), might have been surprised to hear sensation and induction called 'principles of demonstration'; but Simplicius notes that Aristotle offers hypotheses from induction in this stretch of text (*Physics* 1.2, 195a12-14).

Throughout, Simplicius again aims to show that Aristotle is only refuting the apparent meaning of Parmenides and Melissus. He thinks that the real Eleatics (he concentrates on Parmenides) would indeed have to admit that the one is also many, but he takes this, not as a refutation, but as exhibiting the complex structure of the intelligible world, in the way that Plato also shows it in the second part of his *Parmenides*.

Simplicius devotes much energy to the last few lines of *Physics* 1.2, on the people Aristotle calls 'the later ancients'. These people apparently thought there were many beings, but they wanted each of the many beings to be one, and they were worried by the same kinds of arguments that are used against Parmenides to show that what is one must also be many. In order to avoid this conclusion, Aristotle says, they avoid saying 'Socrates is white', perhaps on the ground that if Socrates *is* white and Socrates *is* musical, he would be two things; so they say instead either that 'Socrates has gone white' or just that 'Socrates white', without the verb 'is'. Aristotle does not think highly of these people, and they might seem like a minor footnote. But they become important because the commentators, in explaining Aristotle's text, introduce the names of Zeno of Elea and Plato. Eudemus and Alexander think the 'later ancients' were replying to *Zeno's* arguments that whatever is hypothesized as one is really many. This raises two disputes: did Zeno argue just that whatever has many *parts* is many, or also that whatever has many *attributes* is many? More importantly, did Zeno argue just that *each one of a hypothesized many* is itself many and not really one (so that he would be defending Parmenides by refuting Parmenides' pluralist opponents), or did he argue, as the Peripatetics suggest, that *any hypothesized one* is many and not really one (so that he would be refuting Parmenides himself)?

Simplicius works hard to 'save' Zeno by showing that (as Plato says in his *Parmenides*) Zeno's book was intended to defend Parmenides, not to criticize him. Also, Eudemus and Alexander suggest that *Plato* is one of the 'later ancients'

20 Editors' Preface

to whom Aristotle refers, or at least that he has important agreements with them: this would be why, for instance, Plato's *Timaeus* refuses to say that any part of the 'receptacle of becoming' *is fire*, but only that it *has been inflamed*. So Simplicius 'saves' Plato: first he shows that Plato, like Aristotle, is contemptuous of people who are worried about 'easy one-many problems' which argue that a single sensible thing is many because it has many parts or many attributes; then he argues that Plato solves not only these 'easy one-many problems' but also the 'hard one-many' problems, like those that the character Parmenides raises against Socrates in the first part of Plato's *Parmenides*, which argue that a single *intelligible* thing is many. Simplicius concludes that this text of Aristotle, rather than *refuting* Plato, encourages students to turn toward deeper studies in Plato, which go beyond physics, and also beyond Aristotelian metaphysics, in revealing the complex structure of the intelligible world. And precisely because the world of *nous* (Reason) is not a single simple thing but a complex structure, there must be a simple One beyond it.

4.5 Antiphon and Hippocrates of Chios

The next portion of Simplicius' commentary (53,30-69,34) addresses *Physics* 1.2, 185a14-17, and specifically what Aristotle means by saying that 'it belongs to the geometer to solve the squaring [of the circle] by means of segments, but [to solve] Antiphon's [squaring] doesn't belong to the geometer'. Simplicius discusses a strategy for squaring the circle, by an infinite process of approximation, attributed to Antiphon, but focuses primarily on the 'squaring by means of segments' that he attributes to Hippocrates of Chios (after Alexander, whose report Simplicius augments with Eudemus); Simplicius also addresses whether and how these strategies are fallacious, and how they relate to the principles of geometry.

Simplicius gives us in full Alexander's account of Hippocrates' fallacy: Hippocrates showed how to square one kind of lune (a lune is a concave crescent-moon-shaped figure bounded by two arcs of circles), and Hippocrates showed that if a *different* kind of lune could be squared then a circle could also be squared. Alexander shows how these constructions worked, but because they concern different kinds of lunes they do not imply that a circle can be squared. But Simplicius goes back beyond Alexander to Eudemus, whose account is broadly similar but different and more complicated: Eudemus reports that Hippocrates gave four different squarings, not just two, and the details are different from what Alexander reports. Simplicius rightly realizes that Eudemus'

Editors' Preface 21

report is likely to be closer to the historical Hippocrates, and he reproduces it in detail. This report is now by far our most important surviving source on the history of Greek geometry before 400 BCE. Simplicius, in preserving Hippocrates' constructions as reported by Eudemus, also preserves 'an archaic style of geometry eclipsed by later Euclidean "elementarization"', even though Simplicius himself adds citations from Euclid to fill in what are from a later point of view missing steps in Hippocrates' arguments. Menn agrees with Simplicius that when Aristotle speaks of 'the squaring by means of segments' he is referring to Hippocrates' constructions. This is based in part on Aristotle's testimony about 'the diagrammatic fallacy of Hippocrates' at *SE* 11, 171b14-16. But Simplicius' report shows that Hippocrates argued ingeniously, carefully, and correctly. It is very unlikely that Hippocrates himself fallaciously argued that in squaring one kind of lune, and squaring the area composed of a circle and a *different* kind of lune, he had thereby squared the circle. But this fallacy came to be tagged with his name (see Menn 83).

The mathematical content of this section is carefully annotated in the translation's endnotes to support the reader, but the detailed discussion (§ 4.5) and Appendix in Menn's *Introduction* volume will be particularly useful for closer study. The most complex elements of the mathematical discussion involve Eudemus' arguments that, in the different lunes that Hippocrates squared, the outer circumference is in one case a semicircle, in one case less than a semicircle, and in one case more than a semicircle. These arguments, while they are significant as evidence of the state of geometry in Eudemus' time, are not directly relevant to the central mathematical and philosophical questions, and are also not evidence for Hippocrates. Menn emphasizes that less mathematically-inclined readers may safely pass over those sub-arguments in particular.[14]

4.6 Simplicius and Philoponus on *Physics* 1.1-2

In concluding this section, Menn offers a comparison of the counterpart commentary by Simplicius' contemporary John Philoponus. Philoponus' commentary on these chapters is about half the length of Simplicius', and involves far less consultation of early sources, although Philoponus also does a certain amount of 'saving' and 'harmonizing' of earlier philosophers. Philoponus' commentary on these chapters is, as Menn suggests, likely to be heavily based on Ammonius' lectures, supplemented by some excerpts from Themistius' paraphrase, with very few of the personal and often polemical contributions which are a striking feature of Philoponus' comments on some later books of the

Physics. Menn concludes that neither Simplicius nor Philoponus knew the other's commentary when they wrote, but 'it is always worth checking Philoponus to see where they agree', perhaps due to a common source, whether oral or written, direct or indirect, and 'where they disagree', particularly where Simplicius adds a point on which Philoponus is silent (92). In these chapters Philoponus often represents, better than Simplicius, a late Neoplatonic 'vulgate' interpretation of Aristotle, what Simplicius expects to be his readers' default interpretation of the text. Simplicius often agrees with this default interpretation, but it is where he corrects it or tries to deepen it – through his careful citation of ancient sources, and through his own solutions, characteristically introduced by *mêpote*, to the problems he poses – that we can see Simplicius' distinctive contributions.

Notes

1 (1) *On Aristotle Physics* 1.1-2, tr. S. Menn, 2021; (2) *On Aristotle Physics* 1.3-4, tr. P. Huby & C. C. W. Taylor, 2011; (3) *On Aristotle Physics* 1.5-9, tr. H. Baltussen, M. Atkinson, M. Share & I. Mueller, 2012; (4) *On Aristotle Physics* 2, tr. B. Fleet, 1997; (5) *On Aristotle Physics* 3, tr. J. O. Urmson with P. Lautner, 2001; (6) *On Aristotle Physics* 4.1-5 and 10-14, tr. J. O. Urmson, 1992; (7) *Corollaries on Place and Time*, tr. J. O. Urmson with L. Siorvanes, 1992; (8) *On Aristotle Physics* 5, tr. J. O. Urmson, 1997; (9) *On Aristotle Physics* 6, tr. D. Konstan, 1989; (10) *On Aristotle Physics* 7, tr. C. Hagen, 1994; (11) *On Aristotle Physics* 8.1-5, tr. I. Bodnar, M. Chase & M. Share, 2012; (12) *On Aristotle Physics* 8.6-10, tr. R. McKirahan, 2001.

2 For an updated discussion of philosophy in this period, see R. R. K. Sorabji, ed., *Aristotle Transformed*, 2nd edn (London: Bloomsbury, 2016), and *Aristotle Re-Interpreted* (London: Bloomsbury, 2016).

3 For difficulties with the rigid periodization of 'Neoplatonism', see for example L. Catana, 'The Origin of the Division Between Middle Platonism and Neoplatonism', *Apeiron* 46.2 (2013), 166–200. Simplicius would not have identified himself by the term 'pagan' (from the Latin *paganus*), a word used primarily by ancient Christian authors to designate their opponents, although there is debate about which term is most appropriate for cults and practices that are affiliated neither with Christianity nor Judaism in antiquity.

4 See in this series Simplicius, *On Epictetus Handbook 1–26*, tr. C. Brittain and T. Brennan (2002); Simplicius, *On Epictetus Handbook 27–53*, tr. T. Brennan and C. Brittain (2002).

5 See P. Hoffmann, 'Damascius', in Richard Goulet, ed., *Dictionnaire des Philosophes Antiques II* (Paris: CNRS Éditions, 1994), pp. 541–93, at 577–9.

Editors' Preface

6 See Menn 124–9, with P. Golitsis, *Les Commentaires de Simplicius et de Jean Philopon à la Physique d'Aristote* (Berlin: De Gruyter, 2008), p. 18.

7 See Menn 123 for discussion of the 'harmonization' thesis in application to Simplicius.

8 As Pantelis Golitsis notes in 'Simplicius and Philoponus on the authority of Aristotle', in Andrea Falcon, ed., *Brill's Companion to the Reception of Aristotle in Antiquity* (Leiden: Brill, 2016), pp. 419–38, at 430; see Menn 125.

9 He mentions Syrianus nine times, and knows Aspasius likely only through Alexander. See Menn 19, 127.

10 On these embedded monographs, see Pantelis Golitsis, *Les Commentaires de Simplicius et de Jean Philopon à la Physique d'Aristote* (Berlin: De Gruyter, 2008).

11 Menn points out that Simplicius' procedure is interestingly related to Plato's etymology of *epistêmê* ('knowledge'), which 'stops (*histêsin*) our soul at (*epi*) the objects' (*Cratylus* 437A2-5; cf. Aristotle, *DA* 1.3, 407a32-33). A discussion of Democritus in Aristotle's *Physics* (2.4, 106a35-b1) illustrates how Aristotle already uses the construction to connote a critique (Menn 27–8).

12 Drawing on the broader distinctions between 'exoteric' works (intended for a wide audience, lacking technical precision), 'acroamatic' works (with technical precision, but often obscure and demanding commentary), and 'hypomnematic' works (notes primarily for the author's own use) (see Ammonius, *in Cat.* 3,20-5,20).

13 As we have seen, Alexander proposed that we begin from universal axioms like the excluded middle, and so deploy general disjunctive descriptions, like 'the principles are either one or not one'. Simplicius thinks that Aristotle wants us to work back from sensible effects to their causes, although disjunction is an important tool.

14 Personal communication.

A Note on the Text and Translation

In translating Simplicius' commentary on the *Physics*, we have started from the only modern edition, that by Hermann Diels in the *Commentaria in Aristotelem Graeca* published by what was at that time the Royal Prussian Academy of Sciences in Berlin (volume 9, prolegomena and *Physics* 1-4, 1882; volume 10, *Physics* 5-8 and indices, 1895). The *CAG* was one of the Academy's prestige series of critical editions of historical sources: it came out of a recognition that the Greek commentators were authors deserving of critical editions in their own right, not merely to be culled for 'scholia' as they had been in Volume 4 of Bekker's complete Aristotle (*Scholia in Aristotelem*, edited by C. A. Brandis, 1836). But the main interest was still to use them as sources for the interpretation of Aristotle, for the history of his texts, and for other Greek writers, especially those no longer extant. The committee in charge of the *CAG* included Adolf Torstrik as chief editor, and Torstrik did much to seek out manuscripts of the commentators and to collate them himself. Torstrik had apparently chosen Simplicius' *Physics* commentary, with its wealth of information about earlier writers, to edit himself as the first flagship volume of the series, but Torstrik died suddenly in 1877, at the age of only 56, and Diels inherited the editorship of the *CAG* and in particular of Simplicius on the *Physics*. He also inherited Torstrik's collations of manuscripts and many proposed emendations, which Diels reports, often but not always accepting them himself.[1] Diels was, of course, very interested in critically assessing the sources for the history of early Greek philosophy and science. His *Doxographi Graeci* of 1879 already drew on his work on Simplicius, and this work would be an important source for his later projects, *Parmenides' Lehrgedicht* (1897), the *Poetarum Philosophorum Fragmenta* (1901), and the *Fragmente der Vorsokratiker* (first edition 1903). Diels had great sympathy with Simplicius as a scholar devoted to preserving ancient learning as the lights went out around him. By contrast, he had little patience with neo-Platonism, and seems to prefer to think of Simplicius, not as a neo-Platonist, but as someone who merely had the poor judgement to transmit some neo-Platonic sources as well as many other more valuable ones.

26 *A Note on the Text and Translation*

In the commentary on the first four books of the *Physics*, Diels reports the Florence manuscript D (Laurentianus 85,2), the Venice manuscripts E (Marcianus Graecus 229) and F (Marcianus Graecus 227), and the Aldine edition a.[2] (The manuscript tradition for the commentary on *Physics* 5-8 is completely different; only codex F and some later copies give [almost] the complete commentary on *Physics* 1-8.) Diels also gives separate reports on two aberrant parts of Codex E, which he calls E^a and E^b, which I will return to below. He also draws on Torstrik's notes; on earlier scholarship on pre-Socratic texts, which included some emendations to Simplicius; and on Hermann Usener's and especially Paul Tannery's notes on Simplicius' report on the mathematician Hippocrates of Chios, which Diels prints as the 'Appendix Hippocratea' to his preface (pp. xxiii–xxxi). The work of David Sider and A. L. Coxon on the tradition of some pre-Socratics, and of Leonardo Tarán and Dieter Harlfinger on Simplicius' *Physics* commentary in general, have brought out significant deficiencies in Diels' editing, including in his reports of the manuscripts, and his edition must be used with caution.[3] But there has been no new edition to replace Diels, except for fragments of some pre-Socratics and Hippocrates of Chios, and the forthcoming edition by Pantelis Golitsis and Philippe Hoffmann of the Corollaries on Place and Time from Book 4.[4] Golitsis and Lutz Koch have begun work on a new edition of the commentary on Book 1 (and we have sent them our suggested corrections to Diels), but for the moment we have only Diels and the manuscripts. A user of Diels' edition should be aware of six kinds of problems.

There are three kinds of problems in Diels' reports of the manuscripts in his apparatus;

(1) Diels was unaware of another primary witness to the first four books, the Moscow manuscript (State Historical Museum, codex 3649) which, following Harlfinger, we refer to as Mo, written by the Byzantine princess Theodora Rhaulaina or Raoulaina (a niece of Michael VIII Palaeologus, who had reconquered Constantinople from the Crusaders in 1261). Mo often agrees with F, and with E when it is no longer following D, but she often has distinctive readings of her own, which often seem to be right.

(2) Because Diels relied on other people's collations of the codices and did not have the opportunity to check their reports against the codices themselves or photographs of them, he sometimes misinterpreted their reports, and in particular sometimes interpreted silences in their reports as implying that the manuscript agreed with a standard edition. This leads to some cases where he reports the reading of a manuscript in places where it is in fact illegible or

missing. Leonardo Tarán in 'The Text of Simplicius' Commentary on Aristotle's *Physics*[5] describes and discusses these errors. (Such errors in reporting are all too common in critical editions before the mid-twentieth century.) Tarán has also called attention to a particularly unfortunate mistake, where Diels must have misinterpreted his own notes, at 86,27. Here Simplicius is quoting the first half of the first line of Parmenides B6 (for which this passage in Simplicius is the only witness): Diels prints '*khrê to legein te noein t' eon emmenai*', and reports that the manuscripts of Simplicius have '*te noein*' but that Simon Karsten in his edition of Parmenides' fragments emends to '*to noein*'; in fact, however, all collated manuscripts of Simplicius have '*to noein*' and Karsten emends to '*te noein*'.[6] Also at 80,2, quoting Parmenides B8 line 28, Diels reports all manuscripts as having the first word '*têde*', when in fact both Mo (which Diels did not know) and E have '*têle*'. Diels and all modern editors think that Parmenides actually wrote '*têle*', but Diels describes this as Scaliger's emendation, when in fact it has manuscript authority.[7]

(3) Diels regards codex E as an independent witness, but it is clear that E switches exemplars at 52,18, and it is quite possible that E is a copy of D up to that point; after that it is an independent witness, but belongs to the same family as F and Mo (although F is probably contaminated from a source in the D family; certainly E and Mo are closer to each other than to F). Dieter Harlfinger in his article 'Einige Aspekte der handschriftlichen Überlieferung des Physikkommentars des Simplikios'[8] gives an excellent discussion of the state of codex E and some potentially misleading aspects of Diels' reports. At some point in codex E's lifetime, its leaves corresponding to *CAG* 52,18-72,11 (in the commentary on *Physics* 1.2) were removed from their natural place near the beginning and were reattached at (almost) the end of the codex; Diels cites this section of codex E in his apparatus to 52,18-72,11 under the siglum E[b], but it has exactly the same status as any other section of E, specifically of the second part of E, after it switches exemplars from D (or a close relative) to the second family. Further complicating the situation, according to Harlfinger's diagnosis, the exemplar of the second part of E (i.e. the now lost manuscript from which the scribe of E copied the leaves corresponding to *CAG* 52,18-795,35) had previously suffered a similar dislocation, perhaps in some accident which also led to the loss of the first part of this manuscript and thereby forced the scribe of E to look to another manuscript for 8,32-52,18.[9] Two sections of the otherwise lost first part of this exemplar before 52,18, corresponding to *CAG* 20,1-30,16 and 35,30–44,19, had been removed and reattached at the end of the exemplar (perhaps they had been rescued from whatever happened to the rest of 1,3-52,18 in this

manuscript), and are therefore copied along with everything else into codex E. Of course the first part of E also includes the passages 20,1-30,16 and 35,30-44,19, copied from a first family exemplar (D or a close relative), so these passages occur twice in codex E, and Diels cites both versions in his apparatus for these passages, citing the first family text from near the beginning of codex E as 'E' and the second family text from near the end of codex E as 'E^a'. (Weirdly, when section 52,18-72,11, 'E^b', was reattached near the end of codex E, it was reattached *in the middle* of E^a, specifically in the middle of the second of the two sections that constitute E^a, yielding a bizarre sequence of texts.)[10] Thus E^a and E^b are not, as Diels apparently thought, further manuscript sources with their own positions on the stemma of manuscripts: rather, they are both parts of E copied from the same second family exemplar as E's text of 72,11-795,35.[11]

In addition to these problems in Diels' reports of the manuscripts,

(4) Diels, and Torstrik before him, were probably too ready to follow the Aldine against the manuscripts, and also too quick to posit lacunae and especially to emend the text, sometimes due to a lack of understanding of neo-Platonism. A lack of understanding of the philosophical issues as Simplicius saw them led Diels in particular to a catastrophic emendation at 18,4 and a false positing of a lacuna and false bracketing of a correct transmitted text at 18,14-15, which managed to make nonsense of a perfectly reasonable paragraph of Simplicius. There are many smaller but similar issues, and a reader or translator should be cautious before accepting one of Diels' or Torstrik's emendations. They were careful readers and are generally responding to real difficulties in the text, and their solutions deserve a respectful hearing, but progress often consists in finding gentler solutions. There is also a specific issue in Simplicius' quotations from earlier authors, especially the pre-Socratics. Diels in principle distinguishes between the question of what some pre-Socratic really wrote and the question of what Simplicius wrote in citing him. (Simplicius will be using a manuscript close to a millennium after the autograph, and he may also misread, quote from memory, or paraphrase.) Diels aims to print what Simplicius wrote, and, if he thinks that the pre-Socratic's original wording differed from Simplicius' quotation, to comment on that in the apparatus rather than changing Simplicius' text. But Diels does not observe this consistently, and in some cases, perhaps from excessive charity to Simplicius, he will print in Simplicius' quotation a text that is probably right for the pre-Socratic but probably wrong for Simplicius.

A Note on the Text and Translation 29

(5) Diels, like editors of classical texts generally, decides what punctuation to print based on his own judgement of what would make sense. The manuscripts of Simplicius do sometimes contain punctuation, but it is hard to say whether the punctuation goes back to Simplicius' autograph or was added by later scribes or annotators. And in any case the people who made the collations that Diels used almost certainly did not report the punctuation, so Diels would not have known about it. Diels' judgement on such matters deserves respectful consideration, but it has no authority, and major interpretive issues may hang on correct punctuation. Simplicius himself explicitly discusses issues of how to punctuate Aristotle's text, notably at 70,3-71,16 on the lemma *Physics* 1.2, 185a17-20. There is a special issue about quotation marks: it is obviously important to know what Simplicius is saying in his own voice and what he is attributing to someone else, and what he is quoting verbatim and what he is paraphrasing. These are often difficult questions, and Diels' judgements cannot be taken for granted. It is a bit disconcerting that Diels often includes words like 'says' within his quotation marks, when they are clearly Simplicius' interruptions of the quotation. It is more disconcerting that sometimes Diels prints a left quotation mark with no corresponding right quotation mark, apparently because he is suspending judgement about how far the quotation extends. Christian Wildberg in an important article has described the quotation marks in the Simplicius manuscripts, has argued that in at least some cases they go back to Simplicius himself, and has shown at least one clear case where we can restore sense if we follow the quotation marks in codex A of Simplicius' commentary on *Physics* 5-8 and realize that a passage that Diels had printed as if it were in Simplicius' own voice is in fact a quotation from his adversary Philoponus.[12]

(6) The lemmas, i.e. the excerpts from the text of Aristotle being commented on, presented above the corresponding commentary, are given more fully in some manuscripts and more sparsely in others. Some manuscripts include the complete text of Aristotle, either in specially demarcated regions of the page or incorporated into the commentary; others apparently assume that you are looking at a separate text of the *Physics* at the same time. Diels says in his preface (pp. x–xi) that he thinks (he doesn't say why) that Simplicius himself just wrote the first and last words of each lemma, connecting them with '*heôs tou*', 'up to', the equivalent of the modern ellipsis '...', and that later scribes copied in more of the lemma from whatever manuscript of the *Physics* they had to hand. Diels does not report what the different manuscripts have in the lemmas, presumably because he thinks it would be useless in establishing the text of Simplicius. Perhaps Diels' general policy is to follow codex E in Books 1–4 and codex A in

30 *A Note on the Text and Translation*

Books 5–8. But his edition cannot be used as a guide either to what the manuscripts have or to what Simplicius himself wrote (or, rather, directed his secretary to write). It is a serious mistake to speak of 'Simplicius' lemmas' to mean 'the portion of each lemma that Diels decided to print': what Diels prints in the lemmas has no authority and is not evidence of Simplicius' intentions. Simplicius' commentary could never have been used without the text of the *Physics*, and it is unlikely that Simplicius intended his readers to be juggling two books at the same time: most likely he expected his secretary to copy out the full text of Aristotle's lemma, if not in the moment of dictation then in a later fair copy, whether or not the secretary actually got around to doing this.[13] Later scribes do whatever they find most convenient.

We have not pretended to produce a new critical edition of the part of Simplicius' commentary that we translated. But we have had to translate *something*, and in each case we have used our best judgement, in the absence of a proper critical edition, on what Simplicius said. In each case where this differs from Diels' text (and sometimes also where we follow him on points of uncertainty) we have signalled this in the endnotes. We have systematically checked codex Mo (which Diels did not know), and we report the reading of Mo in any case where we differ from Diels. We have in some cases checked Diels' reports of codices D, E, and F, but not systematically. Sometimes we accept Diels' or Torstrik's emendations, sometimes we reject them and go back to a text attested in (some) manuscripts, and sometimes we propose a new emendation. There are places where Diels' text does not seem to make good sense, and places where he adopts what we find an adventurous emendation to get it to make sense. There are places where he suspends judgement and obelizes, and there are places, not always the same ones, where we would probably do that if we were editing the text. But since we are not editing but translating, and since we cannot translate an untranslatable text and are unwilling to put obeli in a translation,[14] we in some cases translate an emendation of Diels or Torstrik, or one of our own, even if we have no great confidence in it. In some cases where we would print something different from Diels if we were editing, we accept his text for the purposes of translation, if the change would make no significant difference to the meaning or translation.

Since Diels' text in the lemmas has no authority, and is generally too short to help the reader make sense of Simplicius' commentary, which often depends heavily on textual details of the lemma, we always translate the full text of each lemma. Since there is no good reason to think that the lemmas found in any of the diverging manuscripts reflect what Simplicius thought Aristotle said, we have simply imposed a modern standard, Ross' *editio maior* of the *Physics*.[15] We note the cases where it emerges from Simplicius' commentary that he is reading something different, or where he discusses several possible readings.

Since Diels' punctuation has no textual authority, we have (like Diels) repunctuated, and also in particular reparagraphed, as we thought the sense required. We have often preferred shorter paragraphs than Diels, and sometimes we have found that his paragraph breaks are in odd places. We have added short headings in brackets in front of each paragraph, in the hope that this will help the reader follow Simplicius' argument; it helped us. We have paid special attention to the issue of what to put in quotation marks, and how far each quotation extends. We have often disagreed with Diels on this, or followed a more conservative policy on how much to put in quotation marks even if the quotation *may* extend further. Where we diverge from Diels' quotation marks we have noted the divergence. We have sometimes been tempted to imitate Diels' practice of printing a left quotation mark without a corresponding right quotation mark, but we have never actually done so. One thing that we have not done, but perhaps should have, is to follow Wildberg's lead and study the manuscripts for their punctuation including quotation marks. But Byzantine manuscripts never have enough punctuation for a modern reader, and it is very hard to be sure that a given punctuation mark goes back to Simplicius: a scribe, or simply a Byzantine or Renaissance reader, could easily add such marks, and would have no inhibition about doing so.

Where Simplicius quotes, our aim is to determine and translate the text of Simplicius, not the text of the authors he is quoting. Simplicius often cites what seems to be the same passage, e.g. of Parmenides or Empedocles, several times in the *Physics* commentary (sometimes also in the commentary on *On the Heaven*), and often he seems to quote it in slightly different ways in the different contexts. When Simplicius in our section of the *Physics* commentary cites a lost text (typically of a pre-Socratic) that he also cites elsewhere, we flag the other places (whether in our section or not) where he cites what is apparently the same passage. If he seems to quote it in different ways in different places, we have generally not imposed uniformity, i.e. we have not presumed that the differences are due to later scribes rather than to Simplicius himself. This is especially delicate because in some cases there is a question whether it is really the same passage that he is quoting: this is especially an issue with Empedocles, who often repeats the same line or part of a line either verbatim or with deliberate variations in different passages. We leave these judgements to the editors of the pre-

32   *A Note on the Text and Translation*

Socratics. While Simplicius is, by ancient standards, very accurate in his citations, he is not perfect, and our strong impression is that he is much more accurate (to the manuscript he was using) in his *longer* citations, where he is not tempted to rely on memory.

We have not found it possible to translate in a way that precisely mirrors the structure of Simplicius' Greek while also yielding readable and easily intelligible English. We have had to make some compromises. There is no point in publishing a translation if readers can only guess its meaning by trying to reconstruct the underlying Greek. We have sometimes broken long Greek sentences into shorter English sentences. We have also sometimes had to translate the same Greek term in different contexts by different English words in order to remain intelligible. The Greek–English Index and English–Greek Glossary will allow the interested reader to trace what we have done. We sometimes add an endnote when the translation issue seems especially important. I collect the most important issues here.

We translate '*mêpote*' by 'perhaps', but we add the Greek word in parentheses to flag it as a technical term, marking Simplicius' original proposal for solving some problem that he has raised. We usually translate '*skopos*' by 'object', but sometimes 'aim' where it means not the object that an art or science or text is about, but the activity that it aims at performing: the reader should bear both meanings in mind. '*Ephistanai*'/'*ephistanein*' (with the connected noun '*epistasis*'), marking Simplicius' observations on the text at hand, which serve to criticize previous interpretations and to give a basis for his own, is usually 'remark', 'observe', or 'note', but it has the overtone of 'objecting' against earlier more superficial interpreters. It would be simplest to translate '*on*' by 'being', but because 'being' in English is ambiguous between what *is* and *that* it is, whereas '*on*' always means 'what is', we cannot always make this translation work. Especially when '*on*' is the subject of a sentence, we have often translated it by 'what is' ('Parmenides said that what is is one', but 'being is said in many ways'); we have often translated the plural '*ta onta*' by 'the things that are'. '*Nous*' is 'intellect' only when it means the rational part or power of the soul; when it is the separately existing reason-itself in which souls participate we translate it by 'reason' or 'Reason', and once 'intelligence' to keep a connection with 'intelligible' for '*noêtos*'. (It is also once 'intellectual intuition' as opposed to deductive knowledge, and 'attention' in the phrase '*prosekhein ton noun*', 'pay attention'; it can also mean the 'sense' or thought or argument of a passage under discussion.) But '*noein*' has to be 'think' or 'understand', since the verb 'reason' has the wrong meaning and 'intelligize' is barbarous, so in some passages we must go back and forth between English words from different roots translating different Greek words derived from '*noein*'. We have tried to flag this where it is important and non-obvious. Similarly, we normally translate '*apeiros*' as 'infinite', since this is what it means, and its opposite '*peperasmenos*' as 'finite', but '*peras*' has to be 'limit'; 'end' is '*telos*' or '*teleutê*', but '*telikos*' is 'final'. We prefer to translate '*hupokeimenon*' as 'underlying', but in some contexts there is no choice but to speak of subject and predicate.

There is a particular difficulty in translating Greek verbs of knowing: Greek has many verbs of knowing, the distinctions between them do not map neatly onto distinctions between different English verbs, and each of these verbs can have stricter and looser senses. The most important point is that '*epistasthai*', although it can be used for knowing in general, is very often used technically, contrasting with other knowledge verbs, to mean knowing in the strictest and strongest sense. We have translated '*epistasthai*' by 'scientifically know', and the connected noun '*epistêmê*' by 'scientific knowledge' or 'science'. For a more general sense of 'know', Simplicius standardly says '*gignôskein*', and we have usually translated this by 'know' or 'come to know'. But when, in his discussion of the first lemma of the *Physics, Physics* 1.1, 184a10-16 (from 11,36 and especially 12,14-13,13), Simplicius discusses the relation between the meanings of *epistasthai* and *eidenai* in Aristotle, there is no reasonable alternative to translating *eidenai* as 'know', and so in this passage we translate '*gignôskein*' as 'cognize', or, where 'know' is inescapable, have put the Greek in parentheses to flag that 'know' here translates '*gignôskein*' rather than '*eidenai*'. (Since '*eidenai*' means 'know' only in the perfect tense, '*gignôskein*' is sometimes used to fill in the other tenses, to describe the process whose result is knowledge: the translations 'cognize' and 'come to know' reflect that meaning.) We normally translate the adjective '*gnôrimos*', derived from '*gignôskein*', by 'known' or 'knowable' according to the context, and the verb '*gnôrizein*', derived from '*gnôrimos*', by 'recognize': in Aristotle's commentators, as in Aristotle, '*gnôrizein*' often seems to be equivalent to '*gignôskein*' ('recognize' to 'cognize'), but it may sometimes mean to make something *gnôrimon* (typically, make it *gnôrimon* to oneself).

The word '*phusis*' and its cognates also cause difficulty: '*phusis*' can only be 'nature', but it is hard to avoid translating '*phusikê*' as 'physics', and this threatens to obscure the connection with 'nature'. We have preferred to translate all *phusis* words by nature words: thus '*phusikê*' is 'natural science'. We have translated '*ta phusika*' by '*Physics*' when Simplicius uses it as the title of a book, by Empedocles or Theophrastus or Eudemus, and '*ta meta ta phusika*' by 'metaphysics' as a discipline and '*Metaphysics*' as a book title; but the title of the Aristotelian treatise

34   *A Note on the Text and Translation*

that Simplicius is here commenting on, '*Phusikê akroasis*', is '*Lectures on Natural Science*' when we are translating Simplicius (when we speak in our own voice we call it '*Physics*'). We prefer to translate '*diakrinein*' (with the connected noun '*diakrisis*') by 'differentiate', but have sometimes used 'distinguish' or 'separate'; sometimes *diakrinein* is a cognitive act, sometimes '*sunkrisis*' means combining things and '*diakrisis*' means separating them out into their constituents, and sometimes '*diakrisis*' means a level of being at which things are differentiated, by contrast with a higher level of being at which everything is unified. '*Diaphora*' can mean 'difference', or 'differentia' as opposed to genus, and we have used both of these translations, but sometimes 'variety' or 'variation': Simplicius says that Anaxagoras recognized 'a threefold variety [*diaphora*] of all forms' (34,18-19), meaning that forms exist at three different levels of being. Like most translators of Greek texts, we have given up on finding a single English equivalent of '*logos*': we have preferred 'account', and 'argument' when it means 'argument', but have resorted to a range of translations as the context seemed to demand.

We give references in the endnotes to standard modern editions of the pre-Socratics and of other authors whom Simplicius cites (e.g. FHS&G for Theophrastus, Wehrli for Eudemus, Smith's Teubner for Porphyry, the Oxford Classical Text for Plato), and we refer the reader to those editors' discussions of the problems of establishing and interpreting the text, and of the other ancient witnesses to the text besides Simplicius, where there are any. For the pre-Socratics we always cite DK, but often also more recent editors for a fuller and more up-to-date discussion. Some of these editors, notably Coxon for Parmenides and Sider for Anaxagoras, have themselves done good work on the manuscripts of Simplicius, and we are particularly grateful to them. André Laks' and Glenn Most's Loeb Classical Library edition of the fragments of early Greek philosophy came out too late for us to use.

Notes

1   For the story of how the Academy, and specifically Diels, came to edit the *CAG* in general, and Simplicius on the *Physics* in particular, see Karl Praechter's review of the *CAG*, in Sorabji, ed., *Aristotle Transformed*, pp. 31–54. Diels' edition of Simplicius on *Physics* 1-4 and Hayduck's edition of [Ps.-]Simplicius on *On the Soul* were the two first volumes in the series, both in 1882; I don't know which was published first, although Hayduck's preface is dated two months before Diels'. Simplicius had long

A Note on the Text and Translation

35

been seen as the best source of scholarly information (Alexander was of course also highly valued), and had already been heavily used by editors of pre-Socratic fragments, especially C. A. Brandis and Simon Karsten. This had already led Karsten to edit Simplicius on *On the Heaven* (Utrecht: Kemink, 1865), of which there had been no earlier edition except the fake Aldine of 1526 (a Greek retranslation of a Latin translation, passed off as the Greek original); in other cases, before the *CAG*, people had relied on Renaissance editions or Latin translations.

2 D stops p. 347, in the middle of Book 2. E starts after the proem, 8,32, and stops just short of the end of Book 4.

3 See David Sider, *The Fragments of Anaxagoras*, 2nd edn (Sankt Augustin: Academia Verlag, 2005); A. H. Coxon, *The Fragments of Parmenides*, 2nd edn (Las Vegas: Parmenides Publishing, 2009); Leonardo Tarán, 'The Text of Simplicius' Commentary on Aristotle's *Physics*', in Hadot, ed., *Simplicius, sa vie, son oeuvre, sa survie*, pp. 246–66; and Dieter Harlfinger, 'Einige Aspekte der handschriftlichen Überlieferung des Physikkommentars des Simplikios', ibid., pp. 267–94. We follow Harlfinger on the relations between the different manuscripts.

4 See Pantelis Golitsis and Philippe Hoffmann, 'Simplicius et le 'lieu': À propos d'une nouvelle édition du Corollarium de loco', *Revue des Études Grecques* 127/1 (2014), 119–75.

5 In Hadot, ed., *Simplicius, sa vie, son oeuvre, sa survie*, pp. 246–66.

6 See Simon Karsten, *Parmenidis Eleatae Carminis Reliquiae* (Amsterdam: Müller, 1835; a series title page describes this as *Philosophorum Graecorum veterum, praesertim qui ante Platonem floruerunt, Operum Reliquiae*, vol. 1, pt. 2), p. 32, for the text he prints (it's his line 43), and p. 77 for his explanation of how he is emending the text we read in Simplicius. (Karsten may be proposing this only as the correct text of Parmenides and not also of Simplicius.) Diels' mistake here had particularly unfortunate consequences: in later work, relying on his own edition of Simplicius, Diels drops the reference to Karsten's alleged emendation *to noein* and keeps only the reference to the alleged manuscript reading *te noein*, which is in fact Karsten's emendation and has no manuscript support. This is unfortunately propagated at DK 28B61.

7 See our note to the translation at 40,1, Simplicius' first citation of this verse. The correct reading of E here had been noted before us by Coxon, *The Fragments of Parmenides*, in his apparatus to B8 line 28, and the reading of Mo by David Sider, 'Textual Notes on Parmenides' Poem', *Hermes* 113 (1985), 362–6, at 366.

8 In Hadot, ed., *Simplicius, sa vie, son oeuvre, sa survie*, pp. 267–94.

9 Why he did not copy the proem 1,3-8,30 is unclear, although there are also some other manuscripts of Greek commentaries which skip their proems. It is also possible that it was his exemplar for 8,32-52,18 that was damaged, forcing him to change exemplars at 52,18. If so, then the fact that the second exemplar was also damaged is just a coincidence.

36   *A Note on the Text and Translation*

10 E^b is folios 408–15. E^a begins in the middle of folio 402, continues through the end of folio 407, and resumes after E^b with folios 416 to some way down 418. Then the text of the commentary on *Physics* 4 resumes, 787,31-795,35, at which point it finally breaks off shortly before the end of *Physics* 4. The jump between the two disjoined sections of E^a, 20,1-30,16 and 35,30-44,19, happens within folio 407, i.e. before the mechanical interruption by E^b, and passes from 30,16 to 35,30 as if there were nothing missing. Presumably 20,1-30,16 and 35,30-44,19 were on different folios in E's exemplar, but the scribe of E copied them together without noticing that there was anything missing between them, just as he seems not to have noticed that these texts did not belong inside a commentary on *Physics* 4.

11 A. H. Coxon, 'The Manuscript Tradition of Simplicius' Commentary on Aristotle's *Physics* i–iv', *Classical Quarterly* 18 (1968), 70–5, has some useful observations on particular passages but should be used with great caution. Coxon does not understand the difference between the relations of E to D in different parts of the text, or the relation between E and E^a, and this vitiates many of his conclusions. For some other cautions see Tarán's article cited above.

12 See Christian Wildberg, 'Simplicius und das Zitat: zur Überlieferung des Anführungszeichens', in *Symbolae Berolinenses* (Amsterdam: Hakkert, 1993), pp. 187–99.

13 But see Mirjam E. Kotwick, *Alexander of Aphrodisias and the Text of Aristotle's Metaphysics* (Berkeley: California Classical Studies, 2016), pp. 38–45, for an argument that Alexander inserted a 'lemma' containing only the *first sentence* of each passage selected for commenting into the text of his *Metaphysics* commentary, and that these original 'lemmas' are *sometimes* reflected in our extant manuscripts.

14 But we actually do so once, at 33,9, in a fragment of Empedocles (B21, line 4).

15 Listed as 'Ross' in the Abbreviations; the text and apparatus are reproduced apparently unchanged in Ross' Oxford Classical Text of 1950.

Simplicius

On Aristotle Physics 1.1–2

Translation

The Commentary of Simplicius the Philosopher on Aristotle's *Lectures on Natural Science*, Book One

1,1

[*1,3: To learn the object of the Physics, we must divide the parts of philosophy and the parts of the soul they perfect.*][1] One can easily learn the object of Aristotle's *Lectures on Natural Science* if we recall his division of the natural-scientific part of philosophy.[2] But perhaps it's as well to set out the whole division of philosophy 5 according to him. For philosophy is a perfecting of the soul, as medicine is of the body; and part of the soul is irrational and part is rational; and of the rational part, part cooperates with the irrational, such as what he calls the potential intellect, while part of it is separate, such as the actual intellect; and the power of all the soul is double, the one being desiring and the other cognitive. So the part 10 of philosophy which perfects the desiring part in the irrational soul and in the potential intellect which cooperates with the irrational desires – all this, the Peripatetics call 'practical', since it is occupied with practice and has as its end the choice and attainment of the good. On the other hand, the part of philosophy which perfects the cognitive part of the soul, and which has truth as its end, they call, in general, 'theoretical'.

[*1,14: The parts of theoretical philosophy, matched with their objects and the parts of the soul.*] But as much of it as perfects the potential intellect's cognition, which 15 [*sc.* cognition], accompanied by sensation and imagination, extends over[3] forms which are enmattered and inseparable from matter, this they [the Peripatetics] call 'natural-scientific', because nature is demonstrated to be concerned with such things and in them. But as much of it as is concerned with forms entirely separated from matter, and with the pure activity of the actual intellect and with the activity of the potential intellect which [*sc.* activity] is lifted up with the actual intellect, this they call 'theological' and 'first philosophy' and 'metaphysics', 20 as being ranked beyond natural things.[4] And the part that is concerned with forms which are in one way separate and in another way inseparable from matter, this they call 'mathematical' and '*On the Soul*'. For they say that mathematical substance is intermediate, since inasmuch as it's universal it's something separate 2,1 from matter, but inasmuch as it's extended and differentiated it's inseparable. And in the same way, they think the soul has much that is enmattered in regard to its sensations and imaginations and potential intellect; but in regard to the

40   *Translation*

5   actual intellect, which Aristotle shows to be itself the highest part of the soul,
      even if Alexander disagrees, they say that the soul has separability from matter.[5]
      But the other parts [*sc.* of philosophy] will get a more precise differentiation in
      the appropriate treatises.

      [*2,8: Division of natural science.*] But of the account of nature, one part is
      concerned with the principles of all natural things insofar as they are natural,
10   that is to say bodily,[6] and with the things that are necessarily consequent on such
      principles, and the other parts are concerned with the things that arise from the
      principles. And since of these things some are simple and some are compounds,
      the treatise *On the Heaven* teaches concerning the simples, discussing the fifth
      substance ('the heaven' in the strict sense) in the first two books, and
      demonstrating among other things its eternity, while in the remaining two it
15   discusses the four sublunar elements: these are taken up there insofar as they too
      are simples and move with simple motions.

      [*2,16: Criticism of Al. on the object of On the Heaven; a correct division of natural
      science confirms that its object is simple natural bodies.*] For I think it's better to
      speak this way, and not as Alexander does when he says that the *On the Heaven* is
      concerned with the eternal and rotating body, and also with all natural body
      universally or with the cosmos. For he himself agrees that the present treatise is
20   concerned with what is natural insofar as it is natural. Moreover, what is compound
      is also natural, and there is no discussion there of what is compound, but rather of
      simples, as Aristotle himself has made clear in the third book of the treatise [*On
      the Heaven*] when he says, 'Well then, we have said of the first of the elements, both
      what sort of thing it is in its nature and that it is imperishable and ungenerated.
      What remains is to speak of the [other] two'[7] – meaning by 'two', the two pairings
25   of the four elements determined by their two forms of motion, the one away from
      the centre and the one towards the centre, calling the simples 'elements'. And since
      all the compounds are generable and perishable, while of the simples some are
      eternal and some are generated and perish, he has talked about the eternal ones in
      the first [two books] of *On the Heaven*, and concerning the generable and
      perishable ones as simples in the third and fourth books of that treatise.[8]

30

      [*2,30: Division of the study of generated things.*] But setting out to speak about
      generated things,[9] he first wrote the two books *On Generation and Perishing*,
      teaching about the things consequent in general on all generated and perishing
3,1   things as such. But there are also different attributes that apply in particular to

different [*sc.* generated and perishing] things. And in his treatise on *Meteorology* he taught the ones that are constituted in the place immediately above us; while of the things in the place around us, since some are ensouled and some have no soul, they [*sc.* Aristotle and Theophrastus] teach about those which have no soul in the treatises *On Minerals*.[10] And of the ensouled, some are animals, some are 5 plants, and some are zoophytes. Well then, they discuss animals in the various sorts of treatises on animals, sometimes reporting about them empirically, as in the *Historia Animalium*, and elsewhere teaching with causal explanations, as in the *Generation* and *Parts* and *Motion* and *Sleep* and so on of animals.[11] In the same way they also taught about plants by this double method. So then in sum 10 the division of the natural part of philosophy according to the Peripatetic school is something like this.

[*3,13: The object of the Physics: the principles of natural things in common and what must be discussed together with them.*] But the object of the treatise at hand is to teach concerning the things which belong in common to all natural things inasmuch as they are natural – that is to say, bodily. And what belongs in common 15 to all are the principles, and the concomitants of the principles. And the principles are the causes strictly speaking and the auxiliary causes; and the causes, according to them, are the efficient and the final, and the auxiliary causes the form and matter and the elements generally.[12] But Plato adds the paradigmatic to the causes, and the instrumental to the auxiliary causes.[13] And that the object of the treatise is concerned with the things that belong to all natural things in common, 20 the introduction makes clear straightaway, when he says that it's necessary for the natural scientist 'first to determine things concerning the principles' (184a15-16). He also makes this clear at the beginning of Book 3 when he says, 'So it's clear that both for these reasons and because these things are common to all and universal, those taking the matter up must examine each of them. For the study of what is particular is posterior to the study of what is common' (3.1, 200b21-25). But since it will be shown that nature, as a kind of proximate efficient cause of 25 natural things, is a principle of motion, and since every natural thing, being a body, has a principle of motion within itself, an account of motion is necessary for the natural scientist. And since what is moved is measured by a time, in regard to its motion, and, being a body, is in a place, it's also necessary to teach about time and place. And since body and place and time and motion are 30 continuous, it's also necessary to take up the continuous. These are the 'concomitants' of the natural principles. And enquiries concerning the infinite and concerning void are also included: concerning the infinite, because it's

42   *Translation*

necessary that natural bodies, motion, place, and time, since they are continuous
4,1   and have extension, be divisible ad infinitum, and either be infinite or finite or
possess infinity in one way and finiteness in another.[14] And since place seemed
to some to be a certain empty interval, devoid of body, the discussion of void is
reasonably included with that concerning place, and also because some of the
5   natural scientists, and not just any chance ones,[15] set down void in the role of a
principle. These things, then, are the object of the *Lectures on Natural Science*
[i.e. the *Physics*]: the ones which belong in common to all natural things – or
which seem to, but don't.[16]

[*4,8: The title.*] As for the rest, the reason for the title is clear. For, since it teaches
about the things that belong in common to all natural things qua natural, it
10   reasonably received the common name, being entitled *Natural Science*; and
Lectures as being worked out with enough precision as to be put forward for the
hearing of others.[17] But Adrastus, in the *On the Order of Aristotle's Writings*,
reports that the treatise was entitled by some, *On Principles*, and by others,
Lectures on Natural Science, and he says that yet others entitled the first five
15   books *On Principles*, and the remaining three *On Motion*.[18] And it appears that
Aristotle himself often refers to them in this way.

[*4,17: Utility of the topic: above all, the study of natural science instills virtue.*] The
study of nature is valuable, not only in matters of everyday life, providing
principles to both medicine and mechanics, and helping the other arts (for each
of them needs to investigate the nature and the natural varieties of its subject
20   matter); and not only because it perfects the form of the soul in us corresponding
to the knowledge of natural things, as theology does the intellectual and highest
part; but also because it makes the greatest contribution towards the other
perfections of the soul. For it also assists the practical virtues: justice, since, by
revealing that the elements and parts of the universe give way to each other and
25   are content with their own ordering and preserve geometrical equality, it excludes
selfish excess;[19] and temperance, by showing the nature of pleasure, that it is not
at all a principal good but rather a by-product which, so long as it seems urgent
and choiceworthy, is to that extent still mixed together with a great deal that is
contrary to nature. And moreover, occupation with the study of nature easily
30   turns the soul away from bodily pleasures and excitement over external things.
From these things come temperance and justice and honesty in transactions.
And who would be as courageous as someone who has come to know from the

study of nature that our living body[20] is no perceptible part of the whole,[21] nor is the measure of our life [a perceptible part] of all of time, and that perishing necessarily follows upon every generated thing, being a dissolution into the simples and a restoration of the parts to their proper wholes, and a renewal of things grown old and a recovery of things grown weary. And to perish now or in a few years would be of no account to one who has recognized the infinity of time. And if he considers the separate superiority of the soul and compares it to the concerns that attach to it from the body, then he would be fully content with death. And at what other apparently dreadful thing would a person so disposed towards death tremble? And it [the study of nature] is immediately productive of practical wisdom, which is closely akin to the cognitive part of the soul. And it makes people great-souled and great-minded, by persuading them to deem no human thing great.[22] And it renders people liberal, as being satisfied with little, and for this reason sharing readily what they have and not needing to take anything from others. But the greatest good of it is that it is the finest path to the knowledge of the substance of the soul and the study of the separate and divine forms, as Plato too makes clear when he proceeds from natural motions towards the discovery of the self-moved substance and of the intellectual and divine existence, and also Aristotle when in this very treatise he seeks out the unmoved cause of all motion starting from the eternity of the circular motion.[23] It also especially kindles reverence towards the divine superiority, awakening us well to the wonder and majesty of the Maker, from a precise grasp of the things made by him. Affinity towards god and steadfast trust and hope follow together upon this wonder. For these reasons above all one must practise the study of nature. So then since the study of nature is so valuable, the present treatise would rightly be most valuable, since it teaches us the principles of the whole study of nature, principles without which it is impossible to have scientific knowledge of nature, as Aristotle itself has indicated by saying, immediately at the beginning of the text, 'we think that we know each thing when we recognize its first causes and first principles and as far as the elements'.[24]

[5,26: *The ordering of the work, i.e. its logical place in the scheme of Ar.'s works.*] And if it's also necessary to speak of the ordering of the work, it's obvious from the statement quoted that it comes first of all the natural-scientific works, since it teaches natural principles; and the natural-scientific treatises should be taken up after the ethical treatises which train our character and the logical treatises which supply us with the criterion of truth.

44 *Translation*

[*5,32: Authenticity.*] That the book is a genuine one of Aristotle's, it is superfluous to establish, since it is uncontested, and reference is made to it by Aristotle
6,1 in many of his uncontested works, and his most important students and everyone from his school refer to it, and some of them made summaries and synopses of it.

[*6,4: Internal structure.*] The treatise as a whole being primarily divided into two,
5 Adrastus says that the first five books are about all the natural principles and the things that follow from them, and the things that get caught up in the investigation.[25] And, taking up the discussion of motion from the sixth book on, in the last three books he [Aristotle] hands down all manner of natural-scientific theorems concerning motion. Hence Aristotle was accustomed to call the first
10 five books *On Principles* and the succeeding ones *On Motion*. In the first book of *On Principles*, he teaches about the auxiliary causes – I mean matter and form and the privation opposed to the form. In the second book he teaches about the proximate efficient cause, which he says is the nature, and indeed also about the final cause. Since there are also some apparent efficient causes, which have this
15 character accidentally, like luck and spontaneity, he does not leave the definitions of even these things unarticulated. Having defined nature as a principle of motion and in general of natural things characterized by motion, he teaches in the third book what motion is, both in general and each species of it. Since natural motion is continuous and the continuous is divisible to infinity, he
20 discusses both the continuous and the infinite in the third book. And since natural things are bodies and have position, they need a place in which to exist and be moved. Hence he will also go into detail about place in the fourth book. And since some people suppose that place is empty (*kenon*) interval, and some posit void (*to kenon*) in the role of a principle, he reasonably enough raised
25 questions about void. And since all motion is measured by time, it was also necessary for the natural scientist to concern himself with time. And thus he brought the fourth book to a conclusion. In the fifth book he distinguished motion precisely from the other kinds of change, and determined the opposition of kinds of motion to each other, and of kinds of rest to kinds of motions and to
30 each other, and delineated what a single motion is.

[*6,31: Aristotle in relation to his predecessors.*][26] After adding a few more comments, I'll turn to the text. For of those who philosophized before Plato, people like Thales and Anaximander and their followers[27] (since philosophy then, after the flood and the provision of necessities, was first beginning in

Translation 45

Greece) investigated the causes of things which arise by nature, and, since they   35
began from below, studied the material and elemental principles and brought
them to light without distinction, as if they were bringing to light the principles
of all existing things. But Xenophanes of Colophon and his student Parmenides   7,1
and the Pythagoreans handed down a most complete philosophy of their own as
regards both the natural things and the things above nature, albeit in a riddling
way. Anaxagoras of Clazomenae posited Reason (*nous*) as the efficient cause, but
made hardly any use of it in his causal explanations, as Socrates charges in the   5
Phaedo.[28] But perhaps there's nothing odd about this. For both Timaeus himself
and the character Plato depicted, although they began by hypothesizing an
efficient and a paradigmatic and a final cause of the things that come-to-be,
nevertheless gave their accounts of bodily causes starting from planes and shapes
and in general from the nature of the elements.[29] Except that Plato, bringing   10
forward Pythagorean and Eleatic [thought] into a clearer light, both celebrated
in a worthy fashion the things above nature and, in natural and generated things,
distinguished the elemental principles from the others.[30] Indeed, as Eudemus
reports, he [*sc.* Plato] himself was the first to give the name 'elements' to principles
of this sort, and he also distinguished the efficient and final causes, and in
addition the paradigmatic, i.e. the ideas, having recognized them himself.[31] For   15
he discovered matter by using the same notions as Aristotle did later on, and
similarly form.[32] And he posited the divine Reason as the efficient cause and his
goodness as the final cause, on account of which he [*sc.* the divine Reason] made
the sensible universe resemble the intelligible paradigm.

[*7,19: Ar.'s improvements on the natural scientists.*] But Aristotle surpassed the
natural philosophers before Plato not only in positing the efficient cause but   20
because he also considered the material causes in a more fundamental way. For
while they hypothesized either the homoiomeries, or one of the four elements or
several or all of them, or went as far as the atomic bodies, he himself resolved
both the homoiomeries and the four elements and analysed bodily nature itself
into matter and form, as Plato did before him, and before Plato the Pythagorean   25
Timaeus, when they made the four elements proximate [causes], and made the
planes [causes] prior to them, and made matter and form the first elemental
principles.

[*7,27: The superiority of Ar. in natural science to all his predecessors, including
Plato.*] Aristotle also surpassed both Plato and all those before Plato alike: while
they either discussed natural subjects as if discussing all of the things that are (as

46 *Translation*

30 some of those before Plato did), or raised the questions that are treated here as if they were questions about the cosmos and its parts and did so in writings on the cosmos (as Plato himself and some of those before him did), Aristotle both distinguished what rank natural things have among the things that are and also teaches, as if there were no cosmos, about natural body itself in its own right.

35 Also, among the elements he demonstrated that privation is something other

8,1 than matter, whereas Plato failed to distinguish privation from matter.[33] And while the others omit the efficient cause, and Anaxagoras and Plato (which is the same as to say the Pythagoreans),[34] posited the divine Reason [as efficient cause], Aristotle, seeking the proximate efficient cause of the things that arise by nature,

5 says that it is nature, which Plato had set down among the instrumental causes as being moved by another and moving others.[35] Not, however, that Aristotle stopped at the level of nature either, as if it were the first efficient cause, or the principally efficient cause; rather, he himself went up to the unmoved cause that moves all things, and at the end of this treatise he made all moving things depend on this.[36] Also the form of this man's study of nature surpassed those more

10 ancient, inasmuch as he turned their riddling manner into something clearer, and added precision to the demonstrations; he surpassed Plato, inasmuch as he makes the necessities in the demonstrations more manifest, and is careful to take their principles from sensation and from opinions close to hand; and he surpassed all of them alike in working out all the parts of the study of nature,

15 down to the most particular.

[8,16: *Division of Ar.'s works into exoteric and acroamatic.*][37] His writings are divided into two groups: the exoteric, like the historical works and the dialogues and in general those which are not concerned with the highest degree of precision, and the acroamatic works, which include the present treatise. In the acroamatic works, he practised an obscurity with which he fends off more careless readers, so that in comparison with [the exoteric works] they seem not

20 even to have been written up.[38] Indeed when Alexander wrote to him after the overthrow of the Persians, he said: 'Alexander to Aristotle: Fare well. You have not done rightly in publishing the acroamatic discourses. For in what will we still surpass others, if the discourses in which we were educated are going to be common to all? I would prefer to be superior to others in experience with the

25 best things rather than in power.' And Aristotle replied: 'Aristotle to Alexander the King: Fare well. You have written to me about the acroamatic discourses, thinking that they should be kept secret. Know, then, that they have been both published and not published. For they are comprehensible only to those who

Translation   47

have heard us. Be strong.' Plutarch of Chaeroneia in his *Life of Alexander* says
that these things were written on the occasion of the publication of the   30
Metaphysics.[39]

184a10-16[40] Since knowing (*to eidenai*) and scientific knowing result, in all the
disciplines of which there are principles or causes or elements, from recognizing
(*gnôrizein*) these (for we think that we cognize (*gignôskein*) each thing when we
recognize its first causes and first principles and as far as the elements),[41] it is
clear that in the science of nature too we must try first to determine what
concerns the principles.

[*8,32: The lemma worked out as a syllogism; why the first premise goes unargued.*]
The introduction straightaway reveals the object of the work, that it is about the
natural principles: for, he says, we must first try to determine what concerns
the natural principles. And he exhibits clearly the necessary use of the account
of the principles, using roughly the following syllogism: Natural things have   9,1
principles; Scientific knowledge of things that have principles results from
recognizing their principles; therefore scientific knowledge of natural things
results from recognizing their principles. Therefore, knowledge of the principles
of natural things is necessary for whoever is to have natural-scientific knowledge.
But that there *are* principles of natural things, the whole subsequent discussion   5
will show, and it is not in need of demonstration now. And for this reason, I
think, he omitted this premise.

[*9,7: Alternative explanations of why Ar. provides no demonstration of the premise
that natural things have principles.*] However, Theophrastus, at the start of his
own *Physics* demonstrated even this, saying 'But that there are principles of
natural things is clear from the fact that natural bodies are compound, and that
every compound has as principles the things out of which it is composed. For
everything which is by nature either is a body or at any rate has a body, and both   10
are compound.'[42] But Porphyry says that it does not even belong to the natural
scientist to investigate whether there are principles of natural things, but to
someone more elevated.[43] For the natural scientist uses his principles as given.
And he [Porphyry] might be even more inclined to say that it belongs to the
more elevated [*sc.* scientist] to investigate *what* the principles are. For neither the
geometer nor the doctor demonstrates his own principles, but they use them as
existing, and being such as they are. So then how is it that almost all of the   15
natural scientists investigate the principles of natural things? Perhaps because it
belongs to the natural scientist to demonstrate that natural things have principles

48 *Translation*

and have *these* principles, in the same way that it belongs to the doctor to demonstrate that the human body is composed out of the four elements (*stoikheia*) and that it belongs to the grammarian to demonstrate that speech is composed out of the twenty-four letters (*stoikheia*). But what power each of the
20 elements has, belongs to the more elevated [*sc.* scientist]: in the case of the letters, the poetic theorist; in the case of the human body, the natural scientist; in the case of the natural principles, the first philosopher. Hence Aristotle too, having shown that matter and form are principles of natural things, says that matter is known by analogy, even though the first philosopher also shows it from the
25 causes; and he says, 'concerning the formal principle, whether it is one or many, and what it is or what they are, it is the task of first philosophy to determine with precision. So let it be put off until that occasion' (*Physics* 1.9, 192a34-b1).

[9,27: *Discussion of the claim that we know things which have principles, causes, and elements by recognizing those principles, causes and elements.*] That scientific knowledge of things that have principles results when their principles are known, he has also posited as an axiom. And hence he uses the so-called connective
30 conjunction ['since'],[44] according to which the antecedent is taken as agreed. For if scientific knowledge is knowledge through demonstration, and a demonstration is a syllogism, and this is from principles, it is clear that scientific knowledge is knowledge through principles. But he also tries to make it persuasive from induction and from common belief. 'For', he says, 'we think we know each thing
35 when we recognize its first causes and first principles and as far as the elements.' Nor did he add the conclusion, 'therefore having scientific knowledge of natural things results from recognizing their principles', but rather what follows from the
10,1 conclusion: we must, he says, 'in the science of nature first determine the [questions] about the principles', in which he comprehends the conclusion too. However, Eudemus, at the beginning of his *Physics*, adds an argument higher up,[45] and, after showing that for practice it is more useful to know individuals,
5 but for contemplation to know what is common, he says that 'in the sciences what is most common seems to be the [account] of the principles: for each science has principles. These things being so, it is necessary for the person giving an account of nature to investigate the principles first.'[46]

[10,7: *Problems about the meaning and denotation of the key terms 'principle', 'cause', and 'element', starting with the mistaken view of Al. and Eudemus that the final cause is not a principle and the form is not an element.*][47] And this is the overall sense of the words.[48] But it is worth investigating what is a principle and

Translation 49

what is a cause and what is an element. For Alexander says that these differ from each other in that the efficient [cause], that from which motion begins, is especially called a principle,[49] whereas the for-the-sake-of-which and the form (which *is* the for-the-sake-of-which in things that are by nature) are especially called 'cause', and the constituent as matter is especially called 'element'. Alexander seems to be following Eudemus, who says:

> 'cause' being said in four ways, 'element' is said in the sense of 'matter': for the elements seem to be present in a thing, like the letters in speech, and this is the way in which bronze is said to be a cause of the long-lastingness of its products. And that whence the motion is also called a cause, and we call this a 'principle', and for this reason strife is the principle of insult.[50] Thus they call the principle and the element causes, but the for-the-sake-of-which does not admit the account of an element, for it is not present in what it causes, e.g. health in walking, nor does health seem to be a principle of walking, but rather a cause. And the for-the-sake-of-which and the form seem to be very close and often the same. So for this reason the for-the-sake-of-which seems most to be a cause.[51]

Thus far Eudemus. But it would be surprising if the form is not present in what it causes, unless by 'form' they mean the universal.

[*10,25: Another mistaken view about the scope of 'principle': Porphyry on the relation of 'principle' to 'cause'.*] Porphyry, however, says:

> in one way he [Aristotle] calls[52] that from which the first motion arises a 'principle'. And that-from-which is of this sort, as the first step[53] is the principle of a journey. And likewise also the keel of a ship and the foundation of a house. And 'finish' is opposite to 'principle' in this meaning. In another way, [something is called a principle] as that by which (*huph' hou*), as nature is a principle of natural things and art of artificial things. And the for-the-sake-of-which is also a principle, as victory is a principle of athletic training. And, in another way, the first constituent out of which (*ex hou*) a thing comes-to-be, as stones and logs are the principle of a house as matter. And the shape and figure and in general the form are also a principle. But Aristotle, having considered only the form which is in matter, said that this was a principle, while Plato, having recognized in addition to this also the separate form, introduced in addition the paradigmatic principle. So 'principle' is [said] in four ways according to Aristotle: either the out-of-which as the matter or the according-to-which as the form or the by-which as the agent or the on-account-of-which as the end. According to Plato there is also the [looking] towards-which (*pros ho*), as the paradigm, and the through-which (*di' hou*), as the instrumental. And 'cause' is said in as many ways

50 *Translation*

5 as 'principle'. And both are the same in the subject [that they denote] but differ in conception. For something is conceived as a principle (says Porphyry) inasmuch as it precedes, but as a cause inasmuch as it makes something and produces what comes after it, the cause being virtually principial, and the principle being virtually productive.[54] Hence also the conception of principle precedes the
10 conception of cause. And principles and causes being said in so many ways, not all of them exist in all cases.[55] Rather, some are principles of coming-to-be, like matter and form or the agent and patient or some one of the elements which each of the natural scientists considered; and others are principles of knowledge, [such as] the immediate[56] and indemonstrable premises; and others are principles of substance, in the way that the Pythagoreans said the limited and the
15 unlimited or the odd and the even [were principles]; and either the agent or the end are principles of action.[57]

[*11,16: Corrections of Al. and Eudemus and of Porphyry on the points just discussed.*] Having recounted these things, it should be said in reply to Alexander, and to Eudemus before him, that the for-the-sake-of-which, which is an end, is also a principle in every way, and principle in a stricter sense than the efficient, especially for these people [i.e. Peripatetics] who say that the unmoved first
20 cause is the end but not the efficient cause of all things; and they will [have to] agree that it is the principle of all things, if they say that it is the very first of all things. And how [can] they say that only matter is an element, if they think that the compound is [composed] out of matter and form? For even if the form is something final, it is even more elemental. And in reply to Porphyry, first, by the distinctions which he too has drawn,[58] 'cause' and 'principle' are not said in the
25 same number of ways; rather every cause is also a principle, but the principle of a thing like a journey or a drama would not be called a cause. Second, 'principle' is not even conceptually prior to 'cause', if, on the one hand, the cause must exist prior to the effect, and, on the other hand, the principle, if it is taken either as a part that precedes or as an element, exists together with the effect.[59]

[*11,29: S. gives his own view as to what kinds of 'principles', etc. Aristotle means.*]
30 So perhaps (*mêpote*)[60] Aristotle, having taken 'principle' as the common term, divided it into causes in the strict sense, such as the efficient and the final, and into what some people call 'auxiliary causes', such as the elements.[61] And this is why he says further on 'when we recognize the first (*prôta*) causes and the first (*prôtas*) principles', because the things which are primarily (*prôtôs*) and in the strict sense called causes are the same as the things which are primarily and in
35 the strict sense called principles. 'And as far as the elements', he says; that is, as

far as the things which are called causes and principles in the lowest way.[62] And so he says 'of which there are principles, either causes or elements'.[63] It's also possible that he said 'the first causes and the first principles' because some causes are proximate and individual, and others are *first*, and the person who cognizes[64]   12,1
the proximate ones but is ignorant of the first ones does not even know (*eidenai*) the proximate ones in the strict sense, since he is ignorant of the first causes, which are causes also of these [proximate causes]. So scientific knowing results when we recognize all the causes and all the principles, both the first ones and the proximate ones, which are elements.   5

[*12,5: Scientific knowledge requires knowledge of the principles common to all sciences, but this is not what Ar. refers to here.*][65] But since some first principles are appropriate to each [science], as in geometry the definitions and postulates,[66] and others are common to all [things], Alexander says that whoever is going to possess scientific knowledge must cognize these common principles. And this is a Platonic thing to say: for Plato will not allow to be called 'sciences' in the strict sense those which reach some conclusion by means of a hypothesis. In the present text, however, in saying 'we must try first to determine what concerns   10
the principles', Aristotle seems to be talking about the principles of the study of nature – the principles which he does in fact determine in the present treatise, not the common principles which are assigned to the first philosopher.

[*12,14: Why Ar. says 'knowing and scientific knowing': Plato and Ar. both distinguish eidenai and epistasthai, but treat the latter as the strict sense of the former.*] Alexander rightly remarks that 'knowing' (*eidenai*) and 'scientifically knowing' (*epistasthai*) have not been said in parallel, when he says 'things that are   15
said in parallel have a difference of words alone, the object being the same, and for this reason any one of them has the same force as all of them; but "knowing and scientifically knowing" does not have the same force as "knowing" alone: for we are said to "know" even the things that come through sensation and opinion and immediate premises, none of which we know by demonstration, that is to say, by scientific knowledge.' And thus far he is right. But he [Alexander] did not   20
go on to add in what way they [*sc.* 'knowing' and 'scientifically knowing'] are both used here; but he [Aristotle] seems to put 'knowing' before 'scientific knowing' as its genus, as if he were to say 'to cognize scientifically'. This is like saying 'someone who says something, and says in such a way as to assert, speaks either truly or falsely': for 'saying' is the genus of 'asserting', as 'knowing' (*eidēsis*), that is, 'cognition' (*gnôsis*), is of 'scientifically knowing'. That he acknowledged   25

52   *Translation*

'knowing' as said also of sensation is made clear by the introduction to the
Metaphysics: 'all human beings by nature desire to know (*eidenai*), as is made
clear by the delight in the senses.'[67] But perhaps (*mêpote*) in the present passage
Aristotle takes 'knowing' (*eidêsis*) in the strict sense and identifies it with scientific
30   knowledge: for Plato too says that the mathematicians do not know (*eidenai*)
their own principles, clearly meaning that they do not know scientifically,
on the ground that the strict sense of knowing is scientific knowing: 'For, when
someone has a principle which he does not know, and intermediates and a
13,1   conclusion from what he doesn't know, how is it possible to call his "knowing"
(*eidenai*) scientific knowledge?'.[68] And he clearly says that opinion is other
than knowledge (*gnôsis*) when he says 'What then if this person who we
say has opinion but does not know (*gignôskein*) is angry at us?' (*Rep.* 5, 476D8-
9); and likewise he distinguishes the opinable from the knowable when he
says 'we agreed beforehand that if something should turn out to be of this sort,
5   it should be called opinable rather than knowable (*gnôston*)' (*Rep.* 5, 479D7-8).
But that Aristotle does not add 'knowing' (*eidêsis*), that is to say cognition
(*gnôsis*), in the broad sense but rather in the sense of scientific knowledge,
is also clear from what he adds: 'for we think that we cognize (*gignôskein*)',
he says, 'each thing when we recognize its first causes and first principles',
thus meaning by 'cognition' (*gnôsis*) the knowledge derived from the
10   principles, that is, scientific knowledge. That opinion is one thing and scientific
knowledge is another, Socrates showed in the *Theaetetus* from the fact that there
is both true and false opinion, whereas scientific knowledge is only true;[69] and
Alexander now makes use of the same demonstration.

[*13,14: Al. on why Aristotle adds the 'of which there are principles or causes or
elements'.*] But how is that, having said 'knowing and scientific knowing result in
15   all the disciplines', he adds 'of which there are principles or causes or elements'?
Perhaps he added this as being proper to all scientific kinds of knowing.[70] For
scientific knowledge, being a demonstrative syllogism, is certainly from
immediate premises as principles. But if so, since we know the immediate
premises without demonstration (since otherwise there would be an infinite
regress), then we will also know the principles of natural things without
20   demonstration. And yet he will try to communicate them through demonstrative
syllogisms.[71] So Alexander says, 'since principle and element differ (for the
element is matter), and not all [sciences] have matter, e.g. the mathematical
[sciences do not], what he is saying here would be to make clear that although all
sciences have some one of these [*sc.* principle, cause, element], not all sciences

Translation

have all of them, but some have principles *and* causes *and* elements and others do not, [namely] those which are not about generable things and do not have their being in matter. And there are also some in which there is no for-the-sake-of-which, as seems to be the case for geometry: for there is neither a principle in ungenerated things, nor matter in immaterial things.'[72] 25

[13,28: *Al.'s reading is wrong about what sciences involve 'elements' and final causes.*] But, although Alexander says these things in these very words,[73] we must remark:[74] how [can it be that] only matter is an element and only material things are out of elements? For we speak of elements of speech,[75] and the philosophers 30 have written about the elements of speech; but if an element is that out of which, being present in a thing, something first comes-to-be, and into which it is last resolved,[76] and if the compound comes-to-be out of matter and form, it is clear that the form too is an element of the compound. And how do the mathematical sciences not have as matter numbers and intervals and sounds, whose forms they investigate? And it is even more worth remarking: how is there no for-the- 14,1 sake-of-which in geometry? For it was taken up for the sake of utility in life, both in itself and as supplying principles to mechanics; moreover, it makes the greatest contributions towards astronomy and towards accustoming us to the incorporeal nature.[77] And if, from the fact that it is cognitive and not practical, it follows that 5 it has no end, then the study of nature too will be aimless, and so will all of theoretical philosophy, whose end is the ascent to the first good, and to turn the soul from something human into a god as far as possible, as Aristotle himself communicates in Book 10 of the *Nicomachean Ethics* (*EN* 10.7, 1177b27-1178a8).

[14,9: *The puzzles presented by the relative clause 'of which there are principles or causes or elements' revisited.*][78] 'One possibility', says Alexander, 'is that he is now using "scientific knowledge" in a broader sense which also includes the 10 discernment of the principles, which do not [themselves] have principles, and [then, in the restrictive clause] distinguishes scientific knowledge [which comes] from principles from this [discernment]. But that "scientific knowledge" is not intended in a more general sense is made clear by the fact that he adds "scientific knowing" after "knowing".[79] It is also possible that 'of which there are principles or causes or elements" is said as being proper to all scientific kinds of knowing (*epistêmonikê eidêsis*). For scientific knowledge, being a demonstrative syllogism, is certainly from immediate premises as principles. But 15 if so, since we know the immediate premises without demonstration (since otherwise there would be an infinite regress), then we will also know the

54 *Translation*

principles of natural things without demonstration. And yet he will try to communicate them through demonstrative syllogisms.'[80]

[14,18: S.'s own explanation of the scope of the sentence: the restrictive term here is methodos, so that Ar.'s claim is that all knowledge belonging to a discipline comes about from principles.] So perhaps (*mêpote*) we should attend to Aristotle himself when he says precisely that scientific knowing results not 'about (*peri*) all the
20 things that are' or 'in (*peri*) all the [kinds of] knowledge', but 'in (*peri*) all the disciplines'. For if, as Alexander says, a discipline (*methodos*) is any disposition for contemplating the things that fall under it with an account (*meta logou*), that is, with a cause, or, to say the same thing, the progression (*proodos*) to the knowable by a well-ordered path (*hodos*), it is clear that the knowledge of the principle would not be a discipline, but only the scientific knowledge which
25 arises from the principles and causes of the knowable [object]. So of those knowable [objects] which have principles, either as causes or as elements, as is the case for natural things, scientifically knowing these things results from recognizing their principles: for scientific knowledge is knowledge (*gnôsis*) from principles.

> **184a16-b14** For the path is naturally from the things that are better known and clearer to us to the things that are clearer and better known by nature. For the same things are not knowable to us and without qualification. Hence we must advance in this way from the things that are less clear by nature, but more clear to us, to the things that are clearer and better known by nature. At first it's rather things which are confused which are manifest and clear to us. Later on, starting from these things, the elements and principles become knowable as we divide them. Hence it's necessary to progress from the universal to the individuals. For the whole is better known by sensation and the universal is a kind of whole. For the universal comprehends many things as parts. The same thing in a way happens with names in relation to a definition (*logos*). For they signify a kind of whole without differentiation, like 'circle', whereas the definition divides it into individuals. And little children initially address all men as fathers and all women as mothers, while later on they distinguish each of these.

30 *[14,30: Ar. will begin by explaining how we know principles.]* Having shown that the person who is going to have scientific knowledge of natural things must examine the principles of natural things, and turning in what follows to teaching about the principles, he first determines the manner of this teaching. For the
15,1 question arises (*zêteitai*) whether it is possible to learn anything about the principles at all: for if 'all teaching and all discursive learning'[81] arises from

principles, and it is impossible to grasp principles of the principles, learning would be precluded. So he himself explains to us the manner of knowing the principles.

[*15,4: How knowledge of principles is possible.*] We must begin from a bit further back [i.e. from more general considerations]. Everything known is either self-warranting, and because it is agreed on is [i.e. is uncontroversially usable as] a principle of knowledge, like definitions and the so-called immediate premises, or else is known through some pre-existing knowledge of definitions and immediate premises, like everything that is known through syllogisms and demonstration. Thus clearly also for the principles of natural things (these things being compounds),[82] that they are not self-warranting is clear from the differing conjectures of the natural scientists, since different natural scientists hypothesize different principles, as we will learn; and if they are demonstrable, they must be demonstrated from things that are better known. For 'all teaching and all discursive learning' – that is, all learning which does not come about by sensation or from intellectual intuition but is syllogistic and demonstrative, 'arises from pre-existing knowledge', as we have learned in the *Posterior Analytics*.[83] And 'the things that are better known' are assumed either as principles and causes of the things demonstrated, which is what happens in demonstrations in the strict sense (for these arise from the principles and causes of the thing, as when we deduce that the world is beautiful from the Demiurge's being good, or deduce the immortality of the soul from its self-motion); or else [they are assumed] as necessary consequences of the things which are demonstrated, which they in this way [mutually or reciprocally] entail.[84] The things that are better known are assumed in this latter way when for instance we show that the god is good from the world's being beautiful and ordered, this being closer to hand to us as regards sensation, or when we show that the soul is self-moved from ensouled bodies' being moved from within, and this manner of syllogism is sign-inferential rather than demonstrative.[85] And the things which are assumed towards this kind of confirmation (*pistis*) are not principles of the thing demonstrated (for they follow on it rather than preceding it), but principles of this kind of demonstration, since they are better known and more manifest, and the confirmation (*pistis*) of the thing demonstrated arises from them. Therefore also the principles of natural things – principles[86] in the sense of causes – must certainly be demonstrated from some things which are better known. But sometimes [they will be demonstrated] from things which are also more principial[87] by nature and have the role of causes; [such demonstration] is not appropriate to the natural scientist

56   *Translation*

16,1 (for it exceeds his measure[88] to know the causes of the appropriate principles [for his science]); rather, it belongs to the science more elevated than his, first philosophy:[89] for this science, using self-warranting principles, demonstrates the principles of the other sciences that are taken as causes. It is also possible in a way to deduce what concerns the principles of natural things from what follows from the principles and is composed of them, [deducing] not from causes but from things better known (*gnôrimôtera*), so that we would not know [the

5   principles] scientifically but merely recognize (*gnôrizein*) them. And this is why he says [184a11-12] not 'from knowing the principles scientifically' but 'from recognizing (*gnôrizein*)' them, because the knowledge (*gnôsis*) of them comes from the things which follow from them. And there follow from the more principial and elemental things the things which are compounds of them, and from the parts the wholes.

[*16,8: How sensible particular wholes are 'better known'.*] And the compound and 'confused' things are better known to us than the simple things which compose

10   them, since we recognize compounds through sensation, and most people have this kind of knowledge closer to hand, whereas simples are of such a nature as to be grasped from the compounds. For we readily recognize each animal and plant, that *this* is a human being or a horse, and that *this* is a fig-tree or a vine, but it does not belong to everyone to know that these things are composed out of the

15   four elements; and *how* the elements are disposed so as to make an animal, and *this* animal, and how so as to make a plant, and *this* plant, would belong only to those who have attained the summit of philosophy.

[*16,17: In what way universals are better known than particulars.*] And also in this way common and universal things, the knowledge of which is cruder[90] and more manifest, are better known to us than the individuals: for it is easier to discern that what is approaching from a distance is an animal than that it is a human being, and easier to recognize that it is a human being than that it is

20   Socrates. The universal resembles the whole in containing confused within itself the articulation of the many things that compose it, as the parts are contained within the whole: for in animal too [is contained] the variety of the species of animal without distinction; and so the universal as compound and confused is better known to us,[91] and first in knowledge as regards us, just as by nature this

25   too is posterior, if indeed it is a by-product of the individuals.[92] For the simpler things are clearer and better known by nature, as being pure and unmixed; and this is why the science of dialectic is accustomed to examine what each '[thing]

itself' is, philosophizing among simple forms, inasmuch as it proceeds in tandem with the nature of beings, according to which simpler things are better known and more manifest than compound ones, and pure things than confused ones.　30

[*16,31: Explication of Ar.'s first example: name and definition.*] That what is indistinct and confused, like the whole, seems better known to us, he confirms by taking each name as a kind of whole, and taking the definition of the name as conveying the articulation of the parts and elements of the name. For it is clear that the knowledge of the circle by its name is close to hand even for most people, but that the definition of the circle – that it is a plane figure bounded by a single　17,1 [curved] line, such that all the [straight lines] falling on this [curved line] from a single point are equal to each other[93] – this definition, which conveys the individuals (*ta kathekasta*)[94] of the circle and goes through its parts and elements, is no longer close to hand for all. Now this example [*sc.* name and definition] is　5 appropriate to the compound and whole – for all the parts and elements in the definition are synthesized and confused in the name as in a single whole – but it is not appropriate to the universal. For the universal fits each of the things which fill it out (for both human being and horse are animal[s]), whereas the name fits all of the things contained in the definition together, but not each of them　10 individually. For figure is not a circle, nor is bounded-by-a-single-line a circle, nor is any other one or several of the things contained in the definition, but only all of them together.

[*17,13: The second example.*] This is why he adduced the second example, what is observed from progress in growing up. For young children, whose knowledge (*gnôsis*) is still crude and confused, address all men as fathers and all women as　15 mothers. But as time progresses they articulate what is crude into what is proper to the particular, and in this way they acquire a precise knowledge (*eidêsis*) of their parents. So we too, as long as we discern things by following what is crude and confused in sensory cognitions, are in no way unlike young children who　20 call all the men they meet fathers; but when we progress from confused things to pure ones, from compound things to simple and elemental ones, then we would be progressing closer to scientific knowledge, inasmuch as we recognize not only things knowable by sensation but also things knowable by reason, and not only the compound effects but also their causal elements.　25

[*17,25: Al.'s reading: S. repeats and engages with this at 19,29 ff.*] 'And it has been said', says Alexander, 'that it is possible that by universals here he also means the

58   Translation

axioms, which on account of their obviousness we use in [establishing] everything that is to be shown, but which are not proper to any of the things that are shown by means of them: such as that either the affirmation or the denial holds in each case, and that when equals are taken away from equals, the remainders are equal. For these are universal, through being applicable to many [cases], and each of the things which are shown by them is embraced by them as a part.'[95]

30

[*17,31: Start of detailed observations on the lemma and Physics 1.1 as a whole.*] So then this is the overall reasoning and arrangement of the things said in the introduction [*sc. Physics* 1.1]. But it is worth observing (*epistêsai*) about them, first that the example of the whole and the compound is proper to the present topic, but not the example of the universal. For the universal is not composed out of the individuals as of elements, like the whole and the compound: for no element accepts having the compound predicated of it, as the individuals [accept having] the universal predicated of them.

35

[*17,38: Second observation: two kinds of cognitions of wholes.*] Second, it is worth observing (*epistasis*) that there is a twofold cognition of the whole and of the universal, just as there is of the name: one kind of cognition is crude and confused and arising from a bare notion of the thing known – and this is rougher than cognition according to the definition – and another [kind of cognition] is synthesized and united and comprehends the particulars, the latter being intellectual and simple, whereas the former is imaginative[96] and restricted.[97] This crude [kind of cognition] is familiar to the many, the other to those at the summit.[98] For the many understand the universal, as what is common in the particulars, grasping by abstraction its bare specificity, which shines out when the commonality dominates the differences. The others intellectually synthesize the whole grasp of its particulars and the traversal of all of them and the commonality which synthesizes the differences. And [likewise] when the many hear the name (for example, 'human being') they are brought back to [i.e. reminded of] the crude imagination; but the philosopher synthesizes the definition in a single simplicity, so that he thinks the multiplicity of the definition united, and grasps simultaneously the multiplicity and the one. And this is proper to scientific knowledge, as was hinted also by Socrates in the *Theaetetus*.[99] The cognition according to the definition and through the elements is intermediate between the two, being, rather, discursive or else opinionative,[100] surpassing the inferior kind of cognition in its precision, but falling short of the

18,1

5

10

15

superior kind of cognition through being divided and also through being more or less lacunose. And in this way too the crude cognition of the common things precedes the articulation of the differences, but the precise cognition arises afterwards by synthesizing the differences in the commonality. So whenever Aristotle says that the cognition of common things is first in relation to us, but posterior by nature, he means this crude cognition arising from abstraction of the bare commonality, which also does not subsist by itself.

[18,24: *Third observation: Knowledge of principles of natural things is not demonstrative.*] Third, it is worth observing (*ephistanein*) what sort of thing demonstration about natural things is. For if knowing (*eidenai*) something about natural things belongs to those who have come to know (*gignôskein*) the principles and causes of natural things, and if we discover these from the things which are already compound and confused, which cannot be precisely cognized unless their causes have been precisely cognized, then it is clear that cognition about the principles is sign-inferential and not demonstrative. And Plato rightly said that to give an account of nature is to give a probable account;[101] and Aristotle too bears witness to this when he would have it that demonstration in the strict sense is from immediate and self-warranting principles and from causes in the strict sense and from things prior by nature.[102] But giving an account of nature should not be dishonoured on these grounds; rather, we must rest content with what is in our nature and our power, as is also the opinion of Theophrastus.[103]

[19,1: *A puzzle: how can the common things be less clear, and therefore posterior by nature?*] Fourth, in addition to the things that have been said, it is worth investigating what Aristotle means by saying that the common things are clearer in relation to us but less clear by nature.[104] For if they are less clear by nature, it is evident that they are also more remote and posterior by nature. But common things, when they are destroyed, destroy also the things that fall under them, and not vice versa; and we say this is characteristic of things that are prior by nature.[105] And even Alexander of Aphrodisias agrees that the common and universal is prior by nature to the things under it, e.g. animal is prior by nature to man in destroying it when it is destroyed and not vice versa.[106] And this much Alexander says reasonably enough; but after saying that 'the universal is first by nature', he adds 'but not first in the strict sense, since it is not even a substance; and this is why the cognition of the common [features] of a thing[107] is posterior to the cognition through [features] that are proper to it, if indeed the [features] that

60   *Translation*

reveal the proper nature of each thing are *first* in it.' However, one might wonder
how it could be that what is first by nature would not be first in the strict sense.

[*19,12: S.'s own solution to this puzzle.*] So perhaps (*mêpote*), just as Aristotle says
that the elements and parts are prior by nature to the whole and the compound,
while as confused and graspable by sensation the compounds are first in relation
15   to us, so too he is taking the [universals] which are posterior and [produced] by
abstraction as 'common'[108] – things which do not strictly destroy the particulars
when they are destroyed, since they are taken as bare properties and not as
comprehending the particulars. So if someone can give a yet more persuasive
account of this, let him do so.

[*19,18: What 'common things' does Ar. say are better known to us? Al. claims that
they are universal truths about the principles.*] But since Aristotle says that we
must work back up from things that are common and compound and clearer to
20   us to the principles of natural things, it is worth investigating what are the
common things, and what are the things prior by nature, which are also principles
of natural things. Well then Alexander says: 'he will show first that the principles
are several, and neither one nor infinitely many, then that there must be both a
contrariety in them and something that underlies the contrariety; then, making
a transition from these [assertions], which are common, he will show what they
[the principles] are: for the person who knows these [general characterizations
25   of the principles] does not yet know what the principles are.' But it is worth
remarking: if 'whether the principle is one or several' and 'whether they contain
a contrariety or not' and 'whether something underlies them or not' are said
about the principles themselves and not about the things that are composed out
of them, how will this procedure send us up from the compounds to the
principles? 'And it has been said', says Alexander, 'that it is possible that by
30   universals here he also means the axioms',[109] which we have mentioned before
[17,25 ff. above]. He now invokes these [axioms]: for that the principle must be
either one or several is equivalent to its being either one or not one, and this is
subordinated to [the axiom that] of each thing either the affirmation or the
negation ought to be predicated. But these common things [*sc.* the axioms] too
are not compounded from the principles of natural things, which is what
35   Aristotle's precept requires, but rather they too are observations about the
20,1   principles;[110] and we were supposed to come to know, from the things which are
compound and better known to us, whether the principle is one or several, and
whether they are contraries or not, and what they are.

[20,3: S.'s own explanation of how Ar. thinks we come to grasp principles of natural things, viz. via observation of natural things.] So perhaps (*mêpote*) it is better to find the principles of natural things starting from the attributes which hold, obviously and knowably by sensation, of natural things, as Aristotle himself thinks. For instance, that the principle is not one [we come to know] by means of the variety of the things that are, as we will learn: for, he says, if there are among the things that are both substance and quantity and quality, whether detached from each other or not, then the things that are are many.[111] We will learn the precise [details] of what has been said a little later on. And that the principles are not unmoved he shows from the obvious motion of natural things: 'for let us suppose', he says, 'that some or all natural things are moved; and this is clear from induction.'[112] And that the principles are contraries is shown from the agreement of the natural scientists about this, and that they are form and privation and something underlying is shown from the change in natural things. For if change is not from any chance thing to any chance thing, but the musical [comes-to-be] from the unmusical, and in general [something comes-to-be] from what is not such but is naturally suited to be such, and if every change must occur in some persisting underlying thing, then it is clear both that [the principles] are contrary, as form and privation, and that they are in a formless subject. And overall, to put it in general terms, we must track down the truth about natural principles [starting] from the senses and sensible things, being persuaded also by Theophrastus who, investigating this in the first book of his *Physics*, wrote as follows: 'since it is not possible[113] to talk about even one thing without motion (for all the things of nature are in motion), nor to talk about the things around the centre [of the cosmos] without alteration and qualitative change, with a view to these things and speaking about them it's not possible to do without sensation, but rather we must try to consider [these things] beginning from this [i.e. sensation], either grasping the phenomena in themselves or [starting] from them, if perchance there are any principles stronger than them and prior to these.'[114] And I think it would be better for the transition from the things better known to us to the principles to take place in this kind of way. But let us turn to what comes next.

184b15 The principle must necessarily be either one or several.[115]

[20,29: Puzzle about why Ar. apparently skips prior question of whether natural things have principles: the answer of 'the commentators'.] It would be in sequence first to investigate whether there are principles of natural things at all, and then what and how many they are; for this was the order of problems which he handed

62 *Translation*

down to us in the *Apodictics* [= *Posterior Analytics*]. 'But this [*sc.* whether there are principles of natural things]', they say, 'belonged not to the natural scientist but to the more elevated [*sc.* scientist, i.e. the first philosopher] to consider:[116] for

21,1 the natural scientist uses this as given. For this reason he straightaway says in the introduction, as positing that there are principles of natural things, "since ... of the things which have principles or causes or elements" [*Phys.* 184a11], someone who is going to have scientific knowledge about these things[117] must first "recognize these [principles etc.]" [184a12], so too among the things "belonging to the science of nature we must try first to determine what concerns the

5 principles" [184a14-16].' So say the commentators on Aristotle.[118] But it is worth observing that perhaps (*mêpote*) even the question 'how many and what are the principles?' and the account of principles in general seem to belong to the more elevated [*sc.* scientist] according to this account.

[*21,8: S.'s own solution.*] But perhaps (*mêpote*) it's also necessary for the natural scientist to know that natural things are bodies, and that every body is a compound, and that what is compound has as principles the things out of which

10 it is composed, as Theophrastus too demonstrated.[119] So presumably it is better to say that 'whether it is' is not investigated in all problems, but [only] in those in which this is contested, e.g. whether the void exists, but not whether a human being exists: for this too has been determined in the rules of logic.[120] And while all the natural scientists agree that there are principles of natural things, they investigate what they are. For he says that also those who investigated what is

15 were investigating the principle of what is [cf. *Physics* 1.2, 184b22-25]. For those who philosophized about the principles were investigating them as principles of things that are: some did so without distinction, not distinguishing natural things from the things that are above nature; others did so distinguish, like the Pythagoreans and Xenophanes and Parmenides and Empedocles and Anaxagoras, but through their obscurity this escaped most people's notice. For

20 this reason Aristotle argues against [the latter group], as against the apparent sense, in order to come to the help of those who took [them] superficially. And in demonstrating that the principles are such or so many, at the same time he also demonstrates simultaneously that there are principles in the first place (*holôs*).

[*21,22: Ar.'s division of the ancients' theories of principles.*] So having shown, given that there are principles, that knowledge about the principles is necessary, and having conveyed the manner of approaching them, he thinks it reasonable not to

Translation

express his own opinion about the principles before he has examined the opinions of the more ancient thinkers. And having assumed as a disjunctive axiom 'the principle is either one' or many (for it is necessary on account of the axiom of contradiction that it be either one or not one; and if not one, then many)[121] and (he says) that 'if it is one', it must in turn be either 'moved ... or unmoved', he next arranges the opinions that had been laid down previously [i.e. by earlier thinkers] under the sections of the division. For either it is one and unmoved, as Parmenides and Melissus seemed to be saying, or one and moved, as the natural scientists did. 'But if the principles are several, either they are finite' in number 'or infinite, and, if finite ... either two or three or determined by some other number';[122] if infinite, then either of the same kind or else opposite in kind. And though it would be possible to divide also those who said [that the principle was] one into [those who made it] infinite and finite, and to divide those [who said that the principles were] many into [those who made them] moved or unmoved, Alexander says, 'he subjoined to each [section] of the division what was more appropriate to it', and being moved or not moved is more appropriate to the one [principle], and being finite or infinite to the many. But one must know that later down in the arguments against them, after arguing against Parmenides and Melissus, he takes up those whom he calls natural scientists and divides them in this way: either they say that what is, or the element, is one, or that it is one-and-many: one, if it is one of the three elements [i.e. fire, air, or water] or something intermediate; one-and-many, like Empedocles and Anaxagoras; and he also ranks among these people Democritus, who says [that there are] the void and the atoms.[123]

[22,9: Al. is wrong to think that Ar.'s restriction here of the application of 'moved/ unmoved' and 'finite/infinite' to the one and the many respectively expresses their irrelevance to the other branch of the division.] But one must observe that 'infinite and finite' in plurality, which was appropriate to those who say that the principles are many, is one thing and 'infinite or finite' in magnitude is another. He both examines the latter in the arguments against Melissus and Parmenides, and also applies it to Anaximander and Anaximenes, who hypothesized that the element was one, but infinite in magnitude. And 'moved and unmoved' also applies to the division both of those who said that the principle was one and of those who said that the principles were several. For this reason Eudemus says, 'however the principles may be, they are either moved or unmoved.'[124] But Aristotle passes over this disjunction,[125] because there never was an opinion that said that the principles were many but unmoved. But he seems to skip here 'finite and infinite'

64 *Translation*

in the case of the one for the sake of concision; in any case, as I have said, he puts these [*sc*. 'finite and infinite' as said of a single principle] too to the test in his
20 arguments against Parmenides and Melissus. But it is presumably better first to encompass all the opinions through a more complete division, and then having done so to go back to the text of Aristotle.

[*22,22: The fuller, more systematic division undertaken: excursus on Xenophanes, whose principle does not fit the division.*] Well then: the principle must necessarily be either one or not one, that is to say, several, and, if one, either unmoved or moved.[126] And if unmoved, either infinite, as Melissus of Samos seems to say, or
25 finite, as does Parmenides, son of Pyres, of Elea;[127] however, these people were talking not about a natural element, but about what really is. But Theophrastus says that Xenophanes of Colophon, the teacher of Parmenides, posited that the principle is one, or that what is is one and all, and neither finite nor infinite, neither moved nor at rest, while he [*sc*. Theophrastus] grants that the mention of his doctrine belongs more to some other enquiry than to the enquiry into nature.
30 For Xenophanes said that this one and all is god, whom he shows to be one from the fact that he [*sc*. god] is most dominant of all things.[128] For, he says, if they [*sc*. gods] were several, it would necessarily belong to all of them alike (*homoiôs*)[129] to dominate; but god is what is most dominant and best of all things. He showed that [god] is ungenerated from the fact that whatever is generated must be
23,1 generated either out of something like or out of something unlike. But, he says, what is like cannot be affected by what is like (for the like is no more suited to generate its like than to be generated out of it). If it were generated out of something unlike, what is will be out of what is not. In this way he showed that [god] is ungenerated and eternal. And [he showed that god] is neither
5 infinite nor finite, because what is not is infinite, as having neither beginning (*arkhê*) nor middle nor end, and the many limit each other.[130] In much the same way he takes away both motion and rest [from god]: for what is not is unmoved (for neither will anything else come to it, nor will it go to anything else [i.e. change]), and the things that are more than one are moved (for one thing changes into another). Thus when he says that it remains in the same
10 [place] and is not moved:

> and it remains always in the same [place], moved in no way
> nor is it appropriate for it to proceed at different times in different directions[131]

he does not mean that it 'remains' in the sense of the rest which is opposed to motion, but in the sense which transcends motion and rest. But Nicolaus of

Translation 65

Damascus, in *On the Gods*,[132] records him as saying that the principle is infinite and 15
unmoved and Alexander [mentions him as saying] that it is finite and spherical. But
from what has been said already it is clear that he shows it to be neither infinite nor
finite; rather he calls it finite and spherical on account of its being alike from all
sides. And he describes it as thinking (*noein*) all things when he says:

> But far from effort it shakes all things by the intelligence (*phrên*) of its thought 20
> (*nous*).[133]

[*23,21: Those who say that the principle is one and moved and finite.*] Of those who
say that the principle is one and moved, whom he especially calls 'natural
scientists',[134] some say that it is finite. In this way Thales, the son of Examyes of
Miletus, and Hippo, who seems to have been an atheist, said that the principle was
water, being led to this conclusion by the things that appear to the senses. For the
hot lives by the moist, and things that are dead dry out, and the seeds of all things 25
are moist, and all nourishment juicy; and each thing is naturally nourished by that
out of which it is; and water is the principle of the moist nature and holds all things
together (*sunektikon*).[135] This is why they supposed that water was the principle of
all things, and declared that the earth rests on water.[136] Thales has come down to
us as the first person to have brought to light the enquiry into nature for the 30
Greeks: there were many others before him, as Theophrastus too thinks,[137] but he
so surpassed them as to eclipse all who had come before him; he is said to have left
nothing in writing except the so-called *Nautical Astronomy*.[138] Hippasus of
Metapontum and Heraclitus of Ephesus too said that [the principle] was one and 24,1
moved and finite, but they made the principle fire, and they make the things that
are come from fire by condensation and rarefaction, and they resolve them again
into fire, on the grounds that this one nature is what underlies: for Heraclitus says
that all things are an exchange for fire.[139] And Heraclitus also makes a certain order
and a determinate time of the change of the cosmos according to a certain fated 5
necessity.[140] And it is clear that these people too acquired this opinion from
observing the life-generating and craftsmanly and concocting [power] of heat,
pervading all things and altering all things. For we do not have [any evidence] that
they set it down as infinite. Furthermore, if 'element' is the minimal thing out of
which other things come-to-be and into which they are resolved, and fire is finest- 10
grained of all things, this would be most of all an element.[141] So these are the
people who said that the element is one and moved and finite.

[*24,13: Next branch of the division: the principle as one and moved and infinite.*][142]
Of those who said that [the principle] is one and moved and infinite, Anaximander

66 *Translation*

the son of Praxiades of Miletus, the successor and student of Thales, said that the
15   infinite was the principle and element of the things that are, being the first to
introduce the word 'principle'.[143] And he says that it [*sc.* the principle] is neither
water nor any other of the so-called elements, but a certain other infinite nature,
out of which all the heavens and the worlds within them come-to-be: and the
things that are perish into the same things out of which they come-to-be,
according to necessity. For they pay the just penalty and render recompense to
20   each other for their injustice according to the order of time – saying these things
thus in rather poetic words.[144] So it is clear that this man, having considered the
change of the four elements into each other, did not think it fit to make some one
of these the underlying thing, but rather something else beside these. And he
makes coming-to-be [happen] not when the element is qualitatively altered, but
25   when the contraries are separated out through the eternal motion; and this is
why Aristotle groups him together with Anaxagoras and his followers.[145]

[24,26: *The 'one, moved, infinite' branch continued: Anaximenes.*] Anaximenes the
son of Eurystratus of Miletus, who was a companion of Anaximander, also says
that the underlying nature is one and infinite, as he did, but not indeterminate, as
he did, but determinate, saying that it is air: and it differs in rareness and density
among the different substances. When it is rarefied it comes-to-be fire, when
30   condensed wind, then cloud, when yet more [dense] water, then earth, then
stones; and the other things [come-to-be] out of these. And he too [*sc.* like
Anaximander] makes motion eternal, on account of which also [this] change
25,1   comes-to-be.

[25,1: *The 'one, moved principle' branch of the division completed: Diogenes of
Apollonia.*] Also Diogenes of Apollonia, who was pretty much the most recent of
those who devoted themselves to such things, wrote most things in a jumbled-
together way, saying some things in accordance with Anaxagoras, others
in accordance with Leucippus; and he too [*sc.* like Anaximenes] says that
the nature of the universe is air, infinite and eternal, out of which the shape
5   of other things comes-to-be when it is condensed and rarefied and changed
in its affections. This is what Theophrastus reports on Diogenes, and
his [Diogenes'] treatise entitled *On Nature*, which has come down to me,
clearly says that that out of which all other things come-to-be is air.[146] Nicolaus,
however, reports that he posited the element as intermediate between fire
and air.[147]

Translation   67

[*25,9: Conclusions on the 'one, moved principle' branch.*] And these people
[Anaximenes and Diogenes] thought that the easily affected and easily   10
[qualitatively] altered [character] of air was suitable for change; this is why
they did not think it at all fit to posit earth as a principle, since it is hard to move
and hard to change.[148] And this is the division of those who said that the
principle is one.

[*25,14: The division continued: those who say the principles are many, beginning
with those who say they are of finitely different kinds.*][149] But of those who said
that the principles were several, some posited that they were finite and others
that they were infinite in multiplicity. And of those who said that they were finite,   15
some said that they were two, as Parmenides (in what he wrote with regard to
appearance (*doxa*)) posited fire and earth, or rather light and darkness, or as the
Stoics posited god and matter, clearly not intending god as an element, but rather
one [principle] as agent and the other as patient; others said that they were three,
as Aristotle did with matter and the contraries; others four, like Empedocles of
Agrigentum, who was born a little later than Anaxagoras, and was an admirer   20
and associate of Parmenides and even more of the Pythagoreans. He makes the
bodily elements four: fire and air and water and earth, which are eternal in
muchness and littleness,[150] but change through being combined and separated.
And he posited as principles in the strict sense, by which these things are moved,
Love and Strife. For the elements must continue to be moved in alternate ways,
being combined at one time by Love, and separated at another time by Strife. So   25
according to him the principles are six. For he sometimes gives the efficient
power to Strife and Love, when he says:

> at one time all things coming together through Love into one
> at another time again all borne asunder through Strife's hatred[151]   30

And at other times he ranks these too as coordinate with the four, when he says:

> then again they grew apart to be many out of one: 26,1
> fire and water and earth and immense height of air
> and accursed Strife apart from them, each equivalent,
> and Love amidst them, equal in length and breadth.[152]

[*26,5: Plato's (finitely many) principles.*][153] And Plato posits that the causes in the
strict sense are three, the efficient, the paradigm, and the end; and that the
auxiliary causes are also three, the matter, the form, and the instrument.
Theophrastus, however, after first reporting on the others, says that 'After these

68   *Translation*

came Plato, who was before them in fame and ability but after them in time: he
10   occupied himself mostly with first philosophy, but also devoted himself to the
phenomena [i.e. sensible things] and touched on the enquiry into nature, in
which he means to make the principles two, one underlying as matter, which he
calls the all-recipient,[154] and one as cause and mover, which he attaches to the
power of god and of the good.'[155] Alexander, however, records Plato as saying that
the principles are three, the matter and the efficient and the paradigm[156] – even
15   though he had clearly added the final cause when he says 'let us say then on
account of what cause the composer composed coming-to-be and this whole
universe. He was good, and in no one who is good does grudgingness about
anything ever arise.'[157] And I think he clearly conveys the enmattered form too
where he also [does] the immaterial form, writing about both of them as
20   follows:[158] 'these things being so, it must be agreed that one form has its existence
in the same state, ungenerated and indestructible, neither receiving anything
from elsewhere into itself nor itself going anywhere into anything else; and this,
since it is invisible and otherwise non-sensible, is what it falls to the lot of
intellection to examine. But the second is what shares the same name and is
similar to this, sensible and generable and carried around, always coming-to-be
in some place and perishing from it again, comprehended by opinion
25   accompanied by sensation';[159] and he also conveys matter as a third in addition
to these.

[*26,26: Other 'several finite principles' theories.*] Some, however, extended the
principles (even if not the elemental ones) as far as ten, as the Pythagoreans said
that the numbers from the unit to the decad, or the ten pairs of opposites (which
different people have differently written up) are principles of all things. And this
is the division of those who said that the principles are several and finite in
30   plurality.

[*26,31: The 'infinite non-uniform principles' branch of the division.*][160] But of those
who said that they are infinite in plurality, some said that they are simple and
27,1   uniform, others that they are compound and non-uniform and contrary,
characterized by what predominates.[161] For Anaxagoras of Clazomenae, the son
of Hegesibulus, who had shared the philosophy of Anaximenes,[162] was the first to
change the doctrines about the principles and to supply the missing cause [*sc.*
5   *Nous* as efficient cause]. He made the bodily [principles] infinite: for he said that
all homoeomerous things, like water or fire or gold, are ungenerated and
imperishable, and appear to come-to-be and pass away due to combination and

separation alone, all [homoeomerous things] being in all things,[163] but each thing being characterized by what predominates in it. For that in which much is golden appears to be gold, although all [things] are present in it. At any rate Anaxagoras says that 'in everything a portion of everything is present' and 'in whatever thing things are present in the greatest quantity, this one thing is and was most manifestly those things.'[164] And Theophrastus says that Anaxagoras in saying these things stays close to Anaximander: for he[165] says that in the separation of the infinite, kindred things are carried towards each other, and that because there was gold in the universe, gold comes-to-be, and because there was earth, earth, and likewise each of the others, [supposing] that they do not come-to-be but that each was present before. But Anaxagoras posited Reason as the cause of motion and coming-to-be; separated out by it, they [i.e. the homoeomerous things] generated[166] the worlds and the nature of other things. 'And if we take it in this way', he [Theophrastus] says, 'Anaxagoras would seem to make the material principles infinite [sc. infinitely many], while the cause of motion and coming-to-be is one, Reason; but if one were to suppose that the mixture of all things is a single nature indeterminate both in form and in magnitude,[167] it results that he says that the principles are two, the nature of the infinite and Reason; so he seems to make the bodily elements in much the same way as Anaximander.'[168] And Archelaus of Athens, of whom they say Socrates was an associate and who had himself been a student of Anaxagoras, gave the same account of the principles as Anaxagoras, although he tries to contribute something distinctive concerning the generation of the world and other matters.

[27,26: *Summary of the 'infinite in plurality, non-uniform principles' option.*] So these people say that the principles are infinite in plurality and non-uniform, positing the homoeomerous things as principles; and why they thought so, Aristotle will say a bit further on. For refusing to recognize the existence of coming-to-be, on the ground that what comes-to-be must come-to-be either out of being or out of not-being, and that each of these is impossible, they gave an account of the apparent coming-to-be and passing-away through combination and separation.

[28,4: *Atomism, as the 'infinite in plurality, uniform principles' option.*][169] But Leucippus of Elea or Miletus (for both are said of him), who had shared the philosophy of Parmenides, did not follow the same path as Parmenides and Xenophanes about the things that are, but rather, as it seems, the contrary one. For while they made the universe one and unmoved and ungenerated and finite,

70   *Translation*

and refused even to investigate what is not, he hypothesized the atoms as infinite
and ever-moving elements,[170] considering that both coming-to-be and change
10   are uninterrupted among the things that are. He also [hypothesized] that what is
exists no more than what is not, and that both of them are in the same way
causes to the things that come-to-be. For hypothesizing that the substance of the
atoms is solid and full, he called it 'being' and said that it was carried around in
the void, which he called 'not-being', and said that it exists no less than being.
15   Similarly also his companion Democritus of Abdera posited the full and the void
as principles, of which he called the former 'being' and the latter 'not-being'. For
hypothesizing the atoms as matter for the things that are, these people generate
the other things through their differences. And these are three, 'rhythm' and
'turning' and 'intercontact', that is to say, shape and orientation and ordering.[171]
20   For [he says/they say], it's natural that like is moved by like, and things that are
akin are carried towards each other, and each of the figures, when it is arranged
in a different combination, produces a different disposition. So they reasonably
promised that, given that the principles are infinite, they could give an account
of all the affections and substances – what something is generated by and how.
Hence they also say that only for those who make the elements infinite do all
25   things result according to reason (*kata logon*). And they say that the plurality of
figures in the atoms is infinite, because of nothing being any more this than that.
For they give this account of the cause of infinity. Also Metrodorus of Chios
makes the principles almost the same as Democritus and his followers,[172] having
hypothesized the full and the void as the first causes, of which the former is
'being' and the latter 'not-being'; but he takes a distinctive approach to other
30   things. This is a concise overview of the things which are reported about the
principles, written up not in chronological order, but according to which
doctrines are akin.

[28,32: *S. introduces his harmonization of the ancients' theories of the principles.*]
But, hearing of such great variation,[173] one must not think that these are contrary
accounts on the part of those who have philosophized, a thing which some
people,[174] who encounter only reports and write-ups[175] and understand nothing
29,1   of the things said, undertake to criticize – although they themselves are divided
into myriad schisms not with regard to the principles of nature (for of these they
have not even a dream-understanding), but with regard to the desecration of
divine dignity.[176] But perhaps it's not a bad idea, digressing briefly, to display for
those more desirous of learning how the ancients, although appearing to disagree
5   in their doctrines about the principles, nonetheless come together in harmony.

Translation

For some of them were discussing the first intelligible principle, like Xenophanes and Parmenides and Melissus. Of these, Xenophanes and Parmenides said that it was one and finite: for the one must exist prior to plurality, and the cause to all things of boundary and limit must be determined more by limit than by infinity, and what is complete in every way, having received the completion appropriate to it, must be limited, indeed must be the completion of all things, just as it is their principle: for the incomplete, being deficient, has not yet received limit. But Xenophanes places it beyond both motion and rest, and in general[177] beyond every pair of opposites, as being the cause of all things and surpassing all things, just as Plato did in the first hypothesis of the *Parmenides*; while Parmenides, considering its [being] always in the same state and in the same way, and beyond all change, perhaps beyond all activity and power, celebrated it as unmoved and as 'alone', in the sense that it transcends all things:[178]

> ... alone and unmoved it abides, through everything's being a name[179]

And Melissus too considered [its being] unchanging in the same way, but on the basis of the inexhaustibility of its substance and the infinity of its power he pronounced it infinite, just as it is ungenerated.[180] This is made clear by his demonstration of its infinity, which comes about through this conception. For he says:

> So then since it did not come-to-be, it is and always was and will be, and has neither beginning nor end, but is infinite. For if it came-to-be, it would have a beginning (*arkhê*) (for in coming-to-be[181] it would at some time have begun (*êrxato*)) and an end (*teleutê*) (for it would have ended (*etêleutêse*)). But since it neither began nor did it ever end but always was, it does not have a beginning or end.[182]

So then in this way Melissus, looking to its being without temporal beginning or end, and its always existing, pronounced it infinite.

[29,28: *Harmonization of philosophers continued: Parmenides agrees with Melissus that the principle is infinite in having no temporal end, saying that it is limited only in the sense that it is perfect or complete.*] And Parmenides too bears witness for him on this point, when he says through almost these words:

> Being ungenerated it is also indestructible,
> whole and unique and unshaken and unending[183]
> nor was it ever nor will it be, since it now is all together.[184]

So then this man too says that being inexhaustible and ungenerated it is also infinite. He showed his conception of limit through these verses:

72   *Translation*

Remaining the same in the same it lies by itself.
And in this way steadfast it remains there. For mighty necessity
Holds it in the bonds of limit, which encloses it around
For which reason it is not right for what is to be without end (*ateleutêton*).
10   For it is not deficient; and if it were not, it would lack everything.[185]

For if it is being and not not-being, it is non-deficient; and if it is non-deficient, it is complete (*teleion*); and being complete, it has a completion (*telos*), and is not without end (*ateleutêton*). And having an end it has a limit and a bound. So then in this way there would be no contrariety between the conceptions of these men where they are speaking about the same thing.

[*30,14: Parmenides also goes on to discuss sensibles, introducing contrary principles*
15   *and the efficient cause.*] But when Parmenides passes from the intelligibles to the sensibles, or as he himself says from truth to seeming, where he says,

Here I will cease for you trustworthy speech and thought
About truth; from here on learn mortal opinions
Listening to the deceptive ordering (*kosmos*) of my words,[186]

20   he too posits as elemental principles of generated things the primary opposition, which he calls light and darkness or fire and earth or dense and rare or same and other, saying directly after the verses we have cited before:

For they set down two shapes for naming in their judgements (*gnômais*)[187]
Of which it is not right [to posit only] one[188] – in which they have
        wandered astray.
25   And judged them to be contrary in body, and set down signs [for them]
Apart from each other: for the one, aethereal fire of flame,
Being mild and rare, everywhere the same as itself,[189]
31,1   And not the same as the other. But that too [they set down] by itself,
The reverse: unknowing night, dense and heavy in body.

Moreover, a little passage in prose is inserted between the verses as being by Parmenides himself, as follows:[190]

To the former are given as names 'rare' and 'hot' and 'light' (*phaos*) and 'soft'
5   and 'light' [in weight, *kouphos*]; and to the dense, 'cold' and 'dark' and 'hard' and 'heavy'. These things [i.e. the two sides] are each distinguished on each side.

Thus it is clear that he assumed (*elabe*) two opposed elements. Hence he acknowledged that what is, which was earlier [treated as] one, is [also] two; and he says that those who did not see,[191] or did not clearly reveal, the opposition of the elements which constitute coming-to-be have wandered astray. And Aristotle, following him, posited the contraries as principles.

10

And Parmenides clearly conveyed an efficient cause not only of the bodies which are in coming-to-be but also of the incorporeals which complete coming-to-be,[192] when he says:

> The [rings] after these [are filled] with night, and a portion of flame shoots
>> forth.
> In the middle of these [is] the goddess (*daimôn*) who steers all things
> For she rules over the hateful birth and mixture of all things[193]
> Sending female to mix with male and again contrariwise
> Male to female.[194]

15

[*31,18: Empedocles also recognizes principles of both sensible and intelligible worlds, agreeing with Parmenides: his efficient causes, Love and Strife, both operate at both levels.*] But Empedocles too, teaching both about the intelligible and about the sensible world, and positing the former as the archetypal paradigm of the latter, posited in each [world] as principles and elements these four – fire, air, water, and earth – and Love and Strife as efficient causes. But he says that the things in the intelligible [world], being dominated by the intelligible unification, are more brought together by Love, while those in the sensible [world] are more separated by Strife.[195] And Plato (or Timaeus before Plato),[196] following him, says that in the first intelligible paradigm there pre-exist the four ideas which are characterized by the four elements, and which at the last stage produce this four-part sensible world, Strife dominating down here on account of the separation which has fallen away from the intelligible unification.[197] And his [*sc.* Empedocles'] account was common to both worlds, except that he too [i.e. like Plato], having posited the four elements in the role of matter, considered the contrariety of Love and Strife among them. For [as evidence] that it is not the case, as most people think, that according to Empedocles Love alone produced the intelligible world, and Strife alone the sensible, but rather that he considers both of them everywhere in the appropriate manner [i.e. the manner appropriate to each level], listen to what he says in the *Physics*, where he says that 'Aphrodite' or 'Love' is the cause of the demiurgic blending down here too. And he calls fire 'Hephaistos', 'sun', and 'flame', and water 'rain', and air 'aether'. So he says these things many times and [in particular] in these verses:[198]

20

25

30

32,1

5

> And earth encountered these in equal proportions[199]
> Hephaistos and rain and all-shining aether[200]
> Anchored in the perfect harbours of Kupris,

74   *Translation*

Either a little more, or less [encountering] the greater[201]
10   From which blood arises and other forms of flesh.

And elsewhere too, before these verses, he conveys the activity of both [*sc.* Love and Strife] on the same things, saying:[202]

When Strife reached the lowest depths
Of the vortex, Love arose in the centre of the eddy
15   In which all these things come together to be only one,
Not suddenly, but different ones coming together willingly from different
        places.
And countless tribes of mortals flow forth from them when they are mixed.
But many stood unmixed, in alternation with the ones being blended,
The [*sc.* unmixed] ones which Strife above still held. For not yet had all [Strife]
        blamelessly
20   Stood apart at the extreme bounds of the circle.
But some of its limbs remained within, and others had gone outside.
For however much it [Strife] retreats at each moment, so much does
The kindly immortal surge of blameless Love at each moment advance.
Straightaway things grew mortal which had earlier learned to be immortal,
25   And things grew pure which had earlier been unblended, exchanging their
        path.[203]
33,1   And countless tribes of mortals flow forth from them when they are mixed.
Fitted together in all kinds of shapes, a wonder to behold.

So in these [lines] he says clearly that mortal things too have been fitted together by Love, and that where Love predominates, Strife has not yet entirely stood
5   apart. And also in those verses in which he conveys the distinguishing features of each of the four elements and of Strife and Love, he has clearly expressed the mixture of both Strife and Love in all things. They go as follows:[204]

The sun, hot and shining to see in every direction,
And immortals, ones which are † flooded with a shining ray[205]
10   And rain in all things, gloomy and frigid,
And from the earth flow forth [things] close-packed and solid.[206]
And in wrath all things come-to-be unalike in shape and sundered.
But they come together in Love and long for each other.
For from these all the things which were and are and will be
15   Have sprouted: trees and men and women,
Beasts and birds and water-nurtured fish,
And long-lived gods, foremost in honours.

Translation

And a little further on he says:[207]

> They dominate in turn as the cycle (*kuklos*) turns around,
> And they diminish into each other and grow in their turn of destiny.   20
> For these same things *are*, but when they pass through each other
> There come-to-be human beings and the other tribes of animals[208]
> At one time coming together in Love into a single world
> At other times again each thing borne apart by the hatred of Strife,
> Until, grown together into one, the totality comes-to-be below.   25
> Thus insofar as they have learned to grow one out of many
> And again they come-to-be many when the one has grown apart,
> In this respect they come-to-be and have no enduring life,   34,1
> But insofar as these things never leave off constantly exchanging with each
>   other,
> In this respect they always *are*, unmoved through the cycle.

So that both the one out of many, which results through Love, and the many out of one, which arises when Strife dominates, he considers also in this sublunar 5 world, in which mortal things [exist], where clearly Strife dominates at some times and Love at others, in cycles.[209]

[*34,8: Empedocles agrees with Parmenides, posits several levels of intelligibles beyond the sensible world.*] But perhaps (*mêpote*)[210] he is conveying a certain progression of the unification and differentiation of beings, speaking riddlingly of several varieties of the intelligible world above this sensible world [distinguished] according to the greater or lesser dominance of Love, and in the 10 sensible world he displays varieties of the dominance of Strife, distinguished by certain marks, as I have tried to indicate elsewhere.[211] But he too utters nothing contrary to Parmenides and Melissus, rather he considers the opposition of the elements as Parmenides too had done; and while Parmenides posits as a single common efficient cause the goddess who is seated in the middle of all things and 15 is the cause of all coming-to-be, Empedocles considers an opposition in efficient causes as well [as in material causes].

[*34,18: Anaxagoras harmonized: like Parmenides and Empedocles, he discusses both intelligible and sensible principles.*] Anaxagoras of Clazomenae seems to have considered there to be a threefold variety of all forms.[212] One is what is synthesized in the intelligible unification, when he says 'all things were together, infinite both in multiplicity and in smallness.'[213] And again he says,[214] 'before 20

76 *Translation*

these things were separated, all [of them] being together, neither was any colour manifest: for the mixing together of all things prevented it: the fluid and the dry and the hot and the cold and the bright and the dark and much earth being present, and a plurality of infinitely many seeds, not resembling each other in
25 any way. These things being so, it's necessary to believe that all things are one in[215] the totality.' And this totality would be the One-which-is of Parmenides.[216] But he [also] considered a certain [variety of forms] differentiated in the intellectual differentiation, of which the differentiation down here is a likeness. For Anaxagoras speaks thus, a little bit after the beginning of the first book of *On*
35,1 *Nature*: 'These things being so, it's necessary to believe that many things of all kinds are one in[217] all of the things which are mixed together, and seeds of all things, having all kinds of shapes (*ideas*) and colours and savours; and [*sc.* to believe] that human beings and the other animals, all that have soul, have been put together [from these]. And the human beings have well-populated cities and
5 manufactured products, just as among us, and they have a sun and a moon and the rest, just as among us, and the earth grows for them many things of all kinds, of which they gather together the most useful to their dwellings and use them. Well then I have said these things about the separation, that there is not separation only among us but also elsewhere.'[218] And perhaps it will seem to some people
10 that he is not juxtaposing the differentiation that is in [the world of] becoming with the intellectual differentiation, but rather comparing our dwelling-place with other places on the earth. But he would not have said about other places [on the earth] that 'they have a sun and a moon and the rest, just as among us', and he would not have called the things that are there 'seeds and shapes (*ideas*) of all things'.[219] And listen to what he says also a little further on when he compares the
15 two [divisions]: 'these things rotating and being separated off thus by violence and swiftness. And the swiftness makes the violence. Their swiftness is not like any of the things that now exist among humans in swiftness, but altogether many times more swift.'[220] And if this was his conception [*sc.* and it was], he is saying that 'all things are in all' in one way in the intelligible unification, in another way
20 in the intellectual compresence [*sunousiôsis*, i.e. the level of the intellectual division] and in another way in the sensible coordination [*sumpnoia*, i.e. the level of sensibles] and in the coming-to-be out of the same things and resolution into the same things.

[35,22: *The atomists and Plato (and the Pythagorean 'Timaeus') are here added to the harmonization: their bodily principles are more basic than earth, air, fire, and water as elements, but are compatible with them.*] Leucippus and Democritus and the Pythagorean Timaeus and their followers did not contradict [the thesis that] the four elements are principles of compound bodies. But these people too, like the Pythagoreans and Plato and Aristotle, seeing that fire and air and water and perhaps also earth change into each other, looked for causes that would be more principial and simpler than these, by means of which they could also give an account of the qualitative differences among these elements. And in this way Timaeus, and Plato following him, posited surfaces which have some depth and differences of shape as first elements of these four elements, judging that the nature of body [i.e. three-dimensional extension], together with bodily shapes, is more principial than, and is a cause of, qualitative difference.[221] But Leucippus and Democritus and their followers, calling the smallest first bodies 'atoms', [said that] according to the variety of their shapes and orientation and ordering, some bodies come-to-be hot and fiery, those which are composed of first bodies that are sharper and more fine-grained and lying in a similar orientation;[222] and others come-to-be cold and watery, those which are [composed of] the contrary ones; and the former [are, or come-to-be] bright and luminous, the latter obscure and dark.

[36,8: *The monists harmonized: they all looked for similar features in their choice of principle.*][223] And those who posited one element, like Thales and Anaximander and Heraclitus, each of them looked to its active [character] and its suitability for becoming:[224] Thales looked to the generative and nourishing and holding-together and vivifying and easily-shaped [character] of water, Heraclitus to the life-generating and craftsmanly [character] of fire, Anaximenes to the easily-moulded [character] of air and its changing easily in both directions, both to fire and to water; so too Anaximander, if he hypothesized something intermediate on account of its being easily [qualitatively] altered.

[36,15: *The harmonization so far summed up; a strategy announced for dealing with Aristotle's (and Plato's) upcoming criticisms of his predecessors, especially Parmenides.*] So in this way some looked to an intelligible and others to a sensible world-arrangement; some sought the proximate elements of bodies and some the more fundamental ones; some laid hold of the elemental nature in a more particular way and others did so more universally; some sought the elements alone and others sought all the causes and auxiliary causes: [accordingly] they say different things when they give an account of nature, but not contrary things, for someone who is able to judge correctly. And Aristotle himself, who appears to be displaying their disagreements, will say a bit further on that 'they differ

78   *Translation*

from each other in that some took prior and others posterior things [as their principles], and some took things that were better known by reason, others by sensation'; 'so that', he says, 'in a way they are saying the same things as each other, and in a way different things.' [225] But we were compelled to draw this out

25   at greater length on account of the people who are easily inclined to accuse the ancients of disagreement. But since we will hear Aristotle too refuting the opinions of earlier philosophers, and before Aristotle Plato seems to do this, and before both of them Parmenides and Xenophanes, it should be known that these people, being concerned for those who listen more superficially,

30   refuted the apparent absurdity in their accounts, since the ancients were accustomed to express their doctrines in riddles. But Plato makes clear in this way that he admires Parmenides, whom he seems to be refuting: he says that

37,1   his thought requires a deep diver.[226] And Aristotle too is evidently surmising the depth of his wisdom when he says 'Parmenides surely seems to be perceptive (*blepein*).'[227] So these people *seem* to be refuting, when sometimes they are supplying what was left out, sometimes making clear what was said unclearly, sometimes distinguishing what has been said about the intelligibles

5   [by pointing out] that it cannot apply to natural things (as in the case of those who said that what is is one and unmoved), sometimes forestalling the easy interpretations of more superficial people. And we ourselves will try to remark on these in [discussing] Aristotle's arguments against each of them. But now we must take up Aristotle's text (*lexis*) again and articulate the things that are said in it.

10   **184b15-16** The principle must necessarily be either one or several, and if one, either unmoved, as Parmenides and Melissus say ...

[*37,12: Al. on the placement of Parmenides and Melissus in Aristotle's division.*][228] Alexander says that 'having said that we must take our starting point from the things that are better known to us, he then does so: for he began from a disjunction (*diairetikon*) which is complete and obvious and manifest to everyone. For what is clearer than the contradictory disjunction saying "either

15   one or not one", that is, "several"?' But that he [Aristotle] began from a clear disjunction has been said rightly [by Alexander], but not that this is what Aristotle [meant when he] said that we must proceed from what is manifest to unmanifest principles.[229] For those manifest things were composite and better known to sensation, and they were called 'universal' [as being] wholes comprehending the more particular and less manifest things. At any rate,

20   [starting] from the things that are sensible and knowable to us he will both refute

Translation   79

the false opinions about the principles, as we will learn, and confirm the true
ones. 'When he says "as Parmenides and Melissus say"', says Alexander, 'he did
not mean that Parmenides and Melissus posited one principle and said that it
was unmoved. For they did not posit a principle at all: for they said that the all
was one, which is inconsistent with saying that there is a principle. For the people   25
who posit a principle agree that the things that are are several, since they
introduce together with the principle the things of which it is a principle. But
having stated the first disjunction, "the principle is either one or several", with
regard to one [section] of the division he again applies a disjunction, "if the
principle is one, it is either unmoved or moved". And since it is implausible to say
that this principle is one and unmoved, he gave some motivation [for discussing   30
it]: although it is not less but rather *more* implausible than this for the *all* to be
one and unmoved, nonetheless this has Parmenides and Melissus as its
champions, and even if this is not straightway the same as that, it comes to the
same thing.'   38,1

[*38,1: Criticism of Alexander's reading.*] Now although Alexander says in these
very words that the [discussion of the] implausible thesis is being motivated by
the even more implausible thesis, I do not think this would be [worthy] of
Aristotle's greatness of mind. Moreover, neither does he [Aristotle] mention the
opinion of Parmenides and Melissus as another implausible opinion alongside
the opinion that says that the principle is one and unmoved (for he refutes these   5
men [Parmenides and Melissus] as saying this), but rather, Aristotle charitably
interpreted this [doctrine] of these men, saying: 'For those who investigate how
many the beings are also investigate in the same way [as those who investigate
how many are the principles]: for they are investigating primarily (*prôton*) about
the things out of which the beings are, whether these are one or many.'[230] So he
thinks that these men are philosophizing about the principle of the beings, and   10
he marked off their section of the division with the hypothesis that the principle
is one and unmoved. For they said that what really *is*, the unified, which is both
a principle and cause of the many differentiated things, not as elemental but as
having brought them forth, is a 'One-which-is'.[231] For having divided the section
which says that the principle is one by a necessary disjunction, [namely] through
the one [principle] being unmoved or moved, and taking the 'unmoved', he gives
as arguments against those who say that being is one and unmoved the arguments   15
that would [also] be given against those who say that the principle is one and
unmoved: for even if they use different names, nonetheless they too are saying
and investigating the same things.

80 Translation

[*38,18: Relation between Parmenides' 'Truth' and 'Opinion': contra Alexander, Parmenides intends the Doxa to be a valid account of the sensible world.*] Alexander agrees that in the things he says with regard to truth, which are about intelligible

20 being, Parmenides says that being is one and unmoved and ungenerated; 'but when he gives an account of nature according to the opinion of the many and the appearances', he [Alexander] says, 'no longer saying that being is either one or that it is ungenerated, he hypothesized fire and earth as principles of the generated things, hypothesizing earth as matter and fire as efficient cause'; 'and', he says, 'he names fire "light" and earth "darkness"'. And if Alexander had taken 'according to

25 the opinion of the many and the appearances' in the sense that Parmenides intended when he called the sensible 'opinable', then he would be right; but if he thinks that those accounts are entirely false, and if he thinks that light or fire is being called efficient cause, he is wrong. For when he has completed his account of the intelligible, Parmenides adds these [verses], which I have also cited before:[232]

30   Here I will cease for you trustworthy speech and thought
    About truth; from here on learn mortal opinions
    Listening to the deceptive ordering of my words

39,1   For they set down two shapes for naming in their judgements[233]
    Of which it is not right [to posit only] one – in which they have wandered
        astray.
    And judged them to be contrary in body, and set down signs [for them]
    Apart from each other: for the one, aethereal fire of flame,

5   Being mild and rare, everywhere the same as itself,
    And not the same as the other. But that too [they set down] by itself,
    The reverse: unknowing night, dense and heavy in body.
    I proclaim this ordering to you as likely in all things,
    So that no thought of mortals will ever outstrip you.

10 So he calls this account opinable and deceptive, not as being simply false, but as having fallen off from intelligible truth into what is apparent and seeming, the sensible [world].

[*39,12: Also contra Alexander, Parmenides' efficient cause is the daimôn, not fire (cf. 38,27-28).*] And a bit further on, after speaking again about the two elements, he adds the efficient [cause], speaking as follows:[234]

    For the narrower [rings] are filled with unmixed fire,
15   The [rings] after these [are filled] with night, and a portion of flame shoots forth.
    In the middle of these [is] the goddess who steers all things.

Translation

He also says that she is the cause of the gods, saying:[235]

> She contrived Eros first of all gods

and what follows. And he says that she sends souls sometimes from the manifest to the unseen and sometimes vice versa. 20

[39,20: *Parmenides distinguishes intelligible from sensible being; only the former is unmoved.*] But I am compelled to draw these things out on account of the current widespread ignorance of ancient writings. And those who said that what is is one also reasonably said that it was unmoved, if, that is, (*eiper*) they were not[236] talking about natural things. For there would be introduced together with motion that in which the motion [occurs],[237] whether in quality or quantity or something else; and place too would be introduced together with [it], if it were natural motion, and place is something else besides the thing moved. But 25 Parmenides, in speaking about intelligible being, says:

> But unmoved in the limits of great bonds
> It is, unbeginning, unceasing, since coming-to-be and destruction
> Here[238] are utterly warded off: true conviction has driven [them] away. 40,1

And he also adds the cause of [its] immobility:

> And in this way steadfast it remains there. For mighty necessity
> Holds it in the bonds of limit, which encloses it around
> For which reason it is not right for what is to be without end. 5
> For it is not deficient; and if it were not, it would lack everything.[239]

For, he says, just as what is not is lacking in all things, so what is is non-lacking and complete. And what is moved is lacking in that on account of which it moves: therefore what is is not moved.

[40,9: *Correction of Al. on Melissus.*] And Melissus demonstrated that it is unmoved using the same thought again, since if what is were moved, there would 10 necessarily be something void of being, into which what is would withdraw: and he had demonstrated beforehand that there is no void. In his own treatise he speaks thus: 'Neither is anything empty. For what is empty is nothing; but what is nothing would not be. Nor is it moved: for it does not have anywhere to withdraw, rather it is full. For if there were [anyplace] empty, it would withdraw into the empty, but since there is no empty, it does not have anywhere to withdraw.'[240] So, 15 since it is full, it is not moved, not because there can be no motion through a

82   *Translation*

plenum, as Alexander understood the saying of Melissus, but because being itself is full, in such a way that there cannot be anything else alongside it.[241] At any rate, Melissus says, 'one must make this judgement about full and not full: if it makes

20 room for something or receives something, it is not full, but if it neither makes room nor receives, it is full. Now it must be full, if there is no empty: if therefore it is full, it is not moved.'[242]

> **184b16-18** . . . or moved, as the natural scientists say, some of whom said that air and others of whom said that water is the first principle.

[*40,23: A dispute about the scope of 'natural scientists' here.*] Having[243] set out those who say that what is, or the principle, is unmoved, he passes to the other section [of the division], and says 'or moved, as the natural scientists say',

25 contrasting those who say that it is unmoved with the natural scientists, inasmuch as those who abolish motion are not natural scientists at all, which he will say and show more clearly next: for if nature is a principle of motion, how would someone who abolishes nature itself be a natural scientist? People who pursue some part of philosophy either alone or especially are customarily called after

30 that [part], as they called Socrates an 'ethicist', and people like Thales and

41,1 Anaximander and Anaximenes and Anaxagoras and Democritus and their followers 'natural scientists'. Here too I differ from Alexander who, having said earlier that [Aristotle] contrasted the natural scientists with those who say that [what is, or the principle] is one and unmoved, then says later that it was Aristotle's custom to call 'natural scientists' those who philosophized about the truth, since

5 the end of physics too is not action but knowledge. For who does not know[244] that Parmenides too, with whom he says the natural scientists are being contrasted, philosophized about truth, saying clearly:

> Here I will cease for you trustworthy speech and thought
> About truth[245]

[*41,10: Why no division of the monists by whether their principle is finite or*

10 *infinite?*] There is indeed another division among those who say that the principle is one, whether unmoved or moved, [namely the division] that divides into infinite and finite.[246] For of those who say that it is one and unmoved Melissus says that it is infinite in these words:[247] 'Well then since it did not come-to-be but *is*, it always was and always will be and has neither beginning nor end, but is

15 infinite'[248] and also Aristotle himself will show a bit further on in arguing against these people[249] that it is impossible not only to say that the principle is infinite, but also to say that what is is infinite, as Melissus thought. But also, of those who

say that it is one and moved, Anaximander the son of Praxiades of Miletus posited a certain infinite nature which is other than the four elements as a principle, whose eternal motion he said is the cause of the coming-to-be of the heavens, and Anaximenes, the son of Eurystratus of Miletus, also[250] posited a single and infinite principle, saying that it is air, from which, when it is rarefied and condensed, the other things come-to-be. So although there is also this sort of division, Aristotle omits it for now,[251] as Alexander says, 'because this division does not yield a difference in the way that things come-to-be out of [the principle]. For it is not the case that some things will come-to-be if [the principles] are infinite and others if they are finite, in the way that some things will come-to-be if the [principle] is one and others if they are many. For if the principle is one, the things that come-to-be must come-to-be by alteration, and if they are many, by combination. Likewise, "unmoved" and "moved" provide a major differentia, for if it is unmoved, nothing would come-to-be out of it which did not already exist before, whereas if it is moved, nothing prevents coming-to-be from happening either in a linear fashion or in a cycle.'

[41,30: *Differences from Al.*] Thus far Alexander. But perhaps (*mêpote*) Melissus called the principle infinite, not in substance, but through the inexhaustibility of its existence: for, he says, 'Since it did not come-to-be but *is*, it always was and always will be and has neither beginning nor end, but is infinite.'[252] And perhaps (*mêpote*) also [i.e. also against Alexander] the manner [in which things] come-to-be will be different according as the principle is infinite or finite: for if the principle is infinite in magnitude either there will be no coming-to-be or the things that come-to-be can come-to-be out of it to infinity in a linear fashion, whereas if it is finite, coming-to-be must either go in a cycle or be exhausted at some time.

> **184b18-20** And if several, either finitely or infinitely many. And if finite, but more than one, either two or three or four or some other number.

[42,7: *Why Ar. skips 'moved' vs. 'unmoved' as a division of the 'several' option.*] In the case of those who said that the principles are several, the other[253] disjunction 'unmoved or moved' has no place: both because it is impossible for something to come-to-be out of several principles if they are not moved (for they need to be involved with (*koinônein*) each other), and because this opinion, due to its manifest impossibility, did not even have a champion. For which reason even Democritus, who says that the atoms are unmoved by nature, says that they are moved by a blow.[254] But the eloquent Themistius says in his paraphrase of this

84   *Translation*

passage that the several too are 'either moved or unmoved and either finite in number or infinite'.[255] And Eudemus too, as I also said before, says in his *Physics*

15   that 'however the principles may be, they are either moved or unmoved'.[256] And it is clear that these people [Themistius and Eudemus] have explained the necessity of a division by contradictories. 'And if several,' he says, 'they must be either finite or infinite' in multiplicity.[257] 'And it seems', says Alexander, 'that he does not introduce both divisions in each [section] of the first division so

20   as not to talk repeatedly about the same things; rather, having shown in the case of the one [principle] that the principle cannot be unmoved, from this he will simultaneously [implicitly] demonstrate still more that neither can the several [principles] be unmoved; and for this reason he did not again use "either moved or unmoved" [as a principle of division] in the case of the many. And conversely, having shown in the case of the many that the principles cannot be infinite, he simultaneously demonstrates that no principle at all can

25   be infinite. For not moving is more appropriate to a single [principle], if that were possible, and being infinite is more appropriate to many [principles].' So says Alexander, but I remark that it is one thing to be infinite or finite in multiplicity, which is more appropriate for those who said that the principles are many, and another to be infinite or finite in magnitude, and that this [in turn] fits better those who said that the principle is one. For how would several things be

30   infinite in magnitude, unless a body can pervade another body?[258] Rather it seems that Aristotle made the division in this way for the sake of concision:[259] at

43,1 any rate, in what follows he critically examines Melissus as one who says that the principle is one and infinite. And from the division previously set out we have come to know who says that the principles are several and finite, and who that they are infinite.[260]

[*43,3: Footnote on Al. on Plato, repeating the earlier response to his criticisms at 26,5 ff.*] However, we think that here too Alexander records the doctrines of Plato in a careless way. 'For', he says, 'Plato seems to have two principles, calling

5   one of them "underlying" and "matter", and the other, as cause and mover, which he calls "god" and "Reason" and "the good".[261] And', he says, 'there would also be a third principle according to him, the paradigmatic.' For it is surprising that Alexander did not observe that Plato clearly ranked the final cause first of all things, when he says 'let us say then on account of which cause the composer

10   composed coming-to-be and this whole universe. He was good'.[262] So if it was on account of goodness, it is clear that goodness is the final and most principal cause. And does he not also trace back the different structures of the parts[263] to

the differences in their use, and to that for the sake of which each of them has come-to-be? But Plato also clearly communicates the formal cause, not only the one that is separate from matter, but also the inseparable, when he says, '[it must be agreed that] one form has its existence in the same state, ungenerated and indestructible, neither receiving anything into itself nor itself going anywhere into anything else; and this, since it is invisible and otherwise non-sensible, is what it falls to the lot of intellection to examine. But the second is what shares the same name and is similar to this, sensible and generable and carried around always.'[264] And a bit further on, 'so these things then being so in their natural condition, he first arranged them by forms and numbers.'[265] And the twofold formal cause, separate and inseparable, is made clear through these passages. 'So just as Reason perceives which and how many ideas are present in what-animal-is,[266] he also intended that this universe too should have so many and such [ideas].'[267]

184b20-22 And if infinite, either, as Democritus [thought], one in genus but differing in shape or form, or even contrary.[268]

[*43,27: Al. vs. Porphyry et al. on the parsing of the lemma.*] All the interpreters agree that Aristotle thinks that Democritus hypothesized that the principles were homogeneous, and said that the atoms were out of the same substance but differing in shape and in form in the sense of shape. But as for the '*or* even contrary', Porphyry and Themistius think that it is the counterpart [clause] to '*either*, as Democritus [thought] . . .', and refers to Anaxagoras. For of those who hypothesized that the principles are infinite, Democritus and his followers, having hypothesized that the atoms are of the same substance (since they are considered according to a single genus, the full), say that they differ in shape and orientation and ordering, whereas Anaxagoras and his followers posit that they are contrary even in their substances: for they hypothesize hotnesses and coldnesses, drynesses and wetnesses, rarenesses and densenesses, and the other qualitative contrarieties in the homoeomeries, by which they say that the homoeomeries (which according to them are principles) differ, the contrariety being considered principally in qualities rather than in shapes. However, Alexander of Aphrodisias was aware of this interpretation too but does not accept it; rather, he thinks that the whole thing refers to Democritus, [saying] that he posited that the principles are one in genus, that is, one according to their underlying nature, but that in shape or form they are differing or even contrary. For that Aristotle records Democritus as saying that the principles are contrary, he makes clear[269] through these words: 'and Democritus [takes as principles] the

86   *Translation*

full and the void, of which he says that the one exists as being and the other as not-being; furthermore, by orientation, shape, and ordering; and these are genera of contraries, of position [the contrary species being] above and below and front and back, and of shape, straight and round in angle.'[270] For even if Aristotle
20   himself denies that shape is contrary to shape, it does not follow that Democritus also must have been of this opinion. And Alexander so sympathized with this interpretation that he says the choice is between two options: either to say that the text is wrong, and that the 'either',[271] which demands a counterpart to Democritus, has slipped in[272] superfluously (for it ought to be: 'and if infinite, as
25   Democritus [said], one in genus, but differing in shape and form or even contrary'); 'or, if the text is right,' he says, 'then he omitted giving as a counterpart those who say that the principles are not the same even in genus, as Anaxagoras and his followers said.'

[44,27: *S.'s solution: Al.'s two options are both unacceptable, as is the Porphyry/ Themistius reading.*] So[273] if [a] it's absurd to athetize texts which agree in all the manuscripts, and [b] it's also no less absurd to render the account defective both
30   in its expression and in relation to the sections of the division,[274] especially since the opinion of Anaxagoras – against which Aristotle offers many arguments – has been left out, and [c] it does not seem easy to accept athetizing Aristotle's opinion about Democritus [i.e. take the 'or even contrary' as referring exclusively to Anaxagoras] when he clearly thinks that he hypothesized contrariety in the
45,1   principles, as the other commentators [Porphyry and Themistius] do, then [d] perhaps (*mêpote*) he has on the one hand given the 'differing in shape and in form in the sense of shape' as distinctive of Democritus since Democritus said that the atoms do not differ in substance; and on the other hand, the 'infinite principles not only differing but even being contrary', which belongs not only to the position[275]
5   of Democritus but also to that of Anaxagoras, he has attributed to both positions in common. So he would be saying: 'either, as Democritus [said], one in genus but differing in shape or form – or not only differing in shape and in form in the sense of shape, but also contrary', on the ground that Democritus posited contrariety in shape and position, but Anaxagoras also in substance and genus. For if this way
10   of taking the text has some justification, we need neither correct the text nor criticize the account as lacking a [grammatically required] counterpart, nor turn one's back upon [what is said elsewhere] about contrariety in Democritus.

184b22-25 And the people who investigate how many the beings are investigate in the same way: for they investigate first[276] concerning the things out of which the beings are, whether these are one or many, and if many, [whether they are] finite or infinite, so that they are investigating whether the principle and the element are one or many.

[*45,15: Al.'s reading of the lemma.*] 'As we,' he says, 'before philosophizing about natural things themselves, were compelled to investigate about the principles of natural things, how many and what they are, so too the natural scientists, although setting out to investigate about the beings, how many they are, were compelled first to investigate about the principles of the beings, since the knowledge of the beings depends on these. And this is intended by him [Aristotle] to show that an account of the principles is necessary, since even people who did not set out to investigate these things were confronted by them first, since otherwise they could not come to know about the beings.' So Alexander interprets the text, and he says that this is said about all the natural scientists. 15

20

[*45,23: S. vs. Al.: Ar. is talking not about the natural scientists but about Parmenides and Melissus.*] But perhaps (*mêpote*) the account is not about all the natural scientists, nor [does it claim that] although they set out to investigate other things, another investigation, about the principles, confronted them before those things. Rather, since Parmenides and Melissus investigated about what is, whether it is one or many, and if one, whether it is unmoved or moved, even they, he [Aristotle] says, investigated not about the things that are, as one might think, but rather about the principle of the things that are: Aristotle is charitably attributing this to them. For he would never think that these people were ignorant of the multiplicity in the things that are, or for instance whether they had two feet;[277] rather, their account was about what really is, and *is* in the strict sense, which is a principle and cause of all the things that are in any way whatever. And for this reason he immediately takes up the opinion of Parmenides and Melissus, of those who philosophize about what is. For whether they are investigating about the principle or about what is, whether it is one or many, they are investigating the same things, even if they use different names. So[278] the things that are said [here, by Aristotle] in response to those who say that what is is one, would also be said against those who say that the principle is one. So since he himself has made the division with respect to the principle, saying 'the principle must necessarily be either one or several',[279] he reasonably added that those too who investigate about the things that are, how many they are, are investigating about principles, even if they use a different name.[280] For which reason he posits this as a single doctrine and argues against it.[281]

25

30

46,1

5

88 *Translation*

184b25-185a5 So then to examine whether what is is one and unmoved is not to
10 examine about nature. For as for the geometer too there is no arguing against
someone who abolishes the principles, but [such arguing belongs] either to
another science or to one common to all, so too [such arguing does not belong]
to one who [investigates] the principles. For there is no longer a principle if there
is only one thing and one in this way. For the principle is of something or of
some things.

[*46,10: Al.'s reading of the lemma.*] 'With this discussion', says Alexander, 'he also
adds the problem apparently set aside, whether there are principles at all, in
arguing against those who posit that there is no principle of natural things at all.
For those who say that what is is one and unmoved abolish the principles of
15 nature and nature itself. For the principle is a principle of something or of some
things, and introduces multiplicity together with itself; and if motion does not
exist, neither does nature, for nature will be demonstrated to be a principle of
motion.'

[*46,16: S. vs Al.: Ar. takes the opposing view to treat the One as a principle of
nature.*] But perhaps (*mêpote*) the following interpretation is more carefully
considered: Aristotle does not with this discussion set out to show that there are
principles of nature, but rather, taking this as agreed by them as well, if that is
they took 'being' in the sense of 'principle', on this basis he tries to confound
20 those who say that what is is one, [understanding them] as speaking about the
principle. For there is no longer a principle, if what is is only one, and one in the
way that most people think is meant by 'What is is one', [i.e.] in such a way that it
alone [exists].[282] For a principle is a principle of something or of some things, so
that it also introduces multiplicity together with itself. So at the same time that
he refutes their thesis he also charges those who posited it, that although they
25 seem to be examining about nature they abolish nature. And having collected
the first sections of the division – that is, if the principle is one and unmoved –
he finds as champions of this opinion Parmenides and Melissus, who say that
what is is one, substituting 'being' for 'the principle'.[283] And he immediately argues
against these people,[284] first by combining the notion of 'principle' and the notion
of 'being' which he conjectured they meant. Then he [argues] according to the
30 notion of 'being' which it was likely most people would think on hearing the
name. Then, finally, he argues from [the notion of] the one. And[285] he seems first
to criticize [them] on the ground that, in saying that the principle of being is one,
they said that being is one, and with the notion of 'being', 'principle' is abolished,
47,1 and that while speaking[286] about the principle of the things that are, in saying

Translation 89

that what is is one and unmoved they abolish both 'principle' and 'nature'; and if nature and the principles of nature are taken away, so is the whole study of nature.

[47,4: *How to defend principles of natural science against the 'One-which-is' option.*] And since not every account is worth arguing against, and since he intends to argue against them, he first indicates this: in what respect their 5 account is not worth arguing against, and, on the other hand, in what respect, even though this is so, nevertheless nothing prevents arguing against it. For no art or science is able to confront scientifically, using its own account, the person who rejects its principles and its whole constitution. For if the natural scientist (as the case may be) must, qua natural scientist, demonstrate from the principles 10 of nature and in a natural-scientific way everything that he shows, and neither the principles nor the study of nature are conceded [by the opponent], how would the natural scientist, qua natural scientist, still [be able to] demonstrate? But nor will the geometer dispute as a geometer with someone who rejects the principles of geometry and the constitution of geometry: for he will not have principles from which to dispute. If he wants to establish[287] the principles, he will establish them either from things that are prior or from things that are posterior; 15 if from things that are prior, it is clear that it won't be from natural things, nor in a natural-scientific way; if from posterior and natural things, he must postulate these [posterior things], since they are not yet clear, because the principles from which it is possible to show them have been rejected, as is the case with what the geometers call postulates.[288]

[47,19: *The solution: recourse to a higher science, or to dialectic.*] Rather, either the principles of each of the sciences must be validated by the immediately more 20 elevated sciences (as it belongs to natural science to validate the principles of medicine, and to geometry those of mechanics), or those [principles] of all by some one common [science], such as the dialectic of the Peripatetics.[289] For he has also said in the *Topics* that this discipline is also useful for the philosophical sciences: 'for being capable of examining,' he says, 'it has a path to the principles of all the sciences.'[290] And this is reasonable, if indeed the aim of dialectic is to 25 make deductions from plausible [premises] about any object which is put forward.[291] For the dialectician will show, as the case may be, that the point is without parts, and the line is a length without breadth, and the plane has only length and breadth, beginning by assuming[292] as a common axiom that body is three-dimensionally extended and that every boundary has one less dimension

90 Translation

30 than what it bounds. And first philosophy will demonstrate the principles of all [the sciences]: and this is why it is proclaimed[293] as an art of arts and science of sciences.[294] So it does not belong to the natural scientist to dispute against the person who rejects the principles of natural science.

[47,33: *What about debating someone who denies all first principles? Eudemus on the regress of the sciences.*] And perhaps it would not belong to anyone to dispute against those who reject all principles universally. And those 48,1 who say that what is is one only, and one in such a way that nothing else exists beside it, are rejecting all principles. For the principle in every case introduces together with itself something or some things of which it is a principle. And Aristotle investigates in the *Metaphysics* whether there is one science in each case that shows the principles of each science, or 5 whether it belongs to some one common science to consider about all the sciences. And Eudemus at the beginning of his *Physics* investigates the problem impressively, but defers the solution to other more complete enquiries. He says as follows:

One might raise the puzzle whether each science discovers and passes judgement on its own principles, or a different one in each individual case, or whether there 10 is a single one which does this for all. For the mathematicians indicate their proper principles, and define what they mean by each [term]; and someone who has seen nothing [of geometry] would seem ridiculous investigating what a line and each of the other things is. But concerning the principles such as they themselves assert, they do not even undertake to declare them;[295] rather they deny that it belongs to them to examine these things, but when these are conceded they show what comes after them. And if there is a different science 15 concerned with the principles of geometry, and likewise with those of arithmetic and each of the other sciences, is there some one science about the principles of all the sciences, or a different one for each case? And whether there is one common one or one proper to each, there will have to be some principles in these sciences too. So it will be investigated in the same way in turn, whether these [sciences] are of their own proper principles, or some others are. So if they 20 always turn out to be different [i.e. if another science must always prove each science's principles], they will proceed to infinity, so that there will be no sciences of the principles: for there seem to be always higher principles. If, on the other hand, they come to a stop, and there are several or indeed just one science proper to the principles, an investigation and an account will be needed: why is it [this science] about both the principles beneath it and its own, when the others are 25 not. For this peculiarity seems artificial, if there is no difference involved.

Anyway these things would be more appropriate for another [branch of] philosophy to determine with precision.[296]

[*48,26: Solution and summation.*] I have cited this text of Eudemus, which clearly sets out the whole difficulty pertaining to the problem, for those more inclined to investigate. And Eudemus, as I have said, deferred the resolution to more complete enquiries [i.e. those on first philosophy]. But let it be said concisely that of the principles in each art and science, some are self-warranting and are for this reason knowable even by the very sciences whose principles they are, like the so-called common notions in geometry, and also the definitions (*horoi*).[297] For these too are supposed to be themselves indemonstrable. For this reason demonstrations in the strict sense proceed from definitions (*horismoi*) as immediate premises. Other [principles] are hypothetical, such as the existence of the terms (*horos*). For that the point satisfies the notion of something without parts, and the line the notion of length without breadth, is self-warranting; but that something without parts exists at all in things with parts, and something without breadth in things extended in breadth – this the geometer takes as a principle without demonstrating it, while the first philosopher demonstrates it from indemonstrable self-warranting principles. And this person is the dialectician in Plato's sense; the dialectician in Aristotle's sense, who makes deductions from plausible [premises] about anything put forward, as has been said before, uses plausible principles. And in this way neither will we go to infinity positing principles prior to principles (for they will arrive at indemonstrable and self-warranting principles), nor will scientific knowledge of the principles belong to the person for whom they are principles, since scientific knowledge is demonstrative deduction, and deduction is from principles already known; rather, one person's principles are known to another person by scientific knowledge, because he demonstrates [them] from other self-warranting and indemonstrable principles.

[*49,16: Summation, with a correction to follow.*] So it would not belong to the natural scientist to dispute against people who reject the principles of nature. For [he will dispute] either from prior [things], as has been said, and no longer as a natural scientist, or from posterior [ones], [in which case] he will be postulating that the principles exist, to which the things he demonstrates from are posterior. For if the principles do not exist, the things which are posterior to the principles will also not exist. 'For this reason', as Alexander says, 'even Aristotle himself, when he speaks against those who say that what is is one and unmoved, who

92   *Translation*

reject the principles of nature, will not be speaking qua natural scientist, but qua philosopher.'

[*49,23: S. corrects Al.: the natural scientist could defend the principles of nature which he uses.*] But perhaps (*mêpote*), while the natural scientist is incapable of arguing scientifically against the person who rejects the principles of nature –
25   scientifically in the sense of arguing from the principles of the object (for qua natural scientist he does not know other principles higher than the principles of nature) – he is able to show [the disputed principles] from principles of demonstration. The things that appear from evident sensation are also principles of demonstration – both sensation of particular things and so-called induction in general. For this reason Aristotle too confronts those who say that what is is one by showing that among the things that are there are substance and also
30   quantity and also quality, and these are not one; and against those who say that it is unmoved, he says, 'Let us hypothesize that some or all of the things which are by nature are moved: it is clear from induction.'[298] So the natural scientist will not be at a loss for all argument against one who rejects the principles of nature: for in fact he will not [be at a loss for argument] from the principles of demonstration, but [only for argument] from the principles of the principles. And, Alexander
50,1   says, Aristotle takes up this opinion [that of Parmenides and Melissus] first, because it rejects nature and the principles of nature; so after he has got rid of it and confirmed that nature exists and that there are principles of natural things, he will thus pass on to the other opinions which have been professed about the principles of nature.

5   **185a5-10** To examine if it is one in this way is like disputing against any other thesis asserted for the sake of argument, like that of Heraclitus, or if someone should say that what is is one human being, or solving an eristic argument, which is what both of the arguments are, both that of Melissus and that of Parmenides. For they both start from false premises and are non-deductive.

[*50,7: False theories which reject the principles of a science are not to be argued against within that science.*] There are many modes of argument against which someone who disputes in a philosophical and law-abiding way should not argue. He should not argue either against modes which abolish the principles of the objects which are the subject-matter for the discussants, nor against ones
10   which assert paradoxical and counter-intuitive things: of this kind are theses[299] such as when Heraclitus appeared to assert[300] that good and bad agree in the same thing in the manner of a bow or a lyre[301] – which appeared[302] to assert a

Translation

thesis because it speaks in this way without distinction. But he was indicating the harmonious mixture of contraries in [*sc.* the world of] coming-to-be, which is also how Plato records Heraclitus' doctrine in the *Sophist*, comparing to it that of Empedocles as well. He says: 'Afterwards certain Ionian and Sicilian Muses   15
agreed that it is safest to interweave both and to say that what is is both many and one, and is held together by hatred and love. "For in differing it is brought together,"[303] say the stricter of the Muses' (calling Heraclitus' Muses 'stricter' and 'Ionian'); 'but the softer Muses' (for he calls Empedocles' Muses 'softer' and 'Sicilian'), these, he says, 'relaxed on its always being in this way, but they say that   20
the universe is in turn at one time one and loving under Aphrodite, and at another many and at war with itself on account of some strife.'[304] And since Heraclitus' doctrine is rather obscure, Aristotle introduced a clearer and at the same time more appropriate example of paradox, saying 'if someone should say that what is is one human being': for this example of paradox is more appropriate   25
to the matters at hand.[305] And there is also another mode [of paradoxical argument], which does not merely assert paradoxes declaratively, but also seems to deduce them – not, however, out of true or even out of plausible premises, but out of ones that *appear* to be plausible: this is what sophistical paralogisms are like.[306]

[*50,29: Strategies for dealing with different categories of opponents proposing false opinions.*] And, to sum up, each of those who introduce a false opinion either preserves the principles of the subject-matter of the opinion and the natural   30
scientists must contend against him; or else he abolishes [these principles] and   51,1
the natural scientist has no argument against him. Again, either he will introduce [this opinion] declaratively, or he will also seem to use a deduction. And if he introduces it declaratively, either he says something that would be easily accepted and persuasive, and then it is necessary to argue against him, since he is not of himself unpersuasive even if he is speaking falsely; or he is saying something   5
counter-intuitive and paradoxical, and the person who assents to the truth would have no argument [against him]; for neither would it belong to the dialectician to argue against someone who says that the just is the porch. But if in speaking falsely he also contentiously undertakes to offer deductions, if he produces his deduction out of plausible premises, one must refute the deception, if not on one's own account then on account of the superficial hearers. But if the   10
premises are not even plausible, but are brought forward merely eristically, then arguing against it would belong more to those who are relaxing than to those who are engaged in serious business. So if the argument of Parmenides and

94 *Translation*

Melissus both abolishes the principles of nature and posits something paradoxical and counter-intuitive in saying that what is is one, and also in deducing what it
15 claims not only assumes false premises but also concludes invalidly, then for all these reasons it would not be worth arguing against, especially for the natural scientist whose principles it abolishes. But since the vice of a deduction, or indeed of anything compound, is twofold, one arising from the components and one from the way they are composed, he criticizes these arguments on both grounds. For the premises are falsely assumed and also the manner of
20 composition goes wrong as to syllogistic form and is among those that do not conclude anything with necessity.

[*51,21: According to Al., the position of Heraclitus to which Ar. here alludes is a paradoxical thesis, while that of Parmenides and Melissus is an eristic argument.*] However, Alexander says that Aristotle is saying these things in the following way: 'while the thesis of Heraclitus is paradoxical, and of the same kind as if someone were to say that what is is one human being, the argument of Parmenides and Melissus is "eristic", that is to say sophistical, because of the proof; but it
25 belongs to "those which are said for the sake of argument", that is, those for which there is no evidence from the objects which they are discussing, but which are false and empty.'

[*51,27: Al. is wrong: Ar. classes the views of Parmenides and Melissus as 'theses' too.*] Although Alexander says these things and in these very words, I remark that he [Aristotle] thinks that it is not only Heraclitus' assertion that is a thesis similar to the one that says that what is is one human being, but he also discards these assertions too [*sc.* those of Parmenides and Melissus] as being theses
30 similar to that of Heraclitus, or still more closely similar to [the thesis] that says that what is is one human being. Anyway, he [Aristotle] says 'To examine if it is one in this way is like disputing against any other thesis' and what
52,1 follows, [on the grounds that] this too is a thesis. And I am surprised that Alexander, who thinks that these assertions are said merely for the sake of argument, nonetheless does not think that they are theses, but only eristic assertions, although Aristotle has in this way clearly said that theses are said only
5 for the sake of argument, without evidence from the objects.[307]

> **185a10-12** The argument of Melissus is rather vulgar and involves no aporia; but one absurdity being granted, the others follow. And this is nothing difficult.[308]

Translation 95

[*52,8: Why Melissus is vulgar, and his motivations for saying that what is is infinite or unlimited.*] He says that the argument of Melissus is more vulgar, because he said not only that what is is one and unmoved, as Parmenides did, but in addition also posited that it is infinite; for this reason, having argued against both of them together, he added, 'Melissus says that what is is infinite; therefore what is is a quantum.'[309] So it is vulgar because it has introduced quantity, which must be in something underlying, i.e. substance,[310] even though he posited that what is is one. And he says 'involves no aporia' on account of its being easy to resolve and not causing puzzlement on account of its superficiality. For a sharp argument is one that bites and causes puzzlement, as is said in the *Sophistical Refutations*.[311] 'But one absurdity being granted,' he says, 'the others follow'. For it must also be unmoved, if it is one, and one in such a way that only it exists, for if it is moved it will also have motion and change and whence and whither, whether[312] from disposition to disposition or from place to place or however; and it must be infinite, for if it has a limit it will have both limit and [that which is] limited. For this reason Plato too shows from Parmenides' saying that what is is a whole and like a ball:

> Like the bulk of a ball well-rounded on all sides[313]

that it is not one, since it has a middle and extremes and parts. And this is written in the *Sophist*:[314]

> So if [what is] is a whole, just as Parmenides says,
>
> 'Like the bulk of a ball well-rounded on all sides
> Equally balanced in every direction from the middle. For it must not be
> Any greater or any less here than there'[315]
>
> then what is, being like this, has a middle and extremes, and having these it must by all necessity have parts; or is it not so?
> – It is so.
> However nothing prevents what has parts from having the affection of unity over all of its parts, and, since it is all and whole, being in this way one.
> – Why not?
> But is it not impossible for what has these things as an affection to be itself the one itself?[316]

He [Aristotle] says that it is nothing difficult, but rather necessary, that on one absurdity, once it has been posited, other absurdities should follow; or, perhaps, that it is nothing difficult to see how on one absurdity, once it has been granted, the other absurdities follow.

96   *Translation*

185a12-14 Let us hypothesize that the things which are by nature are moved, either all or some of them: it's clear from induction.

10   [*53,10: Ar.'s strategy of arguing inductively against the Eleatics.*] So they [Parmenides and Melissus], having hypothesized that what is is one and unmoved, fell into many absurdities; let *us* hypothesize that the things which are by nature are moved, either all or some of them. This hypothesis is not a thesis, nor does it introduce anything paradoxical or counter-intuitive, nor is it confirmed by solving the arguments to the contrary; rather, it is knowable from induction, for we also see that many of the things which are by nature are moved.

15   For *all* things which are by nature are moved, if indeed nature is a principle of motion; but let what is uncontested be hypothesized, that *some* of the things which are by nature are moved. For animals and plants all are evidently moved, and the simple elements and the heaven and the stars in the heaven; and it is likely that he said 'all or some' because the poles and centres and axes of the

20   universe, although they too are by nature, are unmoved;[317] or, as Alexander says, the soul. But what is being hypothesized now is not that the principles of nature are moved, but rather things which are by nature, whose principles he is seeking.[318] But here too Alexander agrees that 'he takes this as a principle, not the principle by nature, but the principle in relation to us, which is clearly not the principle of the object (for it would be first by nature),[319] but rather [a principle] of demonstration, which is taken also from things that are posterior, but

25   evident,[320] just as induction from the particulars confirms the universal, which is not posterior by nature, but prior.'

> **185a14-17** At the same time it is also not appropriate to solve all [eristic arguments], but only the ones someone uses to argue falsely from the principles, and not the others. For instance, it belongs to the geometer to solve the squaring [of the circle] by means of segments, but [to solve] Antiphon's [squaring] doesn't belong to the geometer.

[*53,28: Introduction to a very long digression on attempts to square the circle, presented in order to explain Ar.'s references in the lemma.*] Having opposed to the thesis that says that what is is one and unmoved [the hypothesis that] the things

54,1   that are by nature are moved, either all or some of them, which is attested by evident [experience], then, lest someone should say 'you have hypothesized the thing sought as if it were agreed', he adds the justification for hypothesizing what is true before refuting what is false. For one thing, it's easy and involves no

Translation   97

difficulty to see what follows from the absurdity which has been hypothesized [by Melissus], and also it is not appropriate to solve *all* the things that are said   5
falsely, but only those which someone says falsely in arguing from the principles of the interlocutor, and not the others. But those who said [that what is is] one and unmoved do not preserve either a principle or nature. So there is nothing absurd in hypothesizing things witnessed by evident experience, even before solving the arguments to the contrary, if indeed it is not even necessary to solve all [the arguments to the contrary]. And what this difference is between those   10
falsehoods which must be solved and those which need not be, he shows in the case of some diagrammatic fallacies[321] in geometry. For while many people sought the squaring of the circle – that is, to construct a square equal to a circle – both Antiphon and Hippocrates of Chios falsely thought that they had found it. But, as we shall learn, it does not belong to the geometer to solve Antiphon's falsehood, because it did not proceed from geometrical principles, whereas it   15
does belong to the geometer to solve that of Hippocrates, because he went wrong while preserving the principles of geometry. For one must solve only those arguments which reason fallaciously while observing the principles appropriate to the discipline, whereas the principle-destroying arguments through which people go wrong should not be solved.

[*54,20: Antiphon's squaring of the circle, which uses a kind of exhaustion.*][322] Now   20
Antiphon, having drawn a circle, inscribed in it some one of the polygonal areas which can be inscribed in it. Let what is inscribed be, as it may happen, a square. Then, bisecting each of the sides of the square, he erected lines at right angles from the point of division to the circumference; each of these lines clearly bisects   25
the segment of the circle in which it is. Then he joined straight lines from the point of division [*sc.* of the circumference] to the ends of the sides of the square, so that there come-to-be four triangles on the straight lines, and the whole   30
inscribed figure is an octagon. And likewise again by the same method, bisecting each of the sides of the octagon and erecting [a line] at right angles from the point of division to the circumference and joining straight lines from the points   55,1
where the lines at right angles touched the circumference to the ends of the divided straight lines,[323] he made the inscribed [figure] a 16-gon. And again by the same rule dividing the sides of the inscribed 16-gon and joining straight lines and doubling the inscribed polygon,[324] and continually doing this, he   5
thought that,[325] the surface [i.e. the interior of the circle] being at some time exhausted, in this way there will be inscribed in the circle a polygon whose sides

on account of their smallness are fitted to the circumference of the circle. And since we can construct a square equal to any polygon, as we learned in the *Elements*,[326] [then] because it is hypothesized that the polygon which is fitted to the circle is equal to it, we will also be constructing a square equal to a circle.

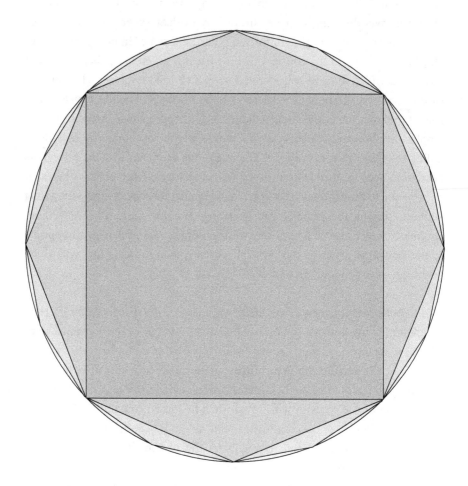

[55,12: *Criticism of Al. as to which principle(s) of geometry Antiphon abolishes.*] And it is clear that the inference goes against the principles of geometry, [but] not in the way that Alexander says, 'since the geometer hypothesizes as a principle that the circle touches the straight line at a point, whereas Antiphon abolishes this.' For the geometer does not hypothesize this, but rather demonstrates it,[327] in the third book [of the *Elements*].[328] So it is better to say that it is a principle that it is impossible for a straight line to be fitted to a circumference; rather a straight line outside a circle will touch it at one point and a straight line inside a circle [i.e. a chord] touches it only twice and no more, and the contact takes place at a point.[329] Moreover, by continually cutting the surface between the straight line and the circumference he will not exhaust it, nor will he ever attain the circumference of the circle, if indeed the surface is divisible ad infinitum. And if he does attain it, the principle of geometry will be abolished which says that magnitudes are divisible ad infinitum. And Eudemus too says that this principle was abolished by Antiphon.

[*55,25: The squaring 'by means of segments': introduction to Hippocrates' squaring, following Al.*][330] He [Aristotle] says, 'it belongs to the geometer to solve the squaring by means of segments'. Then he would mean by 'the squaring by means of segments' the squaring by means of lunes, which Hippocrates of Chios discovered.[331] For a lune is a segment of a circle. The proof is as follows:

About the straight line AB, he says, let semicircle AGB be circumscribed; and let AB be bisected at D.[332] And from D let DG be erected at right angles to AB, and from G let GA be joined, which is a side of a square inscribed in the circle of which AGB is a semicircle. And about AG let semicircle AEG be circumscribed,[333] and since the [square] on AB[334] is equal to the [square] on AG together with the [square] on the other side of the square inscribed in the semicircle AGB, namely GB (for AB is the hypotenuse of a right triangle);[335] and as the squares on the diameters are to each other, so are the circles and the semicircles about them (as has been shown in the twelfth book of the *Elements*).[336] Therefore the semicircle

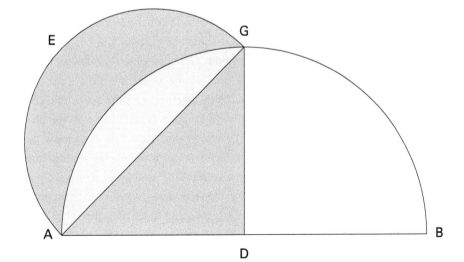

100   *Translation*

15   AGB is double the semicircle AEG. And the semicircle AGB is also double the
      quadrant AGD. Therefore the quadrant is equal to the semicircle AEG. Let the
      common part, the segment contained by the side of the square and by the arc
      AG, be taken away. Therefore the remainder, the lune AEG, is equal to the
      triangle AGD, and the triangle is equal to a square.[337]

      And having shown by these means that the lune is squared, he next tries by
20   means of what has already been shown to square the circle, as follows:

      [*56,22: Hippocrates' squaring cont'd: how to go from squaring a lune to squaring a
      circle.*] Let there be a straight line AB, and let a semicircle be circumscribed
      about it. And let [the straight line] GD be constructed double of AB, and let a
24   semicircle be circumscribed about GD, and let there be inscribed in the
57,1 semicircle sides of a [regular] hexagon inscribed in the circle, GE and EZ and
      ZD. And about these [sides] let semicircles be circumscribed, GHE and EQZ
      and ZKD. Therefore each of the semicircles about the sides of the hexagon is
      equal to the semicircle AB; for [the line] AB is equal to the sides of the hexagon.
5   For the diameter is double the radii, and the sides of the hexagon are equal to the
      radii.[338] And GD is double AB, so that the four semicircles are equal to each
      other. Therefore the four [semicircles taken together] are four times the semicircle
      AB. And the semicircle about GD is also four times [the semicircle] AB. For
      since [the line] GD is double AB, the square on GD is four times the square
10   on AB; and as are the [squares] on the diameters, so are the circles and
      semicircles about them. So the semicircle GD is four times [the semicircle]
      AB. Therefore the semicircle GD is equal to the four semicircles, the semicircle
      about AB and the semicircles about the three sides of the hexagon. Let there
      be taken away, both from the semicircles about the sides of the hexagon and
15   from the semicircle about GD, the common segments, which are contained by
      the sides of the hexagon and by the arcs of the semicircle GD. Then the
      remainders, the lunes GHE, EQZ and ZKD, together with the semicircle AB,
      are equal to the trapezium [i.e. the half-hexagon] GEZD. And if we take
      away from the trapezium the excess [i.e. the amount by which it exceeds the
      semicircle AB], that is, what is equal to the lunes (for it was shown that there is
20   a rectilineal figure equal to a lune),[339] and we leave the remainder, which is equal
      to the semicircle AB, and if we double this remaining rectilineal figure, and
      the double is squared (that is, we take a square equal to it), then the square will
      be equal to the circle about the diameter AB; and in this way the circle will be
      squared.

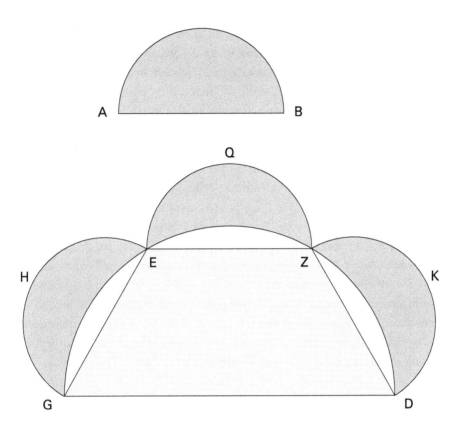

[57,25: *Verdict on Hippocrates, apparently following Al. (cf. 68,32 ff. for S.'s own considered view).*] Well, this is a noble attempt; the diagrammatic fallacy arises from assuming what has not been shown universally as if it had been shown universally.[340] For not every lune has been shown to be squared, but, if at all, the [kind] that is about the side of the square inscribed in the circle;[341] but these lunes [i.e. the ones that the argument assumes to have been squared] are about the sides of a hexagon inscribed in the circle.

[58,1: *Another way of trying to square the circle by means of lunes, viz. by dividing the circle into lunes.*][342] There was also the following proof claiming to square the circle by means of lunes, which is simpler and is not refuted by this diagrammatic fallacy occurring in it.[343] For having discovered the squaring of the lune about the side of the square, these people too thought that by this means they had discovered the squaring of the circle, on the ground that the whole circle can be divided into lunes. For multiplying the square equal to the lune as many times as all the lunes into which the circle[344] is divided, they thought that the square equal

102   *Translation*

to these lunes would also be equal to the circle, assuming the falsehood that the whole circle can be divided into lunes. For in the division of the circle into lunes

10   there is always something gibbous left over in between in the middle, contained by the lines [i.e. the boundary-arcs] of the lunes on both sides; since this is neither a lune nor squared, the whole circle would also not be squared.

[*58,13: A correction of the preceding diagnosis.*] But the objection against this kind of squaring is not sound.[345] For there is no need for the person who squares

15   the circle by means of lunes to divide the whole circle into lunes, nor, even if this did happen, would the circle in this way be squared by means of lunes, for it has not been shown that every lune is squared. And conversely [even] if the whole [circle] is not divided into lunes, it will be squared, if the lunes circumscribed about the sides of the hexagon inscribed in the circle are agreed to be squared,

20   and not only the lunes about the sides of the square.[346] So here too the cause of the diagrammatic fallacy is that, having squared only the lune about the side of the square, they proceeded in their proof as if all the lunes into which the circle is divided, of whatever kinds they might be, had been squared. So much, then, for the diagrammatic fallacy by means of lunes.

25   [*58,25: Al. discusses a bizarre arithmetical strategy for circle-squaring.*] 'Some people think', says Alexander, 'that if they should show that a circular *number* is square, they would also have found the squaring of a circle among [geometrical] magnitudes. And', he says, 'a number is square which is equal times equal; and they called numbers circular which were composed of successive odd [numbers] like one, three, five, seven, nine, [and] eleven; and having found that a number

30   among those composed in this way is at once a square and circular, like thirty-six (for it is square because it is generated out of six times itself, and circular because

59,1   it is produced from the composition of the odd [numbers] one, three, five, seven, nine, eleven), they thought that they had also found the squaring of the circle. But the proof', he says, 'is not from the principles of geometry but from those of arithmetic: for that thus-and-such a number is circular and thus-and-such is square are arithmetical principles.'

[*59,4: S. denies that anyone could have meant this: the correct conception of 'circular' numbers.*] Alexander says this, but it is worth remarking, first, that the

5   arithmeticians do not posit 'circular number' on the basis of [i.e. do not define circular number as a] composition out of successive odd [numbers], but on the basis of its ending in the same [number] from which it [arose].[347] For twenty-five

is a circle because five times five is twenty-five, and thirty-six because six times six is thirty-six, but neither four nor nine nor sixteen is a circle, although they arise from the composition of successive odd numbers. Rather, these are just squares; for squares arise from the cumulative composition of odd numbers.[348] And perhaps the person who originally handed down this method did not assert without qualification that all [the numbers] which arise by cumulative composition of successive odd numbers are circular, but rather that the circular [numbers] are found in the cumulative composition of successive odd numbers.[349] But even this does not always happen, for 125 is circular, as arising from five times twenty-five, and 216 as arising from six times thirty-six, but these do not arise from cumulative composition of successive odd numbers: unless, perhaps, these numbers are not 'circular' but 'spherical', as having been circularly deepened [i.e. made three-dimensional] out of plane circles. And it is also worth remarking on this point that it is not likely that those who discovered that the same numbers are at once circular and square would think that they had thereby also discovered the squaring of the circle among magnitudes. But perhaps, having discovered that among numbers the same number is at once a square and a circle, they came to the notion of seeking the squaring of the circle among magnitudes as well.

[59,23: *Ammonius notes that geometric figures are fundamentally different in kind, unlike numbers.*] But our teacher Ammonius used to say that it is perhaps not necessary, if this is found in the case of numbers, that it should also be found in the case of magnitudes. For the straight line and the circumference are magnitudes of unlike kinds.[350] 'And', he says, 'it is nothing surprising that no rectilineal figure has been discovered equal to a circle,[351] if indeed we find this also in the case of angles. For there would not be a rectilineal angle equal either to the angle of the semicircle or to the remainder in the right angle, which is called the horn angle.[352] And perhaps for this reason', he says, 'the theorem,[353] even though it has been sought by such famous men down to the present, has not been discovered, not even by Archimedes himself.'[354]

[59,30: *S.'s response to Ammonius, defending the in-principle possibility of squaring the circle.*] But I said to the teacher that if indeed the lune on the side of the square is squared (for this much has been concluded without error), and the lune, being composed out of circumferences, is of the same kind with the circle, what prevents the circle too, as far as this goes, from being squared? And even if the surface of the lune is unlike that of the circle on account of its horns, still

104 *Translation*

every lune is also unlike the rectilineal area, and the lune about the side of the
square is squared nonetheless. But the angles of the semicircle and the horn
angles, being both composed out of a circumference and a straight line, are not
only of unlike kind[355] with the rectilineal angle, but also incomparable.[356] So I

5   think that what was said [by Ammonius] is not sufficient to establish a rejection
of [the possibility of] discovering the squaring [of the circle]. For also Iamblichus
in his commentary on the *Categories* says that although Aristotle had not yet
discovered the squaring of the circle,[357] it had been discovered by the

10   Pythagoreans;[358] 'As is clear', he says, 'from the demonstrations of Sextus the
Pythagorean, who had received the method of demonstration from his
predecessors.[359] And afterwards', he says, 'Archimedes by means of the spiral line,
and Nicomedes by means of the [line] properly called the quadratrix, and
Apollonius by means of a line which he himself called the sister of the cochlioid,

15   but which is the same as Nicomedes' [quadratrix], and Carpus by means of a
[line] which he calls simply 'the [line] arising from the twofold motion', and
many others too', he says, 'constructed the problem [i.e. gave a construction
which solved the problem] in manifold ways.'[360] But perhaps (*kai mêpote*)[361] all of
these [people] used a mechanical construction of the theorem.[362]

[*60,18: Introduction to Eudemus' account of Hippocrates, correcting Al.*] So
Alexander, as I have said,[363] thinks that the diagrammatic fallacy is refuted in this
way, to the extent that Hippocrates, having squared only the lune about the side

20   of the square, used this [squaring] as if it had been shown also in the case of the
side of the hexagon. However, Eudemus in his *History of Geometry* says that
Hippocrates showed the squaring of the lune not in the case of the side of the
square, but rather, one might say, universally. For if every lune has its outer

25   circumference either equal to a semicircle or greater or less, and if Hippocrates
squares both the [kind] that has [its outer circumference] equal to a semicircle
and the [kinds where it is] greater or less, then, as it seems, he would have shown
it universally. I will set out verbatim what Eudemus says, adding a few things for
clarity by reference to Euclid's *Elements*,[364] on account of Eudemus' hypomnematic

30   [i.e. series-of-notes] manner, since in the ancient manner he sets out his results
concisely.[365] In the second book of the *History of Geometry* he speaks as follows:

61,1   [*61,1: Eudemus on Hippocrates: the principles used in squaring lunes.*] 'And the
squarings of lunes, which seemed to be not superficial diagrams[366] on account of
the kinship [of the lune] to the circle, were first drawn [i.e. constructed] by
Hippocrates, and seemed to have been properly set out; for which reason, let us

take them up and go through them at greater length. So he took as a starting
point and posited as the first of the things useful for these [squarings], that 5
similar circle-segments have the same ratio to each other that their bases have in
power;[367] and he showed this from showing that diameters have the same ratio
in power that the circles have', which Euclid placed second in the twelfth book of
the *Elements*, giving its enunciation as follows: 'circles are to each other as the 10
squares on their diameters.' For as the circles are to each other, so also are their
similar segments: for similar segments are those which are the same part of the
circle, as a semicircle [is the same part as, and is similar] to a semicircle, and a
third part [of a circle] to a third part.[368] For this reason[369] similar segments also
have equal angles: for the angles of all semicircles are right, and the angles of 15
[segments] greater [than a semicircle] are less than right angles, and less than
right angles by as great [a ratio] as the segments are greater than semicircles, and
the [angles] of [segments] less [than a semicircle] are greater than right angles,
and greater by as great [a ratio] as the segments are less [than semicircles].[370]

[*61,19: Eudemus on how Hippocrates squared the first type of lune.*][371] 'And after
he had shown this, he first drew [i.e. constructed] how there would arise a 20
squaring of a lune having as its outer circumference that of a semicircle. And he
set this out by circumscribing a semicircle about an isosceles right triangle, and 25
circumscribing about the base a segment of a circle similar to those cut off by the
lines that have been joined [i.e. similar to each of the segments cut off of the
semicircle by the legs of the triangle]', which Euclid placed as the thirty-third
theorem [i.e. proposition] of the third book, enunciating it as follows: 'on a given
straight line to draw a segment of a circle having an angle equal to a given
rectilineal angle.' For if he circumscribes [a segment of a circle] about the base in 30
such a way that it has an angle equal to those in the segments cut off by the lines
that have been joined, it will be similar to them. For Euclid in the third book
defined similar segments of circles as those which have equal angles.[372] [Eudemus
says:] 'And the segment about the base being equal to the two segments about the
other sides [of the isosceles right triangle inscribed in the semicircle]', because, 62,1
as has been shown in the next-to-last theorem of the first book of Euclid's
Elements,[373] in right triangles the side that subtends the right angle [i.e. the
hypotenuse] has equal power to the two sides that contain the right angle, and
similar segments of circles are to each other as the squares on the straight lines
[i.e. on the bases of the segments, which are in this case the sides of the right
triangle]. 'And if the part of the triangle above the segment about the base is 5
added in common, the lune will be equal to the triangle; so the lune, having been

shown to be equal to a triangle, would be squared', for it has been shown in the fourteenth theorem [i.e. proposition] of the second book of Euclid's *Elements* how one should construct a square equal to a given rectilineal figure. 'So in this way Hippocrates neatly squared the lune on the hypothesis that the outer circumference of the lune is that of a semicircle.'

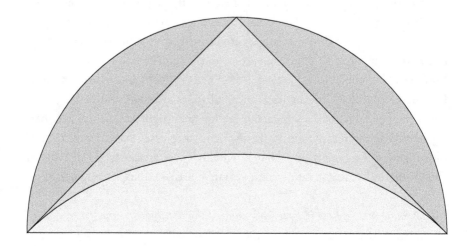

[62,13: *Eudemus on how Hippocrates squared the second type of lune.*] 'Then, next, he hypothesizes that [the outer circumference of the lune] is greater than a semicircle, constructing a trapezium which has three sides equal to each other, and one, the greater of the parallels, three times as great in power as each of those, and encompassing the trapezium with a circle and circumscribing about its greatest side a segment similar to the segments that are cut off from the circle by the three equal sides.' And that the trapezium is encompassed in a circle, you will show in this way: bisecting the angles of the trapezium by the ninth [proposition] of the first book of the *Elements*, and joining the bisectors [i.e. the angle BAG is bisected by AE and the angle DGA is bisected by GE], you will say that since BA is equal to AG, and AE is common [to the triangles BAE and GAE] and the angles [BAE and GAE] are equal [*sc.* because the line AE bisects the angle BAG], etcetera.[374] 'And that the aforesaid segment is greater than a semicircle is clear once a diagonal has been drawn in the trapezium. For since this subtends under two sides of the trapezium,[375] it must be more than double in power the one remaining side.[376,377] For since BD is greater than AG, [the lines] DG and BA, which are equal and join them [i.e. join the parallel lines BD and AG], when they are produced will meet at Z. For if BA and DG, being equal, are parallel, and lines which join equal and parallel lines are themselves equal

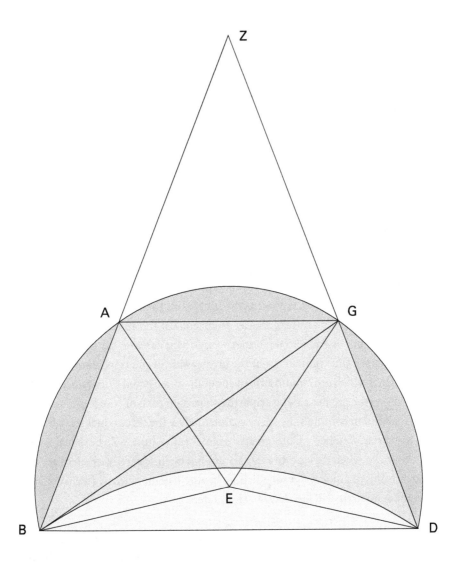

and parallel,[378] AG will be equal to BD, which is impossible.[379] So since BA and DG [produced] meet at Z, the angles ZAG and GAB will be equal to two right angles', by [proposition] 13 of the first book of Euclid. [Eudemus adds:] 'And the [angle] GAB is greater than [the angle] AGZ,[380] the external [angle] of the triangle than the internal', by [proposition] 32 of the first book.[381] 'Therefore angle GAZ is less than angle BAG.[382] Therefore also the line BG is more than double in power either of the lines BA and AG,[383] and so also [more than double in power] of GD. Therefore the greatest side of the trapezium, BD, must be less in power than the diagonal [BG] and that other side under which, together with

108 *Translation*

the diagonal, the aforesaid [side BD] subtends [i.e. GD]. For BG and GD [together] are more than triple in power GD, and BD is triple [in power GD]. 15 Therefore the angle which stands over the greater side of the trapezium [i.e. BGD] is acute.[384] Therefore the segment in which [this angle] is [namely, the segment cut off by BD of the circle circumscribing the trapezium], which is the outer circumference of the lune, is greater than a semicircle.'

[63,19: *The second case of lune-squaring continued.*] Eudemus omitted the squaring of this lune, I suppose as being clear. It would be as follows. The lune 20 together with the segment on the greater side of the trapezium is equal to the trapezium together with the segments cut off by its three equal sides. And the segment on the greater side of the trapezium is equal to the three segments cut off from the circle by the equal sides, since it is hypothesized that the greater side of the trapezium is equal in power to the three [lesser sides taken together], and 25 similar segments are to each other as the squares on their straight lines [i.e. their bases]. And if equals are taken away from equals, the remainders are equal; therefore the lune is equal to the trapezium. Or you can also say more concisely as follows: since the segment about the greater side of the trapezium is equal to the segments which are circumscribed about the three equal sides (since also the 64,1 square on it [the greater side] is triple the square on each of [the lesser sides]), if there is added in common the surface contained by the three equal straight lines and the circumference of the greater segment, the lune will be equal to the trapezium. So when this [i.e. the trapezium] has been squared (since we are able to square any rectilineal figure), the lune having its outer circumference greater 5 than the semicircle will also have been squared.[385]

[64,7: *Eudemus on Hippocrates' preliminary construction for squaring the third kind of lune.*] 'And if it [i.e. the outer circumference of the lune] were to be less than a semicircle, Hippocrates constructed this [i.e. he squared the lune] after
10 first making the following preliminary construction. Let there be a circle whose
15 diameter is AB,[386] and whose centre is K; and let GD perpendicularly bisect BK; and let EZ be placed between this [line GD] and the circumference, pointing towards B and being one and a half times the radii in power;[387] and let EH be
20 drawn parallel to AB. And let [lines] from K be joined to E and Z. And let the [line] which has been joined to Z [i.e. the line KZ], being produced [beyond Z], meet EH at H, and again let [lines] from B be joined to Z and H. So it is clear that EZ, produced, will fall on B (for it is hypothesized that EZ points towards B), and that BH will be equal to EK.'

[64,25: S. supplies an argument for the immediately previous conclusion that BH = EK.] Perhaps someone could show this also in a more immediate way, but it occurred to me to show it from things previously agreed in the following way. It is hypothesized that DG perpendicularly bisects BK. Therefore the centre of the circle to be drawn [i.e. circumscribed] about the trapezium will be on DG by the corollary to the first theorem [i.e. proposition] in the third book of Euclid's *Elements*.[388] And since EH is parallel to KB and GD falls on both, it makes the internal angles equal to two right angles, by [proposition] 29 of the first book. And the [angles] at G are right. Therefore the [angles] at D are also right. So since GD, which passes through the centre [of the circle EKBH], cuts perpendicularly EH, which does not pass through the centre, it also bisects it by the third [proposition] of the third book of the *Elements*.[389] So, since DH is equal to DE and the side DZ is common and the [angles] at D are right, therefore the base ZH is also equal to the base ZE. But also BZ is equal to ZK, because BG is also equal to GK and [the side] GZ is common and the [angles] at G are right. So since the two lines HZ and ZB are equal to the two lines KZ and ZE, and vertical angles are equal,[390] the base HB is also equal to the base EK.

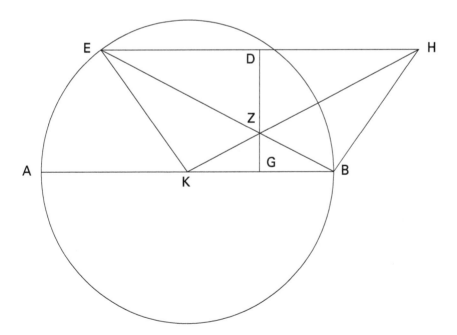

[65,7: Eudemus on Hippocrates' third case, cont'd: how Hippocrates constructs the lune.][391] 'Then, these things being such, I say that the trapezium EKBH will be

10 encompassed by a circle. For the triangle EKH will be encompassed by a circle.' For we are able by the fifth [proposition] of the fourth book of the *Elements* to circumscribe a circle about a given triangle. So if I show that the [line] from the centre to B is equal to the [line] from the centre to K, it is clear that the circle-segment drawn through EKH will also pass through B, and so the trapezium will
15 be encompassed by a circle-segment. This segment will also contain the triangle EZH.³⁹² So taking the centre, call it L, and joining [the lines] LE, LH, LK, and LB, then since the triangle ELH is isosceles (for the [lines] from the centre [including LE and LH] are equal radii), the base angles are equal, LHE to LEH, by the fifth [proposition] of the first book of Euclid's [*Elements*]. And the [angle]
20 BHE is equal to [the angle] KEH, since EB is also equal to KH, as has been shown;³⁹³ therefore also [the angle] BHL as a whole is equal to the whole [angle] KEL; and KE is also equal to BH. Therefore the base KL is also equal to the base LB; therefore LB is equal to the line from the centre LK [which was to be shown]. 'So let the segment have been drawn [i.e. constructed]. So let there be circumscribed around the triangle EZH a circle-segment of which [the part-segment] EZ³⁹⁴ is similar to each of the segments EK, KB and BH.'³⁹⁵

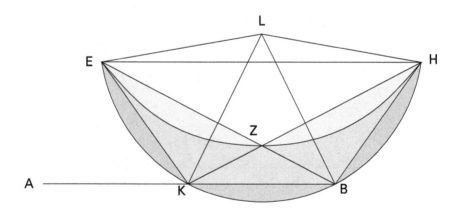

[65,24: *Eudemus on Hippocrates' third case, cont'd: how Hippocrates squares the lune.*] 'These things being such, the lune which is generated, whose outer
25 circumference is EKBH [i.e. and whose inner circumference is EZH], will be equal to the rectilineal area which is composed out of the three triangles BZH, BZK, and EKZ. For the segments cut off from the rectilineal area internally to the lune [i.e. inside the inner circumference of the lune, and therefore not parts of the lune but parts of the pentagon EZHBK] by the lines EZ and ZH are equal to the segments cut off externally to the rectilineal area [i.e. just inside the outer

Translation

111

circumference of the lune, thus parts of the lune but not of the pentagon EZHBK] by the lines EK, KB, and BH. For each of the inner segments is one and a half times each of the outer segments. For it is hypothesized that EZ is one and a half times [in power] the radius [of the semicircle AEB about K], that is, EK or KB or BH.'[396] For it was shown that this too [sc. BH] is equal to EK. So if each of EZ and ZH is one and a half times in power each of the aforesaid three [lines], and the segments are to the segments as the straight lines are to the straight lines [in power], then the two segments are equal to the three. 'So if the lune is the three segments and the part of the rectilineal area apart from the two segments, and if the rectilineal area is [the lune] together with the two segments apart from the three segments, and the two segments are equal to the three segments, then the lune would be equal to the rectilineal area.'

66,1

5

[66,10: *Eudemus on Hippocrates' third case, cont'd: how Hippocrates shows that the outer circumference of this third lune is less than a semicircle.*] 'That this lune has its outer circumference less than a semicircle, he [Hippocrates] shows by the fact that the angle EKH, which is in the outer segment, is obtuse.' For it has been shown in the [proposition] 31 of the third book of Euclid's *Elements* that 'the [angle] in a segment less than a semicircle is greater than a right angle.'[397] 'And that the angle EKH is obtuse, he shows as follows: since EZ is one and a half times the radii in power, and KB is greater than BZ', since the angle at Z is also greater [than the base angles at K and B], as I will show,[398] and BK is equal to KE, it is clear that BE is more than twice BZ in length,[399] and therefore KE will be[400] more than twice as great as KZ in power,[401] on account of the similarity of the triangles BEK and BKZ, for as EB is to BK so EK is to KZ.[402] So EK is more than twice KZ in power, and EZ is one and a half times EK in power; therefore EZ is greater in power than EK and KZ [together]. For if EK were twice KZ in power, and ZE were one and a half times EK [in power], then EZ would be equal to EK and KZ [together] in power, as, in numbers, 6 and 4 and 2 [i.e. if $EZ^2 = 6$, $EK^2 = 4$, $KZ^2 = 2$]; but since EK is more than double KZ in power, as 4 is to 1 [e.g. modify the previous numerical example so that $EZ^2 = 6$, $EK^2 = 4$, $KZ^2 = 1$], since 6 is greater than 5, EZ is also greater than EK and KZ [together] in power. Therefore the angle at K [sc. angle EKH] is obtuse. Therefore the segment in which it is is less than a semicircle. So in this way Hippocrates squared every lune, if indeed he squared the [kind] that has its outer circumference that of a semicircle, and [the kind that has its outer circumference] greater than a semicircle and [the kind that has its outer circumference] less than a semicircle.[403]

10

15

20

25

67,1

5

112 *Translation*

[*67,7: Eudemus' account of Hippocrates' cont'd: how Hippocrates squared a lune and a circle taken together.*][404] But neither [did he square] only the [lune] about the side of the square, as Alexander reported, nor did he try to square the circle

10   by means of lunes about the side of the hexagon, as Alexander also says. Rather, he squared both a lune and a circle [taken] together, as follows:[405] 'Let there be

15   two circles about the centre K, the diameter of the outer circle being six times in

20   power the diameter of the inner circle; and, inscribing a hexagon ABGDEZ in the inner circle, and joining the radii KA, KB, and KG, let them be produced to

25   the circumference of the outer circle and let HQ, QI, and HI be joined. It is clear that HQ and QI also are sides of a hexagon inscribed in the greater circle. And

30   about HI let there be circumscribed a segment similar to that cut off by HQ. So since HI must be triple in power the side of the hexagon HQ (for since the line which subtends under two sides of a hexagon, together with another side of the hexagon, contain a right angle, namely the angle in a semicircle, they [together] have equal power to the diameter; and the diameter has four times the power of

35   [the side] of the hexagon, which is equal to the radius, since things that are double in length are four times in power), and QH is six times [in power] AB, it

68,1   is clear that the [smaller] segment circumscribed about HI turns out to be equal to the segments cut off from the outer circle by HQ and QI and the segments cut off from the inner circle by all of the sides of the hexagon [i.e. is equal to all of these segments taken together].'[406] For similar circle-segments are to each other

5   as the squares on their bases, since similar circles too[407] are to each other as the squares on their diameters. For HI has power three times HQ and QI has power equal to HQ, and each of these has power equal to the six sides of the inner hexagon [taken together], since the diameter of the outer circle was also hypothesized to have power six times the diameter of the inner circle; and as the

10   diameter is to the diameter, so also are the radii, and the radius is equal to the side of the hexagon,[408] as is said in the corollary to the next to last theorem [i.e. proposition] of the fourth book of Euclid's *Elements* [4.15], and as the sides are [in power] so are the segments, 'so that the lune HQI would be less than the triangle of

15   the same letters [i.e. the triangle HQI] by [*sc.* an area difference equal to] the segments cut off from the inner circle by the sides of the hexagon. For the [smaller] segment on HI was equal to the segments HQ and QI and the segments cut off by the hexagon [*sc.* in the inner circle]. So the segments HQ and QI are less than the [smaller] segment about HI by the segments cut off by the hexagon [*sc.* in the inner circle]. So when the part of the triangle [HQI] beyond the segment about

20   HI is added in common, out of this together with the [smaller] segment about HI there will be the triangle [HQI], and out of the same [common added area]

and the segments HQ and QI there will be the lune [HQI]. So the lune will be less than the triangle by the segments cut off by the hexagon. Therefore the lune and the segments cut off by the hexagon are equal to the triangle. And when the hexagon is added in common, this triangle and the hexagon are equal to the aforesaid lune and the inner circle. For the triangle was equal to the lune and the segments cut off by the hexagon from the inner circle. So if it is possible to square the said rectilineal figures [taken together], it is therefore also possible to square the circle together with the lune.'[409]

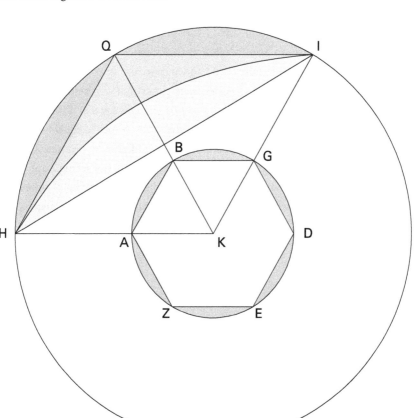

[*68,32: S.'s conclusions on Hippocrates and the 'squaring by means of segments'.*] So for what concerns Hippocrates of Chios, we should rather trust Eudemus to know [*sc.* than Alexander], being closer to the times, and a student of Aristotle. But the squaring of the circle by means of segments, which Aristotle criticizes as [graphically] fallacious,[410] either refers riddlingly to the [squaring] by means of lunes (for Alexander too was rightly hesitant in saying '*if* it is the same as the

114   *Translation*

[squaring] by means of lunes'),[411] or else he is referring not to Hippocrates' proofs but to others, one of which Alexander himself cited, or else he is criticizing

5   Hippocrates' squaring of the circle together with the lune, which indeed he demonstrated by means of segments, the three in the greater and the six in the lesser [circle].[412] For perhaps this demonstration would more strictly be called the demonstration by means of segments than by means of lunes. For Euclid also in the third book of his *Elements* defined a segment of a circle as 'the figure contained by a straight line and the circumference of a circle'.[413] So lunes are not segments in the

10 strict sense. And it would be a diagrammatic fallacy in this [*sc.* demonstration] to square the circle together with the lune rather than by itself, since all the premises of the demonstration have been taken from geometrical principles.[414] But if the squaring of the lune seems to have been handed down as universal by Hippocrates (for every lune has as its outer circumference either that of a semicircle or of a

15 segment greater or less than a semicircle), someone might say that it is possible, by taking away a square equal to the lune out of the square which is equal to the lune and the circle, and squaring the remaining rectilineal figure, to produce a square equal to the circle alone. So how will Hippocrates' squaring still seem [graphically] fallacious, [*sc.* as it must be] if Aristotle thought that [the squaring of the circle]

20 had not yet been discovered? For he says in the *Categories*, 'for instance, if the squaring of the circle is knowable, then knowledge of it does not yet exist, but the knowable exists,'[415] although Hippocrates of Chios was before Aristotle, so that even Eudemus counts him among the 'ancients'. So perhaps (*mêpote*) not every lune universally was squared by Hippocrates. For even if the outer circumference of the

25 lune is determined, still, with that [circumference] held fixed it is possible to draw infinitely many inner circumferences of the lune, or to draw different ones ad infinitum in dividing the surface ad infinitum, so that while the outer [circumference] remains the same, some lunes are greater and others are less. He, however, assumed that the inner circumference was determined: for he assumed that it cuts off a

30 segment similar to the segments constructed in the outer circumference; whence the [segments mentioned in] the first theorem were on the side of a square, and the [segments mentioned] in the other theorems were on [chords] determinate in some other way.[416] So not every lune has been squared, but [only] those which keep their inner circumference similar to the segments which are constructed in the outer circumference and which are themselves determined in some way.

70,1   **185a17-20** However, since it results that they are not speaking about nature but are stating natural aporiai,[417] it would perhaps be right to discuss them a little. For the investigation involves some philosophy.

Translation 115

[*70,3: How to parse the lemma: Al.'s first proposal.*] Having given several reasons why the argument against Parmenides and Melissus is not appropriate to the natural scientist, but wishing to argue against them nonetheless, he first gives an assurance that the argument against them is not pointless. Now Alexander, punctuating in two different ways, has given two different interpretations. First he takes it so that these people are speaking 'about nature,' but the things they said are not 'natural'. For the person who abolishes something, even if he does not use it, is nonetheless speaking (*logous poieitai*) about it. So because their arguments (*logoi*) are in a general way about nature, it would be reasonable for the natural scientist to say something in reply to them; but inasmuch as they are not saying 'natural' things, he will not spend much time on arguments against them. And Porphyry too seems to accept this punctuation when he goes over the passage as follows: 'however, since their argument is about nature, even if they unwittingly abolish nature and even if their aporiai are not "natural", one should spend a little time discussing them.'[418] And this interpretation has much to be said for it, if, as I said before,[419] Melissus even entitled his treatise *On Nature or On What Is.*

[*70,17: Al.'s second, correct proposal.*] 'But it would also be possible', says Alexander, 'to divide the aforementioned passage this way: "however, since [*sc.* they are speaking] not about nature", and then resuming, "but natural aporiai". He says, 'For this manner of expression is also customary with him: anyway, he uses it in the *Sophistical Refutations* when he says "they are not, but appear to be",[420] and again "the others do not do this, but seem to".'[421] He says, 'What is said here would be appropriate.[422] For the person who in the strict sense speaks about something is the person who discourses on what sort of thing it is: anyway, someone who abolishes the soul would not be said to be speaking *about* the soul. However, someone who raises aporiai against there being a soul would seem to be raising aporiai about the soul. In this way one might also call the things raised as aporiai against nature "natural aporiai", but one would not say that this kind of person, the person who abolishes nature, is speaking "*about* nature". And it is consistent with what has been said before', he says, 'to divide in this way: for he [Aristotle] has said, "So to examine whether what is is one and unmoved is not to examine about nature";[423] and "however, since not about nature" harmonizes with that.' And Themistius' paraphrase also harmonizes with this correct interpretation.[424]

[*70,32: Al.'s conclusions here are partly correct, but contradict what he said earlier.*] But Alexander adds to this that 'neither did those people [*sc.* the Eleatics] say

116 *Translation*

71,1 anything about nature: it is not that [despite] having set out to speak about nature they then abolished nature; rather, their abolishing nature followed from what they had said; however, the arguments which they use about motion and about infinity and void involve natural aporiai.'[425] And this much he has said
5 rightly. But how does Alexander say here that those people did not say anything about nature,[426] although he had said earlier in these very words that 'Parmenides in giving an account of nature according to the opinion of the many and according to the appearances, where he no longer says that what is is one or that it is ungenerated, hypothesized fire and earth as principles of the things that come-to-be';[427] and Melissus too, even if [that account was] not about nature in
10 the strict sense or about what is.[428]

[*71,10: Another reason for engaging with the Eleatics.*] And, having given the reason why one should briefly discuss with them, even if the arguments given before hindered our arguing against them, [Aristotle] refers this reason in turn to another more ultimate reason. For in general one must argue against these people, since they are speaking about nature or because they state natural aporiai, and furthermore one must argue against such [opinions or arguments] since 'the
15 investigation involves some philosophy'. For it belongs to no one but the philosopher to investigate about what is in general, or about nature and natural aporiai.

185a20-b5 The most appropriate starting point of all is, since being is said in many ways, how do those who say that all things are one mean it? Are all things substance, or quanta, or qualia; and again are all things one substance, such as one human being or one horse or one soul, or is this one quale, such as white or hot or some other such thing? For these all differ a great deal and are impossible to assert. For if there are going to be both substance and quale and quantum, whether these things are detached from each other or not, then the things that are will be many, and if all things are quale or quantum, whether substance exists or not, it will be absurd, if one should call absurd what is impossible. For none of the others is separable, apart from substance, for they are all said of substance as an underlying thing. Now Melissus says that what is is infinite, so what is will be a quantum, for the infinite is in the quantum, and a substance or a quality or an affection cannot be infinite except per accidens, [i.e.] if they are also at the same time some quanta. For the account of 'infinite' entails quantity rather than substance or quality.[429] So if both substance and quantum exist, what is will be two and not one, and if only substance exists it will not be infinite, nor will it have any magnitude, for if it did it would be some quantum.

Translation 117

[*71,19: Introduction to Ar.'s argument against Parmenides and Melissus.*] The person who argues against some opinion undertakes either of two things: either he is overturning the arguments which support it, or he is abolishing that opinion 20 overall. But the person who only abolishes the supporting arguments has not yet abolished the doctrine: for what if there are other arguments that support it, stronger than the ones that have been abolished?[430] Those, however, who object against the doctrine itself rather than against the supporting arguments, and abolish it overall, securely abolish the doctrine, but leave behind aporiai, unless 25 they also overturn the supporting arguments themselves. For which reason Aristotle, having set out to refute the account of Parmenides and Melissus, first objects against it overall, that what is is not one, if one takes it in terms of the obvious [sense], refuting [it] on the basis of a division;[431] and then he also overturns their arguments, if one takes them as supporting such a 'One-which- 30 is.'[432] And the argument turns out to be dialectical, since it proceeds from the division of beings: for it is possible by making use of dialectic to establish the 72,1 principles of the sciences.[433] And the overall presentation of the argument is as follows. Since they say that what is is one, and each of these, being and one, is said in many ways, each of these individually should be divided. So since being has been shown to be said in ten ways, either as substance or as quale or as quantum 5 or as some other of the ten categories, do those who say that what is is one mean that it is one only in name, but many in reality, so that all things are *called* being[434] although they are in reality ten [categories], or at least several (for let this too be added to the division); or do they mean that it is also one in reality, e.g. a substance or a quale or a quantum, so that all things are numerically one substance? For if 10 they mean that they are generically or specifically [one], it's clear that they will be numerically many. So they mean either[435] that they are one [*sc.* substance] in this way, 'as one human being or one horse or one soul', or else as quale, not the genus (for again they would immediately be many), but 'one this like white or hot or something of this kind'. Now all the ways of taking [the account of Parmenides and Melissus] differ a great deal from each other and all are impossible. For if the 15 being they are talking about is one only in name, but in reality is both substance and quale and quantum, all the genera or some of them, either separated from each other or existing together with each other, the things that are will be many. But if all things are some one genus of the ten, e.g. substance or quale or quantum, and are one for the reason that all things are restricted to one of the ten genera, 20 'then whether substance does or does not exist', something absurd will follow. For if, as is natural, substance first underlies and then one of these [other categories] happens to it, then again what is will not be one, but both substance

118   *Translation*

and quale, or whichever of the ten genera they posit that being is. And if substance
does not exist, this too is impossible, for none of the other genera can subsist
25   apart from substance, since substance underlies the other genera and they have
their existence in it: for let it be added in this way too.[436] Moreover, according to
Melissus and Parmenides, whether it is hypothesized that being is a quale or a
substance (for the argument will be common to substance as well), since the
former says that what is is infinite, the latter finite, quantity too will immediately
30   have been introduced. For the infinite and the finite are in the quantum, and a
substance or a quality or an affection cannot be infinite or finite except per
accidens, [i.e.] if they are also at the same time quanta. For the account of 'infinite'
73,1   and 'finite' entails quantity rather than substance or quality.[437]

[73,2: *Controversy about how the preceding division of being relates to the division of
'one' promised at 72,3-4, and announced by Ar. in the next lemma.*][438] Anyway, I,
following Porphyry for the most part, have taken Aristotle's division and his objection
to each section of the division in this way.[439] However, the very careful Alexander
5   connected the division of 'being' and the division of 'one' as follows: 'those who say
that what is is one, are saying this either on account of the name, since the one name
is predicated[440] of all the things that are, or else in reality. If through the name, then
since the name[441] is said in many ways (for being is said in ten ways), the things that
are and the realities will be many in existence. But if they mean one in reality, [the
10   things will be one] either in genus or in species or in number.[442] But if in genus or in
species, the things that are will be many (for each of these [*sc.* genus and species] is
[said] of many), but if in number, then since "one in number" is [said] in three ways,
he [Aristotle] divided: "[they are numerically one] either as the continuous, or as the
indivisible, or as things whose account is the same"'.[443]

[73,13: *Criticism of Al. for his reading of Ar. as here considering the Eleatic claim
that being is one in genus, as opposed to numerically one.*][444] And yet Aristotle after
the whole division of being added the division of the one, where he says 'again,
15   since one too is said in many ways, just as being is'.[445] He does not even deem it
worthwhile to take up one in genus or species,[446] since these obviously introduce
plurality; rather he concentrates his forces on being as numerically one. But
Alexander failed to notice this, not taking what Aristotle says in a manner
appropriate to his own [*sc.* Alexander's] division. For he [Alexander] thinks[447] that

he [Aristotle] had originally asked in what way they say that what is is one,
20   whether in genus, so as to say that all things are substance or all things are quanta
or all things are qualia or some other of the ten genera; and, if so, then, in turn,

Translation 119

in what way are they each of these things? For instance, if they say one substance, how do they mean this – in such a way as to say that the substance is one man or one horse or one soul? – and likewise in the case of quality and in the other cases. Through this questioning he reveals at the same time the plurality in each genus and the absurdity of the account they have asserted. 25

Now if Alexander had said this and stopped here, he might perhaps have given grounds to suspect that he did not intend 'whether in genus, so as to say that all things are substance' about the hypothesis that says [that all things are] generically one. But instead, after himself rightly interpreting 'if there is going to be both substance and quantity and quality,'[448] he adds,

this does not seem to have been introduced congruously with the things that 30 were said before. For he spoke before as if asking 'in what sense do those who say that what is is one mean [this], as substance or as quality or some other of the ten genera, or as some one of the things [that fall] under some [one] of these genera, as numerically one substance or one quantum or one quale?'. But then, omitting to show the absurdity of each of these, he assumes [for purposes of refutation] 74,1 another [option], which he had neither asked about, nor would it be plausible for those who say that what is is one to say.

Says Alexander, 'But he wanted the disjunction (diairetikon) in his questioning to be complete: for [what is] is one either in name or in what it signifies. So', he says, 'he does not introduce these absurdities as if [following from] what he had asked beforehand, but for confirmation that they must by all means say one of these 5 [i.e. choose one of these options].'[449]

[74,5: *Porphyry is right about the passage.*] But Porphyry says rightly that the original question, asking whether all things are substance or all things are quanta, indicates this: whether they mean[450] that there is one name of all things, although they are many realities, or also that all things are some one reality, and clearly an individual, like one man or one horse: for if they mean a genus or a species, then since each of these is said of many, they will be admitting a plurality of things 10 that are. For if this is not what he [sc. Aristotle] was asking, what is the use of beginning by assuming that being is said in many ways? And if the absurdity for those who hypothesize thus was obvious, since many realities would be posited under a single name from the start, we shouldn't be surprised that he hypothesizes even something obviously absurd for the completeness of his division (diairesis). But then why did he argue against this and not refrain from asking it?[451] In 15 general, the whole thesis of those who say that what is is one, if one interprets it

120   *Translation*

in this superficial way, is paradoxical and counter-intuitive, but nonetheless, out of consideration for the simpler-minded Aristotle deemed it worth arguing against.

[*74,18: Eudemus' counterpart passage.*] However, Eudemus undertakes to argue more concisely as follows:[452] 'For since', he says, 'being is said in many ways (for
20   we say that both substance and quality and quantity and the rest of the divisions *are*), besides which one of these will there not be anything else?' That is, if *what* exists will it be possible for the others not to exist? 'And clearly', he says, 'one would most [plausibly] say, besides substance [nothing else exists]. For the others always appear in something, so that if they exist, that in which [they are] would also exist; but if substance exists,[453] nothing seems to underlie. But if nothing
25   underlies, but animals exist, will walking and acting and moving not exist, or beautiful or any other such thing? How is this not absurd? And it is not possible for them not to make the quantum one of the things that are: for [in that case] they judge that what is is neither infinite nor finite, if indeed these are affections of quantity.'

[*74,29: S. adds his own interpretive observations about the lemma.*] But having
30   recounted what Eudemus says, let us add some things worth observing as regards the text. To first distinguish the meanings of 'being', which is now put forward for
75,1 investigation, is also the appropriate precept of one who takes care in each problem to first define what the name means and learn what each thing is. And this is also consistent with what Plato says in the *Phaedrus*, 'About everything, my child, there is one starting point, to know what it is we are taking counsel
5   about, for otherwise we must miss it altogether.'[454] For the person who is ignorant of it would not be able even to raise objections about it.[455]

[*75,6: Second observation.*] 'Since[456] being is said in many ways' is not [the saying] of a questioner,[457] but of someone who takes a premise from what is obvious and who confidently bases himself on the division in the *Categories* and enquires further whether, since being is said in many ways, those who say that what is is one can be speaking truly in any sense [of being].[458]

10   [*75,10: Third observation.*] After saying rightly that it is absurd for all things to be a quale or a quantum, he added 'if one should call the impossible "absurd."'[459] For even the simply false [can be] absurd, but impossibility is an intensification of falsehood. For the absurd is the opposite of the plausible, signifying either the

paradoxical, what one would not guess,[460] or what there is no place for;[461] whereas the impossible is the opposite of the necessary. So how is this impossible? Because if substance exists, either substance and quale will be the same thing, or what is will be simultaneously both one and not one; and if substance does not exist, since the quale is not separate from substance, it would not exist either. So as the necessary is an intensification of the plausible, so the impossible is an intensification of the absurd. And he first stated the absurdities that follow for those who say that all things are a quale, or some one of the other genera, whether substance does or does not exist. For if it exists, both it and the other genus will exist, and if it does not exist the accidents will exist apart from substance.

[75,21: Fourth observation: Ar.'s discussion of Melissus confirms that a position with these absurd consequences was instantiated.] But that anyone had ever suggested that what is was some other genus beside substance, he confirms from the fact that Melissus said that what is is infinite, which is proper to quanta. And he criticizes those who say that what is is something else beside the quantum by saying that they are not in agreement with Parmenides and Melissus, of whom the former hypothesized that what is is finite, the latter that it is infinite. And in this way he refutes those who said that what is is substance by the same argument as those who said that it was quale or anything else beside quantum, by their no longer being able to call it infinite. And, clearly, not finite either, which presumably he left out here as being clear; a bit further on he added this too.[462] And he will also add other absurdities for those who say that what is is one as a substance, when he sets out to examine 'what just is' (to hoper on).[463]

[75,30: A fifth observation.] But here [i.e. 185a32] he uses 'of an underlying thing' (kath' hupokeimenou) not as meaning the universal but in place of 'in an underlying thing' (en hupokeimenôi):[464] for he is in the habit of calling things which do not exist by themselves, but require something else in order to exist, 'of an underlying thing', as being said of the things which underlie them. For the underlying things are not predicated of the accidents, but the accidents of the underlying things. 'So', says Alexander, 'all those things are said of an underlying thing which need some underlying thing in order to exist. For he says that the things which are in the strict sense "of an underlying thing"[465] are also like this, since he does not acknowledge any separate universal.'[466]

[76,7: A sixth observation.] But what does he mean by saying that the infinite is in the quantum [sc. at 185a33-34]? Perhaps as being in the genus of quantity: for

122   *Translation*

some quantity is infinite and some is finite. Or perhaps because 'infinite' is predicated per se only of the quantum, and not of any of the other genera. For

10   whatever things are included in the defining account of something are predicated per se, as animal is predicated per se of man; and so are the things which are included in the defining account of the things that belong to them,[467] as even belongs to number per se, since number is included in the account of even. For in defining 'even' we say 'number divisible into [two] equals'.[468] And these things

15   have been shown in the *Posterior Analytics*. And if someone takes even as a species of number and does not consider it to be an accident of it, let him take nose and snubness as an example. For nose is included in the definition of snubness, when we say that snubness is concavity in a nose. And infinite is predicated of quantum per se, since quantum is included in the account of

20   infinite. 'Infinite' is twofold [i.e. ambiguous] in the same way that 'white' is,[469] and 'infinite' meaning infinity is an affection of quantity, while the 'infinite' in the sense of the thing having infinity as an affection [i.e. the infinite object] is an untraversable quantum. So from every point of view the infinite also entails the definition of quantum. Therefore it belongs per se to it, and so to it alone: for it is

25   not possible for the same thing to belong per se to several non-homogeneous things. For which reason, as he himself says, 'the account of "infinite" also entails the quantum, not substance or quale'.[470] And if someone who says that what is is substance should say that it is infinite, the infinite would belong to the substance per accidens, not inasmuch as it is substance but inasmuch as it is quantum: so that what is would not be one, since it is quantum and substance.

[76,29: *Seventh observation: why does Ar. already single out Melissus at 185a32?*] But,

30   given that he is now replying universally and intends afterwards to reply [specifically] to Melissus and his followers when he says 'it is also not difficult to solve the [reasons] from which they argue',[471] how is it that nevertheless he now already seems to be enmeshing Melissus' opinion in absurdity? Perhaps he did not

77,1 now mention [Melissus' doctrine] primarily [i.e. as his main intention], but rather, having taken up the hypothesis which says that what is is a quantum or a quale, in order not to appear to be hypothesizing something that no one believes, he adduced Melissus' account. And perhaps (*mêpote*) his argument was universal: for one must hypothesize either that what is is finite or that it is infinite, and either way one must

5   say that what is is a quantum, and he cites Melissus as a witness for the hypothesis; and next he also lines up Parmenides alongside him. And in some manuscripts it is written thus: 'Now Melissus says that the one is infinite, so the one will be a quantum'.[472] And he would mean their 'one' [i.e. the Eleatic one], which is being.[473]

Translation

123

[*77,9: Start of engagement with Al.'s arguments against the Eleatics, through to 80,18.*] And since Alexander of Aphrodisias also sees fit to argue by his own arguments against those who say that what is is one, let us consider briefly in what way he too seems to be speaking rightly, and [in what way] the ancient philosophy remains unrefuted.[474] 'Against those', he says, 'who say that the other things, which are in coming-to-be,[475] do not exist, on the ground that they sometimes are and sometimes are not, and that only the eternal substance exists, since it in no way participates in not-being, first let us speak on the basis of what is obvious and common conceptions and common usage. For they [*sc.* the things that come-to-be] seem to everyone to be beings, and everyone both thinks and speaks in this way. Next, if they deny that these things are because they come-to-be and pass away, then because what is coming-to-be comes-to-be some being and what passes away passes away from being, both what comes-to-be and what passes away[476] would be among the things that are. For it is not the case that, if they do not exist in the same way as eternal things, then for this reason they do not exist [at all]. And', he says, 'if the reason they do not exist is that they pass away, then when they are not passing away and in whatever respect they are not passing away, they would exist in that respect and at that time.'[477]

10

15

20

[*77,21: S.'s response to Al. in defence of Parmenides.*] Now in reply to these and their like, let the general rule be stated that, just as we call 'white' both what is tinted with white in any way, even if it is jumbled up together with more of the contrary, and we also call 'white' what is unmixed with the contrary, and likewise 'beautiful', and what is purely such is called each of these in the strict sense, but what is mixed together with the contrary [is called each of them] in a crude and loose sense, so too what is being in every respect and all together[478] would be called 'being' in the strict sense. And what comes-to-be and passes away does not yet exist before it has come-to-be, and it no longer exists after it has passed away; and even when it seems to exist, since it has its being in coming-to-be and passing away and never 'remains in the same'[479] even then it would not be called being in the strict sense, but rather coming-to-be and passing away on account of the continuous flow which exchanges all things. Heraclitus spoke of this in riddles with his 'not entering the same river twice',[480] comparing coming-to-be, which has more of not-being than of being, to the continual flow of a river: for being, as Parmenides says, has different signs.[481] And it is better to listen to the very things he [*sc.* Parmenides] states and demonstrates about what *is* in the strict sense. For after criticizing those who jumble together[482] being and not-being in the intelligible [world]:[483]

25

30

78,1

124   *Translation*

Who think that to be and not to be are the same
And not the same[484]

5   and having turned [them?] away from the path that investigates not-being:

But you hold back your thought from this path of enquiry[485]

he adds,

Only one story of a path
Still remains, that it is. And on this [path] there are
10   Very many signs[486]

and then in what follows he hands down the signs of what is in the strict sense:

That being ungenerated and indestructible it is,
Whole and unique[487] and unshaken and unending[488]
Nor was it ever nor will it be, since it now is, all together
15   One and continuous. For what birth will you seek for it?
How and from where did it grow? From not-being,
I will not allow you to say or even think. For it is not to be said nor even
        thought
That it is not. And what need would have roused it
Later rather than earlier to grow, beginning from nothing?
20   Thus it must be either completely or not at all,
Nor will the force of conviction ever admit anything to come-to-be
from not-being alongside it. For which reason Justice has never,
loosening her fetters, admitted it to come-to-be or be destroyed.[489]

[*78,24: S.'s response to Al. continued: Parmenides is discussing 'being' in the strictest
sense.*] So, saying these things about being in the strict sense, he clearly demonstrates
25   that this being is ungenerated: for neither [is it generated] out of what is, for nothing
else that is would have existed prior to it, nor out of what is not, for what is not does
not exist. And just why did it come-to-be at that time and not earlier or later? But
neither [did it come-to-be] out of what is in one respect and is not in another
respect, the way that what is generated comes-to-be: for what is in one respect and
is not in another respect would not exist prior to what is *simpliciter*, but rather has
come to subsist (*huphestêke*) after it.[490] And the Platonic Timaeus says, 'we wrongly
79,1   transfer, unawares, "was" and "will be", which have arisen as species of time, to the
eternal substance. For we say that it was and is and will be; but according to the true
account only "is" is fitting for it, whereas "was" and "will be" should be said with
regard to the coming-to-be which proceeds in time.'[491] So if Alexander wants to

show that the things that are in coming-to-be have some kind of subsistence and 5
are therefore loosely said to be, even if they are jumbled together with more not-
being, and he rests content with the usage of the name among the many, then this
won't require much argument [on his part]. But if he thinks that what comes-to-be
and perishes, in which there is more non-being than being, is being in the strict
sense, then he has not followed closely the signs of being declared by Parmenides, 10
nor is he paying attention to Aristotle, who rightly called the Parmenidean [being]
'what just is' (*hoper on*), that is, what is in the strict sense.

[*79,12: Al. also wrong to claim that being in the strict sense could persist through
change.*] Alexander also criticizes Parmenides and Melissus and their followers
because they show that what is is unmoved on the ground that what is moved
seems to depart from that in which it is; so if what is were also moved, it would
depart from that in which it is; but it is in existence. And what departs from 15
existence perishes, and what is is imperishable. 'But', he says, 'if the only motion
were motion with respect to substance, which one might more strictly call change
rather than motion, perhaps they might say this reasonably. However, not even
what changes with respect to its substance changes to non-being *simpliciter*, but
rather to being not what it was, but something else. But if anything, what changes
with respect to substance *simpliciter*, not with respect to *this* substance [would be
what changes to non-being *simpliciter*]. But since there are several [kinds of] 20
motions, including also motion in respect of quality, which is not in respect of
substance, their fear', he says, 'is empty and vain.' It is surprising that after he
himself had agreed that 'what changes with respect to substance *simpliciter*, not
with respect to this substance' would pass into not-being, he criticizes those who
say that if what is *simpliciter* and is in the strict sense should change, it would 25
perish. For if it [*sc.* being in the strict sense] were being thus-and-such, then when
it departs from thus-and-such, nothing would prevent it from changing into
another thus-and-such;[492] but since it is being *simpliciter*, when it departs from
this, what would it come-to-be? And how would *that* being be altered,[493] which
is always in the same state and in the same way, which neither belongs accidentally
to anything else nor has anything else belonging accidentally to it, but is just
what it is?[494]

[*79,29: Reaffirmation that Parmenides and Melissus are right that being in the
strict sense is unmoved.*] So Parmenides, having first shown by the [arguments] 30
which we have mentioned earlier that what is is ungenerated and imperishable,
rightly added:

126 *Translation*

But unmoved in the limits of great bonds

80,1 It is, unbeginning, unceasing, since coming-to-be and destruction

Are warded off utterly, far away.[495]

– from which it is also clear that he is aware that the sensible, in which there are coming-to-be and destruction, is one thing, and the intelligible being is another. And Melissus too shows the immovability [of what is] after first abolishing what

5 is empty of being, i.e. what is not. For if what is were in motion, he says, there would be something empty of being into which what is would be moved. But there is not, for what is is full. He writes as follows: 'Neither is anything empty. For what is empty is nothing; but what is nothing would not be. Nor is it moved: for it does not have anywhere to withdraw, rather it is full. For if there were

10 [anyplace] empty, it would withdraw into the empty, but since there is no empty, it does not have anywhere to withdraw.'[496] Then, after showing that it is neither dense nor rare, he adds, 'one must make this judgement about full and not full: if it makes room for something or receives something, it is not full, but if it neither makes room nor receives, it is full. Now it must be full, if there is no empty; if therefore it is full, it is not moved.'[497]

[*80,15: Conclusion of S.'s rebuttal of Al.'s arguments against the Eleatics (77,9 ff.),*

15 *clarifying the sense in which they hold that being is one and unmoved.*] Well then, I have been compelled to draw these things out at greater length because Alexander, the most genuine interpreter of Aristotle, takes the doctrines of the ancients rather uncharitably and carelessly – doctrines in emulation of which Aristotle himself also demonstrated that the first [being] is unmoved.

185b5-25 Again, since 'one' itself also is said in many ways, just as 'being' is, we must examine in what way they [the Eleatics] say that the all is one. What is called one is either the continuous or the indivisible or things the formula of whose essence is one and the same, like liquor and drink. So then if it is continuous, the one[498] will be many: for the continuous is divisible to infinity. (There is a difficulty about the part and the whole, perhaps not relevant here but in itself a difficulty: whether the part and the whole are one or several, and in what way they are one or several, and if they are several, how they are several, and also about non-continuous parts. And if each [part] is one with the whole as indivisible, [the difficulty arises] that they will also be one with each other.) But if [it is one] as indivisible, nothing will be quantum or quale, so that what is will neither be infinite, as Melissus says, nor finite like Parmenides. For the limit is indivisible but the limited [i.e. finite] is not. But if all the things that are are one in formula, like cape and cloak, they will turn out to be holding the Heraclitean

Translation 127

account. For to be good and to be bad will be the same thing, indeed to be good and not to be good – so that good and not-good will be the same, and human and horse, and it won't be an account of the things that are being one but of their being nothing. And being such and being so much [i.e. having a quality and having a quantity] will be the same.

[*80,20: Against Porphyry, Ar.'s division of 'one' is not the categorial division; introduction of a trilemma: something can be numerically one by being continuous, or indivisible, or having the same formula.*] Having hypothesized that what is [is said] in many ways, and having taken up by division the opinions on which it would be possible to say that what is is one, he in turn hypothesizes that 'one' too is said in many ways, and shows that according to each sense of 'one' it is impossible to say that what is is one. He uses a division which is appropriate to 'one', and, I think, he does not agree with what Porphyry says here. For he [Porphyry] says: '"one", too, signifies many things, in the first place those which "being" also signifies; and by dividing "one" into the same [senses] as "being", it is possible to argue in much the same way, demanding what they mean by saying that what is is one, whether as a substance or as a quale or according to some other [category].'[499] For Aristotle has, more precisely, made a division of the meanings of 'being' and another appropriate to the meanings of 'one': for what is one will be one either in genus or in species or in number. But Aristotle did not see fit now to set out what is one in genus or species, since these manifestly introduce plurality: for if they say that what is is one in genus, it will be many in species, and yet more in the number of individuals. And if it is one in species, then, first, by this very fact it will be clear that it is many: for the species is a species of a genus, and the genus is predicated in what-it-is of several and differing species.[500] Furthermore, if it is one in species, it will be several in number, for the one species is predicated of things several in number. Well then, these things are clear even to those who have been introduced to the first [rudiments] of logic,[501] and reasonably enough he did not see fit to mention them. But as for what is one in number, that too is said in many ways: either as the continuous, in the way that I would say that the line is one, or as what is indivisible by nature, like the point and the unit, or as the things which have the same formula even if they may differ in name, like cape and cloak. Again, by another division, something is called one either in potentiality or in actuality, and these are related to each other in [the realm of] coming-to-be in such a way that what is one in actuality is many in potentiality, and what is one in potentiality is many in actuality. Thus in the case of wax, when it is continuous and one in actuality, it is many in potentiality, because it can be divided into many; and

20

25

30

81,1

5

10

128   *Translation*

when it is dispersed and many in actuality, it is one in potentiality, because it can
15   be made continuous.

[*81,16: If what is is one by being continuous, then there are many.*] So for these
reasons, if they are going to say that what is is one as continuous, it will be one in
actuality, but many and infinite in potentiality. For that is continuous whose parts
touch at one common boundary, and which is divisible into [parts which are]
always themselves divisible.[502] So if they call it one because its parts are unified,
20   they will also call it many, because the parts which are unified are many, and
because it is divisible to infinity they will call it infinitely many or multiplied to
infinity. So if what is is one as continuous, and the continuous is many, the one will
be many. And the many are not one; so the same thing will be both one and not
one. Furthermore, since there are several [kinds of] continuum, how will what is
25   be one, if it is one as continuous? As some line, as a surface, as a body, as a place,
as a motion, as a time? For all of these are continuous. And each of these has many
species. For of lines, some are straight, others are round; of surfaces, some are
plane, others are concave, others are convex, and there are many shapes of plane
surface. And there are many species of solid bodies and of the places that have
30   the same shapes as they; and likewise of time the past and the future and
the present, and hours and days and months and years [are species], and one
motion is in a straight line, another in a circle; all of these things are continuous,
and all of them taken together are many in actuality, and each of them is many in
potentiality.

[*81,34: Refutation of the possibility that what is is one by being indivisible: it is
not indivisible either by being not yet divided or by being impassive.*] And if what
is is one as indivisible,[503] since 'indivisible' [is said] in many ways, [it would be]
35   either what has not yet been divided but is capable of being divided, like each
continuous thing, or what is not of such a nature as to be divided at all because
82,1   it has no parts into which it would be divided, like a point or a unit, or because it
has parts and magnitude but is impassive on account of its hardness and solidity
like each of Democritus' atoms. So then[504] if what is is one as continuous, then,
again, what is will be many; if what is is one as the atom, then, first, it is absurd
5   and counter-intuitive to say that all things are one atom; and furthermore, it too
will be continuous and divisible to infinity and for this reason potentially many.
Furthermore it will have the quantity of its magnitude and the quality of its
figure,[505] e.g. angular, straight or round, and motion; and thus again it will be
many.

Translation 129

[*82,8: Refutation of the possibility that what is is one by being indivisible, completed: it is not indivisible by being partless.*] And if what is is one and indivisible like a unit or a point, then none of the things that are will be a quale (for qualia are divided along with the bodies [to which they belong] and especially with natural bodies), nor a quantum; for the indivisible is the *limit* of a quantum. So neither will 'what is be infinite, as Melissus says, nor finite as Parmenides' thinks.[506] For everything infinite or finite is a quantum, and nothing which is indivisible in plurality and in magnitude is a quantum: 'For the limit is indivisible but the limited [i.e. finite] is not.'[507] And here too Aristotle deemed only *this* meaning of 'indivisible' worth arguing against, on the ground that the others are easy to resolve. And against this, he did not argue as against a point, as the commentators do, but rather as against the sort [of indivisible one] that Parmenides and his followers actually hypothesized, which is without quantity or quality.

[*82,20: Refutation of the possibility that what is is one by being one in formula: completion of the trilemma at 185b7-9.*] But if what is is one like liquor and drink or cape and cloak or in general many-named things (for this meaning of 'one' is still left over), then all things will be one many-namedness and quale will be the same as quantum and all things will be the same as each other, and the account of Heraclitus will be true which says that the good and the bad are the same. And contradictories will occur together: for the same thing will be good and not good, if the bad is not good. And observe that here too he passes from the affirmation of the contrary [e.g. that what is good is also bad] to the contradictory opposition [e.g. that what is good is not good],[508] which is greater.[509] And the same thing will be both human and horse, so it will be both human and not human, and one and not one; so that the account and the investigation will no longer be about what *is* being one but about its being nothing, if indeed in the case of each thing its negation and its affirmation are likewise true, or, as Porphyry infers, if indeed what is is not.[510] For just as human and not human will be true together [i.e. will hold of the same thing], so too will being and not-being. And I think that this [i.e. Porphyry's *reductio ad absurdum*] would follow, if being were some one of all things, such as a human; for then all other things would be not-beings. So in sum what is is not one in this way either. Therefore if what is cannot be one according to any of the meanings of 'one', then we should not say that what is is one at all; rather, the things that are are several, just as the phenomena bear witness. So the sequence of the division and of the responses to the sections of the division would go thus.

130   *Translation*

[*83,6: Why does Ar. introduce the aporia about part and whole at 185b11-16?*] But after responding to the first section of the division, which says that what is is one as continuous, he has made the argument rather unclear by inserting, before solving the remaining [sections], an aporia about the whole and the part, whether they are the same or other, or rather whether both are one.[511] Now Porphyry says

10 that this aporia has been posed as if people were going to object to him [Aristotle] that he had mentioned three modes of existence of the one but had not mentioned the fourth which some people had introduced in the belief that a part which is not continuous with another part is one with the whole, e.g. that Socrates' hand and Socrates are one, which is not the same as any of the previously mentioned

15 modes of 'one'.[512] So he first refutes these people, on the ground that their belief is absurd, and then passes to the refutation of the one as indivisible. And the refutation of these people is that if Socrates' right hand and Socrates are one, and if, again, the left hand and Socrates are one, then the left hand and the right hand will also be one; for this was [what he means by] 'and if each [part] is one with the whole as indivisible, that they will also be one with each other' [185b15-16].

20 Alexander, however, says that he [Aristotle] solves the aporia about the part and the whole (which says that the part is the same as the whole) in order that, by showing that it is not the same, he may hold more firmly that the parts come-to-be several not only when they have been divided from the whole, but also when they are taken in continuity [i.e. when they are undetached], if indeed they are other both than each other and than the whole. But he says that the 'perhaps not

25 relevant here' [185b12] is said, although the things that have been said *are* relevant, because what was said beforehand was sufficient to refute those who say that what is is one as continuous. And perhaps also because the aporia on both sides was exoteric to the argument, as Eudemus also says, belonging rather to dialectic.[513]

[*83,28: Aporia of part and whole cont'd: why does Ar. say 'one' rather than 'same'?*] I will also cite a bit later the text of Eudemus,[514] which clearly manifests the object of the discussion; for now let the words of Alexander be set before us. He

30 says: 'Admittedly, what has been shown is more customary with "the same": for things that are the same as the same are also the same as each other.' And for this reason Eudemus too gives the demonstration in this form, and so do the commentators on Aristotle, taking 'the same' in the place of 'one'. And yet Aristotle, proceeding (it seems to me) in a more precise manner, kept 'one': for things that are one with the same thing are also one with each other, much more

84,1 than things that are the same as the same thing are also the same as each other.

For this reason he also says 'each of them is one as indivisible' [185b15]; for the one, more than the same, unifies whatever things it accrues to.

[*84,3: Aporia of part and whole cont'd: restatement in terms of whether the part can be the same as the whole.*] Furthermore, what is one will be many, if each of its parts is the same as the whole, and the whole will be composed of many wholes and will be a part of itself. For the part is a part of a whole: so if the part and the whole are one, the whole will be a part of itself, and the part, since it is the same as the whole, will itself be [composed] of many wholes, and the whole will be a part of the part. And that the part is not the same as the whole has been shown from these [considerations].

[*84,9: The other side of the aporia of part and whole: why the whole is not other than the part.*] It should next be shown that the difficulty also remains if it is hypothesized to be other [i.e. if the part is supposed to be other than the whole],[515] in order to make clear why Aristotle adds 'There is a difficulty about the part and the whole, perhaps not relevant but in itself a difficulty' [185b11-12]. For if it is hypothesized that the part is other than the whole, it is clear that each of the parts will be other than the whole; so they all will; but all the parts are the whole; so the whole itself will be other than itself. Furthermore, things that are other seem to be separated from each other, but the whole is inseparable from the parts.

[*84,15: Aporia of part and whole cont'd: Al. replies to a possible solution by reposing the dilemma.*] Aristotle, having begun his aporia with continuous parts, says that the aporia is similar also in the case of discrete parts – for these are the ones 'which are not continuous' [185b14]. For the brick too is either the same as the house or other than the house; and if it is the same, the brick will be a house and the house a brick. But if it is other, then so too all the parts out of which the house is [constituted] would be other than the house. However, all the parts seem to be the house, and so the house will be other than itself. And since it is easy for anyone to have the thought that it is not the parts *simpliciter* that are the whole, but the parts together with the order and composition, Alexander zealously poses the aporia in this way too: 'if the foundation thus somehow disposed and ordered[516] is other than the house, but also the wall atop the foundation is other than the whole house, but also the roof thus placed atop the walls is other than the whole house, thus each of the parts together with the appropriate order is other than the house: so all the parts together with

132   *Translation*

the appropriate order are other than the house. However, the house is all the parts together with such an order of them; so the whole house will be other than itself.'517

[84,29: *Aporia of part and whole cont'd: one solution.*]518 But perhaps (*mêpote*)
30   Aristotle did not add to no purpose that such an aporia exists also in the case of discrete parts: for if the same aporia applies even in cases where it is agreed that the parts are other, besides the whole, and a plurality is seen, then one should not abolish plurality on account of the aporia even in the case of continuous parts. So the aporia proceeds on both sides in this way; the solution is that [the
35   inference] is not sound that if each of the parts taken on its own is other than the
85,1 whole, then all of them taken together are still other than the whole. For 'all of them' is other than each of the things in it, just as the whole is [other than each of the parts].

[85,2: *Aporia of part and whole cont'd: Al. on why Ar. mentions the case of non-continuous parts.*] 'Someone might also', says Alexander, 'take "and also about parts which are not continuous" [185b14] as being said with regard to those parts of a continuous thing which are not connected with each other, such as a
5   hand and a foot, [asking] whether they too are the same as each other or not. For if they are not the same, they are other, and the continuous [whole] would be several; but if the continuous [whole which is constituted] out of these is said to be the same as these parts, these too would be the same as each other; which seems absurd, to say that the hand is the same as the foot.' Porphyry, however, thinks that the whole aporia is posed about these parts, although Aristotle clearly
10   added 'and also about parts which are not continuous' as being about something *else*. 'And if someone says', says Alexander, 'that in the case of continuous homoeomerous things the part is the same as the whole, but not in the case of anhomoeomerous things, he will find that even in the case of homoeomerous things they are not the same, if he takes the sameness of part and whole [to be] because they are continuous. For if he says that because they are continuous the
15   whole is one and the same as its own parts, the case will be the same for anhomoeomerous things too (for these too are continuous); and if they are divided from each other, then it will be agreed that homoeomerous things too are many. And if in the case of anhomoeomerous things which are continuous they do not say that they are the same, then even in the cause of homoeomerous things they will not say that they are the same on account of continuity.' Thus far
20   Alexander.519

Translation 133

[*85,21: Aporia of part and whole cont'd: Eudemus' interpretation.*] Eudemus, however, clearly says that these things have been said because the continuous has been shown not to be one;[520] but he himself sometimes mentions discrete parts and sometimes continuous ones. The text of Eudemus is as follows:[521] after showing that what is is not one as indivisible (which he calls 'atomic'), he adds, 'but also not by continuity: for discrete parts will not be the same. This involves 25 an exoteric aporia.[522] For if each part of the line is the same as the whole, they will also be the same as each other: for things that are the same as one thing are likewise the same as each other.[523] But if each of them is other than the whole, then they will also all be [other than the whole].[524] If so, how will they be the whole [line]?[525] But let these be dismissed.' Here he [Eudemus] shows by another 30 approach, I think, that not even if what is is said to be continuous will it be one. 'For discrete parts', he says, 'will not be the same' as the continuous ones;[526] so even if someone concedes that what is continuous is one, since the discrete parts are other than the continuous ones, the things that are will be many and not one.

[*85,34: Aporia of part and whole, concluded.*] And there is an aporia about the parts, which he [Eudemus] calls 'exoteric', and Aristotle says is 'not here relevant' 86,1 [185b12]. For it is rather dialectical, arguing plausibly on both sides, and it is not sufficient to cause trouble for the account of 'continuous' which says that the continuous is what is divisible into things always divisible. For, as has been shown, the aporia is easy to resolve. But Eudemus sets out the aporia only in the 5 case of continuous parts, and posits the arguments on both sides and the absurdities which are inferred from them; whereas Aristotle says that the same aporia exists also in the case of parts which are 'not continuous' but rather, clearly, discrete[527] and posits only the absurdity which follows for those who say that the part is one and the same as the whole. This [Aristotle's introduction of non- 10 continuous parts], I think, is also what made Porphyry say that he [Aristotle] responds in passing to those who introduce a fourth mode of unity.[528] But it is not a fourth mode, but rather a part of the aporia, [a part which is] trying to show that what is continuous is one.[529] For which reason Aristotle mentions the whole aporia, saying 'There is a difficulty about the part and the whole . . . whether the part and the whole are one or several' [185b11-13], but he adds only the 15 absurdity which follows for those who say that [the part and the whole are] one, both because these people are wrong (for those who say [that the part and the whole are] other are right) and because this assertion [that the part and the whole are one] seemed to refute the [claim that] the continuous is many and divisible into things always divisible.

134 *Translation*

[*86,19: Taking up again the thread of 81,16-83,5, with Ar.'s trilemma: does Parmenides mean that what is is one by being continuous, indivisible, or one in account? Answer: Parmenides intends all of these.*] And I for one wonder at

20 Aristotle's arguing against these meanings of 'one', meanings which Parmenides indeed says apply to the One-which-is. For he celebrates it as continuous:

> The continuous is all,[530] for what is draws near to what is[531]

and

> it is indivisible, since it is all alike.[532]

25 But Parmenides also says that the account of all things is one and the same, [namely] that of being, in these [verses]:[533]

> one must say and think that being is; for it is capable of being,
> and nothing is not.[534]

So if whatever one says or thinks is being, then all things will have one account,

30 that of being:

> for there neither is[535] nor will be
> anything else outside of being, since fate bound it

87,1   to be whole and unmoved; wherefore it has been named all things.[536]

[*87,2: What is, even if indivisible, can have a limit in the appropriate sense.*] And the things Aristotle adduces as absurdities against these hypotheses, those men would accept, if they are interpreted charitably. For their One-which-is, being indivisible, will be neither finite (*peperasmenon*) nor infinite (*apeiron*) as a body:

5 and in fact Parmenides places bodies among the objects of opinion, and Melissus says 'being one, it must not have a body; if it had thickness, it would have parts, and would no longer be one.'[537] And so what is indivisible will not have a limit (*peras*) as the limit of a body, but rather as the end of all things and the principle [or beginning] of the things that are; and [to put it] simply, [it will have a limit] in the same way that Aristotle himself says that his Reason (*nous*) or first cause

10 is some one [thing],[538] proclaiming 'the rule of many is not good',[539] and showing that it is partless and unmoved and the end of all things and at once intelligence (*nous*) and intelligible (*noêton*) and intellection (*noêsis*), taking this not only from Plato, but also from Parmenides, who says:

> the same thing is to think (*noein*) and that of which (*houneken*) it is a thought
> (*noêma*)

Translation

135

for not without being, in which it is expressed
will you find thinking (*noein*).[540]

   15

For thinking is for the sake of (*heneka*) the intelligible, or, which is to say the same, of being, which is its end.[541] But Aristotle, by taking 'whole' and 'part' and 'continuous' in the sense in which they apply to bodies, has adduced absurdities. But if they are taken according to those men's intention, they would accept of a certain rank of being both that it has parts, since he [Parmenides] says that it is a whole – 'whole and unique'[542] – and that it is divisible to infinity on account of its continuity:

   20

> The continuous is all, for what is draws near to what is.[543]

And Plato's Parmenides accepted this absurdity more clearly in the case of the One-which-is, when he said in the second hypothesis:

   25

> What then: do either of these portions of the One-which-is, the one and being, depart, either the oneness portion from being or being from the oneness portion?
> – They would not.
> So in turn each of the portions also possesses both oneness and being and even the smallest portion will in turn be out of two portions. And thus always in the same way, whatever portion is generated will always possess these two portions. For being always possesses unity and unity, being. So necessarily, being always two, it will never be one.
> – Absolutely so.
> So in this way the One-which-is would be an infinite multiplicity.
> – So it seems.[544]

   88,1

[88,4: *So there is no real absurdity, if Parmenides' views are understood correctly; S. invokes Proclus' theory of the internal structure of the One-which-is.*] But that all things there [i.e. among the intelligibles] have one and the same account, that of being, and are the same as each other, is nothing absurd. For if that [i.e. the Parmenidean One-which-is] is the cause of all things, and *is* all things before all things, it is clear that all things have been embraced in it beforehand, being contained in the single unification of the One-which-is, on account of which each thing is all things, differentiated without partition. And, I think, Aristotle himself believes this, since he says that his first Reason is the cause of all things, and since he says that order is twofold, one in the cause and one in the effect.[545] And unless I would seem to some readers to be redirecting [Ar.'s meaning] in an overly subtle way, I would say that Aristotle too, being aware of the third level of Parmenides' One-which-is, alludes to it in this way:[546] the summit is indivisibly

   5

   10

136   *Translation*

unified; the middle, having relaxed its unification into continuity, has become
15   whole and parts (which is why Aristotle put the aporia about the whole in the
account of continuity); and the third thing, in projecting the differentiation of
the forms in a unified way, has displayed all things beforehand in itself in a causal
manner.[547] But on account of the fact that the differentiation is intelligible, all
things are dominated by the unification of the One-which-is; and whatever
someone might take as differentiated, if he holds on to this he will find the
20   intelligible unification of the One-which-is. And since differentiation has been
somehow displayed in a causal manner [among the intelligibles], even the
progression ad infinitum of the parts of coming-to-be has received from there
its inexhaustible multiplication.[548]

[*88,22: Ar. argues against these doctrines because they cause trouble when
introduced into physics.*] So how, someone might say, does Aristotle see fit to
argue against these divine doctrines? Perhaps because they seem to deviate from
the truth when they are introduced into the study of nature. For the sensible
25   dispersal does not receive intelligible unification. And while in the intelligibles a
unified existence contains causally a multiplied differentiation, so that
[differentiation] can be considered there too, it is not in the same way possible to
see in sensible things the One's complete unification. So indivisibility here [in the
sensible world], and continuity here, and sharing in a single account here, do not
fit the One.[549]

[*88,30: More on how Ar. could have criticized Parmenides: he is following Plato.*]
30   And that [Aristotle's] argument against Parmenides did not arise from
contentiousness is clear also from Plato, who in the *Parmenides* accepts the One-
which-is of Parmenides, and [starting] from it discovers what is above it, which
he does not see fit even to call 'one',[550] and then hands down the ranks of unity
after it. But in the *Sophist* he clearly argues against [Parmenides] when he
89,1   [Parmenides] says that what is is one, and [Plato] separates the One from what
is, as superior to what is, showing that what is is first unified by participation in
the One, and subsequently differentiated and multiplied by otherness. And
perhaps it would not be a bad idea, for the sake of preliminary preparation in
5   Plato's thought,[551] to cite what he says in the *Sophist*:[552]

> What then? Shall we not ask, to the best of our ability, of those who say that the
> all is one, what they mean by 'being'?
> – Why not?

Translation

So, let them answer this. 'You say that only one [thing] is?' – 'Indeed we say so', they will reply, won't they?
– Yes.
What about this: 'Do you call being something?'
– 'Yes.'
'Do you call that the same as the one, using two names for the same thing, or what?'
– What's their answer to this one, Stranger? 10
It's clear, Theaetetus, that for someone who has made this hypothesis, it's not the easiest thing to answer the question we have now asked – or any other.
– How so?
After you've posited that nothing but one [thing] exists, to agree that there are two names is a bit ridiculous –
– Yes, isn't it?
And even to agree with someone who says that there is some name wouldn't be reasonable.
– How so?
In positing that the name is other than the object, he's surely saying that there 15
are two [things].
– Yes.
And yet if he posits that the name is the same as the thing, either he will be compelled to say that it is a name of nothing, or, if he says that it is of something, it will follow that the name is a name only of a name and not of anything else –
– So it will.
And that the one is a one only of a one, being itself one of the name.[553]
– Necessarily.
What about this: will they say that the whole is other than the one that is, or the same as it? 20
– Of course they'll say so [sc., that it's the same], and they do.[554]
So if it's a whole, just as Parmenides says:

'Like the bulk of a ball well-rounded on all sides
Equally balanced in every direction from the middle. For it must not be
Any greater or less here than there'[555]

then what is, being like this, has a middle and extremes, and having these it 25
must by all necessity have parts; or is it not so?
– It is so.
However nothing prevents what has parts from having the affection of unity over all of its parts, and since it is all and whole, being in this way one.

– Why not?

But is it not impossible for what has these things as an affection to be itself the One itself?

– How so?

Surely what is truly one must be said, according to the right account, to be entirely without parts?

– Indeed it must.

But something of this sort, since it consists of many parts, won't agree with the account.[556]

– I see.

Will the whole,[557] having unity as an affection, be in this way one and a whole, or shall we say that what is is not a whole at all?

– You're posing a difficult choice.

[90,4] You're absolutely right. For if what is has unity somehow as an affection, it will appear to be not the same as the one, and so all things will be more than one.

– Yes.

And yet if what is is not a whole by being affected in this way by it [i.e. if what is fails to participate in unity], but there is a whole itself, it follows that what is falls short of itself.

– Very much so.

And according to this argument, what is, being deprived of itself, will not be what is.

– That's so.

And won't all things turn out to be more than one, since what is and the whole each have their own separate nature?[558]

– Yes.

But if the whole does not exist at all, not only will these things hold of what is, but also, in addition to not being, what is would never come-to-be.

– How so?

What comes-to-be always comes-to-be as a whole, so that someone who does not posit the one or the whole among the things that are must not speak of being either as coming-to-be or as existing.[559]

– This certainly seems to be so.

And yet neither must what is not a whole be of any size; for if it were of some size, it would necessarily be as a whole of whatever size it was.

– Absolutely.

And for someone who says that what is is either two things or only one thing, everything will turn out to involve countless other inextricable difficulties.[560]

Translation 139

– The ones which are just dawning on us show that pretty clearly. For on each there follows another, which brings with it a greater and more difficult confusion about the things said before in each case.   20

But even if these things involved a rather long digression, let it be granted as an indulgence to our eros; and now let us turn to what comes next.

185b25-186a3 The later ancients also were disturbed lest the same thing should turn out for them to be at the same time one and many. For this reason some took away 'is', like Lycophron, and others refashioned their manner of expression, [saying] not that the human being 'is white' but that he 'has been whitened', and not that he 'is walking' but that he 'walks', so that they would not make the one many by attaching 'is',[561] on the assumption that 'one' or 'what is' is said only in one way. But the things that are are many, either in account (for instance, being white and being musical are different, but the same thing is both: so the one is many) or by division, like the whole and the parts. And here [i.e. in the case of the whole and parts] already they were in aporia and confessed that the one is many – as if it were not possible for the same thing to be both one and many without being opposites, for there is 'one' both in potentiality and in actuality.

[*90,24: Attempts of the 'later ancients' to escape the conclusion that one is also many.*] Having said that, according to each of the meanings of 'one', the same thing is shown to be one and many (for what is one as continuous is divisible ad   25 infinitum, and, being a whole, has a multiplicity of parts which are other than the whole; and he shows that things that are the same in account are each one and many, if indeed a human, being human, is also a horse and an ox and the other things which have the same account as them, [namely] that of being; and even what is indivisible and without parts is a limit and a beginning and many other things) – having said these things, and that they fall into contradiction, he adds   91,1 that this absurdity which follows for those who say that what is is one, [namely] that the same thing is one and many, disturbed not only those people [i.e. Parmenides and Melissus] when it was put forward, but also those who came after them. For even if these [later] people did not say that what is is one, nonetheless, positing that each of the sensibles, such as Socrates, is one, and then   5 saying that he is many on account of the categories of accidents (that he is snub-nosed and that he is a philosopher and that he is white, if it so chance), they were disturbed as to how it could be possible that the same thing is at the same time one and many. And for this reason they predicated 'is' of substance,[562] saying 'Socrates is', but they took 'is' away from the things that belong accidentally to substance, on the ground that 'is' together with substance does not produce a   10

140   *Translation*

plurality (for the same thing is said [i.e. predicated] of itself),[563] whereas when 'is' is added to accidents, it makes them too exist, i.e. gives them substantial being, and also interweaves them with the substance,[564] as when I say 'Socrates is white': for he becomes two beings [since I am saying that he is both Socrates and white, both of which *are*]. For this reason Lycophron took away 'is' from the predicates, saying 'Socrates white', on the ground that the accidents by themselves, without

15   'is', do not produce an addition of being. However, if they did not produce an addition, it would be the same to say 'Socrates' and 'Socrates white'. Furthermore, this kind of utterance does not produce a declarative sentence: for it does not display either truth or falsehood. Nor, however, does it produce any other form of sentence, nor will it be a sentence at all: for it is not imperative or interrogative or optative; so that in addition to not escaping the original aporia, they have

20   fallen into others.

[*91,20: Further strategies for avoiding saying that what is one is many.*] Others, wanting to produce a declarative sentence, reshaped the predicates into verbs, saying not that a human being 'is white' but that he 'has been whitened', and not 'is walking' but 'walks', so that they would not make what is many by attaching 'is',[565] but so that it would rather be clear that accidents have a diminished nature,

25   just as the verb manifests action or passion, which are diminished relative to substance. And it is clear that these people too did not escape the aporia, even if they did produce a predication by bending and refashioning their manner of speaking: for every verb is analysable into a participle and 'is': 'walks' [is analysable into] 'is walking'. But the Eretrians were so afraid of the aporia that they said that

30   nothing is predicated of anything, but rather that each thing is said itself by itself, e.g. 'the human being human being', and 'the white white'.[566] But not even they escaped the aporia – for a human being is many things, and white is many things, as the definitions manifest – and they also fell into the other absurdity of

92,1   abolishing declarative sentences. But they thought that in this way they would escape from each sensible thing's being many by having many things predicated of it, not recognizing that being and the one do not become many through predication alone. Rather [a one becomes many] both in this way [i.e. through predication], when things that differ in formula, and are many for this reason,

5   belong to one and the same thing and are predicated of the same subject; and also in another way, when what is continuous and whole, being one in actuality, is many in potentiality because it can be divided into many parts, and conversely when what are many and divided in actuality are potentially one continuous thing because they can be connected, like many pieces of wax. And with regard

Translation   141

to the former [way in which one becomes many] they thought that they had
found the aforesaid methods of escape, but with regard to the latter, not being
able to say anything, they gave in and admitted the absurdity that the same thing   10
is both one and many.

[92,11: *Explanation of the difficulty.*] But the cause of their error and of their
giving in to the aporia was their not seeing that it is possible for the same thing to
be both one and many, not in the same respect, but as being one in subject and
many in accidents, which are not opposed to each other, or as being actually one
and potentially many, like what is continuous. For these things too are not opposite   15
to each other,[567] since they are not [referring] to the same thing, and for this reason
they can coexist. For things are opposed which both belong in actuality to the
same thing in the same respect,[568] as when someone says that Socrates at the same
time has one finger and several. For it is nothing absurd for one and many to
coexist at different times in respect of the same part, or at the same time in respect
of different parts. Moreover the potentially [one and many] can coexist both at   20
the same time and in the same respect. For the actually childless person would be
said to potentially have both one and many children. And for this reason they [the
potentially one and potentially many] are not opposed either to the actually one
or to each other, and thus they also coexist: for if something potentially sleeps and
stands, it would be said to potentially be awake and sit.[569]   25

[92,25: *The first part of a long quotation giving Porphyry's reading of 185b25-
186a3, as Ar.'s response to anonymous objectors.*][570] The intention of Aristotle's
text, taken in the most obvious way, seems to be like this. But since Porphyry has
gone over the text in a novel way, it would be worthwhile not to omit his opinions,
abridging some of the things he says, and citing the others verbatim. So he says:

> Having exhausted the difficulties which are introduced corresponding to each
> meaning of 'one', he adds another aporia which arises against himself. For   30
> someone might say: 'You have raised these aporiai on the hypothesis that one
> and being are said in many ways; but if [they are] not, perhaps you would not   93,1
> have [been able to] introduce these difficulties.' To these people he makes a reply
> which is both forceful and overlooked by all the commentators, saying that if it
> is not hypothesized that being is said in ten ways, then not only Parmenides and
> Melissus and their followers, but everyone else too will be disturbed. For let us   5
> see what kind of one in the strict sense we encounter. Is it not clear at once that
> it is something simple and without parts and indivisible, inasmuch as it is
> conceived as one? So when they say that animal is one in genus and many in

142   *Translation*

species, and that human is one in species and many in number, and that Socrates
is actually one and potentially many both through his parts and through his
accidents, aren't they naming [these things] 'one' in name, but in no way agreeing

10   with the notion of the one? For there is much partition seen in these cases, even
if a genus or species is said in the singular, just as 'plurality' itself, or 'cavalry', even
if they are said in the singular, express a plurality. So it is reasonable that there
was an aporia in these cases, e.g. in the first place, in the case of subjects and
accidents. For if Socrates is white, how is this one? For either the white is nothing,

15   and then predicating it of Socrates will be nothing more [than Socrates]; or, if
the white also is, why won't 'Socrates white' be two? For if [you say that] white is
nothing because it's predicated, why not rather [say that] because Socrates is the
subject he'll be nothing? For both of them are.[571]

[*93,17: Porphyry cont'd: problems about manyness arise even for the 'later ancients', from
parts and genera.*] And likewise in the case of what is actually one and potentially many.
For what shall we say? That the parts are nothing? Then how will the whole not also be

20   nothing, since the whole is constituted out of the parts? – Rather, the parts are. Then
how is Socrates not many? And [likewise] in the case of [terms predicated] as genus and
species. For does animal belong (*sumbebêke*) to human, and human to Socrates, as
nothing? Then how do we say that animal differs from not-animal, and human from
horse? – Rather, animal is something. Then how is human not many, being both animal

25   and human? And why does human belong to Socrates, but not Socrates to human? So
there will be much disturbance, not only for Parmenides and his followers, but in
general for all who hypothesize that being is univocal and hypothesize it as one, but are
unable to preserve the pure conception of unity with regard to it.

[*93,29: Porphyry cont'd: thus the later ancients' attempts to exclude manyness fail.*][572] So
for these reasons Lycophron did not attach 'is', supposing that some absurdity resulted

30   from this; and some people reshaped the predicates into verbs to express that they are
lesser and merely accidents. But the Eretrians say that nothing is predicated of anything,
but rather only each thing of itself, e.g. 'human human'. But neither the earlier [thinkers]
nor these escaped the question.[573] For the question would apply to the human himself;

94,1   but they say that it should not apply: for if he were divided in actuality, he would be
many, but as it is he is one. But the argument and the question were about the undivided
[thing] and its parts. Are they something or nothing, so long as they are in it?[574] So the
question is not solved.

5   [*94,5: Porphyry cont'd: Ar.'s solution through distinguishing senses of being.*] Aristotle
alone saw how to solve such and so great an aporia. For he says that the beings are not
beings in the same way, and that for this reason being is not their genus. Rather, there is
one [kind of being] which is also capable of existing by itself, expressing a peculiar
character;[575] while the others, though they are beings, have not received a like share of

being, but rather exist in a different mode, through existing in those things [i.e. substances] and depending on them for their existence. For father and son, and master and slave, exist by chance.[576] For this reason he said that being [is said] in many ways, but the other [predicates] belong accidentally to the substance according to which the subject is characterized. This is why some people abolished the others, as the Stoics did, contrary to evident [truths];[577] but he who says that the others are [each] one in the same way as substance commits a greater error. For he will make the beings many and heap them up like the atomic bodies; whereas he who says that they in a way *are*, through being considered as applied to substance and being together with substance, and in a way *are not*, through not being able to subsist without substance, has laid hold of the correct [view].[578] So going through the modes of 'one', we will no longer say that the one is many, since the parts are not called one in the way that Socrates is, but in a different way: for he expresses in himself peculiarity of character, whereas the parts would not subsist without the whole, but are in such a way as to be together with the whole. So Socrates remains one. Likewise with regard to the species, he is not multiplied by also being human, since the species would never subsist by itself, nor does human subsist in the same way as the primary substances, but rather in a different way. However, one wouldn't say that this addition [e.g. the predicate 'human' or 'white'] is absolutely nothing at all besides Socrates,[579] even if it is not such as Socrates himself is, but exists according to him and along with (*meta*) him. For being is also not equivocal in the manner of chance equivocals, but rather as those which are [derived in various ways] from a single [meaning]. And white *is* when it is *of* something else, and it has being in this, [namely] in being *of* something else. For just as a surface, being *of* a body, has taken its quasi-bodily existence from the body, so too we must understand the subsistence of the other beings: for they have their subsistence in being *of* something else. For this reason, white Socrates is no longer many, nor he himself and his parts: for it is not the case that some other things, when they have come together, as oxen to a yoked team or humans to a chorus,[580] constituted Socrates; rather, he being a subject, the things which belong accidentally to him will subsist insofar as they are of something else [namely him],[581] and their existence too will be on account of it. So if they, I mean the accidents, were indeed many and existed along with something else, then the problem would remain.[582] And from this the aporia about being and not-being emerges. For substance is a being, but the accidents, as being in it, are not beings; but in another way, and as being *of* it, to that extent they too are beings.

[*95,6: Porphyry cont'd: how the same thing is unproblematically one and many.*] And you would say that the same thing [i.e. the substance with its accidents] is one and many, but not many in the same way in which it is one, for it is not multiplied out of *this* kind of units. Likewise in the case of the parts of Socrates, for these too are not beings in the way Socrates is, but rather as of him and by being of him,[583] not in the way that he is. And Socrates is both animal and human in this way, not by there being Socrates *and* a human

144 *Translation*

and an animal, the result produced by those who posited that being is univocal; nor that produced by those who rejected the others from the [domain of] beings, [i.e.] those who said that what is is one.[584] So Socrates is neither three nor only one. For neither are the others nothing, since they *are* through being *of* Socrates, though not in the same way as

15 Socrates. And thus again Socrates is both many and not many but one – not the one which is absolutely pure of even conceptual composition, but rather the one which gives a single subsistence and introduces one substance, not as brick is one by being one in name but rather through unity's being present, and through its admitting being indicated as 'this'.[585] For the many are one if we interpret 'one' equivocally, as Aristotle was the first

20 to recognize. So the things that are are many, first through the categories, such as substance and quality and the others; and in all of these categories, some are many in potentiality, others in actuality, and furthermore either in genus or in species or in number; and, further, by division or by formula or by name. And there is nothing absurd in the same thing appearing and being called one in one way, and many in another, and

25 simultaneously one and many, but not opposites.[586] The reason is that neither being nor one is said in only one way, but each of them in several ways. And since the people before Aristotle did not see this, they were disturbed, some of them saying that the things that are are many and infinite and detached from one another, others saying that [what is is] one – when it is neither one as simple and unextended, nor many as a chorus, but rather,

30 as has been said, both one and not one in the way that we have explained.[587]

[*95,31: Caveat about Porphyry's reading: Ar.'s solution to the 'aporia from the accidents' turns on the way that things can be 'many in formula and one in subject', not on the different ways of 'being' corresponding to the categories.*] Thus the most philosophical Porphyry has excellently written up these things, which in themselves, I think, deserve much attention, both for investigations into nature and for the division of the categories, perhaps taking as his starting point for this

96,1 effort the phrase 'on the assumption that "one" or "what is" is said only in one way. But the things that are are many' (185b31-32). But if he [Aristotle] had added 'many in the categories', it would have been likely that he was taking up the division of being as said in many ways [as the starting point for] the solution of the aporia. But, as it is, he says that the things that are are many and one, either

5 as many in formula and one in subject, as in the case of substance and the things that accidentally belong to it (and for this reason he took both of his examples of accident from the same genus, quality), or else in potentiality and in actuality. However, if someone raised the additional aporia, if both substance and the so-called accidents are beings in the same way, how it is possible for the same thing, and in the same respect (*kata to auto*), being one to also be many – that is to say,

10 both one and not one – then someone would plausibly add this solution to the

aporia, based on the difference between being as said of (*kata*) substance and said of (*kata*) accidents. And perhaps, even as it is, he [Aristotle] hints riddlingly at this when he says that there is nothing absurd in the same thing being both one and many – many in respect of (*kata*) the accounts of the many accidents, one in respect of the subject and the substance – which, itself remaining one, is many in respect of those [the accidents].[588]

[*96,15: The 'aporia from the accidents', with Al.'s discussion.*] For there being two aporiai that conclude that the same thing is one and many, one [aporia] from the plurality of accidents belonging to a single substance, and the other from the continuous, which is one in the whole and many by division, the latter is solved by means of the difference between potentiality and actuality. For it is actually one and potentially many. But the former, according to the other commentators [*sc.* other than Porphyry], has not been solved [by Aristotle in this text]: for they do not take 'the things that are are many, either in account' (185b32) as a solution to the aporia. At any rate Alexander, when he puts this passage forward for commentary, adds the following:

> either he is dividing the ways in which each thing is simultaneously one and many, showing that 'one' is not said in only one way, as he has already said, or else he is saying how Zeno showed that each of the sensibles is many, the argument by which they [*sc.* 'the later ancients'] were disturbed. For either they are many in account, being one in subject, as musical [Socrates] and white Socrates are many in account (for there is one account of musical and another of white), but Socrates is one in subject; or else the same thing is simultaneously many and one as the whole and the parts: for as a whole it is one, but as the parts out of which the whole [is constituted] it is many, since it has been shown that the part is not the same as the whole.

And Alexander, after saying this, later adds [comments] by which he indicates that the aporia from the accidents has not been solved, but only the aporia from division, saying:

> so in the case of things that are many in account, as has been said, those people whom he has called 'the later ancients' thought that they were accomplishing something, some by taking 'is' away from the accidents, others by warping and refashioning the manner of speaking. But in the case of [the one and many] as whole and part, not having any such defensive move against the sophism, they gave in. But (he says) the whole is both one and many, not in the same respect, but one in actuality and many in potentiality.

146 *Translation*

So if the aporia from the accidents was also going to be solved, Porphyry has well
5   thought out and exhibited what Aristotle hinted at in the words 'as if one or
being were said in only one way; but the things that are are many'. Eudemus too
had in a way indicated something like this, although his solution was confined to
potentiality and actuality.

[*97,9: Eudemus' reading of the one-many aporia introduced.*][589] Perhaps it would
not be a bad idea to cite from Eudemus, in order to observe more [fully] the
10   things he says. His text after the responses regarding the meanings of 'one' is as
follows:[590]

> So is it the case that this is not one, but that there is some one?[591] For this was an
> aporia. And they say that Zeno said that if someone could give him an account
> of what the one is, he would be able to say the [many] things that are.[592] And he
> [*sc.* Zeno] was in aporia, as it seems, because each of the sensibles is called many
15   > both predicatively and by partition, and because he posited the point as not even
> one: for what neither makes something larger when it is added, nor makes it
> smaller when it is taken away, he thought was not something that is.[593] And if
> someone added on the other categories, he would make the argument still more
> persuasive; for the point does not seem to produce either substance or quality, or
> anything else in the divisions [i.e. any other category]. But if the point is like this,
20   > and each of us is said to be many (e.g. white and musical and many other things),
> and likewise the stone (since each thing can be broken ad infinitum), how would
> the one exist?[594]

> [*97,21: Quotation from Eudemus cont'd: Zeno's challenge answered.*] Now some people,
> among them Lycophron, thought that one should not add 'is' in predications; rather,
> they said that human is but denied that human is white, and likewise for each of the
> others. For they nowhere attached 'to be', except to one thing in each case.[595] But Plato
25   > thought that 'is' [*sc.* in predications of other categories] did not signify what it does in
> the case of human, but rather that as 'is prudent' signifies being-prudent and 'is seated'
> signifies being-seated,[596] so too in the other cases, even if the names are not available
> [i.e. even if there is no corresponding verb]. So they [Lycophron, Plato, etc.] replied in
> this way to the aporiai that make the one many predicatively, but they had no solution
> to those [aporiai] by partition. And, as it seems, determining in how many ways each
30   > thing is said is the first [step] towards the truth. For Plato, by introducing the 'twofold'
98,1   > [i.e. by distinguishing two senses of a term], solved many aporiai about the realities
> which the sophists now take refuge in, just as [he introduced it into?] the Forms; and
> in addition to these things he distinguished the name from the accounts.[597] And for
> the aporia about the one, the division of being appeared as a cure. But this [*sc.* division]

Translation 147

was difficult for the philosophers, and they did not make much use of it – but what's wise is to use each thing well. For those who do not[598] make use of the principles do 5 not make progress (for the principle is fertile), and those who make non-principles principles[599] are unable to progress, since they do not have any starting point. And they spoke of 'knowing' and 'courageous' and so on, but not of 'one' or 'many', as actual and potential.[600] And yet this division [sc. between an actuality sense and a potentiality sense] appears in just about everything. For if we had to count the 10 things that sleep, we would immediately enumerate human and horse, even though many [of each of these] are not sleeping, since we would have regard to their potentiality, but about fish we would be in aporia and would go to the fishermen. But if we were counting those who are sleeping within the house, we would leave out many humans and horses, if they were present and were not sleeping. So it is clear that in the former case we would have regard to potentiality and in the latter case to actuality. 15 In this same way also one and many are both in potentiality and in actuality. So they never both belong to the same thing in actuality, but what is actually one is potentially many, if it has parts. This seems absurd, but it is not, for these are not contraries. And in this way there will be many things in the same stone, Hermes and Heracles and thousands of others: for all these things are in it in potentiality, but in actuality [there 20 is] only one thing. But things which are many in actuality are not in the same way one in potentiality. But as many things as are composed, but in formula, e.g., standing and sitting,[601] would be simultaneously in one thing in potentiality, but not in actuality. 99,1 And if Zeno were present to us, we would say to him about the one in actuality that it is not many: for the former [sc. being one] belongs to it in the strict sense, the latter [sc. being many] in potentiality. So in this way the same thing becomes both one and many, but in actuality only one [of these two] and never both simultaneously. And if by speaking in this way we persuaded him, we would deem that we had delivered what 5 was demanded.[602]

[99,7: Al. misinterprets Eudemus both on Zeno and on Plato.] Zeno's argument here [sc. as reported by Eudemus] seems to be a different one from the one contained in the book which Plato also mentions in the Parmenides. For there he shows that there are not many, [arguing] from the opposite to come to the aid of Parmenides who says that there is one; whereas here, as Eudemus says, he even 10 abolished the one (for he speaks of the point as the one), and he concedes that there are many. Alexander, however, thinks that here too Eudemus mentions Zeno as abolishing the many. 'For as Eudemus reports', he says, 'Zeno the companion of Parmenides tried to show that it is not possible for the things that are to be many, on the ground that there is no one among the things that are, and 15 that the many are a plurality of units.' But that Eudemus is not now mentioning

148 *Translation*

Zeno as abolishing the many is clear from his own words; and I think that neither in Zeno's book was there contained such an argument as Alexander says.[603] And I think it is also clear from what has been said that Eudemus too solved

20 the aporia by means of the difference between potentiality and actuality. And perhaps Eudemus also indicates the solution from the difference in being [i.e. from the different senses of being corresponding to the different categories] where he says 'and for the aporia about the one, the division of being appeared as a cure. But this [*sc.* division] was difficult for the philosophers, and they did not make much use of it' – 'difficult' perhaps because they did not divide rightly, but only used it a little. And whether these things are so or not would be worth

25 investigating.

[*99,25: Al. is wrong to take Plato to have been among those 'later ancients' seriously disturbed by the problem of how one thing can have many predicates.*] But where Eudemus says that Plato thought that 'is' in the predication of accidents did not signify participation in being, but only the accidental disposition, as 'is prudent' signifies nothing other than being-prudent and 'is seated' signifies nothing other than being-seated – where Eudemus says these things, Alexander says that Plato

30 is the person who refashioned the manner of speaking regarding the accidents, perhaps because Eudemus mentioned this opinion after those who abolished 'is' [*sc.* at 97,21 ff.]. But that Plato was not among those who were disturbed by this aporia, nor is Aristotle hinting at him, is clear from the fact that in the *Philebus*

100,1 he says that such disputation is the idle talk of boys playing with words,[604] and that in the *Sophist* he sets out the whole aporia clearly and entirely sports with those who have pursued it seriously, writing as follows:[605]

> Surely we speak of a man calling him many names, applying to him colours and
> 5 shapes and sizes and vices and virtues: in all of these, and in countless others, we
> say not only that he is a man but also that he is good and infinitely many other
> things. And having posited each of the other things as one in the same way, we
> again speak of it by many names.[606]
> – You're right.
> And with this I suppose we have provided a feast for the young, and for late-
> learners among the elderly. For it lies immediately at hand[607] for everyone to take
> 10 hold of, that it's impossible for the many to be one and for the one to be many.
> And indeed they delight in not allowing [anyone] to say that a man is good, but
> rather [*sc.* only allowing them to say] that the good is good and the (*ton*) man is
> a man.[608] For I suppose, Theaetetus, you often encounter those, older people,[609]
> who have pursued such things seriously: on account of the poverty of their store

Translation   149

of wisdom they marvel at such things, and think that they have found in this
something surpassingly wise.   15

[*100,15: Plato on one and many, both in sensible and in intellectual things.*] And he
himself solves this aporia, by showing that the Forms both participate in each other
and have by themselves their own proper characters and proper domains, and that
by their participation and mixture and blending with each other there comes-to-be
some one whole, as from many letters mixed with each other [there comes-to-be]
a noun or a verb or even a whole sentence; but inasmuch as each of them is in itself
distinct from the others and is not what the others are, they make a plurality. For in   20
being, wherever there is plurality, there is also not-being. For this reason Parmenides
too, wanting to show that what really is – and perhaps also what is above being – is
one, first abolished not-being; and then Plato, wanting to show not-being in the
things that are, and not only in sensible being but also in intellectual [being], first
communicates the differentiation and plurality of the forms.[610]   25

[*101,26: Plato on the easy one-many problems.*] And also in the *Parmenides*,
saying that the aporia that asks how the same thing among sensibles is both one
and many involves nothing serious, he solves it by saying that [something] is one
through participation in the one, and many through participation in the many.[611]
But it would not be a bad idea to listen to Plato's own words:

> If someone will demonstrate that I am one and many, what's surprising [about   30
> that]? He'll say, when he wants to reveal [that I am] many, that my right side is
> different from my left side, and my front is different from my back, and top and
> bottom likewise. For I suppose I do participate in multiplicity. But when [he   101,1
> wants to reveal that I am] one, he will say that despite being seven (*hepta ontôn*)
> I am one man, also participating in the one.[612] Thus both things he reveals are
> true. So if someone undertakes to reveal that the same thing is many and one, in
> cases like these – stones and wood and such things – we will say that he
> demonstrates that something is one and many, not that the one is many or the
> many one, nor does he say anything surprising, but just what we all would agree.   5
> But if someone first does what I was just now mentioning, distinguishing
> separately, by themselves, forms such as likeness and unlikeness, multiplicity and
> the one, rest and motion and all such things, and then reveals that these things
> are capable of being blended and separated (*diakrinesthai*) among themselves –
> then, Zeno, he said, I would be surprised and amazed.[613]   10

[*101,10: Plato on the harder one-many problem, for the 'intellectual Forms'.*] So
you see that he says that there is nothing surprising in the same thing among

150   *Translation*

sensibles being both one and many, just as [it is nothing surprising if they are] both like and unlike, but that to display such a mixture and blending in the intellectual paradigms of these things – as he himself has done in the *Sophist*, saying that this is proper to the philosopher[614] – *that* would be very noteworthy.

15   For the person who demonstrates these things must consider both the unconfused unification and the undispersed differentiation (*diakrisis*) of the forms. So we have the solutions to this aporia, how the same thing is one and many, in Plato too. One solution, in the case of intellectual forms, is stated in the *Sophist*:[615] [they] are one by mutual participation – or rather by the sameness and unification according to which each not only participates in the others, and is

20   not only *the same* as they, but being *unified* with them[616] each one is all[617] (which is what Socrates in the *Parmenides* wishes to be displayed)[618] – but [they are] many, when each is considered according to its own peculiar property. And we have another solution, in the case of sensible things, in the *Parmenides*, in terms of the same thing's participation in the paradigms of both the one and the many [cf. *Parmenides* 129b5-6].

        [*101,25: Ar.'s solution to the one-many problem turns on the priority of sensible substance (such that accidents, parts, universals do not add a further being); some*

25   *Platonist scruples about this.*] Aristotle's solution, which Porphyry explained, is also in the case of sensible things, but arises from the difference of the things that are [i.e. the different senses in which things are said to be], which are not univocal but rather derived from one [primary meaning].[619] And for this reason substance, being naturally such as to subsist by itself, and therefore underlying, remains what it is, and the whole is one on account of it. But accidents or parts, subsisting

30   in the substance and the whole, are provided in multiplicity: not that the one is
102,1   multiplied (for they do not add anything to it, since they are not able to subsist by themselves), but rather what is multiplied is as it were a certain lesser and derivative subsistence of what is. For the substance has not been multiplied out of such units.[620] And it is worth remarking that this solution also rightly establishes the cause on account of which substance is not in the quale, but the

5   quale in the substance, and *this* is a substance and *these* are accidents. But if genera and species and accidents are second in comparison to individual substance, as subsisting in it, what would individual substance be in itself, considered separately from these things?[621] For how would Socrates exist without human and animal and the accidents that complete Socrates, if these things are

10   'second' in the way that parts are 'second' in comparison to the whole even though they are what completes the whole? For these [*sc.* genus, species, and

accidents] too are parts of the individual substance, which is an assemblage and is given substantial being in accordance with this. For this reason there is no paradigm which is primarily productive (*prôtourgon*) of these individuals as wholes, since they subsist as assemblages, and the soul knows them by the impact from sense, projecting their concurrence into the constitution of a single thought.[622]

15

Notes

1   Simplicius [henceforth 'S.'] here begins his proemium with discussion of the object (*skopos*) of the work discussed, as is standard: other standard topics include the reason for the title, its utility, authenticity, and place in the order (*taxis*) of the author's works. The *skopos* is the aim or primary object of a discipline or a text, to which everything else treated must be somehow related. See the *Introduction* for details, and cf. Jaap Mansfeld, *Prolegomena: Questions to be Settled before the Study of an Author or a Text* (Leiden: Brill, 1994).

2   At 4,8 ff., S. takes the title of the work under discussion to be 'Lectures on Natural Science' (*Phusikê Akroasis*): he there briefly discusses the meaning of that and alternative suggested titles.

3   Reading *katateinomenên* with DFMo; the alternative is to read with Diels (and codex Laur. 85.1, a copy of F) *katageinomenên*, 'is concerned with'.

4   Simplicius is etymologizing the word 'metaphysics', or rather the phrase *meta ta phusika*, literally 'after the natural [objects or disciplines or treatises]'. 'Beyond', *epekeina*, is intended to recall the Form of the Good, which is *epekeina tês ousias* at *Republic* 6, 509B9.

5   S. and Alexander [henceforth 'Al.'] agree that the 'actual intellect' which Aristotle [henceforth 'Ar.'] describes in *On the Soul* 3.5 is separable from matter, but S. is insisting that on the true opinion of the (older) Peripatetics it is part of the human soul, against Al. who identifies it with god. This is an important issue because Ar. says that only the actual intellect is immortal, so only on S.'s reading does he affirm human immortality.

6   Ar. does not usually identify natural and bodily things (artefacts are bodily but not natural), but see *On the Heaven* 1.1, 268a1-6.

7   *On the Heaven* 3.1, 298b6-8; S.'s citation differs trivially from modern editions.

8   At the beginning of *in Cael.* S. argues at length both against Al. and against Iamblichus, who thinks that the object of *On the Heaven* is the fifth body, i.e. the naturally rotating substance of the heavens.

9   Diels here obelizes unnecessarily.

10 S. seems to be referring both to the *Peri Metallôn* mentioned by Diogenes Laertius in his list of Theophrastus' works (where perhaps the title means *On Mines*) (5.44) and to Ar.'s *Meteor.* 4. Cf. frr. 197-205 FHS&G.

11 This sounds like a list of titles, in which case S.'s title for Ar.'s *On Sleep* is *On the Sleep of Animals*.

154   *Notes to pp. 41–4*

12 S. here ascribes to Ar. the later Platonist view that form and matter count as elements and thus as mere auxiliary causes. The view becomes canonical with Proclus (cf. Proclus, *in Parm*. 888,15-35). S. has a fuller discussion of causes and auxiliary causes below at 11,29-12,3. It was controversial which causes should be classified as merely auxiliary.

13 A reading along these lines (complete with phrasing oddly suggesting that Plato is adding to Ar.'s system) is cited from Porphyry at 10,32-11,4 (fr. 120 Smith); but Porphyry does not there use the *aition* ['cause']-*sunaition* ['auxiliary cause'] distinction, presenting the instrumental cause as an *aition*.

14 Translating Diels' text; F would give the sense: 'either be infinite or, being limited, have infinity in a way and limitedness in a way'.

15 The respectful reference is presumably to Leucippus and Democritus.

16 This discussion covers mainly *Physics* 1–4: S. is partially following what Ar. says about his agenda at the start of Book 3. S.'s discussion here resembles, but is more precise than, the parallel discussions by Philoponus at *in Phys*. 2,13-16 and *in GC* 1,5-8.

17 S. thus uses 'acroamatic' for works of this kind: cf. 8,16 ff. below. For a full classification of Ar.'s works along these lines, cf. Ammonius, *in Cat*. 3,20-5,30.

18 Adrastus' title refers to the proper order for study, not the chronological order of composition. S. will return to the internal structure of the *Physics* at 6,4, again citing Adrastus (whom he seems to know only through Porphryry's report, cf. 122,33-123,1). S. himself in his earlier commentary on *On the Heaven* had identified the *On Principles* as the first four books and the *On Motion* as the remaining four (226,19-21), following Porphyry (*in Phys*. 802,7-13; Porphyry fr. 159 Smith); this structure is also adopted by Philoponus (cf. Philoponus, *in Phys*. 2,16-21).

19 Cf. Plato, *Gorgias* 507E6-508A8.

20 Literally, 'our animal'.

21 S. here draws on the astronomical axiom that the radius of the earth is no perceptible fraction of the distance between the earth and the sun.

22 Cf. Plato, *Theaetetus* 173C6-175B7.

23 Cf. Plato, *Laws* 10 and Ar., *Physics* 8.

24 For discussion of S.'s sources in this paragraph, see Philippe Hoffmann, 'La triade chaldaique éros, alètheia, pistis de Proclus à Simplicius', in Alain-Philippe Segonds and Carlos Steel, eds, *Proclus et la Théologie Platonicienne* (Paris: Les Belles Lettres, 2000), pp. 459–89, and Marwan Rashed, 'Alexandre d'Aphrodise, lecteur du *Protreptique*', in his *L'héritage aristotélicien* (Paris: Les Belles Lettres, 2007), pp. 179–215.

25 On the division of the *Physics* into two main parts, see above, 4,8 ff.

26 Cf. Ar.'s history of philosophy in *Metaphysics* 1, Plato's *Laws* 3 (on the flood and the recovery of civilization), and Proclus' *Platonic Theology* 1.4.

Notes to pp. 44–6   155

27 Literally, 'the people around (*hoi peri*) Thales and Anaximander and people like them
   [*sc.* Thales and Anaximander]'; but *hoi peri* X typically includes X, and is often just
   an elaborate way of referring to X.

28 *Phaedo* 97B-98D.

29 S. accepts as authentic the pseudepigraphic work of 'Timaeus Locrus' (edited in
   Walter Marg, *Timaeus Locrus, De Natura Mundi et Animae* (Leiden: Brill, 1972)), the
   alleged Pythagorean source of Plato's *Timaeus*.

30 S. will go on to discuss which principles are elemental, concluding that the matter
   and enmattered form of natural things are elements (10,7-12,3). Others, including
   Eudemus and Al., think that only material principles are elements: all are agreed that
   the efficient, final and paradigmatic causes are not.

31 Wehrli prints lines 10-19 as Eudemus fr. 31. It is unclear how much is from
   Eudemus; perhaps only that Plato was the first to call such principles 'elements'
   [*stoikheia*].

32 We emend the text by reading *hais husteron* instead of *es husteron*; Diels' text is
   grammatically possible, but would mean that *Aristotle* discovered matter, which S.
   does not believe. *Hais* and *es* would be similarly pronounced, and *es husteron* is a
   common phrase, so the corruption is easily explained.

33 This charge is made by Ar. himself at the start of *Physics* 1.9; cf. S., *in Phys.* 245,7. We
   emend the text by excluding *ê kata tên hulên* as a gloss and adding *ouk* before
   aphorisamenou. The transmitted text would read 'Plato having defined privation
   from matter or according to matter', which would seem to involve taking
   aphorisamenou in two different and contrary senses ('distinguished from' and
   'defined in terms of'). Torstrik (reported in Diels), also excluding *ê kata tên hulên* as
   a gloss, proposes emending the resulting text to say 'Plato having defined privation
   as the same as matter'. If an *ouk* (before *aphorisamenou*) dropped out, the text would
   cease to make sense, helping to explain why *ê kata tên hulên* would be inserted.

34 S. again has in view the *Timaeus*, which he takes to represent both Platonic and
   authentically Pythagorean thought: this does not imply that Plato and the
   Pythagoreans are interchangeable on all topics.

35 S. is following Proclus' discussion of *Laws* 10 at *Platonic Theology* 1.14, which
   interprets the moved movers, contrasted with the soul as self-moved mover, not as
   bodies but as the natures immanent in bodies.

36 S. here defends Ar. against Proclus' criticisms at *in Tim.* 1,215-229.

37 Compare 4,8 ff. above, with reference to Ammonius; for a full discussion of the
   ancient classifications of Ar.'s work, see Paul Moraux, *Les listes anciennes des ouvrages
   d'Aristote* (Louvain: Éditions Universitaires, 1951).

38 Or 'so that to [more careless readers] they seem not even to have been written up'.
   Either way, the contrast is with exoteric works which have been written in a more
   polished way: on the stylistic elaboration involved in 'writing up' series of notes

156 *Notes to pp. 46–8*

(*hupomnêmata*) into published works, cf. Ammonius, *in Cat.* 3,20-5,30, Simplicius, *in Cat.* 4,10-5,2, Arrian's introductory letter to Epictetus' *Discourses*, and, for full discussion, Tiziano Dorandi's *Le stylet et la tablette* (Paris: Les Belles Lettres, 2000) and *Nell' officina de classici* (Rome: Carocci, 2007). The obscurity (*asapheia*) of the work discussed is a common topic in prolegomena, in explanation of why a commentary is needed.

39 *Life of Alexander* 7. (Note that some modern editions of Plutarch print Xylander's – certainly mistaken – emendation *Peri ta Phusika* for *Meta ta Phusika*, so that the claim would be about the publication of the *Physics*.) The forged letters between Ar. and Alexander the Great are also cited by Aulus Gellius (20.5), who cites Andronicus as his source.

40 We consistently give all of each lemma (i.e. of each successive portion of the *Physics* that S. comments on). Diels usually gives only the beginning and end of longer passages; the MSS vary in their practices. See the *Introduction* for discussion.

41 While we have consistently translated *gnôrizein* (in the lemma and in Simplicius) as 'recognize', and while it is possible that the connected adjective *gnôrimon* (here translated 'known' or 'knowable') means 'what can be recognized', it is likely that the dependence is the other way around, and that the basic meaning of *gnôrizein* is 'make something *gnôrimon* (known or knowable or familiar)', to oneself or (in a less common usage) to someone else. *Gnôrizein* the elements would then be a process of becoming familiar with the elements, which we could reasonably describe as learning to recognize the elements, like learning to recognize the letters in a written text.

42 Theophrastus fr. 144B FHS&G.

43 i.e. the practitioner of a more elevated science, namely the metaphysician. S., following Porphyry, speaks of lower sciences taking their principles from 'more elevated' sciences, and ultimately from metaphysics. Cf. Porphyry fr. 119 Smith.

44 i.e. he uses 'since' (*epeidê*) rather than 'if' (*ei*).

45 i.e. a prosyllogism, an extra syllogism to support one of the premises of the main argument.

46 Eudemus fr. 32 Wehrli.

47 While being clear that an element is a principle which is a constituent (*Metaph.* 5.3, 1014b14-15 and 5.1, 1013a19-20), Ar.'s *Metaphysics* provides support for both sides of the dispute between Eudemus (and Al.) and S. as to whether or not form thus counts as an element. (S. will argue at 11,16-12,3 that form as well as matter is an element.) At *Metaphysics* 7.17, 1041b30-33, Ar. holds that the nature, i.e. form, of a natural thing is 'not an element but a principle', and that only the matter counts as an element, implying Eudemus' position; but at 12.4, 1070b22-26, form, matter, and privation are apparently all elements.

48 We take this to mark the transition from S.'s overall discussion of the content of the lemma to the detailed discussion of problems raised by its wording. (Diels'

Notes to pp. 48–50 157

paragraphing here is misleading.) In general, S.'s approach is to first discuss the overall sense of a lemma, then turn to particular difficulties.

49 The word *arkhê*, which we translate 'principle', can also mean 'beginning' or 'starting point', and so is particularly applicable to moving and/or generated things.

50 The text should perhaps be emended to reverse the grammatical roles of 'strife' and 'insult': Ar. repeatedly uses as an example of causality that an insult is the starting point of a fight (*GA* 724a29-30; *Metaph.* 1013a10, 1023a31-32).

51 Eudemus fr. 32 Wehrli (continued).

52 Translating Diels' text. Mo here has *legei en hois*, while the Aldine omits *legei*, both perhaps expressing discomfort with the juxtaposition of *legei* and *phêsin*.

53 Following Mo (*to prôton bêma*); the other MSS have *to prôton*, arguably elliptical for the same.

54 Porphyry means that the concept of cause entails that of being prior and therefore a principle and that the concept of a principle entails being productive and therefore a cause. Diels, following Torstrik, unnecessarily emends *telestikês* to *telikês*, giving the sense, 'the principle is virtually final [i.e. a final cause]'.

55 Mo lacks the negation, reading 'all of them exist in all cases' (*panta en pasin*). Both versions of the text seem to present possible views: with the negation, Porphyry would already be distinguishing the different cases he goes on to discuss; in Mo's version, he would be granting the more general point that every cause is to be found in every kind of object.

56 A premise is 'immediate' if it is not itself established by a syllogism, which would provide a middle term linking the subject to the predicate.

57 Fr. 120 Smith. On the 'metaphysics of prepositions' see Willy Theiler, *Die Vorbereitung des Neuplatonismus* (Berlin: Weidmann, 1930), pp. 17–34, and Heinrich Dörrie, 'Präpositionen und Metaphysik. Wechselwirkung zweier Prinzipienreihen', in his *Platonica Minora* (Munich: Fink, 1976), pp. 124–36.

58 Diels' MSS all have *diestêsato*; Mo apparently has *diesteilato*, which would have much the same sense.

59 S.'s argument is presumably that since the concepts of cause and principle are mutually implying or even mutually presupposing, neither can be conceptually prior to the other.

60 This is the first instance of a common turning-point in S.'s discussions, on which see the *Introduction*: having raised certain problems with a passage, discussed the interpretations of his predecessors and raised objections to them, S. uses *mêpote*, 'perhaps' (often with either *oun*, 'so' or *de*, 'but') to introduce his own positive proposal. The standard meanings of *mêpote* are 'never' and 'perhaps', but the term need not signal doubt (let alone negation) in this context.

61 Those who call the elements (i.e. the formal and material causes) and the instrumental cause 'auxiliary causes' would include Proclus (*Elements of Theology* 75; *in Parm.* 1059,11; cf. *in Tim.* 1,261,15); S. follows them.

158   *Notes to pp. 51–2*

62 S. here uses 'primarily' (*prôtôs*) and 'in the lowest way' (*eskhatôs*) as opposites, so that Ar. is describing a movement *both* to the first principles and in the opposite direction, to the most proximate causes.

63 So far, S. has opted for the more natural reading of *hôn eisin arkhai ê aitia ê stoikheia* as 'of which there are principles or causes or elements'. This new proposed reading expresses the suggestion now being elaborated that Ar. *divides* principles in the way of Proclus, into causes and auxiliary causes such as the elements.

64 Although we usually translate *gignôskein* either as 'know' or as 'come to know' (and the cognates *gnôsis* and *gnôstos* as 'knowledge' and 'knowable'), here on pp. 12–13, where it is very important for S. in interpreting the present lemma to distinguish different verbs of knowing, we translate *eidenai* as 'know' (the only possible choice), and either translate *gignôskein* as 'cognize' or, where this doesn't work, translate as 'know' but put the Greek in parentheses to make clear that the verb here is not *eidenai*. S. wants here to distinguish *gignôskein* from *eidenai* or at least from the strict sense of *eidenai*, but *gignôskein* is close in meaning to a loose sense of *eidenai*. *Eidenai* means 'know' only in the perfect tense (the aorist *idein* means 'see', and there is no present), and Greek writers sometimes use *gignôskein* to supply the missing tenses of *eidenai*, for instance in the present to mean 'come to know'. Simplicius seems to go back and forth between *gignôskein* and *gnôrizein*, 'cognize' and 'recognize' in our translation. We translate *epistasthai*, the strictest verb of knowing, as 'scientifically know' (and the cognate *epistêmê* as 'scientific knowledge' or 'science').

65 This paragraph begins the third and final movement of the first lemma, in which S. engages with Al. regarding what *kind* of knowledge has to start from principles: this revolves around discussion of Ar.'s words for knowing and the grammatical structure of the sentence.

66 Emending *axiômata* to *aitêmata*: on the Aristotelian theory of science, *axiômata* are not proper to individual sciences but universal: cf. 17,25-31 on *axiômata*.

67 *Metaphysics* 1.1 980a21-22, with *dêloi* substituted for *sêmeion*.

68 A very inaccurate citation (Diels says, 'memoriter') of *Rep.* 7, 533C3-5. Plato's text claims that mathematicians do not know (*eidenai*) their principles, or what follows from them, and thus do not have an *epistêmê*.

69 That not all opinion can be knowledge, since some is false, is simply assumed by Theaetetus and Socrates at *Tht.* 187B-C; that the two powers are different in kind, since knowledge is infallible and opinion fallible, is a point made at *Rep.* 5, 477E.

70 This sentence begins a passage extending to 'through demonstrative syllogisms' (*peirasetai*, 13,21) which is, disconcertingly, later repeated at 14,13-18 as part of a quotation from Al. Cf. the *Introduction* and n. 78 below.

71 Al. seems to here suggest and object to a reading of the relative clause as spelling out 'scientific knowledge' as knowledge of things which have principles; this would imply that there is no demonstration, and thus no scientific knowledge, of the principles

Notes to pp. 52–3 159

themselves; but (so Al. claims), Ar. does attempt to give demonstrations of the principles, so he cannot have intended such a restriction. He then goes on, in the direct quotation, to give an alternative interpretation according to which the point of the relative clause is to restrict the scope of the discussion to sciences which do have principles *and* causes *and* elements.

72 For the argument that mathematical (and more generally unmoved) objects have neither efficient nor final causes, cf. *Metaph.* 3.2, 996a21-b1. It is not so easy to find decisive Aristotelian evidence for the claim that mathematical objects do not have matter. Presumably the reason for saying that ungenerated things do not have a 'principle' or 'starting point' is that they never began.

73 'In these very words' (*autêi lexei*) is a common Simplician form of words used to emphasize that the passage he is about to criticize (usually from Al.) has been quoted accurately and without distortion (cf. *in Cael.* 112,24, 132,18, 171,35, 183,30, 187,6; *in Cat.* 152,13; *in Phys.* 38,1, 51,27, 71,6, 110,20, 113,1, 416,31, 437,6, 454,16-17, 675,14, 739,22, 758,24-25, 802,12, 1052,8, 1052,21, 1159,5).

74 S. commonly uses *epistêsai* (here, 'remark') and its cognates to call our attention to something that has escaped the notice of Al. or some other predecessor. It typically serves to raise a difficulty for their solution to a problem and motivate S.'s new proposal: see the *Introduction*.

75 The 'elements of speech (*logos*)' are standardly the various grammatical classes of word: cf. S., *in Cat.* 10,24 (citing Theophrastus); Chrysippus *SVF* 2.148; Apollonius Dyscolus, *Synt.* 7,1, 313,6; Ammonius, *in Int.* 64,26-7. But see also S. in *in Cael.* 85,23, where the elements of *logos* are the letters, which are standardly called elements of *phônê*.

76 A somewhat standardized formula for the role of the elements: cf., e.g., *Metaph.* 1.3, 983b8-9.

77 Adding a conjunction to read *pros te sunethismon*; Diels' text would mean 'contributions towards astronomy towards accustoming us to the incorporeal nature'. The phrase *pros sunethismon asômatou* or *pros sunethismon asômatou phuseôs* is a quotation or close paraphrase from Plotinus 1.3.3,5-7, and is often cited by later Neoplatonists.

78 More precisely, S. here restates (1) Al.'s objections at 12,14 ff. to taking scientific knowledge broadly for all knowing, and the relative clause as restrictive; and (2) Al.'s objections at 13,14 ff. to taking scientific knowledge as knowledge of things derived from the principles, so that there can be no scientific knowledge of the principles themselves. The latter involves verbatim repetition, here as a direct quotation, of what was earlier presented as paraphrase of Al. (cf. n. 70). S.'s purpose earlier was to motivate Al.'s solution to the problem; here it is to motivate his own.

79 The point seems to be that *to epistasthai* would only be added to secure the stricter conception of knowledge as scientific knowledge.

160   Notes to pp. 54–7

80 'As being proper to all scientific kinds of knowing' (*hôs idion pasôn . . . stoikheia* at 14,13-14) is an almost exact repetition of 13,16; and the following 'For scientific knowledge . . . through demonstrative syllogisms' (*hê gar epistêmê . . . peirasetai*) in 14,14-18 is an exact repetition of 13,17-21.

81 These are the first six words of the *Posterior Analytics*.

82 Diels here marks a lacuna and suggests a supplement with the sense: 'they are either self-warranting or demonstrated. And . . .'. We translate the transmitted text, which is awkward, but the sense of which is clear (and would not be importantly affected by the supplement). We break up a long sentence into two for easier parsing.

83 This completes the first sentence from the *An. Post.*

84 More literally, 'introduce together with themselves' (*suneisagein*); thus, 'entail', and S. often uses *suneisagein* for cases of mutual entailment, as here. The distinctive property (*idion*) *suneisagei* the essence, the effect *suneisagei* the cause, positing a principle *suneisagei* the things of which it is a principle.

85 On sign-inferential or 'tekmeriodic' syllogism, see Donald Morrison, 'Philoponus and Simplicius on Tekmeriodic Proof', in Daniel A. Di Liscia, Eckhard Kessler, and Charlotte Methuen, eds, *Method and Order in Renaissance Philosophy of Nature: The Aristotle Commentary Tradition* (Aldershot: Ashgate, 1998), pp. 1–22.

86 Diels' seclusion (following Torstrik) of *arkhas* seems unnecessary.

87 *Arkhoeidesteron*: i.e. having the status and role of a higher principle.

88 Cf. Heraclitus DK 22B94.

89 Cf. 9,12-13 above, following Porphyry.

90 S. here, and repeatedly over the next two *CAG* pages, speaks of starting from *holoskherês* knowledge, which we have translated 'crude' but might equally be translated 'coarse', i.e. coarse-grained as opposed to fine-grained, and refining it into more precise knowledge.

91 Diels writes *kata to sunkekhumenon*, correcting DEF which have *kai to sunkekhumenon*; we follow Mo (and the Aldine), which has *kai sunkekhumenon*.

92 Following Proclus, S. distinguishes three kinds of universals: the universal existing before the particulars as a paradigm in *Nous*, the universal existing immanently in the particulars, and the universal generated after the particulars; the last of these exists only in the soul, when it grasps through abstraction what is common to the many particulars. See Proclus, *in Euc.* 50,16-51,9 and S., *in Cat.* 82,35-83,10.

93 A somewhat abridged version of Euclid, *Elements* 1, definition 15. We follow Diels' deletion (following Torstrik) of 'on the circumference of the circle': the definition of circle should not include a reference to 'circle'. (On the other hand, Euclid's MSS also have the offending phrase; this is usually excluded by editors, but perhaps the gloss had worked its way into the text of Euclid used by S.)

Notes to pp. 57–9

94 Here not, as would be normal, the individuals instantiating a universal but the logical components of the definition. The oddity of the phrasing here is due to Ar.'s own usage at 184b11-12.

95 Diels' text, following DE, is difficult (and he notes various suggested improvements): *hekaston tôn hup' autôn periekhetai*, 'and each of the things beneath them is embraced'. We follow Mo, which has *hekaston tôn hup' autôn deiknumenôn hôs meros hup' autôn periekhetai*.

96 S. here contrasts the intellectual with the imaginative (*phantastikê*), i.e. dependent on the faculty of *phantasia*, which processes mental images derived from the senses.

97 We translate the following text: *phantastikê de mallon ekeinê kai apestenômenê*. Diels, following the MSS, puts a *kai* before *phantastikê*, which we omit (following the Aldine). Diels also emends the MSS' *ekeinê* to *ekeinês*. So the latter part of the sentence, as Diels presents it, would mean: 'and another kind of cognition which is synthesized and united and comprehends the particulars, being intellectual and simple and also more imaginative and restricted than the former'. So on Diels' view, S. would not be contrasting an intellectual with an imaginative cognition, but would be lumping the two together, presumably in contrast to cognition of a crudely sensory kind. Another possibility, as David Sedley suggests, would be to keep the MSS' *kai* before *phantastikê*, while still rejecting Diels' emendation, and translate: 'the latter being intellectual and simple, while the former is both imaginative and restrictive'. For a discussion of textual and interpretive issues in this passage, see Stephen Menn, 'Simplicius on the *Theaetetus* (*In Physica* 17,38-18,23 Diels)', *Phronesis* 55 (2010), 255–70.

98 Diels brackets *holoskheres* ('crude') here, possibly rightly. On the kind of understanding reserved for those at the 'summit', see 16,14-17 above.

99 S. is presumably thinking of Socrates' Dream in the *Theaetetus*, with its discussion of whether knowledge comes from having a *logos* of some object which spells out its elements; S. takes Socrates to be hinting that such a *logos* is inadequate for knowledge in the strict sense, for which we must also grasp the elements as *united*.

100 Diels brackets the phrase 'according to the definition and through the elements' and posits a lacuna. Diels thinks that S. wrote something like: 'there is another kind of cognition which is intermediate between the two, being discursive or else opinionative', and that the bracketed phrase is a scholiast's gloss on 'the two'. Against this, see Menn, 'Simplicius on the *Theaetetus*'.

101 *Tim.* 29B-D.

102 *An. Post.* 1.2, 71b19-22. The term 'self-warranting' is not taken from Ar. but might be a paraphrase of things he says at *An. Post.* 1.2, 72a25-b4.

103 Theophrastus fr. 142 FHS&G.

104 S. seems to here substitute *ta koina* ('the common things') as equivalent to *ta katholou* ('universals') in Ar.'s text.

162   *Notes to pp. 59–61*

105 i.e. when man ceases to exist, Socrates ceases to exist, but when Socrates ceases to exist, man does not thereby cease to exist. Cf. e.g. *Metaph.* 5.11. We here expand on S.'s phrasing; he uses *sunanairein* to mean 'co-destroy', i.e. x *sunanairei* y if when x is destroyed y is destroyed along with it.

106 For Al. on common and universal things and their priority relations, see *Quaestiones* 1.3 and 1.11.

107 We here translate Diels' *hê tôn koinôn gnôsis tinos* ('the knowledge of the common [features] of a thing'), but *hê dia tôn koinôn gnôsis tinos* ('the knowledge of a thing *through* its common features') is perhaps preferable.

108 See n. 92 on the different kinds of common things or universals recognized by S.

109 Diels prints this quotation from Al. as extending continuously down to 'ought to be predicated' (*kategoreisthai hupotetaktai*, 19,33). However, the earlier occurrence of this quotation, at 17,25 ff., diverges after *axiômata* ('axioms'), and the *peri hôn eirêtai proteron* is most naturally taken as referring back to S.'s own discussion not long before. So we take the quotation to end at 19,30, although it is possible that some of the material down to 19,33 reflects Al.'s reasoning.

110 Accepting Diels' seclusion (following Torstrik) of *to mian ê ou mian einai* as a gloss.

111 A close paraphrase of *Phys.* 185a27.

112 An almost verbatim rendering of *Phys.* 185a12-13.

113 The meaning is the same whether we delete the first *ouk* with Torstrik and Diels or leave it in with FHS&G.

114 Theophrastus fr. 143 FHS&G.

115 S. here begins his discussion of Aristotle's division of opinions about the principles (*Physics* 1.2, 184b15-22, plus Aristotle's comment on this division at 184b22-25): he discusses some general issues about the division, then describes each of the opinions (mostly following Theophrastus) and says who held it, and then he delves into each pre-Socratic's deeper meaning and tries to show that they are all in harmony. Diels prints here a very short lemma, just 184b15, with an extremely long commentary (20,29-37,9), followed by four more lemmas from 184b15-22 with much shorter commentaries (37,12-40,21; 40,23-42,5; 42,7-43,23; 43,26-45,12; plus 45,15-46,8 on 184b22-25). But what S. covers in his commentary on the present lemma goes far beyond 184b15, and it may be that his intended lemma here was all of 184b15-22 (or 184b15-25). If so, the relation of his commentary on this lemma to what Diels prints as his commentaries on the subsequent lemmas would be like the relation between the *theôria* and the *lexis* sections of the commentary on each lemma, as found in Philoponus' *Physics* commentary and in many other sixth-century commentaries: the *theôria* section gives a general overview of the thought of each lemma, and then the *lexis* section discusses problems of detail arising from its wording. S. does not follow this pattern very often, but he does so in his

Notes to pp. 61–4

commentary on the first two lemmas of the *Physics*, marking the transition from *theôria* to *lexis* in the first lemma at 10,7-9 and in the second at 17,31-34, and he may be doing so here in the third lemma as well.

116 Cf. 15,32-33, also 9,12 following Porphyry; the language of 'more elevated' sciences seems to be Porphyrian.

117 The phrasing here is briefly reminiscent of Al. at 12,7; cf. also 9,4.

118 Presumably Al. and Porphyry (cf. preceding notes, and the *Introduction* on S.'s citations of his predecessors).

119 Theophrastus fr. 144b FHS&G, cf. more fully Philoponus, *in Phys.* 4,8-5,6 (= fr. 144a).

120 Cf. *Phys.* 2.1, 193a1-9.

121 By 'contradiction' S. means a pair of contradictory opposites. The 'axiom of contradiction' here seems to be the principle of excluded middle, not the principle of non-contradiction.

122 *Phys.* 184b18-20, with minor omissions and S.'s addition of 'determined'.

123 For Empedocles and Anaxagoras, cf. *Phys.* 1.4, 187a21-23; for Democritus, cf. 1.5, 188a19-22.

124 Fr. 33a Wehrli; repeated with trivial variation at 42,13-15 (fr. 33b Wehrli).

125 'Disjunction (*diairetikon*)' is closely connected with 'division (*diairesis*)': a disjunction like 'either moved or unmoved' is a means of dividing principles into moved principles and unmoved principles, or a means of dividing opinions into those positing moved principles and those positing unmoved principles.

126 Cf. Al.'s division at Marwan Rashed, *Die Überlieferungsgeschichte der aristotelischen Schrift De generatione et corruptione* (Wiesbaden: Reichert, 2001), pp. 44–7, with comparanda.

127 Accepting Diels' emendation: some MSS have 'Parmenides the fiery Eleatic', others, memorably, 'Parmenides, fire or some splendour'.

128 FHS&G print 22,22-25,13 as Theophrastus fr. 224-226a. Diels in *DG* presents this as fr. 5 of Theophrastus' *Phys. Dox.* DK prints 22,22-23,20 as DK 21A31. This presentation of Xenophanes closely echoes the *MXG*.

129 God is by definition *most* powerful, ruling over all; if there were multiple gods, each would have to rule over the others. Some MSS have 'unalike': presumably in that case the argument would be that they would have unequal power, so that again some would not be gods at all. Cf. *MXG* 977a23-36.

130 As S. presents him, Xenophanes seems to assume that the One-which-is can share none of the properties either of not-being or of the many: what is not is infinite, and the many are finite, so the One-which-is can be neither. Likewise, not-being is unmoved, the many beings are moved, so the One-which-is is neither moved nor unmoved.

131 DK 21B26 Xenophanes. We follow Diels, but the MSS differ more than is reported in DK: there are two places at which the difference might be significant. In the first

164   *Notes to pp. 64–6*

line, some MSS have *kinoumenos* rather than *kinoumenon*, making the subject of the two verses masculine rather than neuter. In S.'s discussion as well, at several points the MSS diverge between the masculine *auton* and the neuter *auto*. In the second line, instead of 'nor is it appropriate' some MSS have something like 'nor does it turn to proceed'.

132 In the *Physics* commentary S. seems to cite Nicolaus solely for his views on Xenophanes and Diogenes of Apollonia (cf. 25,8; 149,18; 151,21-23); in both cases his citation is of Nicolaus' work *On the Gods* (cf. 151,21), which S. seems to know from Porphyry (cf. 149,13-18; 151,23-24). S., *in Cael.* refers to *On the Philosophy of Aristotle*, by 'Nicolaus the Peripatetic' (3,28-29; 398,36-39,4); in the *Encheiridion* commentary he refers to Nicolaus of Damascus on an ethical topic (83,9-14).

133 DK 21B25.

134 Ar. does not in fact seem to use *phusikos* especially for these figures; S. is perhaps influenced by 184b16-17, which *could* be read as referring to the monists there contrasted with the Eleatics as 'the' *phusikoi*. S. also cites this allegedly special or strict sense of *phusikos* in *in Cael.* 561,1-5.

135 On the *aition sunektikon*, see Carlos Steel, 'Neoplatonic versus Stoic causality: the case of the sustaining cause ("*sunektikon*")', *Quaestio* 2 (2002), 77–96.

136 Cf. Ar.'s account of Thales in *Metaph.* 1.3, 983b20-27.

137 Diels in *DG* prints this paragraph, as far as 'a certain fated necessity', as Theophrastus, *Phys. Dox.* fr. 1; FHS&G has 23,21-24,12 as fr. 225.

138 This sentence = DK 11B1.

139 Part of DK 22B90.

140 Cf. Diogenes Laertius 8.84, which attributes the phrase 'a determinate time of the change of the cosmos' to Hippasus.

141 Cf. 13,31-32 above, for the account of 'element'. For the argument about fire, cf. *Metaph.* 1.8, 988b34-9a5.

142 This paragraph = DK 12A9, incorporating DK 12B1 (the claim that the infinite is the principle of things, plus 'and the things that are are corrupted ... to the order of time').

143 The phrasing here is ambiguous between 'introduced the name "*arkhê*"' and 'introduced "infinite" (*apeiron*) as the name of the *arkhê*'. In the apparently parallel passage at 150,23-24 he clearly means that Anaximander first introduced the term *arkhê* in the relevant sense.

144 This could also be construed as 'in more poetic words [i.e. than these]'; Christian Wildberg, 'Simplicius und das Zitat: zur Überlieferung des Anführungszeichens', in Friederike Berger *et al.*, eds, *Symbolae Berolinenses: Für Dieter Harlfinger* (Amsterdam: Hakkert, 1993), pp. 187–99, has argued that this is the correct interpretation and that Anaximander wrote in verse. Wildberg's interpretation is difficult if we retain the word 'thus' (*houtôs*), but some MSS omit this. Though our reading implies that S. repeats some of Anaximander's language, we do not present

Notes to pp. 66–8 165

these lines as a quotation since the infinitive *didonai* ('pay') in 24,19 seems to indicate indirect speech, picking up infinitives in the previous sentence.

145 *Physics* 1.4, 187a20-23.

146 All of 14,13-25,7 are Theophrastus, *Phys. Dox.* 2 in *DG*; the whole paragraph is part of fr. 226a in FHS&G.

147 Cf. Ar. *Physics* 1.4, 187a13-15; *GC* 2.1, 328b33-329a1 and 2.5, 332a20-23; and S., *in Phys.* 149,17-18. S. has a full discussion of the problem of this intermediate *arkhê* and the difficulties involved in identifying its author at 148,26-153,24.

148 Indeed for such reasons *no one* posited earth as *arkhê*, according to Ar., *Metaph.* 1.8, 989a4-12), despite traditional ideas which might suggest it.

149 25,14-26,4 and 26,26-30 are fr. 227a FHS&G with 26,5-10 as fr. 230. *DG* prints 25,14-26,4 as Theophrastus, *Phys. Dox.* 3.

150 This could mean either that each element is always the same in quantity or that they are always four in number. In the latter case we would translate 'in manyness and fewness'.

151 There are some minor textual variations here: the most important would render the last line: 'at another time Strife holds them all borne asunder again'. These two lines appear twice later as part of much longer quotations: (i) at 33,19-34,3 (= DK 31B26) and (ii) 158,1-34 (= DK 31B17). Both other versions depart slightly from the present one, but the sense is not greatly altered. B17 overlaps with the text of Empedocles preserved in the Strasbourg papyrus; cf. Alain Martin and Oliver Primavesi, ed., tr., and comm., *L'Empédocle de Strasbourg (P. Strasb. gr. Inv. 1665–1666)* (Berlin: De Gruyter, 1999), p. 127, cf. p. 131, and Brad Inwood, ed. and tr., *The Poem of Empedocles*, rev. edn (Toronto: University of Toronto Press, 2001), fr. 25.

152 DK 31B17 continued, lines 17-20 (also at 185,15-19, with some discrepancies).

153 Cf. above 3,13 ff. and the *Introduction* for S. on Platonic causes.

154 Plato, *Tim.* 51A7

155 26,7-15 = Theophrastus fr. 230 FHS&G (= *Phys. Dox.* fr. 9 Diels (*DG*)).

156 This is also the reading of Alcinous, *Didaskalikos* 9-10.

157 Plato, *Tim.* 29D7-E2 with minor textual variants.

158 S.'s use of the following as a proof text for enmattered forms seems to presume that *eidos* is being used as a technical term for 'form', and that the enmattered 'second' shares *that* name (not merely that sensible particulars share the names of Forms they participate in).

159 *Tim.* 51E6-52A7, with minor textual variations (both within S.'s MSS and in relation to Plato's text). Most of S.'s MSS have *eis allo poioun*, 'acting on anything else', where Plato has *eis allo poi ion*, 'going anywhere into anything else'; and *palin ekeithen apolelumenon*, 'detached from it again', where Plato wrote *palin ekeithen apollumenon* 'perishing from it again'. We nonetheless translate Diels' text, which matches Plato's.

166 *Notes to pp. 68–9*

160 Here begins Theophrastus fr. 228a FHS&G, which extends to 27,28
(= Theophrastus, *Phys. Dox.* fr. 4 (*DG*)).

161 Following (with Diels) DE against MoFa, which omit 'others that they are compound and non-uniform.' This elision would leave Anaxagoras characterized as proposing simple, uniform, and opposite principles, which cannot be right; the 'simple, uniform, and infinite' party are presumably Democritus and Leucippus, to be discussed immediately after (cf. also 43,27-45,12 for discussion). S. here seems not to be distinguishing between the homoeomerous gold which is the principle and the compounds in which it predominates, though he does so within a few sentences.

162 At 28,4-5, S. uses the same phrase for Leucippus' relation to Parmenides. Since *philosophia* might suggest a shared activity, S. may mean not that Anaxagoras had shared Anaximenes' opinions but that he was a student of his; if so, this is probably chronologically impossible. But see Philip Thibodeau, *The Chronology of the Early Greek Natural Philosophers* (North Haven: Cosmographia, 2019), for a challenge to the usual dating of Anaximenes, which would make S.'s (probably Theophrastus') connection between Anaximenes and Anaxagoras possible.

163 Compare S.'s fuller treatment, explicitly citing the original text, at 155,23 ff.

164 These quotations are printed by Diels as DK 59B11 and part of DK 59B12 (2,37,22-23; 2,39,6-7), lines 5-6 and 29-30 in David Sider, ed. and comm., *The Fragments of Anaxagoras*, 2nd rev. edn (Sankt Augustin: Academia Verlag, 2005), with minor discrepancies. The first of these quotations is also in somewhat fuller versions at 164,23-24 and 172,4; the latter is at the end of a much longer quote (B12) at 157,4, and also at 165,3-4. The text of the latter quotation is difficult and translations vary significantly; we take the sense to be that if A, B, etc. occur in high concentrations in X, then X is most manifestly A and B, or A and B are most manifestly present in X, although X is not purely A or B, and A and B are also present in other things.

165 The reference here is ambiguous between Anaximander and Anaxagoras (and Theophrastus); Anaximander is the most plausible reading, on grounds both of sense and construction. The sense of the quotation is also ambiguous: where we have 'because (*hoti*) there was gold . . ., gold comes-to-be, and because there was earth, earth', one might translate 'what (*hoti*) was gold . . . comes-to-be gold, and what was earth, earth'.

166 Reading *egennêse* with F (and a correction in E^a) or *egennêsen* with Mo; the alternative *egennêsan*, printed by Diels on the basis of DEE^a a, would entail either assigning a grammatically incorrect plural verb to the neuter plural subject implied by *diakrinomena*, or taking the subject to be Anaximander and Anaxagoras.

167 As Ar. proposes in *Metaph.* 1.8, 989a30-b6.

168 Theophrastus' reading of Anaxagoras is discussed again by S. at 154,14 ff, where the same passage is quoted in a slightly different form.

169 This paragraph is printed as Theophrastus fr. 229 FHS&G = Theophrastus, *Phys. Dox.* fr. 8 Diels (*DG*). The sentences regarding Leucippus, Democritus, and

Notes to pp. 69–71 167

Metrodorus are printed by DK as, respectively, 67A8; 68A38; and Metrodorus 70A3.

170 Here begins a brief passage which we omit (*kai tôn . . . tautên gar*, 28,9-10), which is repeated with two small changes (*en tais atomois* for *en autois*, and *phasi* added after *plêthos*) at 28,25-26 ('And they say that the plurality of figures in the atoms is infinite, because of nothing being any more this than that'). Diels here secludes only the last two words, *tautên gar*, which indeed give no intelligible sense; but the whole seems out of place here. A scribe may have wrongly copied the lines here, but Malcolm Schofield, 'Leucippus, Democritus and the οὐ μᾶλλον Principle: An Examination of Theophrastus *Phys. Op.* Fr. 8', *Phronesis* 47 (2002), 253–63, makes a plausible case that S. himself added the passage from his source, presumably Theophrastus.

171 It was standard to cite these three features of atoms, sometimes using the original archaic terms and sometimes not. Cf. Ar., *GC* 1.9, 327a16; *Metaph.* 1.4, 985b13-19 and 8.2, 1042b11-15.

172 Literally, 'those around (*hoi peri*)' Democritus. This idiom is vague but certainly does not exclude the philosopher himself, and may sometimes just be a roundabout way to refer to him, so that the closest modern equivalent would be 'Democriteans'.

173 Reading *tês* following DEE[a] rather than *tous* with Fa as Diels does.

174 Christians, as will soon become evident.

175 *Historikais . . . anagraphais*: so far S. has been following Theophrastus, but we need deeper enquiry, not a mere 'report', to see whether these philosophers really contradict each other: see the *Introduction*.

176 A reference to schisms regarding the Incarnation. *Kathairesis* ('desecration'), which literally means 'pulling down', would to a Platonist recall the reference to witches (who will pay for it with what is dearest to them) pulling down the moon at *Gorgias* 513A.

177 We read *holôs*, following Torstrik's emendation.

178 In dealing with S.'s quotations from Parmenides (and likewise with other pre-Socratics), our aim is to reproduce the text as S. is likely to have cited it, not necessarily the text Parmenides wrote (as we might reconstruct it from all sources taken together). So we will, except as noted, follow Diels' text of S. in the *CAG*, noting significant variations in the MSS of S.; we will also give references to other citations by S. of the same lines; but we will for the most part not note the other sources for the fragments S. cites, nor discuss conflicts among them and the problems of interpretation they raise. We will comment only on those interpretive issues which seem immediately pertinent for understanding S.'s own text and understanding of Parmenides. For a full treatment of the fragments and testimonia in their own right, see A. H. Coxon, ed., tr., and comm, *The Fragments of Parmenides*, 2nd edn (Las Vegas: Parmenides Publishing, 2009). Our translation is

168   *Notes to p. 71*

adapted from G. S Kirk, J. E. Raven, and M. Schofield, *The Presocratic Philosophers* (Cambridge, Cambridge University Press, 1983).

179 DK 28B8.38. This line is problematic. The text given by Diels is not quite what appears in any MS (including Mo, not known to Diels). All MSS give *hoion*, which gives no good sense here, and *panti onoma* (likewise, and unmetrical too). Diels corrects to *oion* and *pant' onom'* respectively, which presumably means something like: 'alone and unmoved it abides, through all things' being a name'. We follow Diels in opting for *oion*, but prefer the Aldine *pan* in place of the plural *pant'*, in order to preserve subject-predicate agreement. Very different versions of the line are given by S. at 87,1 and in the extended quotation at 146,11, while the present version is repeated at 143,10. The long quotation is overwhelmingly the more likely to represent S.'s accurate representation of what he found in his MS. However, the present version is well suited to S.'s present point: if Parmenides says that it is 'alone and unmoved', rather than 'whole and unmoved', it will be not a complex whole like the One of the second hypothesis of Plato's *Parmenides*, but a bare One-itself like the One of the first hypothesis. Perhaps also if Parmenides says that it is alone and unmoved because everything that could be applied to it would be a mere name, this justifies S.'s conclusion that Parmenides, like Xenophanes, makes it transcend all attributes. The 87,1 and 146,11 versions are for the most part the same as each other, both beginning with *oulon* ('whole'), though differing at the end (and in punctuation): *onom' estai* (87,1) vs. *ônomastai* (146,11, obelized).

180 It seems that by its being 'inexhaustible (*anekleipton*)' S. means not simply that Melissus' being is eternal but that its eternity is due to its intrinsically infinite power (cf. 41,30-42,5).

181 Following Diels and translating *ginomenon*, the present participle; it is more likely that Melissus wrote *genomenon*, meaning 'if it came-to-be'.

182 DK 30B2. Quoted again, with minor variations and an extra line at the end, at 109,20. The MSS end the present citation with 'but is infinite' (*alla apeiron*). Diels rejects this as an interpolation from line 23 above, citing 109,24-25 for the correct version.

183 As Coxon says, to get an acceptable sense here we must 'give an unparalleled and improbable sense to *ateleston*, which elsewhere means "imperfect", "uninitiated", or "untaxed"' (*Fragments of Parmenides*, p. 315). But S. does consistently (and with little significant MSS variation) quote the line in this way when quoting B8 in extenso (i.e. presumably, from his best MSS of Parmenides), at 78,13 and 145,5. Interestingly, when briefly citing the line (likely from memory), he substitutes 'ungenerated' (*agenêton*), (e.g., *in Cael.* 557,18; *in Phys.* 12,23). *Agenêton* is standard in our numerous other sources for B8.4 (see Coxon ad loc.). This however seems to be borrowed from the preceding line. DK follows S.'s reading; other scholars have suggested various emendations.

184 DK 28B8.3-5. This is repeated by S. at 145,3-5 as part of a much longer quotation, and also at 78,12-14; line 4 is also cited at 87,21; 120,23; and *in Cael.* 557,18. DK

Notes to pp. 71–3 169

prints the 145,1 ff. quotation as 28B8, with a very different version of the first half of the second line quoted here (28B8.4), *esti gar oulomeles* ('whole of limb') rather than *oulon mounogenes* ('whole, unique'). However, S. actually has the same text there as here: DK is following citations in Plutarch and others (see Coxon, *Fragments of Parmenides* or DK ad loc.). We follow Diels' text here: the MSS (for this occurrence) differ only trivially from each other, and no emendations are required for a viable sense. The occasion for the citation is presumably 'unending', which supports S.'s claim that Parmenides agrees with Melissus.

185 Quoted later as 40,3-6 (minus the first line) and as 146,2-6 (= DK 28B8.29-33). The last line is unmetrical; DK restores metre by deleting *mê*, turning 'if it were not' into 'if it were [*sc.* deficient]'.

186 B8.50-52: S.'s later extended quotation at 145,1-146,25 ends here. B8.50-61 is also quoted at 38,30-39,9; B8.50-52 at *in Cael.* 558,5-7; B8.50-51 at 41,8-9; and B8.53-59 at 180,1-12.

187 This quote is B8.53-59. DK prints *gnômas* in B8.53, on the basis of 39,1 and 180,1.

188 The sense here is controversial; but 31,7-9 ('he says that those who did not see together … the opposition of the elements which constitute coming-to-be have wandered astray') suggests that S. takes the error to consist in failing to posit a pair of contraries, though who might commit this error (in light of the following line) is unclear.

189 This line is cited three times by S., with MSS disagreement and textual trouble each time (cf. 39,5; 180,5). The line as Diels prints it is unmetrical, and Diels obelizes; DK reads *on* rather than *to* (following Fa), and secludes *araion*. We read *on* and seclude *meg'*.

190 Whatever MS S. uses here presumably marked this passage as *Parmenidou*, 'by/of Parmenides'; this kind of reference, with the genitive, occurs elsewhere in doxographical summaries. This prose statement of Parmenides' position as if it were by Parmenides himself might be comparable to the text cited later as by Melissus but now recognized to be a later reformulation (cf. n. 240). Plato in the *Sophist* refers to Parmenides as having advanced his views both in verse and prose (*pezêi*), but the latter may well be referring only to oral discourse (*Sophist* 237A4-7), although the *Suda* cites Plato as referring to prose works of Parmenides (*katalogadên*, as in S. here), Π675. We thank Gérard Journée for discussion and references.

191 We use 'see' for *sunoran*: this means not to see in a literal sense, but to intellectually grasp or be conscious of something, often in a way which involves seeing how a plurality of things fit together.

192 Presumably these incorporeals are souls: cf. 39,12-20.

193 Diels obelizes; others emend variously. We read *pantôn* in line 31,15 with Mo, rather than Diels' *panta* (which is unmetrical and hard to construe).

194 This quotation = DK 28B12.2-6 (i.e. B12 minus the first line); lines 1-3 are also cited at 39,14-16, and alluded to at 34,14 ff. The 'rings' as subject have to be supplied on the basis of DK 28A37.

170 — *Notes to pp. 73–5*

195 S. assumes that Empedocles' *sphairos* is not a stage in the development of the sensible world, but is an intelligible paradigm for it, like Plato's 'animal itself' in the *Timaeus*. He argues that both Love and Strife are active in both worlds, Love predominating in the intelligible world, Strife down here.

196 Cf. *Tim.* 39E3-40A2, though this is not directly about the four elements but about the four types of animals characterized by them. Plato does discuss forms of elements at 51B6-52A7. Cf. also *Timaeus Locrus* 207,8-14.

197 S. is evidently assimilating the *Timaeus'* opposition between *Nous* and *Anankê* (Necessity) to Empedocles' opposition between Love and Strife.

198 DK 31B98.

199 Translations from Empedocles are indebted to Inwood, *The Poem of Empedocles*.

200 DK 31B98.

201 Following Panzerbieter's emendation of *pleonessin* for *pleon estin* (reported in Diels).

202 DK 31B35.3-17; lines 1-15 are also given by S. at *in Cael.* 528,30 ff.

203 This is translating Diels' text, but the sense of this line is puzzling. MSS have *ta prin akrita* ('things which before were undistinguished, muddled'). Problems: (1) *akrita* is unmetrical; (2) the sense is odd: 'things which before were muddled' gives the needed contrast with '[become] pure' (*zôra*), but this is the reverse of the usual operation of Love. Theophrastus as cited by Athenaeus, *Deipnosphistae* (10.22.26 Kaibel) has *akrêta* ('unmixed'), which is printed by Diels, but this too gives a bad sense. Diels copes by taking *zôra* to mean 'zu (kräftig) gemischten', i.e. powerfully mixed rather than pure, following Sosicles ap. Plutarch, *Quaest. Conv.* 677d (cf. Inwood, *Empedocles*, pp. 116–18).

204 DK 31B21.3-12, quoted in full at 159,13 ff.

205 We translate Diels' text, but none of the MSS give a satisfactory sense and Diels himself obelizes. See also Inwood ad loc. In context, the line should be a description of aether, i.e. air.

206 Our translation deviates from the text Diels prints, which is difficult to make sense of, following rather his suggestions in the apparatus as to Empedocles' original text. Thus we translate *thelumna* 'close-packed' instead of *thelêma*, 'willingly', and *stereôpa*, 'solid', rather than *stereôma*, 'solid body, framework'. *Stereôpa* is found in the fuller quotation at 159,18. DK has *thelêmna* and *stereôpa*.

207 DK 31B26. The last five lines are also quoted by Ar., *Physics* 8.1, 250b30-251a3.

208 Again following Diels' suggestions ad loc. (and likewise DK) as to what Empedocles wrote, thus reading *thêrôn*, 'animals', rather than the MSS *kêrôn* 'dooms'.

209 Empedocles does speak of an alternation of Love and Strife in the sublunar world, but where S. may take for granted that the supralunar world is more governed by Love, Empedocles probably sees Strife as having greater power in the heavens than below during the current phase of the cosmic cycle (cf. B35).

Notes to pp. 75–6 171

210 As usual, *mêpote* introduces S.'s own view, in correction of the one just cited: here he proposes to read Empedocles as saying not that Love and Strife dominate at different times, but that there are different degrees of reality which they dominate to differing degrees. See the *Introduction*.

211 Cf. e.g. *in Cael.* 140,25-141,9; 293,20-294,13.

212 Anaxagoras' three levels seem to run as follows: (1) the 'intelligible unification' (*noêtê henôsis*), which corresponds to Parmenidean One-which-is; (2) the level of 'intellectual division' (*noera diakrisis*), i.e. the world of *Nous*' thinking, where the forms are more distinct; and (3) the sensible world, in which the forms are physically divided. S. here follows Proclus and Damascius in distinguishing between *noêton*, 'intelligible', and *noeron*, 'intellectual'; the One-which-is is intelligible rather than intellectual in that it does not itself think but is the object of thinking. On Anaxagoras cf. 157,5-24; 461,10-17; and *in Cael.* 608,31-609,12; however, these passages seem chiefly concerned to distinguish *two* levels at which forms exist. It is not clear whether in these texts forms also exist within *Nous* itself. See the *Introduction* for discussion.

213 DK 59B1, beginning (= DK 2,32,11-12). S. also cites this at 164,15-16, in somewhat fuller versions at 172,2-3 and *in Cael.* 608,21-23, and as part of a much larger quotation at 155,26-27.

214 DK 59B4, part (= DK 2,34,17-2,35,5). This and the following quotation are treated by Sider as fragments 4b and 4a respectively. All except the last sentence of this quotation are also at 156,4-8, as part of a larger quotation; the last sentence is also cited at *in Cael.* 608,24.

215 Here (in fr. 4b Sider) and at 35,1 just below (fr. 4a), Diels prints *eneinai* ('are [or were] in'; *eneinai . . . en* would mean 'are [or were] present in'), which is found in the parallel passages at 156,2 (fr. 4a) and 159 (also fr. 4a). But apparently all MSS, both here and at 35,1, have *hen einai* ('are [or were] one'; *hen einai . . . en* would mean 'are [or were] one in'). Anaxagoras certainly meant *eneinai*, and that is what editors of Anaxagoras print, but it looks as if S., at least when he wrote the present passage, took him to mean *hen einai*. That seems to be part of his justification for saying that Anaxagoras is here describing the 'intelligible unification' or 'the One-which-is of Parmenides'. It is also possible that S. intended *hen einai* here but *eneinai* at 35,1 and the parallels, which are talking about the 'intellectual division'.

216 Both Parmenides himself, presumably, and the second hypothesis in Plato's *Parmenides*. One ground for the identification would be Anaxagoras' phrase *homou panta*, 'all things [were] together', which would recall Parmenides' *homou pan*, 'all together' (B8.5, cited at 30,3).

217 Here again, as noted above, keeping the *hen einai* of the manuscripts against Diels' *eneinai*.

218 DK 59B4, earlier part (DK 2,34,5-16) = fr. 4a Sider. S. also cites these lines also as part of larger quotations at 156,2-4; 157,9-16; and *in Cael.* 609,5-11.

172 *Notes to pp. 76–80*

219 S. is likely influenced in this reading by the phrase 'among us', used in Plato's *Parmenides* to contrast the sensible world with the Forms (133D-134A), by the word *idea* (used for the Forms), and probably by a parallel interpretation of the 'true earth' of the *Phaedo*.

220 DK 59B9.

221 For further exposition of this reading of the *Timaeus*, which has Proclus' interpretation as its background, see S., *in Cael.* 563,26-573,11. As above, S. there maintains that Plato holds that earth too transforms into the other elements (contrary to *Tim.* 54B-D).

222 Leucippus and Democritus seem in fact to have held that fire atoms are spherical (DK 67A15; DK 68A101); S. is here assimilating their view to that of the *Timaeus*.

223 His claims here recall those regarding Thales at 23,22-29, Thales and Heraclitus at 24,4 ff., and Anaximenes at 25,9-11, for this reading of Anaximander, compare 149,5-28.

224 Following Mo and reading *kai to* rather than *to kai* at 36,8, so that the *drastêrion* 'active [character]' and the *epitêdeion* 'suitability' are distinct features.

225 *Physics* 1.5, 188b30-33 and 188b36-37.

226 As Diels notes, S. here seems to conflate the admiring reference to Parmenides' depth at *Tht.* 184A1 with Socrates' alleged comment that *Heraclitus*' book required 'a Delian diver' to get to the bottom of it (Diogenes Laertius 2.22, cf. 9.11). His 'thought' (*dianoia*) here seems to mean his intended meaning.

227 We here read, with Mo and F *post correctionem, Parmenidês de eoike pou blepein*, as at *in Cael.* 560,2-3. This is a slight misquotation of Ar., *Metaph.* 1.5, 986b27-28.

228 Compare the presentation of Al.'s division in Rashed, *Die Überlieferungsgeschichte der aristotelischen Schrift De generatione et corruptione*, pp. 44–7.

229 This passage is a reference back to Ar.'s earlier discussion of proceeding from what is better known to us, and in particular to S.'s discussion of Al.'s claim that Ar. here has in view axioms and general descriptions of principles (19,18-20,2).

230 *Physics* 184b22-25. The version here varies somewhat from Ross's text of the *Physics*. Ross prints *prôtôn, zêtousi*, giving 'they investigate the first things out of which the beings are', on the basis of Bonitz' emendation; but S.'s later lemma at 45,13-14 (as Diels prints it) is different again, leaving out the *prôton* altogether.

231 S. is careful here to speak of the One-which-is as 'unified', following Damascius; it contrasts with the highest principle, the One Itself, which is beyond being and which is not unified but essentially one. S. takes Parmenides and Melissus to be talking about the One-which-is.

232 DK 28B8.50-61. Parmenides B8.1-52 is quoted at 144,29 ff.; other partial quotations overlapping with the present one include 30,17-19; 30,23-31,2; 41,8-9; 180,1-12; and *in Cael.* 558,5-7. On problems with the text and sense, see our notes to 30,17-31,2.

Notes to pp. 80–1   173

233 Here S.'s MSS (including Mo) have *gnômas* (as also at 180,1) rather than *gnômais* as at 30,23.

234 DK 28B12, lines 1-3: lines 2-6 quoted on 31,13-17; as before, we supply 'rings' on the basis of A37.

235 DK 28B13: also cited by Plato, *Symposium* 178B; Ar., *Metaph.* 1.4, 984b23; Plutarch, *Amatorius* 756E-F. S. follows Ar. in taking Parmenides to have recognized a cause of motion.

236 We follow DE (and the Aldine) in reading a *mê* after *eiper* in 39,22 (against E^aFMo).

237 Accepting Diels' two suggestions (in his apparatus) of *kan* for *kai* in this sentence.

238 DK 28B8.26-28. The lines are again quoted at 79,32-80,2 and at 145,27-146,1. The MSS here have *têde*, 'here', or *tê de*. Diels in his apparatus cites *têle*, 'afar', as the emendation of the sixteenth-century humanist scholar Joseph Scaliger. The reading *têle* is now generally accepted as what Parmenides actually wrote, but it is more problematic what S. wrote, here and in the other places where he cites this verse, and *têle* is definitely not Scaliger's emendation. Scaliger's text is in his (still!) unpublished edition of the fragments of Parmenides, *Parmenidou epê ex Sexto Empirico et Simplicio*, preserved in MS Scaliger 25 at Leiden University: see Patrizia Marzillo, '"Would you check my edition please?" Scaliger's annotations to some poetical/philosophical texts', in Bernhard Huss, Patrizia Marzillo, and Thomas Ricklin, eds, *Para/Textuelle Verhandlungen zwischen Dichtung und Philosophie in der Frühen Neuzeit* (Berlin: De Gruyter, 2011), pp. 399–428. Scaliger in fact writes *tê de*, but in the margin he cites the reading *têle*, and attributes it to 'Cant.', meaning probably the Dutch humanist Willem Canter, or possibly his brother Dirk. We do not know whether Canter himself proposed *têle* as an emendation or whether he simply read it in a manuscript of Simplicius, since, unknown to Diels, it is in fact in some of the manuscripts, not (in any manuscripts that have been collated) here at 40,1 or at 146,1, but at 80,2 in MSS Mo and E (the first unknown to Diels, the latter misreported: see the Note on the Text and Translation). We read *têle* at 80,2: *têle mal' eplakhthêsan* is a clever use of Homeric models (see *Iliad* 8.14 and esp. 22.291), and *têde* would be a banalization and an easy corruption if S. correctly wrote *têle* (lambda and delta are easily confused in uncials). S. *may* have written *têle* in all three citations, but since no MS gives it in the present occurrence, we stick here with the transmitted *têde*. (We thank Patrizia Marzillo for her advice and for sending us her scan of the Leiden manuscript; and we thank Tony Grafton and Glenn Most for identifying 'Cant.' for us.)

239 DK 28B8.30-33, cited earlier at 30,7-10; see earlier occurrence for the textual difficulty in the last line.

240 Part of DK 30B7, given in full at 111,18-112,15 with no significant variations; this and the following quotation are also quoted at 80,7-10 and 80,11-14 respectively

174   *Notes to pp. 81–2*

(again with no significant variations), and are paraphrased at 104,5-7 and 104,10-13 respectively. DK treats all of 103,15-104,15 as a paraphrase of frr. 1, 2, 6, and 7 in succession. Disturbingly, this paraphrase is introduced with a reference to its location at the beginning of Melissus' book (103,13-15, cf. 40,12), and has all the hallmarks of a direct quotation. The canonical quotation of B7 at 111,18-112,15 is also presented explicitly as a direct quotation, complete with comments on Melissus' style. The divergence in wording between the paraphrase and the B7 quotations is much too great to be a matter of ordinary scribal error, either in the manuscript tradition of S. or in different MSS of Melissus which S. might have used. If we assume with Diels et al. that 111,18 ff. represents direct quotation by S. of his best MS of Melissus' own book, only a few and rather unsatisfying explanations seem to be available: either S. is offering his own paraphrase at 103,15-104,15, and misleadingly representing it as Melissus' own words; or S. is drawing the paraphrase from some mediated source (a doxography, a reconstruction, a fake?) and perhaps mistakes his *source's* paraphrase of Melissus for quotation; or Melissus' book was repetitious in the extreme, including multiple versions of the same arguments. (In volume 1 of his edition of S., published in 1882, Diels treats 103,15-104,15 as a quotation from Melissus; but in the index to volume 2, (1895) and in the *Fragmente der Vorsokratiker* (first edition 1903), he follows Arnold Pabst, whose 1889 Bonn dissertation, *De Melissi Samii fragmentis*, argued that 103,15 ff. is not a direct quotation but a paraphrase of otherwise preserved fragments.)

241 S. revisits this disagreement with Al. more fully at 104,2-15 and 110,13-112,15. Al. takes Melissus to argue on natural-scientific grounds that there is no void and thus no room for anything to move; S. takes him to argue that being is full in the sense that it is complete and incorporates any other prospective existents. S.'s argument would apply to all change, not simply locomotion, and would not be liable to the objection that circular motion can take place in a plenum.

242 Repeated at 80,11-14 and (as part of the longer whole B7) 111,12-15, with no significant variations.

243 Diels presents this passage, down to 'and the like' (41,1), as excerpted from Al., in single quotation marks; but though S. may well be agreeing with Al. here there is no particular reason to suppose he is quoting him.

244 Emending *ēgnoei* to *agnoei*, following Torstrik; cf. *in Cael.* 405,5.

245 DK B8.50-51. Also quoted (at greater length) at 30,17-18; 38,30-31; 146,23-24; and *in Cael.* 558,5-6. S. is citing the passage as evidence that Ar. does not use *phusikos* for anyone who philosophizes about truth, since Parmenides does so yet is contrasted with the *phusikoi*. Al.'s talk of those who philosophized about truth recalls Ar., *Metaph.* 1.3, 983b1-3; cf. *Metaph.* 2.1, 993b16-23; *Phys.* 1.8, 191a24-31.

246 The following long parenthesis amounts to a footnote justifying this allusion to a part of the division Ar. skips: the monists too can be divided into those who posited

Notes to pp. 82–5 175

a single finite principle, whether moved or unmoved, and those who posited an infinite one. But Ar. here uses the infinite/finite division only for the pluralists.

247 Accepting Diels' seclusion of *estin*.

248 DK 30B2. This will be quoted again almost immediately at 41,31-42,1; it is also quoted (more fully) at 29,19-29 above and again at 109,20 ff. The 41,31-42,1 and 109,20 ff. versions agree with the present occurrence except that 41,31-42,1 has *gar* ('for', presumably an intrusion in S.'s voice) rather than *toinun* (also at 29,22). The 29,22 version differs in having *te kai* rather than *de*, so that *esti*, 'it is', belongs to the consequent.

249 Cf. *Phys.* 1.2, 185a32-b5, though Ar. there argues only that it is impossible that what is is both one and infinite.

250 Or, 'also a Milesian'.

251 Cf. 22,9 ff. on Ar.'s omissions in his division.

252 From DK 30B2, cited just above at 41,13-14. Cf. 29,19-29 above on Melissus, with notes ad loc.

253 Other than finite vs. infinite.

254 i.e. Democritus is the most plausible candidate for a proponent of many unmoved principles, but even he says they are moved by collisions. Ar. complains about his denial to them of natural motions in *On the Heaven* 3.3, 300b8-16.

255 Themistius, *in Phys.* 2,29, with minor variations.

256 Eudemus fr. 33b Wehrli; the earlier citation (fr. 33a) is at 22,15-16, with minor variations.

257 This repeats the lemma, with 'must' (*anankê*) added in from earlier in Ar.'s text, and with 'multiplicity' (*plêthos*) added to suggest the distinction which S. will soon accuse Al. of overlooking.

258 S. is here using terminology adopted by the Stoics for their doctrine of total mixture (*khôrein dia*).

259 Cf. 22,16-18 above.

260 A reference back to the division starting at 22,22; the 'several principles' branch begins at 25,14, with the 'finite' subdivision including Parmenides, Empedocles, and Plato; and 'infinitely many' (26,31 ff.) including Anaxagoras and the atomists.

261 This is close to the reading given in the quotation from Theophrastus on 26,7-13.

262 *Tim.* 29D (with very minor textual variants), almost exactly as given in the more extensive quotation on 26,16-18.

263 i.e. the parts of an animal body.

264 *Tim.* 51E6 ff., as quoted at 26,20-24 (but cut short and with minor variations) to prove the same point: see nn. 158-9.

265 *Tim.* 53B.

266 i.e. the 'animal itself' of the *Timaeus*.

267 *Tim.* 39E7-9, with 'so many' and 'such' interchanged; S. expands 'this' to 'this universe', leaves out the word 'must', and changes the tense of 'have'.

176 *Notes to pp. 85–7*

268 After 'as Democritus said' the text that S. assumes, and that all Ar.'s MSS share (with one minor variation), reads *to genos hen skhêmati de* (some MSS omit the *de*), then *ê eidei diapherousas ê kai enantias*. In part to resolve the difficulties S. goes on to discuss, Ross, following Torstrik, adds another occurrence of *diapherousas* after *skhêmati de*, giving the sense 'either, as Democritus said, one in genus but differing in shape, or differing or even contrary in species'. The latter option ('or differing or . . .') would presumably refer to a different theory, perhaps that of Anaxagoras, correlative with the opening 'either', as S. suggests.

269 The subject here might be either Ar. or Al.: in the latter case, S.'s claim would be that Al. makes his interpretation clear by citing the following passage of Ar.

270 *Physics* 188a22-26, with (mostly) minor variations. Ar.'s text has 'pointy' (*gegôniômenon*) and 'non-pointy' (*agônion*) in addition to straight and round as opposites in the genus of shape; at *in Phys.* 180,21-25 ad loc. S. paraphrases this accurately. The present version is repeated at *in Cael.* 129,30-130,4 and occurs in some MSS of Ar., but seems impossible to construe. We posit an iota subscript to take *gôniâi* as dative of respect (one could also read *gônian* with Mo) to give the sense translated.

271 Omitting *ê houtôs*, for *ei apeirous hôsper Dêmokritos*.

272 i.e. has been interpolated; cf. Galen, *in Hipp. de Hom. Nat.* 15,11,5 Kühn and *in Hipp. Epid. 1* 17a,253,3 Kühn.

273 In this monstrous conditional, S. first rejects two proposed solutions from Al. ([a] and [b]), then [c] rejects the alternative reading of Porphyry and Themistius, and [d] offers his own solution, introduced as usual by *mêpote*.

274 i.e. Al.'s first option (his suggested emendation) is unacceptable, and so is his second option, which very uncharitably takes Ar.'s text as setting up for a counterpart to Democritus (Anaxagoras or similar) who is never mentioned; this is grammatically wrong (in the *ê houtôs*) and omits a section of the division.

275 *Thesis*, translated 'orientation' in descriptions of atomism: a rare Simplician pun.

276 Ar.'s MSS here differ, some having *prôton zêtousi* and others *zêtousi prôton* (both meaning 'investigate first'). S.'s lemma here as printed by Diels differs from all of them, with no *prôton* reported in any MS; S.'s earlier citation at 38,8 has *zêtousi prôton* (all MSS). Al.'s discussion implies a *prôton*, which we add here though what S. himself read is uncertain. Ross (following Bonitz) emends Ar.'s text to *prôtôn, zêtousi* – i.e. taking the *prôtôn* with the preceding *ex hôn ta onta esti*, giving the sense 'concerning the first things out of which the beings are'. See n. 230.

277 An example also used at *Rep.* 522D1-8.

278 Reading *oun* with DEMo in place of Diels' *goun* (following aF).

279 184b15, the starting point of Ar.'s division of opinions about the principles.

280 Following DEMo, with a slight emendation from *onomati allôs khrôntai* ('use a word differently') to *onomati allôi khrôntai*. Presumably the name in question is *to*

Notes to pp. 87–90

on ('being', 'what is'), which Parmenides and Melissus use to mean *arkhê* ('principle'). aF have *onomasi khrôntai allois*: 'use different names'; Diels prints *onomasin allois khrôntai*.

281 The text as transmitted and printed by Diels seems untranslatable; we follow Torstrik in adding *doxan pros*. The alternative would be to take the *mian* 'one' as referring to the one *arkhê* of the theory in question, in keeping with the preceding lines, and to somehow emend to give the sense, roughly: 'Hence he argues against this theory as setting down a single *arkhê*.'

282 This and the following sentence are elaborated paraphrases of *Phys.* 185a3-5.

283 Accepting Diels' supplement from the Aldine: *tên phusin anêiroun. kai* ('they abolish nature. And'). DEMo omit this, while F has a lacuna. Diels cites 47,1-2 and Themistius 3,11-12. Since, as S. argues, the view attacked by Ar. presents the One-which-is as a principle, it is discussed as a natural part of his division, and not (as Al. suggests in the previous paragraph) in order to get at the question whether there are principles at all.

284 In this sentence S. seems to refer to three Aristotelian arguments, the first of which ends our lemma. The first argues that there cannot be a principle if there is only one thing (in the sense the Eleatics intend) (*Phys.* 185a3-5); the second depends on a broader conception of 'being' (185a20-b5); and the third depends on the concept of the 'one' (185b5-25.)

285 This sentence seems to elaborate on the first of the three arguments noted in the preceding sentence. It resembles Al.'s version of the argument outlined in the preceding paragraph; the difference is that S. takes the opposing view to be committed to conceiving of the One-which-is as a principle, so that to show the view abolishes principles refutes it on its own terms.

286 Accepting Diels' supplement (following the Aldine) of *legontes*.

287 *Sustêsai*, 'establish', is cognate with *sustasis*, 'constitution'.

288 S. apparently means that the geometers postulate things not because they are intrinsically unprovable, like axioms, but because the student does not possess the premises from which they can be proved.

289 Presumably as opposed to the higher Platonic discipline also called 'dialectic': cf. 49,8 ff.

290 *Topics* 1.2, 101a34-b4.

291 This follows closely the first sentence of Ar.'s *Topics*, 100a18-21.

292 Reading *prolambanôn* with DEMo.

293 For the verb *aneuphêmeitai* here, cf. 1360,20, Al., *in Metaph.* 767,30. Damascius in *On First Principles* uses the verb seven times for some philosopher proclaiming some principle or some attribute of some principle.

294 For this conception of philosophy, cf. David, *Prolegomena to Philosophy* 6,31.

295 This sounds odd: surely the mathematicians do declare (*apophainein*) the principles of their science. The text ought to distinguish these from the principles which are

178   *Notes to pp. 90–4*

undeclared, unexamined, and merely used once conceded; the latter are surely the principles of a higher science, or those common to all sciences (for the latter idea one could easily emend to get *hoias koinas autoi legousin* at 48,12-13).

296 Eudemus fr. 34 Wehrli.

297 In this passage S. confusingly combines a range of mathematical and philosophical usage: *horos* for 'definition' is both Euclidean and Aristotelian, *horos* for 'term' and *horismos* for 'definition' is Aristotelian. The idea of existence hypotheses as a distinct class of principles is from *An. Post.* 1.10.

298 *Physics* 1.2, 185a12-14.

299 As in the *Topics*, *thesis* here is evidently restricted to the deliberately paradoxical theses of the philosophers (cf. Ar., *Topics* 1.11, 104b19-24 for *thesis* as 'a paradoxical opinion held by someone famous in philosophy', with Heraclitus and Melissus as examples). S.'s point about Heraclitus seems to be that he only seemed to say that good and bad come to the same thing (without qualification): so properly understood his obscure doctrine is not a thesis at all in the present sense. See following note.

300 Following DEMo. Diels has *edokei . . . legôn*, the reading of F¹ (Aldus has *legón* also, but omits *edokei*). DEMo have *legein*: on our reading, *edokei* is completed by *legein*, so we delete Diels' comma after *edokei*. The two readings give different senses: Diels' text claims that Heraclitus *appeared* to assert a thesis in *saying* that good and bad agree in the same thing; according to DEMo, he only *appeared* to say that good and bad agree in the same thing.

301 Cf. DK 22B51; the reference to good and bad seems to be taken from Ar., *Physics* 1.2, 185b19-22, which Simplicius comments on at 82,23-25.

302 Following DEMoF, which have *ho* rather than Diels' and the Aldine's *hos*, though on this reading it is unclear what exactly is doing the asserting and speaking.

303 Cf. *Symposium* 187A5-6 and DK 22B51.

304 *Sophist* 242D7-243A1. The only variations from the OCT Plato are (i) the omission of a *tauta* in 242E4, which seems to make no difference to the sense, and (ii) in line 18, a *dê* (untranslated) where Plato's MSS and the OCT have an *aei*, 'always': 'For in differing it is always brought together'. Either S. has misread an uncial MS of Plato or our MSS of S. go back to a misreading of an uncial text of S.

305 Following DEMo rather than Diels, whose reading would yield 'a more appropriate example of the paradox at hand'.

306 Ar. speaks of 'apparently plausible premises' (*phainomena endoxa*) as the basis for eristic syllogisms (*SE* 165b7-8; *Topics* 100b24).

307 S. and Al. seem to be disagreeing about the conditions required for a position to count as a paradox or *thesis* in the present special sense: S. takes the (alleged) position of Melissus and Parmenides to count as it is offered only for the sake of argument, while Al. denies this, apparently taking it that a position offered with a supporting argument, however eristic, is not a *thesis*.

Notes to pp. 94–6

308 The force of *mallon* here is unclear. We translate *mallon phortikon* as simply adjectival ('rather vulgar'); S. may read it as comparative ('more vulgar' [*sc.* than Parmenides]). A further alternative (which the word order makes plausible) is to take it as an introductory conjunction: 'Rather, the argument of Melissus is vulgar . . .'.

309 = *Physics* 185a32-33. Ar.'s MSS read *to on apeiron einai phêsin. poson ara ti to on*, which DK prints for Melissus as the first part of DK 30A11. Of S.'s MSS, aF also have *on*, giving the text translated; DEMo have *hen* for the first *on*, giving the sense, 'the one is infinite'. (The only other divergence is that Mo omits the *to* in the second *to on*.) The quotation is repeated at 77,7, where the same disagreement among the manuscripts as to the first *to on/to hen* is repeated. This time, however, Diels prefers *hen* in both the first and the second occurrences (apparently with unanimous MSS support in the latter case): 'He says the one is infinite. Therefore the one is a quantum.' S.'s point at 77,7 is to note an alternative reading, so it makes sense that the two citations would differ, confirming the plausibility of *to on* for both occurrences here.

310 Diels, following Torstrik, deletes *ousia*, against the consensus of the MSS. Mo adds *têi* before the *ousia*. We follow Mo and read the phrase as an apposition: cf. 125,14; 269,1.

311 A paraphrase of *SE* 33, 182b32-33.

312 Here begins a dislocation in MS E: see the Note on Text and Translation, pp. 27–8. For a detailed discussion, see Dieter Harlfinger, 'Einige Aspekte der handschriftlichen Überlieferung des Physikkommentars des Simplikios', in Ilsetraut Hadot, ed., *Simplicius, sa vie, son oeuvre, sa survie* (Berlin: De Gruyter, 1987), pp. 267–94, at 267–86.

313 DK 20B8.43: see n. 315.

314 S. quotes extensively from the *Sophist* in *in Phys.* 1.1-2: for his interpretation of it, see Marc-Antoine Gavray, *Simplicius lecteur du Sophiste* (Paris: Klinksieck, 2007).

315 DK 20B8.43-45. S. cites partial and overlapping versions of these lines (and parts thereof), sometimes directly and sometimes from an intermediate source, also at *in Phys.* 89,22-24; 107,26; 126,21-22; 127,31; 137,16-17; 146,16-18.30. See Coxon, *Fragments of Parmenides* ad loc. for details.

316 *Sophist* 244E2-245A6, with only minor variations from Plato's MSS: in 'being one in this way since it is all and whole', 'one' is added, following Diels, from the text of Plato and S.'s citation at 89,28.

317 We omit *dêlon oun hoti tôn kinoumenôn ta onta*, which would mean something like 'clearly of the moved things, the beings'.

318 i.e. contra Al., soul is not to the point here, as it is a 'principle of nature' rather than a 'thing which is by nature'. S. goes on to note that Al. really agrees with the general point that principles are not in question here: the hypothesis that 'some or all things by nature move' is an *arkhê* only in the special sense of being an *arkhê* for us.

180   *Notes to pp. 96–9*

319 Following the Aldine in reading *èn* for the *ou* of the MSS, which gives no clearly good sense. It would also be possible to read *ou gar èn*, giving the sense 'it was not first by nature'.

320 Emending *enargôs* ('evidently') to *enargôn*.

321 *Pseudographêmata* are fallacies in geometry, which often turn on drawing something falsely (*pseudôs graphein*).

322 Antiphon's method of exhaustion should not be confused with the later, much more sophisticated method of exhaustion credited to Eudoxus and practised in Euclid, *Elements* 12.

323 i.e. the sides of the octagon just divided.

324 i.e. doubling the number of sides, not doubling the area.

325 Following Diels' conjecture of *ôieto* for the MSS *hôste* or *hôs to*.

326 Euclid, *Elements* 2.14.

327 So this is not a principle, and therefore cannot be the principle Antiphon is violating.

328 The reference is to Euclid, *Elements* 3.16, and apparently specifically to something that in many MSS is included as part of the Corollary to this proposition. S. notes later, in his discussion of Eudemus' presentation of Hippocrates, that part of his purpose is to fill out earlier accounts by adding references to Euclid (60,27-30).

329 *Contra* Protagoras (DK 80B7 = Ar., *Metaph.* 3.2, 997b34-998a4).

330 As becomes clear later (60,18-21), S. is following Al.'s commentary from 55,25 at least through to 57,29, and again at 58,25-59,22. After that, S. gives an alternative account of Hippocrates drawn from Eudemus.

331 While Ar. does not name Hippocrates here, S. and Al. before him fill in the reference in the light of *SE* 171b13-14 and/or of Eudemus' description of Hippocrates. See the *Introduction* for a detailed discussion of the issue, and of the whole passage on the squaring by means of segments. Ar. in the *SE* passage mentions a diagrammatic fallacy 'like that of Hippocrates or the squaring by means of lunes': it is possible but not certain that the 'or' is explicative, so that Ar. is identifying Hippocrates' fallacy with the squaring by means of lunes. (It is, however, possible that 'or the squaring by means of lunes' is a gloss, and it is not certain that Al. and S. read it in their texts of the *SE*.) Ar. also refers to the prospect of squaring the circle by means of lunes at *An. Pr.* 2.25, 69a30-34. Despite S.'s explanation in the next sentence, Ar. has been sloppy in calling Hippocrates' method 'by segments'; a lune (i.e. a figure bounded by two arcs) is not properly a segment (a figure bounded by an arc and a straight line); cf. S.'s discussion in 68,32 ff.

332 i.e. given any straight line AB, add a semicircle joining AB with G as midpoint, and add D as midpoint in the line AB.

333 i.e. let a semicircle AEG be circumscribed on the base of the straight line AG, making a larger arc past the arc AG. (E need not identify any particular point, it just marks this out as a new third line between A and G.)

Notes to pp. 99–102 181

334 i.e. any square one might draw with AB as one side.

335 Since the angle AGB is inscribed in a semicircle, the triangle AGB is right; since the sides AG and GB are equal, this triangle is half of a square. Describing the square as inscribed in the semicircle is slightly improper, since only this half of this square is contained in the semicircle.

336 *Elements* 12.2. Euclid proves this only for circles, but the result for semicircles follows trivially.

337 i.e. we know from elementary geometry how to construct a square equal to any given triangle or any other given rectilineal area.

338 There are no radii in the construction; the point is that each side of a regular hexagon inscribed in a circle (the notional circle with the diameter GD) is equal to a radius of that circle. In other words: each of BE, EZ, and ZD is equal to half GD, i.e. AB.

339 *Sc.* therefore we can take away from the trapezium a rectilineal figure equal to these lunes, leaving a rectilineal figure as the remainder. According to the report, Hippocrates is supposing, on the basis of the first half of his proof, that we can construct a rectilineal figure equal to any lune, and specifically the lunes GHE, EQZ, and ZKD. However, the first part of the proof showed only that the particular lune constructed there, the lune on the side of the inscribed square, could be squared. This would certainly be a fallacy, but as S. will go on to show (60,22-69,34), there is a more plausible alternative account (that of Eudemus) on which Hippocrates did not commit it.

340 S., following Al., imports the term *pseudographêma* from Ar.'s reference to Hippocrates in the *SE* (171b13-14: cf. note above at 55,25 ff.).

341 i.e. the kind of lune whose outer arc is a semicircle and whose inner arc is subtended by the diameter of the semicircle, taken as a side of a square inscribed in a circle.

342 We have no evidence as to who might have propounded this very unpromising method of circle-squaring: perhaps it was hypothesized to explain Ar.'s (arguable) reference at *SE* 171b13-14 to a squaring by means of lunes distinct from that of Hippocrates. We also do not know whether S. here follows Al. or draws on some other source; he goes on to qualify the present account in the following paragraph.

343 Diels prints but brackets *toiautê*, following E^bFa. We emend to *toiouto*, modifying *pseudographêma*, so that the claim is that the present method avoids 'this' diagrammatic fallacy, i.e. the one just discussed.

344 Deleting *tou henos*, 'of the one': it is unclear what 'the circle of the one' would mean, and the sentence makes good sense without it.

345 S. means that the objection fastens on a relatively trivial problem with this circle-squaring strategy; he does not mean that the objection is false (let alone that this strategy succeeds).

182 *Notes to pp. 102–4*

346 i.e. that the whole circle be divided into lunes is neither necessary nor sufficient for the squaring of the circle by lunes, so the objection does not bring out the crucial error here, which is to assume that because one kind of lune can be squared all lunes can be squared.

347 i.e. ending in the same digit that it is a power of. For this account of circular numbers and spherical numbers (see below), see Nicomachus, *Introduction to Arithmetic* 2.17.7.

348 By 'cumulative composition of [successive] odd numbers' S. means addition of all the odd numbers, beginning with one, up to some determinate number. This always results in a square.

349 That is, the unnamed proponent of the view that circular numbers are square perhaps did not use 'circular number' to mean a number which is the sum of successive odd numbers, but rather pointed out that circular numbers in the correct sense can be expressed as sums of successive odd numbers, although not all sums of successive odd numbers are circular.

350 For the idea that straight lines and circles are essentially unlike, so that no straight line can be found equal to a circle, cf. Ar., *Phys.* 7.4, 248a10-14 and 248b4-6.

351 Following MoE^{b}a in reading *kuklôi euthugrammon*.

352 By 'the angle of the semicircle' Ammonius means the angle between the circumference of the semicircle and its base; the remainder when this angle is subtracted from a right angle (the 'horn angle' (*keratoeidês*)) would be the angle between the circumference and the tangent.

353 i.e. the squaring of the circle. On the standard terminology some propositions in geometry are theorems, when they state a fact to be proved; others are problems, when they state a task to be accomplished. But S., and apparently Ammonius, call both types 'theorems'.

354 This has some overlap with what Ammonius says in his commentary on the *Categories* (75,10-19): perhaps S. is reporting a discussion which occurred in the context of Ammonius' lectures on the *Categories*.

355 Following MoE^{b}a and reading *anomoiogeneis*, not that there is a great difference in meaning from Diels' *anomogeneis* (following DF), 'of a different kind'. It is possible that at 59,32 a few lines above, *homogenês* 'of the same kind' should be *homoiogenês* 'of a like kind'.

356 One clear sense in which the horn angle is incomparable with any rectilineal angle is that no multiple of the horn angle will be greater than any rectilineal angle. Ar. in *Physics* 7.4 (cf. n. 350) suggests that a circular line and a straight line can never be comparable; S. seems to be disagreeing.

357 A reference to *Categories* 7b30-33 (which S. cites below 69,20-21), where Ar. says that even if the squaring of the circle is knowable, there is no knowledge of it as yet.

Notes to p. 104 183

358 It's unclear whether Iamblichus means to imply that the Pythagoreans had already discovered this by Ar.'s time, though Ar. himself did not find out about it.

359 *anôthen kata diadokhên*, lit., 'by succession from before', i.e. it was transmitted from his predecessors in the Pythagorean school.

360 The quotation from Iamblichus is also found in S.'s commentary on the *Categories*, 192,18-24. S. there adds that this construction seems to have escaped Porphyry's notice, and gives an appropriate quotation from Porphyry; he then adds the comment, 'So perhaps there has been a mechanical but not a demonstrative discovery of the theorem' (192,29-30).

361 S. often uses the phrase to correct what has just been cited and add his own conclusions. He is here adding a qualification to Iamblichus' claim, perhaps in order to suggest that such mechanical methods do not really count as squaring the circle (in the sense that Ar., for instance, would have understood the problem). Similar scruples were often expressed about mechanical solutions to geometrical problems, including the duplication of the cube.

362 Except for 'Sextus the Pythagorean', these are all known geometers who did indeed show how to construct a square equal to a given circle, not by straightedge-and-compass procedures (which is indeed impossible), but by more complicated mechanical procedures. Archimedes does so in the extant *On Spirals*; for the others, and for the history of the problem in general, see W. R. Knorr, *The Ancient Tradition of Geometrical Problems*, (Boston: Birkhäuser, 1986). 'Sextus the Pythagorean' has a Roman name, so if he is a real person he is almost certainly later than Archimedes, Apollonius and Nicomedes, who all lived in the third century BCE (Carpus' dates are uncertain). He might be the person behind the extant *Sentences of Sextus*, but that text contains nothing mathematical. Iamblichus adds Sextus' name in order to suggest that the Pythagoreans were involved in the discovery, and perhaps that the Pythagoreans had handed down this knowledge since before Aristotle's time.

363 Referring back to 56,1-29, culminating in the judgement at 57,25-29, though Al. is not named there and S. apparently presents the judgement as his own.

364 *apo tês ... anamnêseôs*, lit. 'from memory', on the most common sense of *apo*, but the sense seems to be as above. S. will fill in the references to elementary results that Eudemus implicitly assumes.

365 On hypomnematic writings, cf. S.'s remarks at the start of *in Cat.* (4,14-21), where they are the author's provisional notes for his own use, in contrast to syntagmatic writings intended for wider circulation, which include both dialogues and treatises. According to David (or Elias), *in Cat.* 114,1-14, syntagmatic writings are distinguished by having introductions and conclusions, and diction appropriate for published writing.

366 The opposite of 'superficial' (*epipolaios*) might be 'difficult' or 'important'; *diagramma* here presumably refers to the whole geometrical proof rather than

184   *Notes to pp. 104–6*

merely the diagram. While it is elementary to square a rectilineal figure, squaring a curvilinear figure like the lune is much more difficult, and raises the hope that the circle too can be squared.

367 'In power' (*dunamei*): X has a certain ratio to Y 'in power' if X-squared has that ratio to Y-squared.

368 This falls far short of a rigorous proof that similar circle-segments (*tmêmata*) are to each other as their circles; it gives an intuitive argument but a rigorous proof would depend on the method of exhaustion. Also, S. is at best speaking imprecisely in saying that a segment could be a third part of a circle; he may be thinking of a sector (*tomeus*) of a circle.

369 Diels takes the rest of this paragraph as quotation from Eudemus, but this has been disputed by more recent scholars, starting with Oskar Becker's 'Zur Textgestaltung des eudemischen Berichts über die Quadratur der Mondchen durch Hippokrates von Chios,' *Quellen und Studien zur Geschichte der Mathematik, Astronomie und Physik* B3 (1936), 411–19.

370 Here by 'the angle of a segment' Eudemus means the angle inscribed in that segment, not the angle between the circumference and the base of the segment, which is what Euclid calls the angle of a segment. What Eudemus calls the angle of a segment, Euclid calls the angle *in* a segment (Book 3, definitions 7-8).

371 Compare Al.'s account at 56,1-19.

372 Book 3, definition 11.

373 *Elements* 1.47.

374 S. is implicitly citing Euclid *Elements* 1.4, and the relevant part of Euclid's conclusion is that the remaining sides are also equal, i.e. EB = EG. We can show similarly that EA = ED. It will follow that the trapezium can be circumscribed in a circle if we also know that EA = EG. S. does not prove this, but it can be easily proved. Produce the lines BA and DG until they intersect at the point Z. We will have ZA:AB::ZG:GD. Since BA = DG, the triangle ZAG is isosceles, so angle ZAG = angle ZGA. Consequently angle BAG = angle DGA; consequently their halves, angles EAG and EGA, are also equal, so triangle EAG is isosceles.

375 In a triangle ABG, the line BG 'subtends' or 'subtends under' the angle BAG; here Eudemus says that the line BG 'subtends under' the lines AB and BG.

376 For instance, the diagonal BG, which subtends under the equal sides AB and AG, is more than double each of these sides in power, since the angle BAG is obtuse. It is therefore also more than double in power the one remaining (non-base) side GD, since the three sides are all equal.

377 It is controversial whether and how far the quotation from Eudemus continues from this point. Becker holds that 63,1-11 is not a quotation but a supplement justifying Eudemus' conclusions, whereas Diels holds that with the exception of the references to Euclid, these lines are from Eudemus. Becker also excludes all letters

Notes to pp. 106–8

in 63,11-18. These proposals would have the effect that Eudemus' account of the
second squaring, like his account of the first, has no letters. Letters would however
remain in his account of the third and fourth squarings. In support of Becker, S.'s
presentation here of the second squaring uses phrases like *hê BD* to mean the line
BD; this is the standard later Greek usage but contrasts with Eudemus' third and
fourth squarings, which use the older phrase *hê eph' hêi BD*, 'the [line] on which
BD', i.e. the line on top of which the letters B and D have been written. S. would not
use the older expression except where it was in his source, but it is possible that
Eudemus goes back and forth between the two expressions; Ar. uses both.

378 'Lines which join equal and parallel lines are themselves equal and parallel': Euclid,
Elements 1.33.

379 It seems to be assumed here that the meeting-point Z lies beyond AG, rather than
beyond BD or in between the two lines. It cannot lie between the two lines if BA
and GD are sides of a trapezium. Because AG and BD are parallel, the triangles
ZAG and ZBD are similar, so since the line AG is less than the line BD, ZA must be
less than ZB, and so Z must lie beyond AG rather than beyond BD.

380 We emend the text here, substituting AGZ for the MSS' GAZ.

381 S. would have done better to cite 1.16, which says that the external angle of a triangle is
greater than either of the opposite internal angles; instead he cites the stronger and
more famous 1.32, which says that the external angle is equal to the sum of the two
opposite internal angles. We do not follow Diels in positing a lacuna before this phrase.

382 Following a proposal of Henry Mendell, we emend to *elattôn*, 'less' in place of the
MSS' *hêmiseia*, 'half'. Since triangle ZAG is isosceles (which S. has not explicitly
shown, but which is easily shown, see n. 374), angle GAZ is equal to angle AGZ, so
angle GAZ too is less than angle BAG, and thus angle BAG is obtuse.

383 This is true because lines BA and AG are equal and BG is greater in power than
lines BA and AG together (by Euclid, *Elements* 2.12, since angle BAG is obtuse).

384 This is because the lines BG and GD are together greater in power than the line BD;
if angle BGD were right, they would be equal in power to line BD, and if angle
BGD were obtuse, they would be less in power than line BD.

385 With this whole account of the second lune-squaring, compare Al., reported above
at 56,22-57,24. Eudemus' and Al.'s constructions both involve a trapezium with
three equal sides inscribed in an arc of a circle. But they are not the same
trapezium: for Al., the long side is double the other sides (i.e. his trapezium is a
half-hexagon), while for Eudemus the long side is three times the others in power.
(Eudemus' third construction will also involve a trapezium with three equal sides,
cf. 64,7-67,6.) Again, see the *Introduction* for details of these constructions.

386 As noted above, Eudemus in this and the next construction says literally '[the line]
on which are AB' (*eph' hêi* or *hê eph' hêi AB*) to mean the line AB. We have not
rendered this construction literally.

186   *Notes to pp. 108–10*

387 A line 'points' (*neuei*) towards a point if it would touch that point when extended. *Neusis*-constructions, i.e. the construction of a line which points towards a certain point and satisfies certain other conditions, were one common way of constructing objects which could not be constructed with straightedge-and-compass alone. (The present figure, however, could have been constructed with straightedge and compass, suggesting that Hippocrates did not share the later preference for 'elementary' construction methods.) In the case at hand, imagine the point Z starting at G and moving along the line GD until it hits the semicircle. The line ZE (that is, the continuation of the line BZ until it hits the circle again) will start by being more than one and a half times the radii in power and will end by going to zero; so at some point in between it will be exactly one and a half times the radii in power.

388 The corollary says that a line which perpendicularly bisects a chord of a circle passes through the centre of the circle. So if the trapezium EKBH is inscribed in a circle, KB will be a chord of that circle, and therefore DG, which perpendicularly bisects KB, will pass through the centre of that circle. S. does not show here that the trapezium is indeed inscribed in a circle, but this can be shown as follows. The triangle ZKB is isosceles, so angle ZKB equals angle ZBK; but because KB and EH are parallel, angle ZBK equals angle ZEH. Therefore angle HKB is equal to angle HEB, therefore the points EKBH all lie on a circle. S., or perhaps Eudemus, will give an argument in the next paragraph that the trapezium can be inscribed in a circle.

389 *Elements* 3.3 says that if a line through the centre of a circle bisects a line not through the centre, then it also cuts it perpendicularly, and if it cuts it perpendicularly then it also bisects it. S. has not actually shown that EH does not pass through the centre, but if it does then D will be the centre and GD will bisect EH. Diels' bracketing of *mê dia tou kentrou* is unnecessary.

390 Since the lines EB and KH intersect at the 'vertex' Z, the angles BZH and EZK are called vertical: all such angles are equal by Euclid, *Elements* 1.15.

391 In the MSS and in Diels' text, this paragraph begins with the sentence we have placed at the end. It is agreed that this sentence logically presupposes steps in the construction carried out in the paragraph and that Eudemus could not have put it at the beginning of the paragraph. Diels, following Usener, supposes that S. moved it to the beginning of the paragraph; we suggest that the mistake is that of a later scribe.

392 It is disputed how much of the preceding two sentences is a quotation from Eudemus: Diels prints the first sentence as a quote, the second as S., while Becker (mainly following the criterion of archaic geometrical usage) takes the words through 'will also pass through B' to be S. and the remainder to be Eudemus.

393 It was shown that EZ = HZ and that ZB = ZK; adding, we have EB = HK; we also showed that BH = KE; so the triangles EHB and HEK are congruent; so angle BHE equals angle KEH, as was to be shown.

Notes to pp. 110–11   187

394 This line is problematic in text and sense (as well as location). After 'So let there be circumscribed around the triangle EZH a circle-segment', E^{b}Mo have 'EZH', presumably in apposition as the name of the circle-segment, which gives the wrong sense (namely that the entire segment EZH would be similar to the segment EK); Diels secludes the 'EZH', but this does not solve the problem. Da have 'EZ', which gives the correct sense to the latter part of the sentence (namely that the segment EZ is similar to the segment EK), but this cannot be in apposition with *tmêma*, so emendation is required. We add *hou* ('of which') to the reading of Da, translating *tmêma kuklou hou to EZ*.

395 This presupposes that the segments EK, KB, and BH, all cut out of the same circle EKBH, are similar, which is true if and only if the lines EK, KB, and BH are equal. But EK and KB are radii of the same circle, and it has been shown that BH is equal to EK. It also needs to be shown that the segments EZ and ZH, cut out of the circle EZH, are similar to these segments. To show this it is sufficient to show that angle EZH is equal to angle EKB; but the triangles ZEH and KBE are both isosceles, and angle ZEH is equal to angle ZBK, since EZB lie on a line and EH and KB are parallel. Therefore the triangles are similar and the result follows. We print two diagrams for this construction, where Diels prints only one more crowded diagram.

396 Diels marks all of this as a quote from Eudemus; Becker (following his criterion of archaic geometrical terminology) marks as S.'s supplements the phrases 'whose outer circumference is EKBH' and 'BZH, BZK, and EKZ' in the first sentence, the 'cut off by the lines BK, KB, and BH' in the second sentence, and the whole of the last sentence.

397 An almost verbatim quotation from Euclid, but what S. needs is actually the converse of this, which does follow from the same proposition.

398 This promise (whoever may be making it) is not fulfilled in S.'s text. But angle KZB is greater than angle ZEK, the external than the internal angle, and angle ZEK is equal to angle ZBK since triangle KEB is isosceles.

399 We translate *phaneron hoti hê eph' hêi BE meizôn esti* where the MSS have *phaneron hoti kan hê eph' hêi BE meizôn ê*, and Diels prints *phaneron hoti kan hê eph' hêi BK meizôn ê*.

400 We translate *estai* where Diels prints a lacuna followed by *hôste*.

401 The MSS, followed by Diels, have 'in length and power', but 'in length' is false, and is neither supported by nor contributes to the argument. Whoever wrote *diplasia mêkei* here, whether S. or a later scribe, was probably influenced by the same phrase in the previous line (66,18).

402 The triangles BEK and BKZ are similar, since they are both isosceles and have the same base angle at B. Thus EB is to BK as BK (or EK) is to KZ. Since EB is more than twice BZ (or KZ) in length, EK (which is the geometrical mean between EB and KZ) will be more than twice KZ in power.

403 Scholars have differed as to how much of this paragraph comes from Eudemus and have offered different reconstructions of Eudemus' text.

188 *Notes to pp. 112–14*

404 S. here reports from Eudemus how Hippocrates squared a figure consisting of a circle together with a lune. Ar. refers to the same or a closely related construction at *Prior Analytics* 2.25, 69a30-34, where he presents it as a step in reducing the problem of circle-squaring: since we can square a figure consisting of a circle together with a lune, we have reduced the problem of squaring the circle to the problem of constructing such a figure equal to a given circle. See the *Introduction*.

405 Diels and Becker attribute the first part of this sentence to Eudemus, but the 'rather' (*alla*) suggests that it is part of S.'s response to Al.

406 By 'the segment circumscribed about HI' (or, later, 'the segment HI') Eudemus and S. mean the segment HI which is similar to the segments HQ and QI and is entirely contained within the triangle HQI, not the larger segment which encompasses the triangle HQI. We follow Diels in printing the preceding as an unbroken quotation from Eudemus, but Becker is probably right that the part in parentheses is S.'s supplement.

407 *All* circles are similar.

408 Diels prints the passage from 'For HI has power . . .' down to here as a quotation from Eudemus. Becker is more likely to be right that it is part of S.'s supplement.

409 Diels prints this whole passage as a quotation from Eudemus, but Becker thinks that the four sentences beginning with 'For the segment HI . . .' and also the sentence beginning 'For the triangle was equal . . .' are S.'s supplements.

410 S. is combining the lemma (185a14-17), which speaks of falsehood but not of graphic fallacies, with *SE* 171b13-14.

411 This does not belong to any of S.'s quotations from Al.; perhaps it is an allusion to 55,26-28.

412 Diels' text, following E^ba, says only 'the three in the lesser [circle]'; but there were six such segments. Manuscript D has *tôn te triôn en tôi elattoni*, which means that the three were to be followed by 'and . . .' but no further phrase is supplied. We emend to *tôn te triôn en tôi meizoni kai tôn hex en tôi elattoni*. Tannery (in Diels) suggests an emendation in the same sense.

413 Book 3, definition 6.

414 Presumably S.'s point would be that if Hippocrates committed a fallacy here it was a properly geometric fallacy, of the kind it belongs to a geometer to resolve. The fallacy would consist in offering as a squaring of the circle a squaring of the circle together with another figure. But there is no reason to believe that Hippocrates offered it as a squaring of the circle.

415 *Categories* 7b31-33, with various minor deviations from the text of Ar. as we have it. S. is quoting in what seems to have been roughly the standard version in the Alexandrian school of his time: see Minio-Paluello's apparatus in the OCT. The version S. cites in his later *Categories* commentary is only slightly different (192,13-15).

Notes to pp. 114–16 189

416 The MSS, and Diels, have *epi aoristôn* ('on indeterminate [chords]'). But as Tannery notes (as cited in Diels, p. xxxi), these chords are in fact determinate. We emend to *epi allôs horistôn*.

417 'About nature' (*peri phuseôs*) has closer to a technical sense than the English, because of *Peri Phuseôs* being used (as S. assumes) as the standard book title for works of Presocratic natural science. The 'not' in the first sentence here could go either with 'speaking about nature', as translated here, or with 'stating natural aporiai', so the sentence (with different punctuation) could be taken either as translated here or as meaning 'since it results that they are speaking about nature but not stating natural aporiai'. S., following Al., will discuss both options; our translation adopts his preferred reading here (i.e. what he lists as Al.'s second reading). S. also notes this issue at *in Cael.* 7,24-26; apparently there as here he favours Al.'s second reading, though Heiberg in his *CAG* edition punctuates so as to imply the other reading.

418 Porphyry fr. 122 Smith.

419 Presumably *in Cael.* 556,25-557,12 (discussing *On the Heaven* 3.1, 298b14-24).

420 *SE* 164b22-23. This and the following citation are of occurrences of the same grammatical construction as Al.'s second reading here (*X men ou, Y de*).

421 *SE* 165a3-4.

422 An expression in a text is 'appropriate' (*katallêlos*) if, under a given interpretation of the author's intent, it is correctly expressed and does not need to be emended or rewritten for clarification.

423 *Phys.* 184b25.

424 Themistius, *in Phys.* 4,15-18.

425 Al. here seems to be taking issue with the interpretation credited to Porphyry above, that Parmenides and Melissus abolished nature 'unwittingly'.

426 Following E^bMoFa in reading *mêden*, against D and Diels, who have *mêde*.

427 Cf. 38,20 above.

428 The Aldine and Diels both offer supplements to the text. Diels, after 'about nature in the strict sense', writes 'nonetheless stated natural aporiai, having entitled his treatise *On Nature . . .*' before '*or On What Is*' (taken as the latter part of Melissus' title). But it is unclear how this would contribute to the present critique of Al.'s inconsistency. S. believes that both Parmenides and Melissus give accounts of changing sensible things, while denying that they are real beings (cf. *in Cael.* 556-60). It is unlikely that he would praise Al. for saying here that Parmenides and Melissus did not talk about nature and criticize him for saying in the earlier passage that they did. More likely, when S. says 'And this much he has said rightly', he is praising Al. only for saying that they raised natural aporiai. While Al. would be right that they are not 'speaking about nature' when they argue that what is is free from motion, he is going too far in saying that they *never* 'spoke about nature', since

190 *Notes to pp. 116–18*

they did give positive accounts of the world of appearances. But when they did that, they were not speaking about nature in the strict sense, since, as Melissus' title implies, nature in the strict sense is what really is.

429 X entails Y, literally 'uses Y in addition' (*proskhrêtai*), if X implicitly presupposes Y, in the way that even and odd implicitly presuppose number.

430 *Anairein* ('abolish') is apparently a generic term for successful critical argument: to *anairein* a doctrine would be to refute it (but *elenkhein* would be more precise); to *anairein* an argument would be to show it to be fallacious (*luein* would be more precise).

431 S.'s discussion of this argument, described as 'dialectical' in the next sentence, extends to the next lemma at 80,19. The argument is presumably dialectical in that it interrogates Parmenides and Melissus as to the nature of their One-which-is. However, as S. notes at 75,6, the division of being on which the attack relies is hardly the work of a neutral 'questioner'. Ar.'s argument against the Eleatic position continues with a matching attack on the Eleatic use of 'One'; he turns to overturning the Eleatic arguments only in *Physics* 1.3.

432 Torstrik (in Diels) suggests *tou toioutou henos ontas* (rather than *toioutou henos ontos*), 'taken as supporting such a one'.

433 Cf. *Topics* 1.1, 101b2-4.

434 Emending *ousian,* reserved for 'substance' elsewhere in the passage, to *on*; Torstrik proposed *hen*, 'one', which gives a reasonable sense but is a bolder emendation. Assuming Simplicius wrote 'being', the sense would be 'all things have the same predicate, namely being, and in that sense they are one [although, since only the name of the predicate is the same, not its meaning, they would not be one in reality]'. Diels' positing of a substantial lacuna seems unnecessary.

435 Reading *ê* with aD rather than *ei* with EFMo.

436 It is unclear why this counts as an addition to the division, given that the point is made in the lemma. Perhaps it applies only to the 'and they have their existence in it', which does seem to be a new point. The phrasing echoes 72,8, but the points do not seem closely related.

437 These two concluding sentences closely follow Ar.'s phrasing in the lemma, with 'finite' added so as to apply to Parmenides as well as Melissus.

438 S., following Porphyry, thinks the passage is a division of 'being', followed by a division of 'one' starting at 185b5-7; Al. thinks that there is one big division of both concepts together, with 185b5 initiating a subdivision of the ways in which something can be numerically one.

439 Here and at 74,5, see Porphyry fr. 123 Smith.

440 The phrasing here (*to hen onoma*) is ambiguous, between 'the name "one"' and 'the one name': the sense will be either that 'one' is predicated as a name or that one name, presumably 'being', is predicated. The latter seems to be what Al. has in mind.

Notes to pp. 118–20 191

441 Tentatively reading *onoma* with EFMoa, rejecting Diels' supplement *hen* ('one'); D
   has *on*, 'if being is said in many ways'.

442 The 'or in number' joins Diels in following F²a.

443 This is a paraphrase of *Physics* 185b7-9.

444 There is a disagreement between Al. and Porphyry regarding the argument of the
   lemma; S. mainly follows Porphyry. On Al.'s reading, when Ar. at *Phys.* 185a22-23
   asks whether all things are substance or quanta or qualia, he means to ask whether
   the Eleatics hold that all things are generically one in the sense of falling under a
   single category. When Ar. then in turn asks (at 185a23-26) whether all things are
   one substance, as one human, etc., he is asking whether they are numerically one.
   Al. also complains that when at 185a27 ff. Ar. would be expected take up each of
   these options and show its absurdity, the first option he discusses, namely that there
   is substance *and* quantity *and* quality, is not in fact one of the options noted earlier
   (nor is it something any Eleatic would say). S., following Porphyry (cf. 74,5 ff.),
   takes it that when in 185a22-23 Ar. asks whether all things are substance, etc., he
   meant from the start to ask whether they are numerically one. And indeed, Ar. does
   not here explicitly address the 'one in genus' option. On the other hand, it is hard to
   make sense of his presentation of the two questions at 185a22-26 without seeing
   oneness in genus as mooted by the first of them: 'Are all things substance, or
   quanta, or qualia?'.

445 *Phys.* 185b5-6.

446 Accepting Diels' emendation *to*, or Torstrik's emendation *to tôi*, for *tôi*.

447 We follow Diels in treating this as a quotation from Al., on the basis of S.'s comment
   at the close, but it cannot be quite verbatim.

448 = *Phys.* 185a27-28 with a slight change.

449 The 'absurdities' here are the possibility that 'there are going to be both substance
   and quale and quantum'; this is equivalent to the option of holding that things are
   one in name only (i.e. that they share in the name 'being', but in different senses).

450 Accepting Torstrik's emendation of *phasi* for *phêsi*.

451 Diels suggests an emendation of *dia touto* ('because of this') for *dia ti* ('why?'); with
   a change in punctuation, this would give the sense: 'Because of this [i.e. for the
   reason just given] he argued against ...' etc. This makes the sentence somewhat
   redundant with the previous one, but the transmitted text raises a question which
   seems to have just been answered (by 'for the sake of completeness').

452 Eudemus fr. 35 Wehrli.

453 MSS EMo, followed by Diels, have a *mê* here: 'if substance does not exist'. This gives
   a reaffirmation of the previous point: 'if substance does not exist, there is nothing
   underlying'. On the reading we adopt, the sense provides a contrast with the
   previous part of the sentence, i.e. 'whereas if substance exists, nothing has to
   underlie it'. Either way there is an abrupt shift in sense in the next line, where 'if

192 *Notes to pp. 120–2*

nothing underlies' refers to the prospect of substances without any predicates to be subjects of.

454 *Phaedrus* 237B7-C2, with omissions.

455 All MSS have *stênai*: it is unclear what this could mean, so we follow the Aldine and Diels in emending to *enstênai*, 'raise objections about'. An anonymous referee suggests retaining *stênai* in the sense of 'take any intellectual attitude towards' (LSJ *histêmi* B2).

456 *Epei*; Ar.'s text as printed by Ross, and S.'s lemma as printed by Diels (70,1), have *epeidê*, but it makes no difference to the sense.

457 That is, Ar.'s argument is not a dialectical argument from what a respondent will concede, but is based on his own positive theory.

458 We read *hontinaoun* in 75,9 (Diels has *hontina oun*, the MSS vary), to give the sense 'in any way whatsoever'. It is hard to see what *oun* would mean here as a separate particle, and it would be awkward to take *kath' hontina tropon* as 'in any way': it would standardly be 'in which way'. If we do take it as 'in which way' then the *ei*, 'if' must then govern the genitive absolute: 'if being is said in many ways, in what way it is possible'.

459 *Phys.* 185a30.

460 Mo apparently confirms Brandis' conjecture (in Diels), *topasai* (hence *a-topon*, 'absurd'); other MSS have *to pasai* or *to pasaito*.

461 Presumably also etymological, with *khôra* standing in for *topos* (both mean 'place').

462 *Phys.* 185b16-19.

463 Cf. *Phys.* 186a32 ff.

464 We follow Diels' text; the MSS vary significantly here, with some extended omissions. Ar. in *Categories* 2, 1a20-b9, distinguishes between being *in* an underlying thing and being said *of* an underlying thing: a species is said *of* its individuals but is not *in* them, while an individual token quality is *in* a substance but is not said *of* the substance. But outside the *Categories*, Ar. generally uses 'in an underlying thing' and 'of an underlying thing' as equivalent, and, as S. says, Ar. here uses 'of an underlying thing' for the accidents of a substance.

465 *Sc.* the species and genera, so described in the *Categories*.

466 Since the next point seems a separate one, we take the quotation from Al. to end here; Diels does not mark the end of the quotation.

467 For instance, number is included in the defining account of even, which 'belongs to' it (i.e. is predicated of it). In strict grammar, S. would be saying that number is predicated per se of even, but what he means, as is clear from context and from the *An. Post.*, is that even is predicated per se of number. For the two different ways in which one thing may be predicated of another, cf. *An. Post.* 1.4, 73a34-b3.

468 Cf. Euclid, *Elements* 7, definition 6.

469 The case of 'white' is in *Metaphysics* 7.6 (1031b22-28) and by implication in *Categories* 5 (2a27-34): 'white' can mean an instance of whiteness or the object which has that whiteness.

Notes to pp. 122–4 193

470 *Phys.* 185b2-3.

471 Start of 1.3, 186a5-6. Ar. is here introducing his objections to the arguments offered for monism, in keeping with S.'s earlier (71,20-28) distinction between arguing against a position as a whole (*katholikê*), as Ar. has so far been doing, and presenting objections to the arguments offered in its favour. S. here seems to use *katholikê* in a somewhat different sense, for argument against the Eleatic position in general as opposed to Melissus' version of it in particular.

472 At 185a32-33, in the lemma above. The difference is *to hen* ('one') for *to on* ('being'): instead of the lemma's 'Now Melissus says that what is is infinite, so what is will be a quantum', these MSS have 'Now Melissus says that the one is infinite, so the one will be a quantum'.

473 As opposed to the Platonic One-itself, which is beyond being.

474 S.'s conclusion at 79,5 will be that Al.'s points are fair enough (but compatible with the 'ancient philosophy', properly read) if he means to claim that what comes-to-be and passes away 'exists' in a weak and 'improper' sense; but he is wrong if he means to claim that it exists in the strict sense.

475 Diels follows the Aldine in adding 'and passing away'; none of the MSS (DEFMo) have this.

476 Or, with some MSS, 'even what comes-to-be and passes away'.

477 Cf. Ar. against the Heracliteans at *Metaphysics* 4.5, 1010a15-22.

478 'All together' (*homou pan*) is an allusion to Parmenides B8.5, cited below.

479 Cf. Parmenides B8.29: Being 'remains the same in the same', without generation and destruction. Cf. also Xenophanes B26.

480 A paraphrase of Heraclitus B91.

481 'Marks' is *sêmeia*, recalling Parmenides DK 28B8.2 ff. on the *sêmata* of Being.

482 Following Mo, who confirms Torstrik's conjecture *sumphurousin*; cf. *sunanapephurtai* at 77,23 and 79,6. Diels prints the other MSS' *sumpherousin*, 'bring together', 'collect'.

483 For our policies and issues raised by S.'s Parmenides quotations, cf. n. 178. Here as elsewhere we follow Diels' *CAG* text except as noted.

484 Parmenides B6.8-9: also included in a longer citation at *in Phys.* 117,12-13.

485 Parmenides B7.2, also cited at *in Phys.* 144,1 and 650,13, and via Plato's *Sophist* at 135,22 and 244,2.

486 B8.1-3, also at 142,34-36 and included in the longer citation of B8 at 145,1 ff. (S.'s longest and presumably most reliable quotation from Parmenides B8 is of B8.1-52 at *in Phys.* 145,1 ff.; smaller sections are repeatedly quoted elsewhere.) Some MSS in some occurrences have *de ti* rather than *eti* ('only'); it is unclear how this would be translated.

487 Translating *mounogenes*; other sources have *oulomeles* ('whole of limb'): cf. also *in Phys.* 30,2 above, with note ad loc.

194 *Notes to pp. 124–8*

488 On 'unending' (*ateleston*) cf. n. 183.

489 B8.3-14. These verses are cited as part of a larger quotation at 145,3-14 and portions of them at 30,1-3; 87,21; 120,23; 143,13; 162,18-22; and *in Cael.* 137,3-6.

490 *Huphistanai* is a standard Neoplatonic term for something less than full existence, used of objects which exist incidentally or as by-products.

491 *Tim.* 37E4-38A2, with several minor variations. For S.'s *anapherontes*, the OCT has *ha dê pherontes*.

492 Following Diels' supplement (following the Aldine) of *eis*, 'into', and further adding an *an* in the consequent for a regular conditional construction: *ouden an ekôlue to eis allo toionde metaballein* or *oud' an ekôlueto* . . . . (The MSS actually have *ekôlueto*, which Diels following the Aldine prints as *ekôlue to*). S. here sides with Parmenides: Parmenidean being, since it is being *simpliciter*, cannot change without ceasing to be. Al.'s point that ordinary substances can change without ceasing to be is apparently irrelevant to being in the strict sense.

493 'Alteration' (*alloiôsis*) is qualitative change, the 'motion in respect of quality' referred to earlier.

494 Or, 'is just "what is"', picking up on the earlier use of 'what just is' (*hoper on*) (79,11) for the Parmenidean being.

495 B8.26-28, also included in the extended citation of B8 at 145,1 ff. and at 39,27-40,1: see n. 238 for the textual difficulty surrounding *têle* ('far away')/*têde*.

496 Cf. 40,12-15 (see note there), 112,6-10, and the paraphrase at 104,5-7. This and the following quotation are parts of DK 30B7, given in full (and with no significant variations) by S. at *in Phys.* 111,18-112,15.

497 Part of DK 30B7, repeated with no significant variations at 40,18-22 and 112,12-15. Cf. also the paraphrase at 104,10-13, on which see n. 240.

498 Some MSS of Ar. have *on*, 'being'.

499 Porphyry fr. 124 Smith.

500 This closely resembles the definition of *genos* given at *Topics* 1.5, 102a31-32, and Porphyry, *Isagôgê* 2,15-16; the latter is what anyone 'introduced to the rudiments of logic' would be familiar with.

501 The sense here seems clear, though the construction is atypical; if necessary, we emend *tois ta prôta tôn logikôn eisêgmenois* to *tois eis ta prôta tôn logikôn eisêgmenois*.

502 For the Aristotelian definition of continuity, cf. *Phys.* 5.3, 227a11-12; for its being divisible into parts that are always themselves divisible, cf. 6.1, 231b15-18.

503 The Greek term *adiaireton* can mean either 'indivisible' or 'undivided'.

504 Adding *oun* with Brandis. Alternatively, we could take the previous sentence merely as listing the senses of 'one as indivisible', and the present sentence as continuous with it, drawing the consequences for 'what is'.

505 Or: 'it will have a quantity, namely its magnitude, and a quality, namely its figure'. Magnitudes are a species of quantity and figures a species of quality.

Notes to pp. 129–32   195

506 *Phys.* 185b17-18.

507 *Phys.* 185b18-19 with minor variation.

508 Reading *antiphaseôs* with DEMo against Diels' *apophaseôs*, which follows Fa.

509 For Ar.'s theory of the four kinds of opposition (contradictories, contraries, possession and privation, and correlatives), see *Metaph.* 5.10; *Categories* 10.

510 Cf. Porphyry fr. 128 Smith.

511 *Phys.* 185b11-16. Cf. Porphyry fr. 125 Smith. At 83,28 ff. S. reiterates his self-correction here: Ar. himself, unlike his interpreters, is careful to frame the argument in terms of whether part and whole are one, not whether they are the same.

512 S.'s discussion of the aporia will repeatedly refer to Ar.'s mention of non-continuous parts (at *Phys.* 185b14), with reference to discussions in Al. and Porphyry. It is indeed unclear what Ar.'s distinction between continuous and non-continuous parts consists in (two interpretations will be distinguished at 85,2 ff.), and why Ar. introduces it.

513 S. apparently understands the phrase translated hyperliterally here as 'exoteric to the argument' to mean something like 'extrinsic to the argument' or 'extrinsic to the discussion'. But when Eudemus is cited directly at 85,26, he calls the aporia simply 'exoteric', not 'exoteric to the argument'. Presumably what Eudemus meant is not so much that it is extrinsic to the present discussion but that it is part of popular discussions outside the Peripatetic school, possibly including non-technical contributions by Peripatetics to these popular discussions. See S. on Ar.'s 'exoteric' writings at 8,16-18.

514 At 85,21 ff.

515 The 'difficulty' (*aporia*) was a dilemma: is the whole one with or the same as the part, or is it other than the part? We have seen the difficulty with the first option; S. now turns to the second.

516 Al. uses the Stoic terminology of 'somehow disposed' (*pôs echon*) in order to argue that Stoicism lacks the resources to solve the aporia. The Stoics say that the whole is neither the parts plus something else, nor simply the parts, but the parts somehow disposed. The aporia about whether the whole is the same as all its parts, or is also something beyond them, goes back at least as far as *Theaetetus* 204A-205A.

517 Diels has the quotation from Al. continue to 85,2, where he immediately follows it with another quotation from Al. This is awkward; and the transition at 85,2 would be awkward within a single continuous quotation as well. The present paragraph does offer a solution to Al.'s reformulation of the aporia in the previous paragraph; and *mêpote* is a standard term used by S. to introduce his own views and solutions, particularly in response to Al. However, Al. also uses *mêpote* in the same way (e.g., at *in Metaph.* 141,14, 289,37, 390,16; *in Pr. An.* 117,9, 117,22, 153,2, 209,9), albeit less frequently, and we cannot exclude the possibility that he continues to be the speaker here.

196   *Notes to pp. 132–4*

518 The solution seems to be that 'the all' (*ta panta*), i.e. all of the parts taken collectively, is other than 'each' one of them taken individually. So even assuming that the all is the same as the whole, the parts (the 'eaches' taken individually) may be other than the whole, and so other than each other.

519 Al. has just mentioned hands and feet as examples of non-continuous parts. He now proposes that Ar. might be responding to someone who argues that homoeomerous parts, because continuous, are the same as their wholes even if anhomoeomerous ones like hands and feet are not; the response is that the distinction between homoeomerous and anhomoeomerous parts does not coincide with the distinction between continuous and non-continuous.

520 Eudemus here proposes that Ar. mentions non-continuous parts to confirm the immediately preceding rejection of the possibility that Being is one by being continuous. We follow Mo's *eirêtai tauta*, 'these things have been said' (aE have *eirêtai*, D *eirêke*).

521 Eudemus fr. 36 Wehrli.

522 Cf. 83,26-27. There, S. cited Eudemus as saying the aporia was 'exoteric to the *logos*'.

523 Accepting Diels' conjecture of *allêlois*, 'each other' for *holois*, 'wholes'.

524 We here retain the MSS' inferential *ara* in place of Diels' interrogative.

525 Adding a *hê* with Torstrik.

526 It is not at all obvious that S. is right in glossing Eudemus' claim that discrete parts will not be 'the same' to mean 'not the same as the continuous ones': Eudemus may well just mean that they are not the same as each other, and therefore not the same as the whole.

527 Diels here inserts a full stop, which is unnecessary and makes the double-barrelled contrast between Eudemus and Ar. harder to see.

528 Cf. 83,9 ff. and 85,8 ff. for Porphyry's reading of the part-whole aporia. On Porphyry's reading, Ar.'s point is to confront the objection that his division of senses of unity overlooks the distinct kind of unity which a whole has with a non-continuous part, e.g., Socrates and Socrates' hand – a reading which thus takes its cue, as S. here notes, from Ar.'s reference to non-continuous parts.

529 Presumably the 'part' of the aporia in question is the reference to non-continuous parts. On S.'s view, Porphyry is wrong to see Ar. as refuting objections that he ignores a fourth mode; rather, Ar. is dealing with opponents who believe that the continuous is one and not many, and who deny that the parts of a continuous thing are other than the whole, or other than each other. Ar.'s response would be that the same argument can be made in the case of non-continuous parts, which are clearly other than each other and must therefore be other than the whole. See 84,29 ff. for S.'s interpretation.

530 The MSS differ here (and at 87,23), with DEMo having *to* ('the') nominative, Fa *tôi* dative. The latter gives the preferable sense 'Thus (*tôi*) all is continuous'; and when S. gives a much longer and almost certainly more reliable citation at 145,26, the MSS

Notes to pp. 134–5   197

unanimously have *tôi*. But here and at 87,23, S. is presumably quoting loosely from memory.

531 B8.25.

532 B8.22, but S. has substituted 'and it is indivisible' for 'nor is it divisible', presumably to make it explicit that Parmenides attributes indivisibility (Ar.'s second sense of unity) to Being. (Diels prints the first part of the line as being in S.'s own voice; but the second half taken alone makes a poor citation for the point.)

533 This is evidently different from what Ar. means in speaking of things being one in *logos*: Ar. thinks that this would entail that e.g., 'hot' and 'cold' would have the same definition, whereas S. here takes it to mean only that all things share a single definition, that of 'being'.

534 B6.1-2; for B6.1-9 cf. 117,4-13 (which however begins in the middle of B6.1, at 'for'), with some textual variants in the second line. The MSS differ as to the phrase here translated 'being', with F having *teon* and DEMo *to on*; we follow Diels (following Karsten's *Parmenidis Eleatae Carminis Reliquiae*, Philosophorum Graecorum Veterum 2.1 (Amsterdam: Müller, 1835)) in interpreting the former as *t' eon*. For the first part of the line all MSS have *khrê to legein to noein*: Karsten's emendation to *te noein* is accepted by Diels here and by DK. Diels here misreports *te noein* as the MSS reading and attributes *to noein* to Karsten; DK reports only *te noein* and does not mention *to noein*. For discussion of the grammar and sense of these difficult and controversial lines, see Coxon, *Fragments of Parmenides* at this passage and John Palmer, *Plato's Reception of Parmenides* (Oxford: Oxford University Press, 1999), pp. 47–9.

535 At 146,9, in S.'s longer citation, the MSS have *oud' ei khronos estin* ('nor if time is'?) rather than, as here, *ouden gar estin* ('there neither is').

536 B8.36-38. Also cited at 146,9-11 as part of S.'s canonical quotation of B8.1-52. A line which agrees (at least in large part) with the last line (B8.38) is also cited by Plato at *Theaetetus* 180E1, and by other authors following Plato; and S. seems to cite this version at 29,18 and 143,10. MSS of S. here differ both from the Platonic version and from each other at the end of the last line, and the sense is controversial. We read *pant' onomastai* ('named all things') according to Coxon's report the consensus reading (with the trivial variation of *ônomastai* in F) at 146,11, and the reading of E and Mo here. MSS DFa, which here have *onom' estai*, are presumably influenced by the Platonic version. For the sense, cf. Myles Burnyeat, 'Idealism and Greek Philosophy: What Descartes Saw and Berkeley Missed', *Philosophical Review* 91 (1982), 3–40, at 19, n. 22.

537 Melissus DK 30B9; cf. the overlapping 110,1-2.

538 Following MoFa and reading *ti* rather than *te*.

539 *Metaph.* 12.10, 1076a4, citing *Iliad* 2.204.

540 B8.34-36, ending where the preceding citation begins; cf. S.'s canonical citation at 146,7-9, and also 143,23-25, with minor MSS disagreements; also cited by Proclus, *in Parm.* 1152.

198   *Notes to pp. 135–6*

541 The text here is puzzling; the sense required is clear, but *telos on autou*, at 87,17-18, might be taken as claiming that thinking is the end of being (since *to noein* is the obvious antecedent for *on*); perhaps *on* should be emended to *ontos*.

542 B8.4, which is also cited at 30,2; 78,13; 120,23; in the long citation at 145,4; and at *in Cael.* 557,18; cf. n. 184.

543 B8.25, cited at 86,22 and 145,26; cf. n. 530.

544 *Parmenides* 142D9-3A3, with only minor divergences from Plato's text. (At 87,27, S. has *morion* where Plato has *moriou*; at 88,1, S. has *gennatai* where Plato has *genêtai*. Also at 88,1, Diels prints *toutôi* (dative) *tô moriô* (dual accusative); here we follow the OCT Plato in reading *toutô tô moriô* ('these two portions'). At 88,2, S. has *on to hen* and *to hen to on* where Plato has *hen to on* and *to on to hen*. At 88,3, S. has *ti plêthos* where Plato has *to plêthos*; at 88,4, *eoike ge* rather than *eoiken*.)

545 S. here reads *Metaph.* 12.10, 1075a11-15 as claiming not (as it seems to) that goodness is twofold, residing in both the general and the order of the army, but rather that the *order* is twofold. This gives S. warrant for attributing to Ar. a view that the ordered multiplicity of the world exists in paradigmatic form in its first cause. Cf. *in Cael.* 87,1-17. The same reading of the passage is presented by Philoponus, *DA* 37,20-26 and 63,7-9, where it seems to be derived from Ammonius; see the *Introduction*.

546 S. here and in what follows assumes Proclus' theory of triads within the One-which-is, drawing heavily on the metaphysics of Proclus' *Platonic Theology* 3.20. The realm of the intelligibles can be described as the One-which-is: this is what is hypothesized in the second hypothesis of Plato's *Parmenides* (and is taken by S. to have been anticipated by Parmenides' One-which-is), but it is divided into three levels, the 'summit' (also more particularly known as the One-which-is), the 'whole', and the 'all' (identified by Proclus with the Platonic 'animal itself', i.e. the paradigm of the sensible world). Each of these levels has an internal triadic structure, though S. does not discuss this here.

547 Since the 'all' is the model for the sensible world, it must contain a plurality of forms but in a unified way. It is bird, fish, etc. 'in a causal manner' (*kat' aitian*) because while not literally a fish or bird it is in one way the causal paradigm of fish, in another way of birds, and so on. Cf. S.'s account of the unity and diversity of all things at different ontological levels in Anaxagoras (34,18 ff.) and Empedocles (31,31 ff.).

548 Thus the inexhaustibility of the generation of each species of animal and plant and of the cycle of the seasons is explained not simply, as Ar. says in *On Generation and Perishing*, by a common material cause which can become each of these things in turn, and by the infinitely repeated rotations of the heavens as their efficient cause, but also by an intelligible paradigm of infinity or infinite power.

549 So Ar. refuses to say that what is is one, because he is afraid that his readers would take it to mean that the sensible world is one; and the sensible world is not strictly

Notes to pp. 136–40 199

speaking one, even though it exhibits a kind of indivisibility, a kind of continuity, and a kind of sharing in a single account.

550 Cf. *Parmenides* 141E10-142A1.

551 Presumably a reference to the Neoplatonic curriculum, in which the study of Plato follows that of Ar.

552 89,5-90,20 are a lengthy citation from the *Sophist* (244B6-245E5). For the most part the MSS of S. here differ only in offering trivial variant readings, which often correspond to variations in the extant MSS of Plato. This suggests that different scribes consulted different MSS of Plato in copying the quotation. Proclus quotes much the same passage (though S.'s quotation is fuller), interspersed with discussion, in *Platonic Theology* 3.20, which generally seems to be a crucial text for S.'s discussion here.

553 Plato's text and sense are disputed in this line, with corresponding MSS variation in S.: see the OCT ad loc. We follow the MSS of both Plato and S., in reading *auto* ('itself') where Diels emends to *au de* ('and in turn').

554 From here S. repeats the quotation already given at 52,25-53,5; the lines are also quoted in the long quotation at 145-146, and 8.43-44 at 126,22-23 and 137,16-17.

555 B8.43-45, also quoted via the *Sophist* at 52,26-28.

556 Following EFMo in omitting *holôi* ('the whole account'), though *holôi* does appear (with some variations) in all the Plato MSS.

557 All MSS of both S. and Plato here have *to holon* 'the whole', though the OCT emends Plato to *to on*, 'being'.

558 In asking the question *ou pleiô* ('won't ... more') S. seems to depart from Plato, whose extant MSS have *au pleiô* ('again they are more').

559 S. here agrees with MS W of Plato but diverges from the text of the other MSS (followed, probably correctly, by the OCT): these MSS have 'should not speak either of being (*ousia*) or of coming-to-be as existing'. The OCT also omits 'the one or' (*to hen ê*) in the phrase 'the one or the whole', following Bekker, but this appears in all the MSS of Plato as well as of S.

560 Repeated by S. at 243,18-20.

561 Our MSS of Ar. have *to hen* ('the one'): 'make the one many'; but judging by 91,24 S. reads *to on* ('what is'), 'make what is many'.

562 Deleting the MSS *ti*, which would give the sense 'they predicated "what-it-is" of substance' (Mo apparently has *ti esti* rather than *to ti esti*).

563 Reading *hautou* for Diels' and the MSS *autou*.

564 Reading *einai* with DEMo rather than *to einai* with Fa and Diels in line 11, reading *poiei* with DEMo rather than *poioi* with Fa and Diels, and emending the MSS *sumplekôn* to *sumplekei*, rather than to *sumplekon* with a and Diels. Diels' text would mean 'the verb "to be", when added to accidents, both qualifies and substantiates them'.

200   *Notes to pp. 140–3*

565 This is a close paraphrase of the lemma as S. cites it, *Phys.* 185b29-31: as noted earlier, S. has 'make what is many' where our MSS of Ar. have 'make the one many'.

566 These, like 'human being white' which S. had previously denied was a declarative sentence, are in fact acceptable Greek sentences. But some philosophers, including S., would say that they are so only because there is an implicit 'is'.

567 Accepting Torstrik's emendation of *tauta* for *ta*.

568 Accepting Torstrik's deletion of *ê*, 'or'. For the principle, cf. *Metaph.* 3.3, 1005b19-20; Plato, *Republic* 436B.

569 S. evidently uses 'potential' here in an inclusive sense, so that what is actually P (sleeping, standing) is also potentially so (since a subject will presumably be *either* waking or sleeping at any given time) (cf. Ar., *De Interpretatione* 13, 23a7-11).

570 Smith prints 92,26-96,4; 96,15-20; and 97,4-8 as collectively fr. 129 (including introductory and concluding contexts) of Porphyry.

571 Text and sense are controversial at 93,13 ff.: we insert an *ou* before *mallon* in 93,16, rejecting Diels' and Torstrik's more radical proposals. As we understand it, the argument is a dilemma with two horns. If white does not exist, then saying 'Socrates white' is saying nothing about him; if white does exist, then saying 'Socrates white' is saying two things rather than one. The opponent is imagined to reply that white does exist, but that when 'white' is used as the predicate term of a sentence it does not posit any being. Porphyry responds that if 'white', which by itself posits that being, loses its function in a sentential context, 'Socrates', which by itself also posits a certain being, should also lose that function.

572 Compare S.'s own account of the 'later ancients' at 91,28 ff. etc.

573 Are the earlier thinkers here Lycophron and the 'some people' mentioned just earlier (93,30), in contrast to the Eretrians; or, in distinction to this whole group, the unnamed earlier thinkers implied by Ar.'s talk of 'later thinkers' at the start of the lemma (*Phys.* 185b26), presumably Parmenides and Melissus?

574 Emending *autois* to *autôi*; the transmitted text seems to say that the human being (e.g.) is *in* its parts, whereas the appropriate question is: are the *parts* something or nothing so long as they are in the undivided whole?

575 Each individual substance has a 'peculiar character' or 'peculiar property', i.e. one which it possesses as a whole and which distinguishes it from everything else. 'The musical one' and 'Socrates' might pick out the same underlying subject, but only 'Socrates' expresses the peculiar character of that subject. (Porphyry is perhaps connecting Ar.'s conception of primary substance with the Stoic concept of the peculiar quality of a thing, its *idia poiotês* or *idiotês*.)

576 These relational terms are apparently used as examples of accidental terms in general: it would be more standard to say that they exist 'by accident' (*kata sumbebêkos*) than 'by chance' (*kata tukhên*).

Notes to pp. 143–6 201

577 Porphyry is presumably thinking not of the Stoic doctrine of qualities, which they take to be bodies, but of the Stoic doctrine that predicates or predicables (*katêgorêmata*) are *lekta* and are therefore things but not beings.

578 Taking *pôs . . . pôs* as unaccented ('in a way . . . in a way').

579 Rejecting the first horn of the dilemma posited at 93,14 ff.

580 Emending *khôran* or *tên khôran* to *ton khoron*, cf. 95,29.

581 Following D in reading *estai* (where Diels following other MSS has *esti*) and in deleting the *hê* or *ê* before *huphestêkota*; and reading *hêi* rather than *ê* after *huphestêkota*, following Mo (95,1-2).

582 It is a bit odd that *meta* + genitive was used earlier for the appropriately unifying relation of accidents to substance (94,17; 94,27), whereas here it seems to go with their being unacceptably many. Presumably what is unacceptable is for the accidents to be alongside *something else* (*meta heterou allou*).

583 Or 'and through his existence' (*tôi ekeinou einai*). The same ambiguity recurs below, where we translate 'they *are* through being *of* Socrates', but it might mean 'they *are* through Socrates' existence'. In 95,10 after *ekeino* we read a full stop, which Diels seems to have inadvertently omitted.

584 That is, those who posit that being is univocal wind up with three distinct beings: Socrates, human, and animal; the reference is perhaps to the 'later ancients', or at least to the implications of their views. As we have seen, Porphyry thinks that before Ar.'s realization that 'being' is said in many ways, everyone was caught in this and similar dilemmas (cf. the aporia at *Metaphysics* 3.6, 1003a9-12 for the result that Socrates is many animals, Socrates and human and animal). The second group, who reject 'the others' (*ta alla*) are presumably the Eleatics, since they say that being is one. At 94,13 it was the Stoics who were said to have abolished 'the others', apparently meaning accidental predicates; here 'the others' must also include genera and perhaps parts as well.

585 'Deixis', 'being indicated', here means either being literally pointed at, or being referred to by a 'deictic' demonstrative pronoun such as 'this'.

586 A quasi-citation from the lemma, *Phys.* 186a1-3.

587 This last sentence is entirely in the accusative-infinitive construction: presumably we are to understand 'Aristotle says . . .' or perhaps (since S. is concluding his long quotation) 'Porphyry says . . .'.

588 Following the Aldine and deleting *to*.

589 In contrast to Porphyry and Ar. himself, Eudemus' presentation of the aporia and its solution gives prominent roles to Zeno and Plato. S.'s own reading of the lemma will give a more elaborate version of Plato's response (99,32-101,24), criticizing Al. for misreading Eudemus regarding it (99,7 ff.).

590 Eudemus fr. 37a Wehrli. The 'responses' here are to Parmenides' and Melissus' conclusion that all things are one; Eudemus' strategy of response follows Ar.'s. His

202 *Notes to p. 146*

first move is to say that being has many senses, and that they cannot say that all things are in any of these senses (Eudemus fr. 35, cited by S. at 74,18-29; cf. Ar., *Phys.* 185a20-b5); next, that one is said in many senses (and that they cannot say that all things are one in any of these senses) (Eudemus fr. 36, cited by S. at 85,21-86,10; cf. Ar., *Phys.* 185b5-25); finally the present passage of Eudemus corresponds to the current lemma of Ar.

591 This question is repeated (again from Eudemus) at 138,30, but without the *hen*, thus reading: 'So is it the case that this is not, but that there is some one?'. Diels proposes to harmonize the two by secluding *hen* here, but it seems better to add it later. The antecedent of 'this' is not clear; perhaps 'what is', perhaps an ordinary sensible object such as a human being (cf. 'each of us' in the last sentence of the paragraph).

592 Eudemus represents Zeno as raising aporiai about the one as much as about the many, which seems to conflict with Plato's portrayal in the *Parmenides*. S. will later defend the Platonic picture. It is possible that Zeno did indeed raise such aporiai, but it is also possible that his aporiai against the one were only intended to show that there were no units from which a many could be composed. The question of Zeno's intentions and the import of his aporiai was controversial in antiquity, and remains so. Cf. Zeno fragments DK 29B1-3 (for all of which S., later in the first book of *in Phys.*, is the source, at 139,9 ff.; 140,34 ff.; and 140,28 ff.); and see discussion in the *Introduction*.

593 Cf. Ar., *Metaphysics* 3.4, 1001b7-13, DK 29B2.

594 For Eudemus on Zeno cf. 99,7-18.

595 Reading *all' ê* with EMo.

596 'Being-prudent' and 'being-seated' are here used to translate the articular infinitives: the Greek infinitives (unlike the predicates we translate 'is prudent' and 'is seated') do not involve any form of *be*. Cf. 99,25-28: Eudemus' point seems to be that the verb forms where available show that predicates are mere accidental dispositions, not involving a further imputation of being (*ousia*).

597 At 115,27; 120,9; and 243,2-3 S. again quotes Eudemus' claim that Plato was the first to introduce 'the twofold' (*to disson*). 115,27 and 120,9 are citing a different passage of Eudemus from the present text; at 243,2-3 the citation runs in full: 'For Plato, by introducing *to disson*, solved many aporiai about the realities (*epi tôn pragmatôn*).' The present sentence seems to be a fuller explanation of this claim, but it cannot be construed as it stands. Following Diels' suggestion (and Wehrli's text of Eudemus fr. 37a), we insert *epi tôn* before *pragmatôn* to make the text match 243,2-3, but neither Diels nor Wehrli nor we have a plausible construal, or a convincing emendation, of *epi tôn pragmatôn hôn nun hoi sophistai katapheugontes* (or, with the Aldine, *katapheugousi*): Diels puts an obelus before (and Wehrli obeli on both sides of) *hôn nun*. Eudemus seems to be recalling *Sophist* 236D3 (*eis aporon eidos . . . katapepheugen*, cf. 260C11-D1) and saying that the sophists take refuge in

Notes to pp. 146–8 203

something impassable, so the sophists are probably taking refuge *in* the aporiai rather than *from* the aporiai, but the text needs some supplement or emendation to get it to say either of these things. There is a further difficulty in understanding the sense of *hôsper epi ta eidê* ('just as [in]to the Forms') and its relation to the rest of the sentence. We take *epi* + accusative here to go with *eisagôn* ('introducing'). Perhaps Plato introduced *to disson* into the Forms to distinguish the sense in which Socrates is prudent from the sense in which prudence-itself is prudent. For Plato's contrast between name and definition cf. *Laws* 895D5, 964A6; *Seventh Letter* 342A7-C1, 343A5-B6: perhaps the implication here is that only the name and not the definition applies to a sensible instance. Alternatively, Eudemus might be thinking of *Sophist* 262A-D, contrasting names with sentences.

598 Adding a *mê*, 'not'.

599 Either following Torstrik's emendation, adding *arkhas* ('principles'), or simply understanding it (as Diels suggests).

600 Eudemus is presumably thinking of passages like Plato's distinction between actually grasping or using knowledge (so knowing in the actuality-sense) and merely possessing it (so knowing in the potentiality-sense) at *Tht.* 197A-B. But, Eudemus says, Plato does not make this a distinction between an actuality-sense and a potentiality-sense of the copula 'is', and does not apply the distinction to predicates like being one or being many.

601 Reading *hosa sunkeitai, tade logôi de, hoion* . . ., emending DE's *logou* to *logôi* (Diels emends to *legô*). On the reading we adopt, Eudemus would be referring to the theory attributed in *Metaphysics* 8.6 to Lycophron and his friends, on which what is named by an infinitive such as 'being-healthy' is composed out of its subject and health, which are united by a formula or assertion. Even if Socrates and health are not actually united, they are potentially united.

602 i.e. presumably we have answered the challenge posed at 97,12.

603 Zeno might 'concede' the many merely as a dialectical hypothesis for purposes of *reductio ad absurdum*. But S. seems to think that, if Zeno denied that being is one, he must have accepted that being is many. (S. does not consider, or rejects, the possibility that Zeno, like Gorgias, argued that nothing exists.) He thus thinks Al. is wrong to take Zeno's argument (and to cite Eudemus is taking it) as: (1) each putative one (e.g. Socrates) is in fact many or nothing; (2) therefore there is no one; (3) therefore there can be no many, since each of the many must be one. S. thinks that Zeno argued against the many to support the claim that being is one, and without using the premise that there is no one. He is willing to accept on Eudemus' authority that Zeno also argued against the one, but he thinks that this must have been on a different occasion, as part of a non-serious dialectical exercise, and was not in Zeno's book. See S.'s fuller treatment of the issue at 138,3-139,23. At 140,27 ff. S. cites 'Zeno's own treatise' at length, which indicates that he has access to Zeno's

204   *Notes to pp. 148–50*

treatise or to verbatim extracts from it, but that, as his tentativeness here suggests, he is not sure that he has the whole contents.

604 The reference is to *Philebus* 14D-E and 15D-16A, though S. is perhaps importing the term *ereskholountôn* from 53E5.

605 100,3-15 are a citation of Plato, *Sophist* 251A8-C6, with largely trivial variations.

606 The MSS of Plato, followed by the OCT, have a *polla* in the last clause: 'we speak of it as many [things] and by many names'.

607 The MSS have *euthus gar ei labesthai*; and Diels places an obelus between *gar* and *ei*. The MSS of Plato have *euthus gar antilabesthai*. We read *euthus gar esti labesthai*, giving the sense above.

608 *Ton*: we here follow S. against the divergent Plato MSS, as does the OCT Plato.

609 Plato's text adds *eniote*, 'sometimes': 'you often encounter those, sometimes older people'.

610 S. assumes, following Proclus and ultimately Iamblichus, that Plato in the *Sophist* is arguing for the complex structure of Being, Motion, Rest, Sameness, and Otherness (and thus for the presence of not-being, since Otherness is a kind of not-being) in the *intellectual* realm, i.e. the realm of *nous*, rather than in the higher *intelligible* realm, the realm of intelligible being in the strictest sense, which is what he thinks Parmenides is discussing (and *perhaps* Parmenides was also aware of a One above being). There is 'differentiation' (*diakrisis*) in the intellectual but not in the intelligible realm.

611 *Parmenides* 128B.

612 Following S's text, MS D, *hepta men ontôn*. MSS EF have *hepta menontôn*, 'while seven things remain'. Plato's text has *hepta hêmôn ontôn*, 'we being seven', so that the argument appeals to Socrates' counting as one of seven individuals present. On S's text (in either version), Socrates evidently refers to *himself* as seven (the six parts just listed plus the whole, presumably).

613 *Parmenides* 129C4-E4.

614 *Sophist* 253C-E.

615 There is a grammatical discontinuity here, and perhaps a verb of stating or showing should be added after *kai*: but the general sense seems clear.

616 Reading *auta* instead of Diels' *hauta*.

617 We could also translate 'each is one [and] all'. Either way, we read *hekaston hen* with EFMo rather than *hen hekaston* with D.

618 Cf. *Parmenides* 129B6-C1: S's 'all' here seems to be substituted for Socrates' 'many'. For S's interpretation here and in the next sentence cf. Proclus' *Commentary* ad loc.

619 According to S., Plato's solution does not depend on categorial distinctions in respect of being, whereas Ar's does; contrast Eudemus at 97,21 ff.

620 A reminiscence of Porphyry at 95,7-8.

621 An 'individual substance' (*atomos ousia*) is the primary substance of the *Categories* (e.g. Socrates), according to which genera are 'said of' it and accidental predicates are 'in' it. S.'s rhetorical questions raise the puzzle of whether such a substance could exist as a bare unqualified particular, as Porphyry's version of Ar.'s solution seems to imply.

622 i.e. there is no Form of 'Socrates with all his properties and material parts'; there is a *concept* with that content, but it is posterior to Socrates and dependent on sensation.

Bibliography

Becker, Oskar, 'Zur Textgestaltung des eudemischen Berichts über die Quadratur der Mondchen durch Hippokrates von Chios', *Quellen und Studien zur Geschichte der Mathematik, Astronomie und Physik* B3 (1936), 411–19.

Bekker, Immanuel, *Aristoteles Graece*, 2 vols (Berlin: Reimer, 1831).

Burnyeat, Myles, 'Idealism and Greek Philosophy: What Descartes Saw and Berkeley Missed', *Philosophical Review* 91 (1982), 3–40.

Catana, L., 'The Origin of the Division Between Middle Platonism and Neoplatonism', *Apeiron* 46.2 (2013), 166–200.

Coxon, A. H., 'The Manuscript Tradition of Simplicius' Commentary on Aristotle's *Physics* i–iv', *Classical Quarterly* 18 (1968), 70–5.

Coxon, A. H., ed., tr., and comm, *The Fragments of Parmenides*, 2nd edn (Las Vegas: Parmenides Publishing, 2009).

Denniston, J. D., *The Greek Particles*, 2nd edn, rev. K. J. Dover (London: Duckworth, 1996).

Diels, Hermann, ed., *Doxographi Graeci* (Berlin: Reimer, 1879).

Diels, Hermann and Walther Kranz, eds, *Die Fragmente der Vorsokratiker*, 6th edn, 3 vols (Berlin: Weidmann, 1952).

Dorandi, Tiziano, *Le stylet et la tablette* (Paris: Les Belles Lettres, 2000).

Dorandi, Tiziano, *Nell' officina dei classici* (Rome: Carocci, 2007).

Dörrie, Heinrich, 'Präpositionen und Metaphysik. Wechselwirkung zweier Prinzipienreihen', in his *Platonica Minora* (Munich: Fink, 1976), pp. 124–36.

Fortenbaugh, W. W., Pamela Huby, Robert Sharples, and Dimitri Gutas, eds, *Theophrastus of Eresus: Sources for his Life, Writings, Thought, and Influence*, 2 vols (Leiden: Brill, 1992–3).

Gavray, Marc-Antoine, *Simplicius lecteur du Sophiste* (Paris: Klinksieck, 2007).

Golitsis, Pantelis, *Les Commentaires de Simplicius et de Jean Philopon à la Physique d'Aristote* (Berlin: De Gruyter, 2008).

Golitsis, Pantelis, 'Simplicius and Philoponus on the authority of Aristotle', in Andrea Falcon, ed., *Brill's Companion to the Reception of Aristotle in Antiquity* (Leiden: Brill, 2016), pp. 419–38.

Golitsis, Pantelis and Philippe Hoffmann, 'Simplicius et le "lieu": À propos d'une nouvelle édition du *Corollarium de loco*', *Revue des Études Grecques* 127/1 (2014), 119–75.

Harlfinger, Dieter, 'Einige Aspekte der handschriftlichen Überlieferung des Physikkommentars des Simplikios', in Ilsetraut Hadot, ed., *Simplicius, sa vie, son oeuvre, sa survie* (Berlin: De Gruyter, 1987), pp. 267–94.

Bibliography

Hoffmann, Philippe, 'Damascius', in Richard Goulet, ed., *Dictionnaire des Philosophes Antiques* II (Paris: CNRS Éditions, 1994), pp. 541–93.

Hoffmann, Philippe, 'La triade chaldaique éros, alètheia, pistis de Proclus à Simplicius', in Alain-Philippe Segonds and Carlos Steel, eds, *Proclus et la Théologie Platonicienne* (Paris: Les Belles Lettres, 2000), pp. 459–89.

Inwood, Brad, ed. and tr., *The Poem of Empedocles*, rev. edn (Toronto: University of Toronto Press, 2001).

Karsten, Simon, *Parmenidis Eleatae Carminis Reliquiae*, Philosophorum Graecorum Veterum 2.1 (Amsterdam: Müller, 1835).

Kirk, G. S., J. E. Raven, and M. Schofield, *The Presocratic Philosophers* (Cambridge, Cambridge University Press, 1983).

Knorr, W. R., *The Ancient Tradition of Geometrical Problems* (Boston: Birkhäuser, 1986).

Kotwick, Mirjam, *Alexander of Aphrodisias and the Text of Aristotle's Metaphysics* (Berkeley: California Classical Studies, 2016).

Liddell, H. G., R. Scott, and H. S. Jones, *Greek–English Lexicon*, 9th edn (Oxford: Oxford University Press, 1940).

Marg, Walter, ed. and tr., *Timaeus Locrus, De Natura Mundi et Animae* (Leiden: Brill, 1972).

Mansfeld, Jaap, *Prolegomena: Questions to be Settled before the Study of an Author or a Text* (Leiden: Brill, 1994).

Martin, Alain and Oliver Primavesi, ed., tr., and comm., *L'Empédocle de Strasbourg (P. Strasb. gr. Inv. 1665–1666)* (Berlin: De Gruyter, 1999).

Marzillo, Patrizia, '"Would you check my edition please?" Scaliger's annotations to some poetical/philosophical texts', in Bernhard Huss, Patrizia Marzillo, and Thomas Ricklin, eds, *Para/Textuelle Verhandlungen zwischen Dichtung und Philosophie in der Frühen Neuzeit* (Berlin: De Gruyter, 2011), pp. 399–428.

Menn, Stephen, 'Simplicius on the *Theaetetus* (*In Physica* 17,38-18,23 Diels)', *Phronesis* 55 (2010), 255–70.

Moraux, Paul, *Les listes anciennes des ouvrages d'Aristote* (Louvain: Éditions Universitaires, 1951).

Morrison, Donald, 'Philoponus and Simplicius on Tekmeriodic Proof', in Daniel A. Di Liscia, Eckhard Kessler, and Charlotte Methuen, eds, *Method and Order in Renaissance Philosophy of Nature: The Aristotle Commentary Tradition* (Aldershot: Ashgate, 1998), pp. 1–22.

Pabst, Arnold, *De Melissi Samii fragmentis*, dissertation, University of Bonn, 1889.

Palmer, John, *Plato's Reception of Parmenides* (Oxford: Oxford University Press, 1999).

Praechter, Karl, Review of *Commentaria in Aristotelem Graeca*, tr. Victor Caston, in Richard Sorabji, ed., *Aristotle Transformed* (Ithaca: Cornell University Press, 1990), pp. 31–54.

Rashed, Marwan, *Die Überlieferungsgeschichte der aristotelischen Schrift De generatione et corruptione* (Wiesbaden: Reichert, 2001).

Bibliography

Rashed, Marwan, 'Alexandre d'Aphrodise, lecteur du *Protreptique*', in his *L'héritage aristotélicien* (Paris: Les Belles Lettres, 2007), pp. 179–215.

Ross, W. D., ed. and comm., *Aristotle's Physics* (Oxford: Oxford University Press, 1936).

Schofield, Malcolm, 'Leucippus, Democritus and the οὐ μᾶλλον Principle: An Examination of Theophrastus *Phys. Op.* Fr. 8', *Phronesis* 47 (2002), 253–63.

Sider, David, 'Textual Notes on Parmenides' Poem', *Hermes* 113 (1985), 362–6.

Sider, David, ed. and comm., *The Fragments of Anaxagoras*, 2nd rev. edn (Sankt Augustin: Academia Verlag, 2005).

Smith, Andrew, ed., *Porphyrii Philosophi fragmenta* (Stuttgart: Teubner, 1993).

Sorabji, Richard, ed., *Aristotle Transformed* (Ithaca: Cornell University Press, 1990).

Sorabji, Richard, ed., *Aristotle Re-Interpreted* (London: Bloomsbury, 2016).

Steel, Carlos, 'Introduction: The Author of the Commentary On the Soul', in Priscian, *On Theophrastus on Sense-Perception*, tr. Pamela Huby, with 'Simplicius', *On Aristotle's On the Soul 2.5-12*, tr. Carlos Steel (Ithaca: Cornell University Press, 1997), pp. 105–40.

Steel, Carlos, 'Neoplatonic versus Stoic causality: The case of the sustaining cause ("sunektikon")', *Quaestio* 2 (2002), 77–96.

Tarán, Leonardo, 'The Text of Simplicius' Commentary on Aristotle's *Physics*', in Ilsetraut Hadot, ed., *Simplicius, sa vie, son oeuvre, sa survie* (Berlin: De Gruyter, 1987), pp. 246–66.

Theiler, Willy, *Die Vorbereitung des Neuplatonismus* (Berlin: Weidmann, 1930).

Thibodeau, Philip, *The Chronology of the Early Greek Natural Philosophers* (North Haven: Cosmographia, 2019).

von Arnim, Hans, ed., *Stoicorum Veterum Fragmenta*, 3 vols (Leipzig: Teubner, 1903–5).

Wehrli, Fritz, ed. and comm., *Eudemos von Rhodos*, Die Schule des Aristoteles 8, 2nd edn (Basel: Schwabe, 1969).

Wildberg, Christian, 'Simplicius und das Zitat: zur Überlieferung des Anführungszeichens', in Friederike Berger *et al.* eds, *Symbolae Berolinenses: Für Dieter Harlfinger* (Amsterdam: Hakkert, 1993), pp. 187–99.

English–Greek Glossary

16-gon: *hekkaidekagônon*

ability; power; potentiality: *dunamis*
abolish; take away; reject; destroy:
    anairein
abridge: *suntemnein*
abstraction: *aphairesis*
absurd: *atopos*
absurdity: *atopia; to atopon*
accept: *epidekhesthai*
accident: *sumbebêkos*
accidentally; per accidens: *kata
    sumbebêkos*
account, to give: *apodidonai*
account: *logos; apodosis*
accuse: *enkalein*
acknowledge: *eidenai; gignôskein or
    ginôskein*
acquire: *lambanein*
acroamatic: *akroamatikos*
action: *praxis*
activity, actuality; action: *energeia*
actual intellect: *nous, ho energeiâi; nous,
    ho kat' energeian*
actuality: *entelekheia*
actually: *energeiâi*
add; adduce: *epagein*
addition: *pleonasma; prosthêkê*
adduce: *paragein*
admire: *thaumazein*
admirer: *zêlôtês*
admit: *epidekhesthai; homologein*
affected, cannot be: *apathês*
affinity: *sumpatheia*
affirmation: *kataphasis*

agent, efficient [cause]: *poioun*
agree beforehand (or previously):
    proömologein
agree: *homologein; sumphônein*
agreement: *sumphônia*
akin: *sungenês*
alike: *homoios; homoiôs*
allude: *apoteinesthai*
alteration: *alloiôsis; alloiôtikê kinesis*
altered easily [qualitatively]: *eualloiôtos*
altering: *alloiôtikos*
alternate ways; in alternation: *enallax*
anchor: *hormizein*
ancient: *arkhaios; arkhaïkos; palaios*
angle: *gônia*
anhomoeomerous: *anomoiomerês*
animal: *zôion*
answer (noun): *apokrisis*
answer (verb): *apokrinein*
antecedent: *hêgoumenon*
apart: *khôris*
Apodictics: Apodeiktika
aporia, to be in: *aporein; aporeisthai*
aporia, to raise: *diaporein; prosaporein*
aporia: *aporia*
apparent sense; appearance; what is
    apparent; thing that appears:
    phainomenon
appear: *phainesthai*
appearance: *doxa*
applicable: *khrêsimos*
appropriate: *oikeios*
archetypal: *arkhetupos*
area: *khôrion*
argue: *epideiknunai; epikheirein*

English–Greek Glossary

argue against: *antilegein*

argument against; arguing against: *antilogia*

argument, to make: *kataskeuazein (ton logon)*

argument: *epikheirêma; epikheirêsis; logos*

arise: *gignesthai* or *ginesthai*

arithmetic: *arithmêtikê*

arithmetical; arithmetician; arithmetic of: *arithmêtikos*

arrange: *diaskhêmatizein*

arrangement: *taxis*

art: *tekhnê*

articulate: *diarthroun*

articulation: *diarthrôsis*

artificial: *plasmatikos; tekhnêtos*

ascent: *anodos*

assert: *apophainesthai*

asserting: *apophansis*

assertion: *logos*

assign; arrange under: *hupoballein*

assist: *sullambanein*

assume: *lambanein; paralambanein; prolambanein*

astronomy: *astronomia*

at greater length: *epi pleon*

at hand: *prokeimenos*

at rest: *êremoun*

atheist: *atheos*

athetize: *athetein*

atomic, atom; individual: *atomos*

attach: *sunaptein*

attain: *katalambanein*

attainment: *teuxis*

attempt: *epikheirêsis*

attention: *spoudê*

attention, to pay: *prosekhein ton noun*

auxiliary cause: *sunaition*

aware, to be: *sunaisthanesthai*

axiom: *axiôma*

axis: *axon*

ball: *sphaira*

base: *basis*

be: *huparkhein*

be aware: *eidenai*

become: *gignesthai* or *ginesthai*

begin, rule over: *arkhein*

being: *on*

belief: *hupolêpsis*

belong to: *huparkhein*

bend: *ekklinein*

between: *metaxu*

beyond: *epekeina*

bisect: *dikha temnein*

bisect: *dikhotomein*

bisector: *diagônios*

blending: *sunkrasis*

blow: *plêgê*

bodily: *sômatikos*

body: *sôma*

bond: *desmos*

bound (noun): *horos*

bound (verb): *periekhein*

boundary: *horos; peratoun*

breadth: *platos*

breadth, without: *aplatês*

briefly: *suntomôs*

bring forth: *proagein*

bring forward: *proagein*

bring to light: *proagein*

bring together: *sunagein*

broad; in the broad sense: *koinos*

bulk: *onkos*

by-product: *parakolouthêma; epigennêma*

capable of examining: *exetastikê*

care, take: *phulassein*

careful, is: *spoudazein*

careful, very: *epimelês*

careless way, in a; carelessly: *aphereponôs*

Categories: *Katêgoriai*

category; predication: *katêgoria*

causal explanation: *aitiologia*

English–Greek Glossary

causal explanations, with: *aitiologikôs*
causal manner, in a: *kat' aitian*
causal: *aitiôdês*
causally: *aitiôdôs*
cause; reason: *aition*
celebrate: *anumnein*
centre: *kentron; mesos*
chance: *tukhê*
change: *metabolê*
character: *kharaktêr*
characterize, be characteristic:
    kharaktêrizein
charge: *episkêptein*
charitably: *eugnômonôs*
choice, school: *hairesis*
circle; cycle: *kuklos*
circular: *kuklikos*
circumference: *periphereia*
cite: *paragraphein; paratithenai*
clarity: *saphêneia*
clear, to make: *dêlôtikos*
clear: *enargês; phaneros*
clearly: *enargôs*
close at hand, easy, obvious, at hand:
    prokheiros
close-packed: *thelumna*
close: *oikeios*
cochlioid: *kokhlioeidês*
coexist: *sunistanai*
cognition; knowledge; [kind of]
    knowledge; knowing : *gnôsis*
cognitive: *gnôstikos*
cognize: *gignôskein or ginôskein*
cold: *psukhros*
collect: *sullambanein*
combine; mix together; compare:
    sunkrinein
combined; combination: *sunkrisis*
come first; precede: *proêgeisthai*
come to be, come about: *gignesthai or
    ginesthai*
come to know: *gignôskein or ginôskein*

come together; bring together: *sumpherein*
come together: *sunistanai*
commentary: *exêgêsis; hupomnêma*
commentator; interpreter *exêgêtês*
common; in common: *koinos*
commonality: *koinotês*
communicate: *paradidonai*
convey: *paradidonai*
companion: *gnôrimos; hetairos*
compel: *anankazein*
complete: *teleios*
completeness: *to teleion*
compose: *sunistanai*
composed, to be: *sunkeisthai*
composed, way of being: *sunthesis*
composer: *xunistas*
composition: *sunthesis*
compound; composite: *sunthetos*
comprehend: *perilambanein*
comprehend: *sullambanein*
comprehended: *perilêptos*
comprehending: *periokhê*
comprehensible: *sunetos*
compresence: *sunousiôsis*
concave: *koilos*
concavity: *koilotês*
concede, agree: *sunkhôrein*
conceive: *epinoein*
conception: *ennoia; epinoia; prolêpsis*
conceptual: *kat' epinoian*
conceptually prior, to be: *proepinoeisthai*
concern: *askholia*
concise: *suntomos*
concisely: *suntomôs*
concision: *suntomia*
conclude: *sunagein*
conclusion, to lead to a: *sumperainein*
conclusion: *sumperasma*
concocting: *peptikos*
concomitant, to be: *parakalouthein*
confirm: *pistousthai*
confirmation: *pistis; pistôsis*

214   *English–Greek Glossary*

confront: *hupantan*

confused: *sunkekhumenon*

confusion; error: *planê*

conjecture; approach; effort: *epibolê*

connect: *sunaptein; sunekhizein*

connective conjunction: *parasunaptikos (sundesmos)*

consequent, to be: *akolouthein*

consider: *theôrein; ennoein*

consistent, to be: *akolouthein*

constituent: *enuparkhon*

constitute: *sunistanai*

constitution: *sustasis*

construct: *kataskeuazein; prographein; sunistanai*

construction: *kataskeuê*

contact: *epaphê*

contain: *periekhein; perilambanein*

contemplating, for: *theôrêtikos*

contend: *agônizesthai*

content, to be: *agapan*

contentiously: *philoneikôs*

contentiousness: *phileristia*

continuity: *sunekheia; sunokhê*

continuous, to make: *sunekhizein*

continuous: *sunekhês*

contradiction, contradictory (disjunction): *antiphasis; antiphatikos*

contrariety: *enantiôsis; enantiotês*

contrariwise: *to enantion*

contrary account: *enantiologia*

contrary; (arguments) to the contrary: *enantion*

contrast: *antidiastellein*

contribution, to make: *suntelein*

convex: *kurtos*

conviction: *pistis*

cooperate: *sunergein*

coordinate: *isostoikhos*

coordination: *sumpnoia*

corollary: *porisma*

correct: *orthos*

correctly: *orthôs*

corresponding: *sustoikhos*

cosmos; world; ordering: *kosmos*

count: *arithmein*

counter-intuitive: *apemphainôn*

counterpart, lacking: *anapodoton*

counterpart: *antapodosis*

courageous: *andreios*

craftsmanly: *dêmiourgikos*

criterion: *kritêrion*

critically examine: *euthunein*

criticize: *aitiasthai; memphesthai; oneidizein*

criticize: *euthunein*

crude way: *holoskherôs*

crude: *holoskherês*

cumulative composition: *episunthesis*

custom; manner: *ethos*

customary: *sunêthês*

cut: *temnein*

cut off: *apotemnein*

decad: *dekas*

deception: *apatê*

deceptive: *apatêlos*

declarative: *apophantikos*

declaratively: *apophantikôs*

declare: *apophainesthai*

deduce, to: *sullogizesthai*

deductions, to make or offer: *sullogizesthai*

deep: *bathus*

deficient: *endeês*

define: *horizesthai*

defining: *horistikos*

definition: *diorismos; horismos; horos*

delight: *agapêsis*

delineate; circumscribe: *perigraphein*

Demiurge: *dêmiourgos*

demiurgic: *dêmiourgikos*

demonstrable: *apodeiktos*

demonstrate beforehand: *proapodeiknunai*

English–Greek Glossary

demonstrate simultaneously: *sunapodeiknunai*

demonstrate; render: *apodeiknunai*

demonstration, without: *anapodeiktôs*

demonstration: *apodeixis*

demonstrative: *apodeiktikos*

denial: *apophasis*

depth: *bathos*

desecration: *kathairesis*

desire (noun): *orexis*

desire (verb): *oregesthai*

desiring: *orektikos*

desirous of learning: *philomathês*

destroy: *anairein*; destroy when it is destroyed: *sunanairein*

destruction: *olethros*

detach: *apoluein*

determine: *horizein*

deviate from: *parallattein*

diagonal: *diametros*

diagram: *diagramma*

diagrammatic fallacy: *pseudographêma; pseudographia*

dialectic: *dialektikê (epistêmê)*

dialectician, dialectical: *dialektikos*

dialogue: *dialogikon*

diameter: *diametros*

difference: *diaphora*

differentia: *diaphora*

differentiate: *diakrinein*

differentiation: *diakrisis*

differing; different: *diaphoros*

difficult: *empodios; khalepos*

difficulty: *aporia*

dignity: *huperokhê*

digress: *parekbainein*

digression: *parekbasis*

disagreement: *diaphônia*

discard: *aposkeuazein*

discern: *diagignôskein*

discernment: *epignôsis*

discipline; approach; method: *methodos*

discourse: *logos*

discrete: *diôrismenos*

discursive: *dianoêtikos*

discuss, dispute; argue : *dialegesthai*

discussant; interlocutor: *prosdialegomenos*

discussion: *logos*

disjunction: *to diairetikon*

disjunctive: *diairetikos*

dispersal: *diaspasmos*

disperse: *diaspan*

display: *epideiknunai*

disposition: *diathesis*

dissolution: *dialusis*

distance: *diastêma*

distinction, without: *adioristôs; adioristos*

distinctive, own: *idios*

distinguish; determine: *aphorizein; diorizein; apokrinein*

distinguishing feature: *gnôrisma*

disturb: *thorubein*

divide: *diairein; sundiairein; diastellein; temnein*

divine: *theios*

divisible: *diairetos*

division: *diairesis*

doctrine: *doxa; gnômê*

domain: *perigraphê*

dominance: *epikrateia*

dominant, most: *kratistos*

dominate: *epikratein*

draw: *agein; graphein*

easily affected: *eupathês*

easily-moulded: *euplastos*

easily-shaped: *eutupôtos*

easily; neatly: *eukolôs*

easy to accept; easily accepted: *euparadektos*

easy to resolve: *eudialutos*

easy: *eukolos*

effect: *apoteloumenon; apotelesma*

efficient; productive; poetic: *poiêtikos*

element: *stoikheion*
elemental: *stoikheiôdês*
Elements (Euclid's): *Stoikheia*
elevated, more: *anabebêkôs; epanabebêkôs*
embrace: *periekhein*
emerge: *anakuptein*
empirically: *historikôs*
empty: *kenos*
emulation, in: *zêlôtês genomenos*
encompass: *perilambanein*
end, without: *ateleutêtos*
end; completion: *telos*
end: *peras*
ending: *katalêxis*
enduring: *empedos*
engaged in serious business: *askholos*
enmattered (said of a form): *enulos*
enquire; apply a question: *zêtein*
enquiry: *historia; pragmateia; zêtêma*
ensouled: *empsukhos*
entail, mutually or reciprocally:
    suneisagein
entitle: *epigraphein*
enumerate: *katarithmein*
equality: *isotês*
equally balanced: *isopalês*
equivocal: *homônumos*
erect: *agein*
eristical: *eristikos*
eristically: *eristikôs*
error, to commit: *hamartanein*
error, without: *anexapatêtôs*
especially: *idiôs*
establish: *kataskeuazein*
establish: *sunistanai*
eternal: *aïdios*
eternity: *to aïdion*
ethical; ethicist: *êthikos*
even: *artios*
evident: *enargês;* evident [truth or
    experience]: *enargeia*
evidently be: *phainesthai*

examine: *episkopein; exetazein; skopein*
example: *paradeigma*
excess: *huperokhê*
exhaust: *dapanan*
exist: *huparkhein*
exist prior to, preexist: *proüparkhein*
exist together with; coexist: *sunuparkhein*
existence, subsistence: *hupostasis*
existing; being: *ousia*
exoteric: *exôterikos*
experience: *empeiria*
explain: *exêgeisthai*
express: *apophainesthai; ekphainein;*
    emphainein
extend: *proagein*
extended: *diastatos*
extension; dimension: *diastasis*
extended in breadth: *peplatusmenos*

fall into: *peripiptein*
fall short: *endeês einai*
false: *pseudês*
falsehood, to speak; speak falsely; say
    falsely: *pseudein*
falsehood: *pseudos*
falsely: *pseudôs*
fame: *doxa*
familiar: *sunêthês*
figure: *skhêma*
fill out: *sumplêrein*
final: *telikos*
fine-grained: *leptomerês*
finish; conclusion; end: *teleutê*
finite; limited: *peperasmenos*
finiteness: *peperasmenon, to*
first abolish: *proanairein*
first place, in the: *holôs*
first; the very first: *prôtistos*
fit, apply to: *epharmottein*
fit: *epharmozein*
follow together: *sunakolouthein*
follow: *akolouthein*

English–Greek Glossary

follow: *katakolouthein; hepesthai; sunagein*
for the most part: *to pleon*
form: *eidos; skhêma; morphê*
formal: *eidikos; kata to eidos*
forms, of the: *eidêtikos*
formula: *logos*
from the middle: *messothen*
full: *pleôn; plêrês*
fully: *teleôs*

general; generally; in general: *koinos;
    holôs; koinôs*
generate, to: *gennan*
generated, generable: *genêtos*
generated, to be: *gignesthai or ginesthai*
generation, coming to be, becoming:
    genesis
generative: *gonimos*
genuine: *gnêsios*
genus: *genos*
geometer: *geômetrês*
geometrical; of geometry: *geômetrikos*
geometry: *geômetria*
get rid of: *aposkeuazein*
gibbous: *amphikurtos*
give an account: *apologeisthai;
    apologizein*
give an account of nature: *phusiologein*
give as a counterpart: *antapodidonai*
give substantial being: *ousioun*
go over: *epitrekhein*
god: *theos*
goddess: *theos, daimôn*
good: *agathos*
goodness: *agathotês*
grant: *homologein*
graphically fallacious, to be:
    pseudographeisthai, pseudographein
grasp: *lambanein; katalambanein;
    katanoêsis; perilêpsis*
great-minded: *megalophrôn*
great-souled: *megalopsukhos*

greatness of mind: *megalonoia*
group together with: *suntattein*
growing up: *hêlikia*
grudgingness: *phthonos*
guess: *topazein*

hand down: *paradidonai*
hard to change: *dusmetablêtos*
hard to move: *duskinêtos*
harmonious: *enarmonios*
harmony, in: *enarmoniôs*
heap up: *sôreuein*
heaven: *ouranos*
hexagon: *hexagônon*
highest part, summit: *akron*
hint: *ainittein*
Historia animalium: *Peri zôiôn historia*
historical work: *historikon*
History of Geometry: *Geômetrikê historia*
hold on: *phulassein*
hold: *huparkhein*
holding-together: *sunektikos*
homoeomerous: *homoiomeres*
homogeneous: *homogenês*
homoiomerybis: *homoiomereia*
honesty: *eusumbolon*
horn angle: *keratoeidês (gônia)*
horn: *kera*
human being: *anthrôpos*
human: *anthrôpeios; anthrôpinos*
human: *anthrôpos*
hypomnematic: *hupomnêmatikos*
hypotenuse: *hupoteinousa*
hypothesis: *hupothesis*
hypothesize: *hupotithenai*
hypothetical: *hupotheseôs, ex*

idea: *idea*
ignorance: *agnoia*
ignorant, to be: *agnoein*
imagination: *phantasia*
imaginative: *phantastikos*

English–Greek Glossary

immediate: *amesos*
immediately: *euthus; prosekhôs*
immobility: *akinêsia*
immortal: *athanatos*
immortality: *to athanaton*
impassive: *apathês*
imperative: *prostaktikos*
imperishable: *aphthartos*
implausible: *apithanos*
important: *spoudaios*
impressively: *philokalôs*
in passing: *metaxu*
include: *paralambanein*
included, to be: *empiptein*
incomparable: *asumblêtos*
incomplete: *atelês*
indemonstrable: *anapodeiktos*
indestructible: *anôlethros*
indistinct: *adioristos*
individual: *kath' hekaston*
individually: *idiâi*
indivisible: *adiairetos*
induction: *epagogê*
inexhaustibility: *to anekleipton*
inexhaustible: *anekleiptos*
infer: *sunagein*
inference: *sunagôgê*
infinite; infinity; infinitely many:
     apeiros
infinity, to; ad infinitum; infinite regress:
     ep' apeiron
infinity: *apeiria*
inscribe: *engraphein*
inseparable: *akhôristos*
insert: *empherein*
instrument: *organon*
instrumental: *organikos*
insult: *loidoria*
intellect, potential: *dunamei nous*
intellect: *nous*
intellection: *noêsis*
intellectual intuition: *nous*

intellectual: *noeros*
intellectually: *noerôs*
intelligence: *nous*
intelligible: *noêtos*
intensification: *epitasis*
intention: *ennoia*
intercontact: *diathigê*
intermediate: *mesos; metaxu*
interpret: *exêgeisthai*
interpretation: *exêgêsis; ekdokhê*
interrogative: *erôtêmatikos*
interval: *diastêma*
interweave: *sumplekein*
introduce together with: *suneisagein*
introduce: *eisagein; paragein; prosagein*
introduce: *proagein*
introduction: *prooimion*
invalidly: *asullogistôs*
investigate: *episkopein; zêtein; epizêtein*
investigate, inclined to: *zêtêtikos*
investigation: *skepsis; zêtêsis*
involve: *empherein*
irrational soul: *alogia*
irrational: *alogos*
isosceles: *isoskelês*

join: *epizeugnunai*
judge: *apophainesthai*
judgement: *gnômê*
jumble together: *sumphurein;*
     sunanaphurein
jumbled-together way, in a:
     sumpephorêmenôs
justice: *dikaiosunê*
justification: *logos*

keep: *phulassein*
kind: *genos*
kindred: *sungenês*
kinship: *oikeiotês*
know: *eidenai; gignôskein or ginôskein*
knowable; thing known: *gnôstos*

English–Greek Glossary

knowable: *epistêtos; gnôrimos*
knowing; knowledge: *eidêsis; eidenai, to; epistêmê*
known: *gnôrimos*

lacking: *endeês*
lacunose: *kekhênôs*
law-abiding: *nomimos*
lead: *proagein*
learn: *manthanein; paralambanein*
learning: *mathêsis*
Lectures on Natural Science (of Aristotle): *Phusikê akroasis*
lectures: *akroasis*
length: *mêkos*
less clear: *asaphesteros*
letter: *gramma*
level: *taxis*
liberal: *eleutherios*
life-generating: *zôiogonos*
life: *bios; zôê*
like: *homoios; enalinkios*
likewise: *homoiôs*
limit: *peras*
limited: *peratoumenos*
line up alongside: *suntattein*
line: *grammê*
linear: *euthus*
living body: *zôion*
logical, of logic: *logikos*
longlastingness: *polukhroniotês*
loss, to be at: *aporein*
lowest way, in the: *eskhatôs*
luck: *tukhê*
lune: *mêniskos*

made, to be: *gignesthai or ginesthai*
magnitude; size: *megethos*
make progress: *proagein*
make: *apotelein*
man: *anthrôpos*
manifest: *emphanês; prophanês; phaneros*

manifestly: *prophanôs*
manner: *tropos*
manner of speaking: *lexis*
manufacture: *kataskeuazein*
manuscript: *antigraphos*
many-named: *poluônumos*
many-namedness: *poluônumia*
many: *polloi; pleiones*
mark: *horos*
marvel, to: *thaumazein*
material (said of a composite): *enulos*
material: *hulikos*
mathematical; mathematical science; mathematician, mathematics: *mathêmatikos*
matter: *hulê*
meaning: *sêmainomenon*
measure: *metrein; metron*
mechanical: *organikos*
mechanics: *mêkhanikê*
medicine: *iatrikê*
meet: *sumpiptein*
mention: *mimnêskein*
metaphysics; *Metaphysics* (of Aristotle): *meta ta phusika, ta*
method: *tropos*
middle: *mesos*
miss: *hamartanein*
mix together: *sunanakerannumai*
mixing together: *summixis*
mixture: *mixis*
mode: *tropos*
moon: *selênê*
more: *pleiones*
motion: *kinêsis*
motivate; give an assurance: *paramutheisthai*
motivation: *paramuthia*
move: *kinein*
mover: *kinoun*
muchness: *plêthos*

220   *English–Greek Glossary*

multiplication: *plêthusmos*
multiplicity: *plêthos*
multiply: *plêthunein*
musical: *mousikos*

name: *onoma*
name, sharing the same: *homônumos*
natural philosopher; natural scientist:
    phusiologos
natural scientific; natural [science];
    natural [thing]; natural scientist:
    phusikos
nature: *phusis*
nature, study or account of: *phusiologia*
necessarily: *ex anankês*
necessary, it is; necessity; must; must
    necessarily; necessarily: *anankê*
necessity, must by all: *pasa anankê*
necessity, with: *anankaiôs*
need: *khreia*
negation: *apophasis*
Nicomachean Ethics: Nikomakheia êthika
non-deductive: *asullogistos*
non-deficient; non-lacking: *anendeês*
non-sensible: *anaisthêtos*
non-uniform; non-homogeneous:
    anomogenês
notion: *ennoia*
noun: *onoma*
nourishing: *trophimos*
novel way: *kainoprepôs*
number: *arithmos*
numerically: *arithmôi*

object of opinion: *doxaston*
object; aim: *skopos*
object [thing]: *pragma*
objection, defensive move: *enstasis*
obscure: *asaphês*
obscurity: *asapheia*
observe, in order to: *epistaseôs heneken*
observe: *ephistanai* and *ephistanein*

observe: *theôrein*
obtuse: *amblus (gônia)*
obvious, evident [truth]: *enargeia*
obvious: *enargês*
obviously: *enargôs*
occupation: *askholia*
occupy oneself with: *pragmateian*
    poieisthai
octagon: *oktagônon*
odd: *atopos*
omit: *paraleipein*
On Generation and Perishing: Peri
    geneseôs kai phthoras
on its own: *idian, kat'*
On the Gods: Peri theôn
One-which-is: *hen on*
one: *hen*
only one way, in: *monakhôs*
opinable: *doxastos*
opinion, to have: *doxazein*
opinion: *dogma*; *doxa*; *doxazein, to*
opinionative: *doxastikos*
opposed, to be; be opposite:
    antikeisthai
opposite: *antikeimenos*
opposition: *antithesis*
optative: *euktikos*
order; ordering: *taxis*
ordering: *diakosmos*
orientation: *thesis*
originally: *ex arkhês*
otherness: *heterotês*
overall, at all: *holôs*; *holos*; *katholikos*
overthrow: *kathairesis*
overturn: *anatrepein*

pair of opposites: *antistoikhia;*
    sustoikhia
pairing: *suzugia*
paradigm: *paradeigma*
paradigmatic: *paradeigmatikos*
paradox: *paradoxologia*

English–Greek Glossary

paradoxical: *paradoxos*
parallel: *parallêlos*
parallel, in: *ek parallêlou*
paralogism: *paralogismos*
paraphrase, to say in: *paraphrazein*
paraphrase (noun): *paraphrasis*
part: *meros; morion*
participle: *metokhê*
particular: *idios; merikos; meros, (to) kata*
particular, in: *idiôs*
partition, without: *ameristôs*
partition: *merismos*
partless: *ameristos*
Parts of Animals: Moria zôiôn
parts, without: *amerês*
passage: *lexis; rhêton*
passing-away: *phthora*
patient: *paskhon*
peculiar property: *idiotês*
peculiar: *idios*
peculiarity: *idion, to; idiotês*
perceptible: *aisthêtos*
perfect: *teleioun*
perfecting; perfection: *teleiôsis*
perish, pass away: *phtheiresthai; apollunai*
perishable: *phthartos*
perishing: *phthora*
perpendicularly: *pros orthas*
persuasive: *pistos*
persuasive: *pithanos*
pervade: *khôrein*
phenomenon: *phainomenon*
philosopher: *philosophos*
philosophical: *kata philosophian*
philosophize: *philosophein*
philosophy: *philosophia*
Physics (of Theophrastus, of Eudemus, of Empedocles): *Phusika, ta*
place: *khôra; topos*
plane: (noun) *epipedos*; (adjective) *epipedikos*

plant: *phuton*
plausible: *endoxos*
plausibly: *endoxôs*
pleasure: *hêdonê*
plurality: *plêthos*
poetic theorist: *mousikos*
point of division: *tomê*
point: *stigma; sêmeion*
pole: *polos*
polygon: *polugônon*
polygonal: *polugônos*
pose, project: *proballein*
posit: *hupotithenai; ephistanai and ephistanein*
position: *thesis*
possible: *dunatos*
Posterior Analytics: Hustera Analutika; Apodeiktika
posterior: *husterogenês*
postulate (noun): *aitêma*
postulate (verb): *aitein*
potentially: *dunamei*
power, in: *dunamei*
practical wisdom: *phronêsis*
practical: *praktikos*
practice: *praxis*
precept: *parangelma*
precise: *akribês*
precisely: *akribôs*
precision: *akribeia*
precluded: *aporos*
predicate (noun): *katêgorêma*
predicate (verb): *katêgorein*
predicatively: *katêgorikôs*
predominate: *epikratein*
pre-existing: *proüparkhon*
preliminary preparation: *proparaskeuê*
premise; enunciation: *protasis*
present in, to be: *enuparkhein*
present; present topic: *prokeimenos*
present: *huparkhein*
presentation: *metakheirisis*

222 English–Greek Glossary

preserve: *phulassein*
primarily productive: *prôtourgos*
primarily: *proêgoumenôs*
principal: *proêgoumenos*
principally: *kuriôs*
principial, fundamental: *arkhoeidês*
principial: *arkhikos*
principle; starting point; beginning:
 arkhê
privation: *sterêsis*
probable account: *eikotologia*
problem: *problêma; zêtêma*
procedure: *tropos*
proceed in tandem: *sumproienai*
proceed: *hormasthai*
proclaimed, to be: *aneuphêmeisthai*
produce: *apotelein; paragein*
progress: *prokopê*
progression: *proodos*
proof, being indicated: *deixis*
proper: *idios*
proper: *oikeios*
properly: *idiôs*
property: *idiotês*
provide, yield: *parekhein*
proximate: *prosekhês*
psychology: *peri psukhês*
publish: *ekdidonai*
punctuate: *stizein*
punctuation: *stigma*
pure: *eilikrinês; katharos*
purely: *eilikrinôs*
pursue: *spoudazein*
puzzle, to raise: *diaporein*

quadrant: *tetartêmorion*
quadratrix: *tetragônizousa*
quale: *poion*
qualitative change: *pathêtikos*
qualitative, in quality: *kata poiotêta(s)*
quality: *poion; poiotês*
quantity: *poson; posotês*

quantum: *poson*
quasi-bodily: *hoion sôma*
question: *zêtêsis; zêtoumenon*
questioning: *erôtêsis*

radius: *kentrou, hê ek tou*
rank (verb): *suntattein*
rank (noun): *taxis*
ratio: *logos*
rational: *logikos*
reach a conclusion: *perainein*
reality: *pragma*
reality, in: *pragmasin; pragmati*
really: *ontôs*
reason fallaciously: *paralogizesthai*
reason, cause; justification: *aitia*
reason: *logos; nous*
reasonable; plausible: *eulogos*
reasonably: *eulogôs; eikotôs; metriôs*
reasoning: *dianoia*
receive: *apolambanein; eisdekhesthai;
 epidekhesthai; metalambanein;
 paralambanein*
receptacle: *pandekhes*
recognize: *ennoein; gnôrizein;
 diagignôskein*
record: *apomnêmoneuein*
recount: *prosistorein*
recovery: *anarrhôsis*
rectilineal figure, rectilineal area:
 euthugrammon
rectilineal: *euthugrammos*
redirect: *metagein*
refashion: *metarrhuthmizein*
refer: *anagein; mimnêskein*
reference: *anamnêsis; mnêmê*
refuse to recognize: *apogignôskein*
refuse: *mê . . . sunkhôrein*
refutation: *elenkhos*
refute: *anaskeuazein; elenkhein;
 dielenkhein*
rejection: *apogignôsis*

English–Greek Glossary

remain: *menein and mimnein*

remainder: *kataleipomenon*

remark: *ephistanai; ephistanein; episêmainein*

remarking, observing: *epistasis*

renewal: *ekneasmos*

reply: *antigraphein; apantêsis*

report, say: *historein*

reports and write-ups: *historikai anagraphai*

reshape: *metaplattein*

resolution: *analusis; epikrisis*

resolve: *dialuô*

resolved, to be; be analysable: *analuein*

respond: *apantan*

response: *apantêsis*

rest: *êremia*

restoration: *apodosis*

restrict: *hupostellein*

result: *apodosis*

reveal: *epideiknunai; proagein*

rhythm: *rhusmos*

riddles, in: *ainigmatôdôs*

riddling: *ainigmatôdês*

riddlingly, to speak; to refer or hint riddlingly: *ainittein*

right: *orthos*

right, to be: *orthôs ekhein*

right (of a triangle): *orthogônios*

right angle: *orthê*

rightly: *orthôs*

role: *logos*

room, to make: *khôrein*

rotating: *kuklophorêtikos*

round: *peripherês*

rule: *logos*

rule of many: *polukoirania*

same kind, of the: *homogenês*

same way, in the: *homoiôs*

satisfy: *parekhesthai*

savour: *hêdonê*

saying: *logos; rhêton*

schism: *skhisma*

scientific knowing, scientific knowledge; scientifically knowing: *to epistasthai*

scientific knowledge of nature; scientific knowledge of natural things: *phusiologikê epistêmê*

scientific knowledge, one who possesses: *epistêmôn*

scientific knowledge; science; scientific knowing: *epistêmê*

scientific: *epistêmonikos*

scientifically know: *epistasthai*

scientifically: *epistêmonikôs*

section: *tmêma*

see: *manthanein*

see fit: *oikeioun*

seed: *sperma*

seek; look for: *zêtein*

seem: *phainesthai*

seeming: *doxa*

segment (in geometry): *tmêma*

self-motion: *autokinêton, to*

self-moved: *autokinêtos*

self-warranting: *autopistos*

selfish excess: *pleonexia*

semicircle: *hêmikuklion*

sensation; sense: *aisthêsis*

sense (of a text): *nous*

sense: *sêmainomenon*

sensible: *aisthêtos*

sensory: *aisthêtikos*

sentence: *logos*

separability: *to khôriston*

separate (out, off): *apokrinein*

separate; separately: *khôris*

separate (verb): *khôrizein*

separated: *khôristos*

separation: *apokrisis; diakrisis*

sequence, to be in: *akolouthein*

set out: *ektithenai; apodidonai*

224 English–Greek Glossary

several: *pleiones*
several ways, in: *pleonakhôs*
shape: *idea; skhêma; morphê*
share, be involved with: *koinônein*
sharing: *koinônia*
sharp: *oxus*
show: *deiknunai*
show first: *prodeiknunai*
side: *pleura*
sign (in Parmenides): *sêma; sêmeion*
sign-inferential: *tekmêriôdês*
signify, mean: *sêmainein*
similar: *homoios*
similarity; likeness: *homoiotês*
similarly: *homoiôs*
simple; simple-minded: *haplous*
simplicity: *haplotês*
simply, without qualification; simpliciter,
at all; in general: *haplôs*
slip in: *parenkeisthai*
snub-nosed: *simos*
snubness: *simotês*
solid: *nastos; stereos; stereôpa*
solidity: *nastotês; sterrotês*
solution, to have: *euporein*
solution: *lusis; epilusis*
solve: *luô; dialuô*
sophism: *sophisma*
Sophistical Refutations: Sophistikoi
elenkhoi
sophistical: *sophismatôdês; sophistikos*
soul: *psukhê*
soul, having no: *apsukhos*
soul, irrational: *alogia*
soul, of the: *psukhikos*
species: *eidos*
specifically: *eidei*
specificity: *idiotês*
speech: *dialektos; logos*
spherical: *sphairikos; sphairoeidês*
spiral: *helikoeidês*
spontaneity: *automaton*

square: *tetragônizein; tetragônon;*
tetragônikos
squaring: *tetragônismos*
start, from the: *euthus*
steadfast: *empedos*
straight: *euthus*
straight line: *eutheia*
straightaway: *euthus*
strict sense, strictly: *kuriôs*
strife: *neikos*
structure: *kataskeuê*
student: *mathêtês*
study: *theôria*
subject: *hupokeimenos; pragma*
subject-matter: *hupokeimenos*
subject, to be: *hupokeisthai*
subjoin: *hupotassein*
sublunar: *hupo selênên*
substance, of the same: *homoousios*
substance: *ousia*
subtend: *hupoteinein*
subtle way, overly: *gliskhrôs*
suitability: *epitêdeion, to*
suitable, to be: *epitêdeiôs ekhein*
superficial: *epipolaios*
superfluous; odd: *perittos*
superior, to be; differ; disagree: *diapherein*
superiority: *huperokhê*
supply: *anaplêrein*
support: *kataskeuazein*
supporting: *kataskeuastikos*
suppose: *hupolambanein*
surface: *epipedos; epiphaneia*
surge: *hormê*
surmise; suspect: *huponoein*
surprised, to be: *thaumazein*
surprising: *thaumastos*
syllogism, deduction: *sullogismos*
syllogism, to use: *sullogizesthai*
syllogistic: *sullogistikos*
sympathize: *sumpaskhein*
synthesize: *sunairein*

English–Greek Glossary

take: *eklambanein; lambanein*
take up: *prokheirizein; paralambanein*
taking: *ekdokhê*
teach: *didaskein; anadidaskein*
teacher: *didaskalos; kathêgemôn*
teaching: *didaskalias*
temperance: *sôphrosunê*
term: *horos*
text: *graphê; lexis; sungraphê*
theological: *theologikos*
theology: *theologia*
theorem: *theôrêma*
theoretical: *theôrêtikos*
thesis: *thesis*
thing with parts: *meristos*
thing: *pragma*
things that are, the: *onta, ta*
think: *noein*
third part: *tritêmorion*
thought, have the: *ennoein*
thought: *dianoia; ennoia; gnômê; noêma; nous*
time: *khronos*
title: *epigraphê*
to fall: *empiptein*
together: *koinôs*
touch: *sunaptein*
trace back: *anagein*
trapezium: *trapezion*
traversal: *diïxis*
treatise: *pragmateia; sungramma*
triangle: *trigônon*
true: *alêthês*
truly: *alêthôs*
truly, to speak: *alêtheuein*
trust: *pistis*
trustworthy: *pistos*
truth: *alêtheia*
turn out to be: *gignesthai or ginesthai*
turn, in: *merei, en*
turn; pass to: *metabainein*
turning: *tropê*

ultimate: *telikos*
unarticulated: *adiarthrôtos*
unchanging: *ametablêtos*
unclear: *asaphês*
uncontested: *anamphilekton*
underlie first: *prohupokeisthai*
underlying: *hupokeimenos*
understand: *noein*
understanding, to have: *epaiein*
undertake to argue: *epikheirein tôi logoi*
undertake: *epikheirein*
undivided: *adiairetos*
unending: *ateleston*
ungenerated: *agenêtos*
unification, union: *henôsis*
uniform: *homogenês*
unify: *henoun; henizein*
uninterrupted: *adialeiptos*
unique: *mounogenês*
unit: *henas; monas*
universal: *katholikos; katholou*
universally: *katholou*
universally, more: *holikôteron*
univocal: *sunônumos*
unlike: *anomoios*
unlike kind, of: *anomoiogenês*
unlikeness: *anomoiotês*
unlimited: *apeiros*
unmanifest: *aphanês*
unmoved: *akinêtos*
unpersuasive: *apithanos*
unrefuted: *anelenktos*
unseen: *aeidês*
unshaken: *atremês*
use: *khreia*
useful: *khrêsimos*
utterance: *prophora*

validate: *epideiknunai*
valuable: *khrêsimos*
variation, variety: *diaphora*

verb: *rhêma*
verbatim: *kata lexin*
vertical: *koruphê (kata)*
virtually: *dunamei*
virtue: *aretê*
vivifying: *zôtikos*
void: *kenon*
vulgar: *phortikos*

warp: *parekklinein*
way of taking: *apodokhê*
way: *tropos*
well-ordered: *eutaktos*
well-rounded: *eukuklos*
what is: *on*
what something causes: *aitiatos*
white, to have gone: *leleukôsthai*
whole: *holos; holotês*

wisdom: *sophia; phronêsis*
withdraw: *hupokhôrein*
witness, to bear: *marturein; summarturein*
witness: *martus*
wonder: *thauma; thaumazein*
word: *lexis; logos; rhêma; onoma; rhêton*
work back up: *anatrekhein*
work: *sungramma*
world-arrangement: *diakosmos*
write: *graphein; sungraphein*
write up (verb): *anagraphein*
write-up (noun): *anagraphê*
writing: *gramma; graphê; sungramma*
wrong, to be; go wrong: *hamartanein*
wrongly: *ouk orthôs*

zealously: *philotimôs*
zoophyte: *zôiophuton*

Greek–English Index

References are to the page and line numbers of the Greek text (indicated in the margins of the translation).

adiairetos, indivisible, 73,12; 81,8; 81,34bis; 82 *passim*; 83,16.19; 84,1; 85,24; 86,23; 87,4.7; 88,13.28; 90,29; 93,6; undivided, 94,2

adialeiptos, uninterrupted, 28,11

adiarthrôtos, unarticulated, 6,16

adioristos, without distinction, 16,22; indistinct, 16,31; *adioristôs*, without distinction, 6,36; 21,16; 50,12

aeidês, unseen, 39,20

agapan, be content, 4,25; 5,5

agapêsis, delight, 12,28

agathos, good, 1,13; 4,27; 5,11; 14,7; 15,18.21; 26,13.17; 43,6.10.11; 50,11; 82,23.25; 87,10; 100,6.11.12

agathotês, goodness, 7,18; 43,10.11

agein, erect 54,25.32; 55,1; 56,4; draw, 62,31; 64,19

agenêtos, ungenerated, 2,24; 13,27; 22,33; 23,4; 26,20; 27,5; 28,7; 29,21; 30,1.4 38,20.22; 43,15; 71,7-8; 78,12.24-25; 79,30

agnoein, be ignorant, 12,2.3; 45,30

agnoia, ignorance, 39,21

agônizesthai, contend, 51,1

aïdios, eternal, 2,17.28bis; 23,4; 24,24.31; 25,4.22; 41,18; 77,12.19; 79,2; *to aïdion*, eternity, 2,14; 5,15

ainigmatôdês, riddling, 7,3; 8,10; *ainigmatôdôs*, in riddles, 36,30

ainittein, hint, 18,14; 99,33; speak riddlingly; 34,10; refer riddlingly, 69,1; speak in riddles, 77,32; hint riddlingly, 69,1; 96,12

aisthêsis, sensation, 1,15; 2,3; 8,13; 12,19.26; 15,13.23; 16,10; 17,23; 19,14; 20,4.23; 26,25; 36,23; 37,18; 49,27; sense, 12,28; 20,18; 23,24

aisthêtikos, sensory, 17,19

aisthêtos, sensible, 7,18; 20,18; 26,23; 30,15; 31,19.23.27; 32,1; 34,9.11; 35,20; 36,15; 37,20; 38,26; 39,11; 43,18; 80,3; 88,24.27; 91,5; 92,1; 96,24; 97,14; 100,24.27; 101,10.23.26; perceptible, 7,18

aitein, postulate, 47,16; 49,18

aitêma, postulate, 12,6; 47,19

aitia, reason, 4,8; 70,3; 71,10.12; cause, 14,22; 15,30.32.33; 16,1.3; 26,16; 27,4.19; 28,26.28; 32,3; 34,16; 35,31; 39,17; 40,2; 41,19; 43,8.9.21; 45,32; 70,3; 102,4; justification, 54,2; *kat' aitian*, in a causal manner, 88,17.20

aitiasthai, criticize, 45,11; 69,1.5

aitiatos, what something causes, 10,19.23

aitiologia, causal explanation, 7,5; *aitiologikôs*, with causal explanations, 3,8

aition, cause, 3,16.17.19.26; 5,6.25; 6,14.15.35; 7,4.8bis.14.17.20.21; 8,2.4.8; 9,24.34; 10,9-12,4 *passim*; 13,8.15.25; 14,14.25.26; 15,16.17; 18,26.28.32; 21,2; 26,5.12.15; 27,16; 28,12; 29,9.12; 31,11.21; 34,15.16; 35,27; 36,18; 38,12.23.27; 43,6.11.13; 58,21; 87,10; 88,5.9.10; 92,12; reason, 95,25

aitiôdês, causal, 17,25; *aitiôdôs*, causally, 88,25

akinêsia, immobility, 40,2

akinetos, unmoved, 8,7; 11,19; 20,9; 21,28.29.35; 22,14.16.17.23bis; 23,7.15; 28,7; 29,16.17; 34,3; 37,5-38,20 *passim*; 39,22.27; 40,9.23.25; 41,3-42,20 *passim*; 45,27; 46,9.14.26; 47,2.21; 49,21.30; 52,9.17; 53,8-54,7 *passim*; 70,29; 79,13.32; 80,4.17; 87,1.11

akhôristos, inseparable, 1,16.21; 2,2; 43,14.21; 84,14

228   Greek–English Index

akolouthein, be consequent, 2,10; 2,32; 15,20; follow, 4,35; 6,6; 31,10.24; 35,29; 71,2; 72,21; be in sequence, 20,29; be consistent, 70,28; 75,3; *katakolouthein*, follow, 10,13; 73,2; *parakalouthein*, be concomitant, 3,16.32; *parakolouthêma*, by-product, 4,27; *sunakolouthein*, follow together, 5,20

akribeia, precision, 4,10; 8,11.17; 9,26

akribês, precise, 2,7; 5,18; 17,17; 18,19; 20,8; 83,33; *akribôs*, precisely, 6,27; 14,19; 18,27.28; 80,28

akroamatikos, acroamatic, 8,18.19.22.27

akroasis, lectures, 1,1; 1,3; 4,6.10.14

akron, highest part, 2,5; 4,21; summit, 16,16; 88,13

alêtheia, truth, 1,14; 5,30; 20,19; 30,15.18; 38,19.31; 39,11; 41,4.6.9; 51,6; 88,24; 97,30

alêthês, true, 13,11.12; 37,21; 40,1; 50,28; 54,2; 79,3; 82,23.30; 100,8; 101,2

alêtheuein, speak truly, 12,24; 75,9

alêthôs, truly, 89,29

alloiôsis, alteration, 41,26

alloiôtikê kinêsis, alteration, 20,22; *alloiôtikos*, altering, 24,7

alogia, irrational soul, 1,8.11

alogos, irrational, 1,7.11

amblus, (*gônia*) obtuse, 66,12.14; 67,2

amerês, without parts, 47,27; 49,4.5; 89,29; 93,6

ameristos, partless, 87,11; *ameristôs*, without partition, 88,8

amesos, immediate, 11,13; 12,19; 13,18bis; 14,15.16; 15,6.7; 18,31; 49,2

ametablêtos, unchanging, 29,19

amphikurtos, gibbous, 58,10-11

anabebêkôs, more elevated, 9,12.13.20; 15,34; 21,7; *epanabebêkôs*, more elevated, 20,32; 47,19

anaisthêtos, non-sensible, 26,22; 43,17

anagein, trace back, 43,12; refer, 71,12

anagraphein, write up, 26,29; 28,31; 95,33; *anagraphê*, write-up, 28,34

anairein, abolish, 40,26.28; 46,14.23.25; 47,1-2.3.3-4; 51,1.13.16; 55,14.22.23; 70,7.13.24.27; 71,2–3.4.20.21.25bis; 77,22.23; 84,33; 92,1; 94,13; 99,11.13.16; take away, 47,3; reject, 47,12.17.32.33;

48,1; 49,16.22.24.33; 50,2.8; 95,12; destroy, 54,19; *sunanairein*, destroy when it is destroyed, 19,4bis.7bis.16-17; *proanairein*, first abolish, 80,4

anakuptein, emerge, 95,4

analuein, be resolved, 13,32; 24,10; be analysable, 91,28

analusis, resolution, 35,21; *Hustera Analutika*, *Posterior Analytics*, 15,15; 76,15

anamnêsis, reference, 60,29

anamphilekton, uncontested, 5,33bis; 53,15

anankazein, compel, 39,21; 89,16

anankaios, necessary, 3,21.28; 6,25; 8,34; 9,4; 10,7; 21,22.26; 38,13; 45,20; 53,5; 59,23; 75,14.17; 90,16; necessity, 6,33; *anankaiôs*, with necessity, 51,21

anankê, it is necessary, 3,31.33; 21,8; 54,10; necessity, 8,13; 24,6; 30,7; 40,3; 42,16; 53,1; must, 11,27; 14,30; 15,11.29; 19,31; 20,15; 28,2; 29,8; 40,20; 41,26; 42,5.17; 44,20; 47,17.19; 52,12.17; 62,32; 63,12; 67,31; 75,5; 77,3.4; 80,13; 101,14; must necessarily, 20,28; 22,22; 37,10; 46,5; necessarily, 22,32; 88,2; *ex anankês*, necessarily, 2,10; *pasa anankê*, must by all necessity, 53,1

anaplêrein, supply, 27,4; 36,21; 37,3

anapodeiktos, indemonstrable, 11,13; 49,1.8.12.16; *anapodeiktôs*, without demonstration, 13,19.20; 14,16.17

anapodoton, lacking a counterpart, 45,11

anarrhôsis, recovery, 5,1

anaskeuazein, refute, 71,29

anatrekhein, work back up, 19,19

anatrepein, overturn, 71,20.26.30

andreios, courageous, 4,32; 98,8

anekleiptos, inexhaustible, 30,4; 88,21; *to anekleipton*, inexhaustibility, 29,20; 41,31

anelenktos, unrefuted, 77,11

anendeês, non-deficient, 30,11bis; non-lacking, 40,7

aneuphêmeisthai, be proclaimed, 47,31

anexapatêtôs, without error, 59,32

anodos, ascent, 14,7

anôlethros, indestructible, 26,20-21; 30,1; 43,16; 78,12

Greek–English Index

anomoiomerês, anhomoeomerous, 85,13.16.18

anomoios, unlike, 23,1.3; 60,1.2; 101,11

anomoiotês, unlikeness, 101,7

anomogenês, non-uniform, 27,1.27; non-homogeneous, 76,25

anomoiogenês, of unlike kind, 59,24; 60,5

antapodidonai, give as a counterpart, 44,26

antapodosis, counterpart, 44,1.23

anthrôpeios, human, 9,18.21

anthrôpinos, human, 5,8

anthrôpos, human being, 12,27; 16,13.19.20; 17,9; 18,10; 21,12; 33,22; 35,3.4.17; 50,25; 51,23.28-29.30; 72,11; 73,22; 91,22. 31.32; man, 19,6-7; 76,11; 100,3.5-6.11.12bis.13; 101,2; human, 82,27.28bis.32bis.33; 90,27bis; 93,7-95,11 *passim*; 97,23bis.26; 98,10.14; 102,8

antidiastellein, see **diastellein**

antigraphein, reply, 8,36

antigraphos, manuscript, 44,28; 77,6

antikeimenos, opposite, 92,15; 95,25; 99,10

antikeisthai, be opposed, 6,12; 23,33; 94,14.16.23; be opposite, 10,28; 21,33; 75,13.14

antilegein, argue against, 21,20; 41,15; 46,8.12.28; 47,4; 49,24; 50,7; 51,4; 71,19; 77,10; 88,22; 89,1

antilogia, argument against, 37,8; 70,5; 71,12; 88,30; arguing against, 47,4.5; 51,12.16; 82,16

antiphasis, contradiction, 21,26; 91,1; contradictory (disjunction), 37,14; 82,24.27

antiphatikos, contradictory, 42, 16

antistoikhia, pair of opposites, 29,13

antithesis, opposition, 6,28; 30,20; 31,8; 34,14.17; 82,27

anumnein, celebrate, 29,17; 86,21

apantan, respond, 83,7

apantêsis, reply, 76,30; 93,2; response, 83,5; 97,10

apatê, deception, 51,9

apatêlos, deceptive, 30,19; 38,32; 39,10

apathês, that cannot be affected, 23,1; impassive, 82,2

apeiria, infinity, 5,2; 29,21

apeiros, infinite, 3,33bis; 4,2; 6,20; 21,31-23,17 *passim*; 24,8.13.15.17.27; 25,4.14; 26,31; 27,4.13.18.22.26; 28,8.9.22.24.25; 29,20.23.28; 30,4; 34,20; 41,11-43,2 *passim*; 43,24; 44,3.24; 45,3; 72,28.30.31.32; 74,28; 75,23.25.28; 76,7-28 *passim*; 77,4.7; 81,17.20; 82,11.13; 87,4; 88,3; 95,27; infinity, 4,2; 28,26; 29,9.20; 48,20; 49,11; 52,10.11.19; 71,3; unlimited, 11,14; infinitely many, 19,22; 69,25; 100,6; *ep' apeiron*, ad infinitum, 4,1; 55,21.22; 69,25bis; 88,21; 90,25; to infinity, 6,20; 81,20; 82,6; 87,22; infinite regress, 13,19; 14,16

apemphainôn, counter-intuitive, 50,10; 51,5.13; 53,12; 74,17; 82,4

aphairesis, abstraction, 18,6.22; 19,15

aphanês, unmanifest, 37,17.19

aphereponôs, in a careless way, 43,4; carelessly, 80,16

aphorizein, distinguish, 8,1; determine, 14,32; 29,9-10

aphthartos, imperishable, 2,23; 27,6; 79,16.30

aplatês, without breadth, 47,27; 49,5-6.7

apodeiktikos, demonstrative, 13,17.20; 14,15.18; 15,14.25; 18,29; 49,14; *Apodeiktika*, *Apodictics* [= *Posterior Analytics*], 20,31

apodeiktos, demonstrable, 15,11

apodeiknunai, demonstrate, 1,17; 2,14; 7,35; 9,7.14.17; 15,12.16.20.26.31; 16,1; 21,10; 40,9; 46,16; 47,10.11.30; 49,7bis.16.19; 55,15; 69,5; 78,1.24; 80,18; 101,4.16; render, 44,29; *proapodeiknunai*, demonstrate beforehand, 40,11

apodeixis, demonstration, 8,11.12; 9,6.31bis; 12,20; 13,12; 15,8.17.27; 18,25.31; 29,21; 49,2.26.27.34; 53,24; 60,10.11; 69,6.12; 83,28

apodidonai, set out, 61,4; 70,3; give an account, 97,13

apodokhê, way of taking, 45,10

apodosis, restoration, 4,36; account, 7,9; result, 60,30

apogignôsis, rejection, 60,6

Greek–English Index

apogignôskein, refuse to recognize, 28,1
apokrinein, distinguish, 13,4; separate
  (out, off), 24,24; 34,21; 35,15; answer,
  89,7
apokrisis, separation, 35,8; answer, 89,10
apolambanein, receive, 29,10.12
apollunai, perish, 26,24; pass away, 27,6
apologeisthai, *apologizein*, give an
  account, 19,18; 35,28
apoluein, detach, 20,7
apomnêmoneuein, record, 23,16; 26,14;
  43,4; 44,15; 50,14
apophainesthai, assert, 12,24; declare,
  48,13; express, 36,30; judge, 74,28
apophansis, asserting, 12,25
apophantikos, declarative, 91,17.21.33;
  apophantikôs, declaratively, 50,27;
  51,2-3
apophasis, denial, 17,29; negation, 19,33;
  82,30.
aporia, difficulty, 48,27; aporia, 52,13;
  70,2.14.19.25.26; 71,4.9.14.16;
  83,7-86,16 *passim*; 91,20-101,16
  passim
aporos, precluded, 15,3
aporein, be at loss, 49,32; be in aporia,
  97,13; *aporeisthai*, be an aporia, 97,12;
  diaporein, raise the puzzle, 48,10; raise
  aporiai, 70,25.26; *prosaporein*, raise an
  aporia, 92,31; 96,7
aposkeuazein, get rid of, 50,2; discard, 51,31
apoteinesthai, allude, 88,13
apotelein, make, 5,10; produce, 11,7; 59,1;
  apoteloumenon, effect, 11,30
apotelesma, effect, 11,28–9; 17,25;
  88,10-11
apotemnein, see *temnein*
apsukhos, which has no soul, 3,4bis
aretê, virtue, 4,23; 100,5
arithmein, count, 69,23; 98,10.13;
  katarithmein, enumerate, 98,11
arithmêtikos, of arithmetic, 59,3;
  arithmetical, 59,3; arithmetician, 59,6;
  arithmêtikê, arithmetic, 48,16
arithmos, number, 13,34; 21,31.32; 26,28;
  42,13; 43,20; 58,25-59,24 *passim*;
  66,26; 73,10.11bis; 76,13.14bis.16;
  80,30; 81,4bis.6; 93,8; 95,22; *arithmôi*,
  numerically 72,10.11; 73,33

arkhaios, ancient, 90,23; 96,33; *arkhaïkos*,
  ancient, 60,30
arkhê, principle, 2,8.10.11;
  3,15bis.16.22.26.27.32; 4,5.13.14;
  5,22.26.28; 6 *passim*; 7,12.13.27;
  8,13-16,6 *passim*; 18,26.29.31; 19,19-
  22,26 *passim*; 23,15-26.30 *passim*;
  27,3-29,11 *passim*; 30,20; 31,10.20;
  35,24; 37,10-38,22 *passim*; 40,23.27;
  41,10-43,26 *passim*; 44,3.9.12.15.27.33;
  45,4-50,8 *passim*; 50,30; 51,13.16;
  53,15-23 *passim*; 54,6-55,23 *passim*; 59,3;
  69,12; 71,8; 72,2; 87,8; 98,6bis.7; starting
  point, 37,13; 61,5; 71,17; 75,4; 98,7;
  beginning, 23,5; 29,23.24.26; 34,29;
  90,29; *ex arkhês*, originally, 59,11; 73,19;
  74,6; 91,20
arkhein, begin, 5,24; 6,35; 20,24; rule over,
  31,15
arkhetupos, archetypal, 31,19
arkhikos, principial, 11,8
arkhoeidês, principial, 15,31; 16,7;
  35,26.31; fundamental, 7,21; 36,16
artios, even, 11,15; 76,14.16
asapheia, obscurity, 8,19; 21,19
asaphês, obscure, 50,23; unclear, 83,9;
  asaphesteros, less clear, 19,2.3
astronomia, astronomy, 14,4
asullogistos, non-deductive, 50,6;
  asullogistôs, invalidly, 51,15
asumblêtos, incomparable, 60,4
askholia, occupation, 4,29; concern, 5,4;
  askholos, engaged in serious business,
  51,12
atelês, incomplete, 29,11
ateleston, unending, 30,2; 78,13
ateleutêtos, without end, 29,27; 30,9.12;
  40,5
athanatos, immortal, 32,24; *to athanaton*,
  immortality, 15,19
atheos, atheist, 23,23
athetein, athetize, 44,28.32
atomos, atomic, 7,23; 85,24; 94,16; atom,
  22,8; 28,9.13.17.25; 36,2; 42,11;
  43,27.32; 45,3; 82,3.4.5; individual,
  74,9
atopia, absurdity, 76 32
atopos, odd, 7,6; absurd, 44,28.30; 54,8;
  74,14.27; 75,10–18; 81,25.29; 82,4; 85,8;

Greek–English Index

92,19; 95,23; 96,12; 98,18.19; *to atopon,* absurdity, 36,29; 53,6.7bis. 11; 54,4; 73,25; 74,1.4.13; 75,19.29; 86,7.9.15; 87,2.19.24; 88,5; 91,2.33; 92,10; 93,30

atremês, unshaken, 30,2; 78,13

autokinêtos, self-moved, 15,23; *to autokinêton,* self-motion, 15,19

automaton, spontaneity, 6,15

autopistos, self-warranting, 15,5;9-10; 16,2; 18,31; 48,30; 49,5.8.12.15

axiôma, axiom, 9,29; 17,27; 19,30; 21,25.26; 47,28

axôn, axis, 53,19

basis, base, 60,7; 61,26.30.34; 62,6

bathus, deep, 36,32; *bathos,* depth, 35,29; 37,1

bios, life, 4,17; 14,2

daimôn, goddess, 31,14; 39,16

dapanan, exhaust, 55,6.20

deiknunai, show, 2,5; 4,27; 9,25; 15,22; 17,27.28; 20,10.13; 22,31; 23,17; 47,9.18; 48,4.14; 49,26.29; 52,24; 54,11; 66,11.14; 79,13; 80,4.22; 85,31; 87,11; 89,2; 90,25.27; 96,23; 99,9.14; 100,16; *prodeiknunai,* show first, 79,30

deixis, proof, 51,25; 55,28; 58,1.23; 59,2; being indicated, 95,18

dekas, decad, 26,27

dêlôtikos, to make clear, 13,23

dêmiourgikos, craftsmanly, 24,6; 36,12; demiurgic, 32,2

dêmiourgos, Demiurge, 15,8

desmos, bond, 30,8; 39,27; 40,4; 79,32

diagignôskein, recognize, 5,2-3; 16,19; discern, 17,20

diagônios, bisector, 62,28

diagramma, diagram, 61,2

diairein, divide, 58,5.9.23; 81,14.35.36.37; 83,22; 85,17; 92,7; 94,1; *sundiairein,* divide, 82,9-10

diairesis, division, 1,4.6; 3,11; 21,28; 22,1.15.20; 37,28; 38,10; 41,10.22.23; 42,16.18.19.31; 43,3; 44,30; 46,25; 58,10; 71,29; 72,1.8; 73,3.4.5.13.18; 74,14.21; 75,7; 80,19.20.22.29; 81,10; 83,4.5.6; 95,22.32; 96,3.17.22.32; 97,19; 98,4.9; 99,22

diairetikos, disjunctive 21,25; *to diairetikon,* disjunction, 22,16; 37,13.15.27.28; 38,14; 42,8; 74,3

diairetos, divisible, 4,1; 6,20; 55,21.23; 81,18.20; 82,5; 86,4.17.18; 87,22; 90,25

diakosmos, world-arrangement, 36,15; ordering, 39,8

diakrinein, differentiate, 2,2; 34,27; 38,12; 88.8.19; 89,3; distinguish, 21,17bis; 37,5; 100,20; separate, 25,26; 27,16; 31,23; 101,9

diakrisis, differentiation, 2,7; 34,8.27; 35,10; 88,16.18.20.26; 100,25; 101,15; separation, 27,7.12; 28,2; 31,28

dialegesthai, discuss, 2,13; 6,20; 7,30; 51,32; dispute, 50,8; argue, 51,7

dialektikos, dialectician, 47,26; 49,9; 51,7; dialectical, 71,31; 86,2; *dialektikê (epistêmê),* dialectic, 16,27; 47,22.25; 71,32; 83,27

dialektos, speech, 10,15

dialogikon, dialogue 8,17

dialusis, dissolution, 4,35

diametros, diameter, 56,12; 57,5.10.23; 61,8.11; 64,12; 67,17.34bis; 68, 5.8.10bis; diagonal, 62,32; 63,13.14

dianoêtikos, discursive, 15,2.13; 18,15

dianoia, reasoning, 17,32; thought, 36,32

diapherein, be superior, 8,25; differ, 10,9; 11,6; 13,21; 24,29; 36,21; 43-45 *passim;* 81,3.9; 92,4; 93,23; disagree, 29,4

diaphônia, disagreement, 36,20.25

diaphora, variety, 4,19; 16,23; 20,5; 34,9.11.19; 36,3; difference, 12,16; 18,7.9.19.20; 28,18; 35,28.29; 36,1; 41,23; variation, 28,32; differentia, 41,27

diaphoros, differing, 5,10; different, 36,19

diarthroun, articulate, 17,17; 37,9

diarthrôsis, articulation, 16,21.33; 18,19

diaspan, disperse, 81,14

diaspasmos, dispersal, 88,24-25

diastasis, extension, 4,1; dimension, 47,33

diastatos, extended, 2,2; 47,29

diastellein, divide, 70,18.28–9; *antidiastellein,* contrast, 40,24-25; 41,2.6

diastêma, interval 4,3; 6,23; 13,34; distance 16,19

232 Greek–English Index

diaskhêmatizein, arrange, 43,20
diathesis, disposition, 28,22; 52,19bis; 99,27
diathigê, intercontact, 28,13
didaskalos, teacher, 22,28
didaskein, teach, 2,12; 3,1.5.8.10.15.30; 4,9; 5,23.28; 6,11; 7,34; 31,19;
 anadidaskein, teach, 6,19
didaskalias, teaching, 14,32.33-34; 15,12
diïxis, traversal, 18,9
dikaiosunê, justice, 4,23.31
dikhotomein, bisect, 62,25
diorismos, definition, 6,16
diorizein, distinguish, 6,29; determine, 3,22; 8,33; 9,27; 10,1; 12,11; 21,4.13;
 diôrismenos, discrete, 84,16.30; 85,22.25.32.34; 86,8
dogma, doctrine, 43,4; opinion, 71,24.25
doxa, opinion, 8,14; 12,19; 13,1.11; 21,25.29; 22,17.21; 24,8; 26,24; 30,18; 36,27; 37,21; 38,4.21.25.31; 42,10; 44,30.32; 45,33; 46,26; 49,34; 50,4.30.31; 71,6.19; 76,32; 80,20; 99,31; appearance, 25,16; fame, 26,8; doctrine, 27,4; 28,31; 29,5; 50,14.23; seeming, 30,16
doxastos, opinable, 13,3.5; 38,26; 39,10;
 doxaston, object of opinion, 87,5
doxastikos, opinionative, 18,16
doxazein, have opinion, 13,3; ***to doxazein***, opinion, 13,10
dunamis, ability, 26,8; 89,6; power, 1,10; 8,25; 9,20; 18,34; 25,27; 26,13; 29,16.20; potentiality, 81,10.12.13.14.17.33; 92,6; 95,21; 96,7.18; 97,3.8; 98,11.15.16.20.22; 99,1.3.20; ***dunamei***, virtually, 11,8; in power, 61,7.9; 62,18; 63,1; 64,19; 66,4-67,36 *passim*; potentially, 82,6; 92,8.14.21.22.24; 93,8.18; 96,19; 98,17; ***dunamei nous***, potential intellect 1,8.11.15.19; 2,3
dunatos, possible, 14,8; 15,1; 16,2; 21,34; 42,3; 47,18; 68,31; 69,15.26; 74,22; 88,27; 91,7
duskinêtos, hard to move, 25,11
dusmetablêtos, hard to change, 25,11

eidenai, know, 12,2.18.27.30.31.32bis; 16,14; 18,25; 19,24.25; 21,8; 49,25; 75,4;
acknowledge, 12,26; 76,6; be aware, 44,11; 80,3; ***to eidenai***, knowing, 8,31; 10,4; 12,14.17.30; 13,1.14; 14,12
eidêsis, knowing, 12,22.25.26.28.31; 13,6.16; 14,13.19; knowledge, 17,18
eidêtikos, of the forms, 88,16
eidikos, formal, 43,13
eidos, form, 1,16.18.22; 2,25; 3,18; 4,20; 5,12; 6,12; 7,17.25.27; 8,9; 9,23; 10 *passim*; 11,1.11.22bis; 13,32.33; 14,1; 16,28; 20,12.17; 26,6.18.19.20; 27,21; 34,18; 43 *passim*; 44,14.25; 45,6.7; 91,18; 98,2; 100,16.25; 101,7.15.17; species, 6,19; 16,22; 73,9.10.15; 74,10; 76,16; 79,1; 80,30bis.32; 81 *passim*; 93,7.8.11.21; 94,23.24; 95,22; 102,6; ***eidei***, specifically, 72,10; ***kata to eidos***, formal, 9,25
eikotôs, reasonably, 4,3.9; 6,24; 39,21; 46,6; 81,6; plausibly, 96,10
eikotologia, probable account, 18,30
eilikrinês, pure, 16,26.30; 17,21; ***eilikrinôs***, purely, 77,25
eisagein, introduce, 51,2.3; 52,12; 53,12; 72,29; 73,16; 80,31; 83,121; 86,11; 98,1
eisdekhesthai, receive, 26,21; 40,19.20; 43,16; 80,13.14
ekdidonai, publish, 8,28bis
ekdokhê, interpretation, 37,6; taking, 72,14
ekklinein, bend, 91,26; ***parekklinein***, warp, 96,34
eklambanein, take, 21,20
ekneasmos, renewal, 4,36
ekphainein, bring to light, 7,1; reveal, 8,32; express, 33,7
emphainein, express, 93,12.31; 94,8.21
ektithenai, set out, 48,26; 60,27; 86,6; 100,2
elenkhein, refute, 36,26; 37,7; 38,6; 58,2; 60,19; 71,27; 75,26; 83,14; 86,17; ***dielenkhein***, refute, 36,30.31-32
elenkhos, refutation, 83,15.16; ***Sophistikoi elenkhoi***, *Sophistical Refutations*, 52,15; 70,19
eleutherios, liberal, 5,10
empedos, steadfast, 30,7; 40,3; enduring, 34,1
emphanês, manifest, 39,19
empherein, insert, 31,3; involve, 48,25
empiptein, be included, 3,32; 4,4; fall, 64,30

Greek–English Index

empeiria, experience, 8,25
empodios, difficult, 98,4; 99,23bis
empsukhos, ensouled, 3,4.6; 15,24
enalinkios, like, 52,23.26; 89,22
enallax, in alternate ways, 25,24; in alternation, 32,18
enantiologia, contrary account, 28,32
enantion, contrary, 20,2.11.16; 24,24; 25,18; 27,1; 28,6; 31,10; 34,13; 36,6.19; 43,25; 44,1-45,7 *passim*; 50,13; 53,13; 77,23.24.26; 82,26; 98,19; (arguments) to the contrary, 54,8; *to enantion*, contrariwise, 31,16
enantiôsis, contrariety, 19,23.24.26; 30,14; 31,30; 44,33; 45,8.12
enantiotês, contrariety, 44,7–8.9
enargeia, evident [experience], 54,1.9; what is obvious, 75,7; 77,14; evident [truth], 94,14
enargês, obvious, 17,27; 20,9; 37,14; 74,12; clear, 37,14.16; 81,5; evident, 49,27; 53,25; 54,1.9; *enargôs*, obviously, 20,3; 73,16; 74,14; clearly, 78,24; 83,28
enarmonios, harmonious, 50,13; *enarmoniôs*, in harmony, 29,5
endeês, deficient, 29,11; lacking, 40,7.8; (*einai*), fall short, 90,2
endoxos, plausible, 49,10; 50,28bis; plausible [premise], 47,26; 49,10; 51,8-9.10; *endoxôs*, plausibly, 86,3
energeia, activity, 1,19; 29,16; 32,11; actuality, 81,11.12.13.14.16.32; 92,6.8.14.17; 94,1; 95,21; 96,7; 97,8; 98,15.16.21; 99,1.2.4.20; action, 91,25; *energeiâi*, actually, 92,22.23; 93,8.18; 96,18; 98,17; *ho energeiâi nous*, actual intellect, 1,18.19; 2,4; *ho kat' energeian nous*, actual intellect, 1,9
engraphein, inscribe, 54,21-58,19 *passim*; 67,20
enkalein, accuse, 36,25
ennoia, notion, 7,16; 18,1; 46,29.32; 49,1.4; 59,21; 93,10; conception, 29,22; 30,5.15; 35,18; 77,15; thought, 40,9-10; 89,5; intention 87,20; 92,25
ennoein, consider, 5,3; recognize, 10,34; 92,2; have the thought, 84,21
enstasis, objection, 58,13; 73,4; defensive move, 97,2

entelekheia, actuality, 97,3
enulos, enmattered (said of a form), 1,16; 2,4; 26,18; material (said of a composite), 13,29
enuparkhein, be present in, 10,14.19; 13.31; 27,15; *enuparkhon*, constituent, 10,12.31
epagein, add, 9,36; 10,3; 13,7.15; 14,12; 17,13; 19,9; 38,29; 39,13; 40,2; 52,10; 70,32; 73,14.29; 75,10; 78,7; 79,30; 80,11; 85,10.25; 86,15; 91,1; 92,30; 96,2.10.22.30; adduce, 17,13; 87,2.19
epagogê, induction, 9,33; 20,11; 49,28.32; 53,13.25
epaiein, have an understanding, 29,2
epanabebêkôs, see *anabebêkôs*
epaphê, contact, 55,18
epekeina, beyond, 1,20; 29,14.16
epharmozein, fit, 55,8.10.17; *epharmottein*, fit, 17,9.11; 88,29; apply to, 37,5
ephistanai, *ephistanein*, posit, 7,4.17.20; 27,16; remark, 12,15; 13,28; 19,25; 37,7; 59,5.18; 102,3; observe, 17,33; 18,24; 21,5-6; 22,9; 43,8; 82,25
epibolê, conjecture, 15,10; approach, 85,31-32; effort, 96,1
epideiknunai, reveal, 4,24; 73,24; display, 29,4; 36,21; 101,12.21; validate, 47,20; argue, 54,6; 76,31
epidekhesthai, admit, 10,18; 95,18; accept, 17,37; receive, 88,24
epigennêma, by-product, 16,25
epignôsis, discernment, 14,10
epigraphê, title, 4,8; *epigraphein*, entitle, 4,10.13.14
epikheirein, undertake, 29,1; 48,13; 51,8; 71,19; 101,3; argue, 46,31; 80,26; *epikheirein tôi logoi*, undertake to argue, 74,19
epikheirêma, argument, 75,27; 77,9; 86,6; 99,18
epikheirêsis, attempt, 57,25; argument, 71,31; 77,3
epikrateia, dominance, 34,10.11
epikratein, dominate, 18,7; predominate, 27,8; 33,4; 34,5.7-8
epikrisis, resolution, 48,28

234   *Greek–English Index*

epilusis, see *lusis*
epimelês, very careful, 73,4
epinoein, conceive, 11,6; 93,6;
   proepinoeisthai, be conceptually prior,
   11,26
epinoia, conception, 11,5.9bis; *kat'*
   epinoian, conceptual, 95,16
epipedos, plane, 7,9.27; 17,2; 47,28; 59,17;
   surface, 35,29; 55,6.20.21; 60,1; 64,2;
   69,27; 81,27.28; *epipedikos,* plane,
   59,17
epiphaneia, surface, 81,25.27; 94,30
epipolaios, superficial, 36,28; 37,6; 51,10
episêmainein, remark, 42,27; 51,27
episkêptein, charge, 7,6; 46,24
episkopein, see *skopein*
epistasis, remarking, 14,1; observing,
   17,38; 74,30; *epistaseôs heneken,* in
   order to observe, 97,10
epistêmê, scientific knowledge, 5,23;
   9,3.30.32.36; 12,20.25.29.33; 13,1.12.17;
   14,9-10.11.12.14.27; 17,23; 18,13; 21,3;
   49,12.13.15; science, 10,1.5; 12,9; 13,23;
   15,34; 16,27; 21,4; 47,7.20.23.24.31bis;
   48,4.5.6.21.22.29-30.31; 72,1; scientific
   knowing, 12,22; scientifically knowing,
   12,25; knowledge, 69,21
epistasthai, scientifically know, 12,14; 16,5;
   to epistasthai, scientific knowing, 8,31;
   12,3; 13,14; scientific knowledge,
   9,2.3.27.28; 13,10; scientifically
   knowing, 12,14.18; 14,12.27
epistêmôn, who possesses scientific
   knowledge, 12,8; 14,30
epistêmonikos, scientific, 13,7.10.16;
   14,13.19.24; *epistêmonikôs,*
   scientifically, 12,23.30-31; 16,5; 47,8;
   49,23.24
epistêtos, knowable, 69,20.21
epitasis, intensification, 75,12.17
epitêdeiôs ekhein, be suitable, 52,10; *to*
   epitêdeion suitability, 36,10
epitrekhein, go over, 70,12; 92,26
epizêtein, see *zêtein*
epizeugnunai, join, 54,28; 55,1.5; 56,5;
   61,27.32; 62,28-29; 63,2.4; 64,20.21.22;
   65,17; 67,24.27
êremia, rest, 6,29; 23,13.14; 29,13;
   êremoun, at rest, 22,27

eristikos, eristical, 51,24; 52,3; *eristikôs,*
   eristically, 51,11
erôtêmatikos, interrogative, 91,19
erôtêsis, questioning, 73,24; 74,2.6
eskhatôs, in the lowest way, 11,35
êthikos, ethical, 5,29; ethicist, 40,29;
   Nikomakheia êthika, Nicomachean
   Ethics, 14,9
ethos, custom, 41,3; manner, 60,30
eualloiôtos, easily [qualitatively] altered,
   25,10; 36,14
eudialutos, easy to resolve, 52,13; 82,10;
   86,5
eugnômonôs, charitably, 38,6; 45,29; 87,3
eukolos, easy, 37,6; 54,3; *eukolôs,* easily,
   36,24; neatly, 62,12
euktikos, optative, 91,19
eulogos, reasonable, 21,23; 70,9; plausible,
   75,17; *eulogôs,* reasonably, 28,22;
   79,17
euparadektos, easy to accept, 45,1; easily
   accepted, 51,3-4
eupathês, easily affected, 25,10
euplastos, easily-moulded, 36,12
euporein, have solution, 97,29
eusumbolon, honesty, 4,31
eutaktos, well-ordered, 14,23
euthunein, critically examine, 43,1;
   criticize, 75,4
euthugrammos, rectilineal, 59,28; 60,5;
   61,30; *euthugrammon,* rectilineal
   figure, 57,19.21; 59,26; 62,10-11; 64,4;
   68,31; 69,17; rectilineal area, 60,2;
   65,25-66,10 *passim*
euthus, straightaway, 3,21; 8,32; 21,1;
   immediately, 5,24; 45,33; 46,28;
   72,13.29; 74,13; from the start, 74,13;
   linear, 41,29; 42,4; straight, 44,18; 82,7;
   eutheia, straight line, 54,29-56,22;
   59,25; 60,5; 61,29; 63,22; 64,3; 66,4.5;
   69,9; 81,27.31
eutupôtos, easily-shaped, 36,11
exêgeisthai, interpret, 45,22; 73,28; 95,19;
   explain, 95,30
exêgêsis, interpretation, 44,11.21; 46,17;
   70,6.15.31; 73,28; commentary, 96,21
exêgêtês, commentator, 21,5; 44,33; 82,17;
   83,32; 93,3; 96,20; interpreter, 43,28;
   80,16

Greek–English Index

exetastikê, capable of examining, 47,23;
  exetazein, examine, 22,11
exôterikos, exoteric, 8,16; 83,27; 85,26

genesis, generation, 3,9; 27,25; coming-to-
  be, 11,11; 24,24; 26,16; 27,16.19;
  28,1.3.11; 31,8.11.12; 34,16; 35,21;
  39,28; 41,19; 42,2.5; 43,9; 50,13; 77,12;
  79,4.5; 80,1.3; 81,11; 88,21; becoming,
  35,10; 36,9; *Peri geneseôs kai phthoras*,
  On Generation and Perishing, 2,31
genêtos, generated, 2,31; 7,12; 30,20; 78,28;
  generable, 2,27.29; 13,25; 26,23; 43,18
gennan, generate, 23,2bis; 58,31; 88,1
genos, genus, 12,22.24; 43.24; 44 *passim*;
  45,6.9; 72-73 *passim*; 74.9; 75,19.21.22;
  76,7.9; 80,29.30.31; 81.2; 93,7.11.21;
  94,7; 95,22; 96,6; 102,6; kind, 21,33
geômetrês, geometer, 9,14; 47,12.18; 49,6;
  55,13.15
geômetria, geometry, 12,6; 13,26; 14,2;
  47,13.21; 48,31; 54,11
geômetrikos, geometrical 4,26; 54,15;
  69,12; of geometry, 47,12; 48,15; 54,16;
  55,12.22; 59,2; *Geômetrikê historia*,
  see *historia*
gignesthai, ginesthai, be generated,
  2,28.32; 22,33; 38,22; 58,31; be made,
  5,18; arise, 6,34; 8,4; 14,25; 15,14; 59,9;
  come-to-be, 7,8; 10,31; 13,31.32;
  24,9.19.30; 25,1.6.8; 26,24; 27,6.14.15;
  28,1.2.12; 29,24; 33,22.25; 34,1; 36,3;
  41,13.21.24.25.26.28.29.32; 42,4bis.9;
  43,13; 54,29; 71,8; 77,16.17bis.18.27.28;
  78,22bis.27.28; 79,9.27; 83,22;
  90,12.13bis; 100,18; come about, 15,13;
  18,1.22; turn out to be, 48,20; 71,31;
  90,10; become, 88,4; 91,13; 92,3; 99,4
gignôskein, ginôskein, know, 5,25; 9,24.34;
  13,3; 15,5.7.8; 49,14.15; 68,33; cognize,
  12,2.7.22; 13,8; come to know, 4,33;
  18,26; 20,1-2; 43,3; acknowledge, 31,8
gliskhrôs, in an overly subtle way, 88,11
gnêsios, genuine, 5,32; 80,15
gnômê, judgement, 30,23; 39,1; doctrine,
  36,31; thought, 39,9
gnôrimos, known, 14,29;
  15,12.15.21.28.31; 16,4.18.23.26.29.31;
  20,1.27; 36,22 37,12.18; knowable,

  37,20; 48,30; 53,14; companion,
  99,14
gnôrisma, distinguishing feature, 33,5
gnôrizein, recognize, 5,25; 9,2.3.34.37;
  11,32; 12,4; 13,8; 14,27; 16,6.9.10.12
gnôsis, cognition, 1,15; 12,25; 13,6.9;
  17,19.39; 18,2.15.18.20.29; 19,10;
  knowledge, 4,21; 5,11; 9,5.31.32; 11,12;
  13,2; 14,24.28; 16,7.11.17.24.34; 17,15;
  21,23; 41,5; 45,19; [kind of] knowledge,
  14,20; 15,5.7.14; knowing, 15,4
gnôstikos, cognitive, 1,10.13; 5,7; 14,5
gnôstos, knowable, 13,4.5; 14,23.25; 17,24;
  thing known, 18,1
gônia, angle, 44,18; 59,26.27.28; 60,4-67,33
  passim
gonimos, generative, 36,10
gramma, letter, 9,20; 10,15; 68,15; 100,19;
  writing, 39,21
grammê, line, 17,2.12; 47,27; 48,12; 49,4;
  54,26-7.28; 58,11; 60,12.14.15;
  81,8.24.27; 85,27
graphê, writing, 23,32; text, 44,22.26.28;
  45,10
graphein, write, 8,20.21.26.30; 20,20; 25,3;
  26,19; 80,7; 100,3; draw, 54,20;
  61,3.20.29; 64,28; 65,14; 69,26

hairesis, choice, 1,13; 90,4; school, 3,12; 6,2
hamartanein, be wrong, 44,22; go wrong,
  51,20; miss, 75,5; commit an error,
  94,15
haplous, simple, 2,11.12.15.21.26.27.29;
  4,35; 16,10.11.26.28.29; 17,22; 18,3;
  26,31; 35,26; 53,17; 58,2; 93,6;
  simple-minded, 74,17; 75,11; *haplôs*,
  simply, 39,10; 60,15; 87,9; 95,28;
  without qualification, 59,11; *simpliciter*,
  78,28; 79,19.23.26; 84,21; at all, 83,1; in
  general, 93,26
haplotês, simplicity, 18,12
hêdonê, pleasure, 4,27.30; savour, 35,3
hêgoumenon, antecedent, 9,30
hekkaidekagônon, 16-gon, 55,3.4
hêlikia, growing up, 17,14
helikoeidês, spiral, 60,12
hêmikuklion, semicircle, 56,2-57,20
  passim; 59,27; 60,4.25.26;
  61,13.14.15.17.22.26; 62,11.14-15.31;

Greek–English Index

63,17; 64,5.8; 66,10.13; 67,3.4.5.34; 69,14.15

hen, one, passim; **hen on**, see **on**

henas, unit, 95,8; 99,16; 102,3

henizein, unify, 84,2

henôsis, unification, 31,22.28; 34,8.19; 35,19; 88,7.24.27; union, 88,14.18.20; 101,14.19

henoun, unify, 81,20; 88,14.25; 89,3; 101,20

hepesthai, follow, 9,37; 16,2.7bis; 17,19; 75,18; 86,9.15; 91,2

hetairos, companion, 24,26; 28,15

heterotês, otherness, 89,3

hexagônon, hexagon, 57,1-58,18 passim; 60,20; 67,9-68,29 passim

historia, enquiry, 22,29; 23,30; 26,11; **Peri zôiôn historia**, Historia animalium, 3,8; **Geômetrikê historia**, History of Geometry, 60,22.31

historikon, historical work, 8,17; **historikôs**, empirically, 3,7; **historikai anagraphai**, reports and write-ups, 28,33-34

historein, report, 4,12; 7,14; 25,6.9; 67,8; say, 99,13; **prosistorein**, recount, 74,29-30

holikôteron, more universally, 36,17

holos, whole, 16,31.2; 17,6.34.36.38; 19,12; 44,12; 52,21.25; 53,4; 54,30; 58,9; 83-97 passim; 100,18.20; 101,29.30; overall, 10,8; **holôs**, generally, 3,18; in general, 6,18; 7,9; 8,17; 10,32; 20,15; 49,28; 71,13.15; 74,15; 82,21; at all, 15,1; 21,6; 37,24; 40,26; 42,24; 46,12.13; 49,5; 81,36; 83,1; overall, 20,17; in the first place, 21,21; in a general way, 70,9

holoskherês, crude, 16,17; 17,15.17.19.39;18,4.11.18.21; **holoskherôs**, in a crude way, 77,25

holotês, whole, 4,36; 17,7

homoiomeres, homoeomerous, 27,5.27; 85,12.13.18.19; **homoiomereia**, homoiomery, 7,21.23; 44,8bis

homoios, like, 12,23; 23,1bis.2bis.3; 28,20bis; 52,21; 101,11; similar, 26,23; 36,4; 43,18; 51,28.29.31; 61,6-62,21 passim; 63,25; 67,30; 68,3.5; 69,29.33; 84,19; alike, 86,24; **homoiôs**, in the same way, 2,2; 3,10; 22,32; 29,19; 38,7; 45,13; 77,24; 94,6; 95,8; 96,8; similarly,

7,17; 28,12; alike, 22,32; likewise, 27,14; 48,15; 81,29; 82,30; 93,17; 94,23; 97,20.24

homoiotês, similarity, 66,20; likeness, 101,7

homogenês, of the same kind, 21,33; 59,32; uniform, 26,31-27,1; homogeneous, 43,26

homologein, agree, 2,20; 9,30; 11,20; 15,6; 19,5; 26,20; 37,26; 38,18; 46,18; 53,22; 54,2; 79,23; 84,31; 85,17; 89,12; 93,10; 101,6; grant, 22,29; admit, 74,11; **proömologein**, agree beforehand (or previously), 13,4; 64,26

homônumos, what shares the same name, 26,23; 43,18; equivocal, 94,28

homoousios, of the same substance, 44,3

horismos, definition, 16,33; 17,1-18,12 passim; 49,2; 76,18.23; 91,32

horistikos, defining, 76,10.12

horizesthai, define, 6,16; 48,11; 76,14; **horizein**, determine, 69,25

hormasthai, proceed, 5,13; 54,15; 72,1

hormê, surge, 32,23

hormizein, anchor, 32,8

horos, definition, 12,6; 15,6.7; 49,1; boundary, 29,8; 81,18; bound, 30,13; mark, 34,12; term, 49,3

hulê, matter, 1,16.18.21; 2,1.6; 3,18; 4,20; 6,11; 7,16.24.27.35; 8,1bis; 9,23; 10,12.14.31.33; 11,1.11.21.22; 13,22bis.25.27.29.32.34; 25,17.18; 26,6.12.14.25; 28,17; 31,29; 38,23; 43,5.14

hulikos, material, 6,35; 7,21; 27,18

hupantan, confront, 45,21.25–6; 47,8; 49,29

huparkhein, belong to, 3,14.20; 4,6.7.9; 18,26; 22,32; 45,4; 76,12.13.24.25; 92,5.17; 96,16; 99,3; be, 5,33; 22,15; 42,15; 72,16; 76,28; be present, 10,23; 95,18; hold, 20,4; 90,12; exist, 28,12; 72,18; **proüparkhein**, exist prior to, 11,27; 29,8; 78,25.28; pre-exist, 31,25; **proüparkhon**, pre-existing, 15,7.14; **sunuparkhein**, exist together with, 11,29; coexist, 92,23

huperokhê, superiority, 5,3.17; dignity, 29,3; excess, 57,18

hupoballein, assign, 12,13; arrange under, 21,28

Greek–English Index

hupokeimenos, subject matter, 4,20; 50,9.30; subject, 11,5; 20,17; 92,5.13; 93,13; 94,13; 95,1; 96,5.13–14.25.27; what underlies, 24,4; underlying, 20,13.16; 24,27; 26,12; 43,5; 44,13; 52,12; 75,31.32.33-34; 76,3.4.5.6; *hupokeisthai*, be the subject, 93,17
hupolêpsis, belief, 9,33
hupolambanein, suppose, 6,23; 23,28
hupomnêma, commentary, 1,2; 60,8
hupomnêmatikos, hypomnematic, 60,29
huponoein, surmise, 37,1; suspect, 73,26
hupostasis, existence, 5,14; 49,3; 73,8; 83,11; subsistence, 94,32bis; 95,17; 102,2
hupostellein, restrict, 72,20
hupotassein, subjoin, 22,1
hupoteinein, subtend, 62,3.33; 63,13-14; 67,33; *hupoteinousa*, hypotenuse, 56,11
hupothesis, hypothesis, 12,9; 29,14; 53,12; 73,28; 77,5; 87,3.25; 89,11; *ex hupotheseôs*, hypothetical, 49,3
hupotithenai, posit, 22,28; 25,10; 100,7; hypothesize, 7,8.22; 22,13; 28,28; 43,26; 44,3.4.33; 53,10.30; 54,9; 75,25; 77,1.4; 80,20; 92,31; 93,27
hupokhôrein, withdraw, 40,10-11.13.14.15; 80,8.9.10
husterogenês, posterior, 19,15

iatrikê, medicine, 1,7; 4,18; 47,20
idea, idea, 7,15; 31,25; 44,22; shape, 35,2.13
idios, particular, 3,25; proper, 13,16; 14,13; 17,17.28; 18,13; 48,18; 75,23; distinctive, 27,25; 28,29; 45,2; 101,13; own, 90,10; peculiar, 94,8; *to idion*, peculiarity, 48,24; *idiôs*, in particular, 3,1; especially, 10,10; 23,22; properly, 60,13; *idiâi*, individually, 72,4; *kat' idian*, on its own, 84,35
idiotês, specificity, 18,6; property, 19,16; peculiarity, 94,21; peculiar property, 101,22
isopalês, equally balanced 52,27; 89,23
isoskelês, isosceles, 61,26; 65,17
isostoikhos, coordinate, 25,31
isotês, equality, 4,25

kainoprepôs, in a novel way, 92,26
katalambanein, grasp, 16,12; attain, 55,20.22

kataleipomenon, remainder, 17,29; 63,27
katalêxis, ending, 59,7
katanoêsis, see *noêsis*
kataphasis, affirmation, 19,32; 82,26.31
kataskeuastikos, supporting, 71,22.30
kataskeuazein, establish, 5,32; manufacture, 35,5; construct, 60,16; 64,11; support, 71,19.21.22.23.26; 72,2; (*ton logon*) make an argument, 97,17
kataskeuê, structure, 43,12; construction, 60,17-18
katêgorein, predicate, 19,33; 73,6; 76,3.9.10.11.19; 81,3.5; 91,9-93,32 *passim*
katêgorêma, predicate, 91,14
katêgoria, category, 72,5-6; 91,5; 95,20.32; 96,2; 97,17; predication, 91,27; 92,3; 97,22; 99,26; *Katêgoriai, Categories*, 60,8; 69,20; 75,7
katêgorikôs, predicatively, 97,14.28
kathairesis, overthrow, 8,21; desecration, 29,2
katharos, pure, 1,18; 93,28
kath' hekaston, individual, 10,4; 12,1; 48,4.9; 73,24
kathêgemôn, teacher, 59,23.31
katholikos, universal, 69,13; 77,3; overall, 71,20.24.28
katholou, universal, 2,1; 3,24; 10,24; 16,17.20.23; 17,8.26.30.34.35.37.38; 18,5; 19,6.8.30; 37,19; 53,26; 69,23; 75,31; 76,6; universally, 2,18; 47,33; 57,26bis; 60,24.26
kekhênôs, lacunose, 18,17
kenos, empty, 6,23; 79,22; 80,5.6.14; 51,27; *kenon*, void, 3,33; 4,3.4.5; 21,12; 22,7; 28,14.16.28; 40,10.11; 44,16; 64,24bis; 71,3
kentron, centre, 53,18; 64,13-14.27.32.33; 65,13bis.16.18.23; *hê ek tou kentrou*, radius, 57,4; 64,18; 66,2.15; 67,14.24.35; 68,10bis
kera, horn, 60,2; *keratoeidês* (*gônia*) horn angle, 59,28; 60,4
kinein, move, 2,15; 8,5.6.8.9; 15,24; 20,11; 21,28.30.35; 22,2.13.16.23.27; 23,8.10.11.21; 24,1.11.13; 25,24.25; 28,8.20; 37,29; 38,16; 39,25;

238   *Greek–English Index*

40,8bis.10.13.16bis.21.24; 41,12-42,25
passim; 43,6; 45,27; 49,31; 52,17–18;
53,8-30 *passim*; 74,26; 79,14.15;
80,5.6.8.14; **kinoun**, mover, 26,12
kinêsis, motion, 2,16.25;
3,9.26.27.28bis.29.31.34; 4,15; 5,13-6,30
passim; 10,10.16.26; 20,10.21bis;
23,7.13.14; 24,24.31; 27,15.19; 29,13;
39,23.25; 40,26.7; 41,19; 46,16; 52,18;
60,16; 71,3; 79,16.17.21; 80,25; 81,31;
82,8; 101,8
khalepos, difficult, 53,5; 76,31; 90,4.20
kharaktêr, character, 94,8.21; 100,17
kharaktêrizein, characterize, 6,17; 27,2.8;
31,26; 94,13; be characteristic, 19,4
khôra, place, 42,7; 75,14
khôrein, pervade, 24,7; make room,
40,19.20; 80,12.13
khôrion, area, 54,21
khôris, apart, 30,26; 39,4; 66,8; 72,21;
separate, 90,10; separately, 101,6
khôristos, separated, 1,9.18.20; 2,1; 5,3.12;
10,34; 43,14.21; 75,16; 76,7; *to*
khôriston, separability, 2,5
khôrizein, separate, 84,14; 89,1
khreia, use, 8,34; 43,12; 74,11; need, 58,14
khrêsimos, valuable, 4,17; 5,21; useful,
47,22; 61,6; applicable, 17,30
khronos, time, 3,29.30.31.34; 4,34; 5,2;
6,25.26; 17,17; 24,5.20; 26,9; 28,31;
29,27; 58,33; 79,1.4; 81,25.30;
92,18.19.20.21
koilos, concave, 81,28; **koilotês**, concavity,
76,19
koinos, common, 3,5.24.25; 4,9; 8,24; 9,33;
10,5bis; 11,30; 12,6.7.12; 16,17;
18,6.18.20; 19,4.5.10.15.18.20.23.33;
31,29; 34,15; 47,21.28; 48,5.17.31;
57,14; 62,5.29; 64,2; 65,2.4; 68,20.26;
72,28; 77,14; 81,18; in common,
3,13.15.20; 4,6; general, 6,18; 77,22; in
the broad sense, 13,6; broad, 14,10.12;
koinôs, in general, 1,14; 2,32; in
common, 4,8; 45,5; in general terms,
20,17; together, 52,10
koinotês, commonality, 18,8.9.19-20.22.
koinônein, share, 5,9; 27,2; 28,5; be
involved with, 42,9
koinônia, sharing, 88,28

kokhlioeidês, cochlioid, 60,14
koruphê, (*kata*) vertical, 65,7
kosmos, cosmos, 2,18; 7,30.31bis.33;
24,5.18; world, 15,18.22; 27,17.25;
31,18.26.29.32; 33,23; 34,6.9; 38,32;
ordering, 30,19; 38,32
kratistos, most dominant, 22,31; 22,33
kritêrion, criterion, 5,30
kuklikos, circular, 5,15; 58,26.27.30.31;
59,4-33 *passim*
kuklos, circle, 16,34.35.38; 17,11; 32,20;
54,12-69,20 *passim*; 81,32; cycle, 34,3;
eukuklos, well-rounded, 52,23.26;
89,22
kuklophorêtikos, rotating, 2,17
kuriôs, in the strict sense, 2,13;
11,30-12,31 *passim*; 15,16; 18,31bis;
19,9.12.16; 25,23; 26,5; 45,31; 49,2;
69,10; 70,23; 71,9; 76,6; 77,24.26.30;
78,1.11.24; 79,8.12.25; 93,5; 99,3;
strictly, 3,16; principally, 8,7; 44,9
kurtos, convex, 81,28

lambanein, take, 5,10; 8,14; 9,30; 16,1;
11,28-29; 19,15.16; 27,18; 36,22; 46,19
bis; 49,6–7; 53,22.25; 65,16; 69,12; 75,5;
76,16.17; 83,23; 84,35; 85,1.14;
87,19.20; 94,31; 96,7; acquire, 17,18;
grasp, 18,7; 20,24; assume, 31,7; 51,15;
58,8; 69,29.30; 74,1
leleukôsthai, have gone white, 91,22
leptomerês, fine-grained, 24,10; 36,4
lexis, text, 6,31; 37,9; 48,26; 74,30; 83,28;
85,23; 92,26.28; 97,10; word, 13,28;
38,1; 51,27; 71,6; 99,17; passage,
70,12.17; manner of speaking, 91,27;
96,30; 99,29; **kata lexin**, verbatim,
60,27
logikos, rational, 1,7.8; logical, 5,30; of
logic 21,13; 81,5.
logos, account, 2,8; 3,28; 5,2; 9,1; 10,19;
14,22; 21,7bis; 31,28; 36,29; 38,27.28;
39,10; 44,29; 45,11.20.24.32; 47,4.5.8;
48,23; 71,27; 73,1.12.25;
76,10.12.13.20.26; 77,2; 79,3; 82,23.29;
86,4.25.29; 88,4.15.28; 90,1.2.28;
96,13.21.24.25.26.27.32; 98,3;
discussion, 2,21; 4,4; 6,7; 9,5; 83,29;
discourse, 8,23.24.27; speech, 9,19;

Greek–English Index

13,29.30; 30,17.26; 38,30; 41,8; argument, 10,3; 22,3.12.20; 44,31; 49,32; 50,7; 51,2.6.12.19.24.25; 52,1.4.14; 53,13; 54,8.17; 70,4-72,28 *passim*; 74,19; 79,8; 83,9.24.27; 90,8; 94,2; 97,17; 99,7; saying, 12,24; role, 4,5; 6,24; 15,32; 31,30; reason, 17,24; 28,24; 36,23; justification, 45,9; assertion, 51,28.29; 52,2.3; 86,17; rule, 55,4; 77,22; ratio, 61,6.9; formula, 81,9; 92,4; 95,22; 96,4; sentence, 91,17.18bis.21; 92,1; 100,19; word, 100,29

loidoria, insult, 10,17

luô, solve, 50,5; 53,13.27; 54 *passim*; 76,31; 83,20; 94,3.6; 96,3.18.20; 97,4; 100,16.27; *dialuô*, resolve, 24,3; solve, 55,26; 83,7

lusis, solution, 48,7; 84,34; 96,3.20; 97,8; 99,21; 101,17.23.25; 102,3; *epilusis*, solution, 96,10; *dialusis*, dissolution, 4,35

manthanein, learn, 1,3; 15,1.11.15; 20,6.8-9; 30,19; 32,24; 33,26; 37,21; 38,32; 54,15; 75,3; see, 90,2

mathêmatikos, mathematical, 1,22; mathematical science, 13,23.34; mathematician, 12,30; 48,10; mathematics, 1,22

mathêsis, learning, 15,2.3.13

mathêtês, student, 6,2; 7,1; 27,24

marturein, bear witness, 29,28; 83,3; *summarturein*, bear witness to, 18,30

martus, witness, 77,5

megalonoia, greatness of mind, 38, 3

megalopsukhos, great-souled, 5,7

megalophrôn, great-minded, 5,7-8

megethos, magnitude, 22,11.13; 27,21; 42,3.28.29; 55,23; 58,26; 59,19.21-22.24.25; 82,2.7.14; size, 100,5

memphesthai, criticize, 46,31; 79,12.24

menein, *mimnein*, remain, 23,10.11.13; 30,7; 40,3; 77,11.30; 94,22; 101,28

mêniskos, lune, 55,26–69,32 *passim*

merikos, particular, 8,15; 17,17; 36,17; 37,19

merismos, partition, 93,11; 97,14.29

meristos, thing with parts, 49,5; 98,18

meros, part, 1,4; 2,6; 4,24.33.36; 7,30; 8,15; 11,28; 16,8.22; 17,5.7; 19,13; 40,28;

52,24; 53,2.3; 61,13; 62,5; 68,21; 81,20.36; 83-97 *passim*; 101,29; *(to) kata meros*, particular, 18,3.6.8; 19,16.17; 49,28; 53,25; *en merei*, in turn, 33,19.20, 55,21

mesos, intermediate, 2,1; 12,32; 18,15; centre, 2,26bis; 20,22; 32,14; middle, 23,5; 31,14; 34,15; 39,16; 52,24; 53,1; 58,10; 88,14; 89,25; *messothen*, from the middle, 52,7; 89,23

metabainein, turn, 14,31; pass to, 40,23; 83,15

metabolê, change, 6,28; 20,13.14.16; 24,5.21; 25,1.10; 28,11; 29,16; 52,18; 79,17

metagein, redirect, 88,11

metakheirisis, presentation, 72,2

metalambanein, receive, 94,9

metaplattein, reshape, 91,21; 93,30

metarrhuthmizein, refashion, 91,27; 97,1; 99,30

metaxu, intermediate, 22,6; 25,9; 36,14; between, 31,3; 55,19; 64,18; in passing, 86,11

methodos, discipline, 13,15; 14,21bis.24; 47,23; 54,18; approach, 28,30; method, 54,32; 59,11; 60,11

metokhê, participle, 91,28

metrein, measure, 3,29; 6,25

metriôs, reasonably, 19,7

metron, measure, 4,34; 15,33

mêkhanikê, mechanics, 4,18; 14,3; 47,21

mêkos, length, 26,4; 47,27.28; 49,5

mixis, mixture, 27,20; 31,15; 33,7; 50,13; 100,18; 101,13; *summixis*, mixing together, 34,22

mimnêskein, refer, 4,16; 6,2; mention, 38,4; 77,1; 81,6; 85,23; 86,13; 99,9.13.17.31

mnêmê, reference, 6,1; mention, 22,30

monakhôs, in only one way, 95,25; 96,1.23; 97,6

monas, unit, 26,27; 81,8; 82,1.8

morion, part, 43,12; 81,17.19; 82,1; 85,4.27; 87,7.26.27bis.28.29bis.30bis; 92,19.20; *Moria zôiôn*, *Parts of Animals*, 3,9

morphê, shape, 10,32; 25,6; 30,23; 39,1; form, 45,2

mounogenês, unique, 30,2; 78,13; 87,21

mousikos, poetic theorist, 9,20-21; musical, 20,15; 96,26.27; 97,20

240   *Greek–English Index*

nastos, solid, 28,13
nastotês, solidity, 82,2
neikos, strife, 10,17; 25 *passim*; 31-34
   passim; 50,24
noein, think, 2,4; 18,6.12; 23,19; 78,17;
   86,27.29; 87,14.16.17; understand, 18,6;
   94,31
noeros, intellectual, 4,21; 5,14; 18,3; 34,27;
   35,10.20; 100,25; 101,12.17; *noerôs*,
   intellectually, 18,9
noêma, thought, 30,17; 38,30; 41,8; 78,6;
   87,14; 102,15
noêsis, intellection, 26,22; 43,17; 87,12;
   katanoêsis, grasp, 5,18
noêtos, intelligible, 7,18; 29,6; 30,15;
   31,18.22.25.28.32; 34,9.19; 35,19; 36,15;
   37,4; 38,19.28; 39,11.26; 78,2.17; 80,4;
   87,12.17; 88,17.20.24.25
nomimos, law-abiding, 50,8
nous, intellect, 1,9.11.15.18; 2,3.4; reason,
   7,4.17; 8,3; 27,16.19.22; 43,6.21; 87,9;
   88,9; sense (of a text), 10,8; intellectual
   intuition, 15,13; thought, 23,20;
   intelligence, 87,11; *prosekhein ton*
   noun, pay attention, 79,11

oikeios, appropriate, 2,6; 12,6; 15,33; 17,6;
   21,35; 22,1.10; 29,10; 32,1; 42,24.25.28;
   48,25; 50,24.25; 54,18; 70,3; 71,17;
   73,18; 75,1; 80,23.29; 84,26.27; proper,
   4,36; 17,34; 19,10.11; 48,10.19.22;
   100,16-17; close, 51,30; *oikeiotês*,
   kinship, 61,2; *oikeioun*, see fit, 77,9
oktagônon, octagon, 54,31.32
olethros, destruction, 39,28; 80,1.3
on, being, 16,29;
   28,1.2.13.14.15.16.17.28.29; 30,11bis;
   34,8; 38,8bis.9.17.19.20.21;
   39,26; 40,10.17; 44,16.17;
   45,13.14.17.18.19.22; 46,19.27.29.30.32ter;
   71,17.31; 72,3.4.7.16.24.27;
   73,5.8.13.15.17; 74,12.20.31; 75,6.8;
   77,8.15.17.18.26.27.30.33bis;
   78,2bis.5.16.21.24.25;
   79,6.8.9bis.10.24.25.26.27;
   80,4.5.6.25.26.28; 82,32bis.33; 83,1;
   90,29; 91,13; 94,6bis.7.8.9.12.15.28.31;
   95,4ter.5.6.9.12bis.25; 96,3.8.11;
   what is, 28,8.12bis; 38,11; 39,22;

   40,7bis.8.10.11.23; 41,16; 45,26.31;
   46,1.2.3.9.13.20.21.22.27; 47,2; 48,1;
   49,29; 50,16.25; 51,14.29;
   52,9.11bis.13.21; 53,1.10.28; 70,17.29;
   71,7.10.15.28; 72,3.6.23.29; 73,5.19.31;
   74,2.16; 75,9.16.22.23.24.26bis.30bis;
   76,27.29; 77,1.3.5.10;
   78,1.11.25bis.26bis.27.28bis.29bis;
   79,11.12.13.14.16.24.25.29.31;
   80,5bis.6bis.20.21.23.27.32;
   81,16.21.24.34; 82,3.4.9.11.20.29.31;
   83,1.2.3; 95,12; 96,1; *ta onta*, the things
   that are, 7,33; 20,6; 24,18; 28,6.11.17;
   45,28bis.30.32; 47,1; 49,30; 72,18;
   73,6.8.10; 74,11.28; 77,18; 83,3; 90,14;
   95,20.27; 96,2.4; 99,15bis; 100,24; *hen*
   on, One-which-is, 34,27; 38,13; 71,30;
   86,20; 87,4.25.26; 88,4.7.12.18.19;
   ontôs, really, 22,26; 38,11; 45,31;
   100,22
oneidizein, criticize, 28,34
onkos, bulk, 52,23.26; 89,22
onoma, name, 4,10; 16,32.33bis.34;
   17,7.10.39; 18,10; 29,18; 38,17;
   46,2.7.30; 72,16; 73,6bis.7bis; 74,3.7.13;
   79,7; 81,9; 89,9-18 *passim*; 93,9;
   95,18.23; 97,28; 100,8 word, 12,16;
   24,21; noun, 100,19
organikos, instrumental, 3,19; 8,5; 11,3;
   mechanical, 60,17
organon, instrument, 26,7
oregesthai, desire, 12,27; *orektikos*,
   desiring, 1,10; *orexis*, desire, 1,11
orthê, right angle, 54,25; 55,1.2; 56,4;
   59,27; 61,15.16; 62,3bis; 63,7; 64,31;
   66,14; 67,33; *pros orthas*,
   perpendicularly, 64,17.27
orthogônios (said of a triangle), right,
   56,11; 61,25; 62,2
orthos, right, 90,1; correct, 94,18; *orthôs*,
   rightly, 8,22; correctly, 36,30; *orthôs*
   ekhein, be right, 44,24; *ouk orthôs*,
   wrongly, 79,2
ouranos, heaven, 2,12.13.17.29; 24,18;
   41,19; 53,17bis
ousia, substance, 2,1.13; 5,11.14; 11,13;
   19,9; 20,6; 24,29; 28,13.23; 29,20; 41,31;
   43,27; 44,6; 45,2.9; 49,29; 52,12;
   72,5–73,1 *passim*; 73,20–74,24 *passim*;

Greek–English Index

75,15-30 *passim*; 76,26.27.28bis.29;
77,13; 79,2.16.18.20.21.23; 80,27; 90,13;
91,8.9.10.12.25; 94,12.14.17.25;
95,5.17.21; 96,5.7.11.14.16; 97,18;
101,27-102,11 *passim*; existing, 90,13;
being, 99,26
ousioun, give substantial being, 91,12; 102,12
oxus, sharp, 36,4

palaios, ancient, 8,10; 21,24; 29,4; 36,25;
69,23
pandekhes, receptacle, 26,12
paradeigma, paradigm, 3,19.25; 11,2;
26,6.15; 101,12.23; 102,12; example,
17,6.14.34; 50,24.26; 76,17; 96,6
paradeigmatikos, paradigmatic, 3,19;
7,7.15.18-19; 10,34; 43,7
paradidonai, hand down, 6,9; 7,3; 69,14;
78,11; 88,33; communicate, 13,21–2;
14,9.18; 43,14; 100,26; convey, 16,34;
17,5; 26,18.25; 32,12; 33,6; 34,9
paradoxologia, paradox, 50,24.26.27
paradoxos, paradoxical, 50,9; 51,6.13.22;
53,12; 74,17; 75,13
paragein, produce, 31,27; adduce, 77,2;
introduce, 95,17
paragraphein, cite, 89,5
paralambanein, take up, 5,31; 14,3; 96,4;
assume, 15,16.21.26; learn, 55,9;
receive, 60,11; include,
76,11.12.14.18.20
paraleipein, omit, 92,27
parallattein, deviate from, 88,23
parallêlos, parallel, 62,17; 63,3.4.5; 64,29;
ek parallêlou, in parallel, 12,14.15
paralogismos, paralogism, 50,29
paralogizesthai, reason fallaciously, 54,18
paramutheisthai, motivate, 38,2; give an
assurance, 70,5
paramuthia, motivation, 37,30
parangelma, precept, 19,35; 75,1
paraphrasis, paraphrase, 70,32;
paraphrazein, say in paraphrase, 40,12
parasunaptikos (*sundesmos*), connective
conjunction, 9,29
paratithenai, cite, 38,29; 48,27; 69,4; 92,28
parenkeisthai, slip in, 44,22
parekbainein, digress, 29,4; *parekbasis*,
digression, 90,21

parekhein, provide, 4,18; 101,30; yield,
41,24; *parekhesthai*, satisfy, 49,4
paskhon, patient, 11,11; 25,18
pathêtikos, qualitative change, 20,22
peperasmenos, finite, 4,2; 21,31-25,15
passim; 26,29; 28,7; 29,8; 41,11-43,2
passim; 72,29.30.31; 73,1; 74,28;
75,25.28; 76,8; 77,4; 82,12.13; 87,4;
limited, 11,14; 29,10; 82,14; *to
peperasmenon*, finiteness, 4,2
peplatusmenos, extended in breadth, 49,6
peptikos, concocting, 24,7
perainein, reach a conclusion, 12,9;
sumperainein, lead to a conclusion,
23,6
peras, limit, 29,9bis.12; 30,5.13; 52,20bis;
82,11.14; 87,9bis; 90,29; end, 54,28;
55,3; *peratoun*, boundary, 47,29;
peratoumenos, limited, 52,20
periekhein, bound, 17,2.12; embrace,
17,31; contain, 56,18; 57,16; 62,3; 64,2;
67,33; 69,8; 88,7.26
perigraphein, delineate, 6,30;
circumscribe, 56,2.8.22.23; 57,2; 58,19;
61,26.31; 62,22; 64,1; 65,12; 67,30; 68,1
perigraphê, domain, 100,17
perilambanein, contain, 17,10.13; 58,11;
comprehend, 18,3; encompass, 22,21;
62,19.24; 65,10bis.15
perilêpsis, grasp, 18,8; overview, 28,30;
perilêptos, comprehended, 26,25
periokhê, comprehending, 19,17
periphereia, circumference, 54,25-55,21;
59,25.33; 60,4.24; 61,21; 62,11; 63,18;
64,3.5-6.18; 65,25; 66,11; 67,6.27;
69,14.25.26.28.30.33; arc, 56,17; 57,16
peripherês, round, 44,19; 81,27; 82,7
peripiptein, fall into, 53,10; 91,20.33
perittos, superfluous, 5,32; odd, 11,4
phainesthai, appear, 4,15; 23,24; 27,8;
50,28; 70,21; 74,23; 77,2; 95,23; seem,
10,5.20.21; 27,22; 36,27; 37,1; be
evidently, 53,17
phainomenon, phenomenon, 20,24; 26,20;
83,3; apparent sense, 21,20; appearance,
38,21.25; 71,6; what is apparent, 39,11;
thing that appears, 49,27
phaneros, manifest, 16,29; 37,14.17.18;
clear, 64,22; 67,17

Greek–English Index

phantasia, imagination, 1,15; 2,3; 18,11

phantastikos, imaginative, 18,3

phileristia, contentiousness, 8,30

philokalôs, impressively, 48,6

philomathês, desirous of learning, 29,3-4

philoneikôs, contentiously, 51,8

philosophein, philosophize, 6,32; 16,28; 21,16; 28,33; 38,10; 41,4; 45,15; 46,1

philosophia, philosophy, 1,4.5.6.20; 3,11; 6,34; 7,3; 9,26; 14,7; 15,34; 16,16; 26,9; 27,3.16; 28,5; 40,28; 47,30; 48,25; 71,15; 77,11; *kata philosophian*, philosophical 47,23

philosophos, philosopher, 1,1; 9,22.24; 13,30; 18,11; 36,26; 49,7.22; 71,16; 91,7; 99,23; 101,13

philotimôs, zealously, 84,22

phortikos, vulgar, 52,6.8.11

phronêsis, practical wisdom, 5,6; wisdom, 100,14

phthartos, perishable, 2,27.29

phthonos, grudgingness, 26,18

phthora, perishing, 4,35; passing away, 28,3; *Peri geneseôs kai phthoras*, *On Generation and Perishing*, 2,31

phtheiresthai, perish, 2,28.32; 5,2; 79,9.15.25; pass away, 77,16–31 *passim*

phulassein, preserve, 4,25; 50,30; 54,8.16; keep, 8,27; 83,34; take care, 75,1; hold on, 88,19

phusikos, natural scientific, 1,4.16.20; 2,8; 5,28.31; 6,8; natural [science], 1,2.3; 2,8.18.19; 47,20.32; natural scientist, 3,22.28; 4,4–5; 9,11.12.15.17; 20,12.32; 21,8.14.30; 22,4; 23,21; 40,22.24.25.27.30; 41,2.3.6; 45,17.23; 47,9.11.12.32; 49,17.22.23.25.32; 51,1.2.16; 70,3.10; natural thing, 1,20; 2,8; 3,14.20.26; 4,6.9.21; 6,17.21.26; 7,2.12.32; 9,5.8.11.16.23.35; 10,29; 13,19; 14,17.26.30.31; 15,9; 16,4; 18,24.25.26; 19,19.21.34; 20,3.4.9.13.29; 21,2.8.13.17; 37,5; 39,22; 45,15.16; 46,13; 47,16; 50,3; natural, 2,9.19.20; 3,11.14.32.33-34; 5,13; 6,5.19; 7,29; 8,33.34; 9,1.3.8.11.21; 15,29; 18,24; 20,18; 22,25; 39,24; 70,7.10.14.19.26; 71,13.16; 82,10; *ta Phusika*, *Physics* (of Theophrastus, 9,7; 20,20; of Eudemus,

10,3; 42,14; 48,6; of Empedocles, 32,2); *Phusikê akroasis*, *Lectures on Natural Science* (of Aristotle), 1,3; 4,6.10.13-14; *ta meta ta phusika*, metaphysics, 1,20; *Metaphysics* (of Aristotle) 8,30; 12,27; 48,3

phusikôs, in a natural-scientific way, 47,10.16

phusiologein, give an account of nature, 10,7; 36,19; 38,21; 71,7

phusiologia, study of nature, 4,17.33; 5,20.21.22; 8,10.14; 14,6; account of nature, 18,30.33; *phusiologikê epistêmê*, scientific knowledge of nature, 5,23; scientific knowledge of natural things, 9,4

phusiologos, natural philosopher, 7,20; natural scientist, 9,21; 15,10.32; 45,24

phusis, nature 1,16.17; 2,23; 3,26; 4,19.26.29; 6,12.17.34; 7,3.10.11.24; 8,4bis.6; 9,10; 10,1.11.28; 12,27; 14,4; 15,32; 16,25.26.28; 18,21.32.33; 19,2–20 *passim*; 20,10.21; 21,4.17; 22,29; 23,27.29; 24,3.17.27; 25,4.7; 26,11; 27,17.20.22; 34,29; 35,30; 36,17; 40,27bis; 41,18; 42,11; 44,13; 46,10.14.16bis.24.25; 47,2bis; 49,31; 50,2.3; 53,11-28 *passim*; 54,7; 70,1-71,16 *passim*; 81,8; 90,10; 91,24

phuton, plant, 3,5.10; 16,12.16bis; 53,16

pistis, trust, 5,19; confirmation, 15,26.29; conviction, 40,1; 78,21

pistos, trustworthy, 30,17; 38,30; 41,8; persuasive, 97,17; *autopistos*, self-warranting, 15,5.9-10.35–6; 16,1-2; 18,31; 48,30; 49,5.8.12.15

pistousthai, confirm, 16,32; 50,3; 53,26; 75,22; *pistôsis*, confirmation, 74,5

pithanos, persuasive, 19,17; 51,4; 74,1; *apithanos*, implausible, 37,29.31; 38,2.3.4; unpersuasive, 51,5

planê, confusion, 90,20; error, 92,11

plasmatikos, artificial, 48,24

platos, breadth, 26,4; 47,28

pleiones, several, 7,22; 17,12; 19,22.26.31; 20,2.28; 21,31; 22,14.23.31; 25,14; 26,9; 34,9; 37,10.15.26.27; 42 *passim*; 43,1; 46,6; 70,3; 72,8; 76,25; 79,21; 81,2.4bis; 83,3.22; 85,6; 86,14; 92,18;

Greek–English Index

243

many, 23,6; 26,1; 33,26.27; 34,4.5; more, 23,8-9; 32,9; 55,18; 77,23.33; 79,6.9; 90,6.9; 93,15; 97,9; *epi pleon*, at greater length, 36,25; 61,4; 80,15; *to pleon*, for the most part, 73,2; *pleonakhôs*, in several ways, 95,26

pleonasma, addition, 94,26

pleonexia, selfish excess, 4,26

plêgê, blow, 42,11

pleôn, full, 40 *passim*; 80 *passim*

plêrês, full, 28,13.16.28; 44,4.16

plêthusmos, multiplication, 88,22

plêthunein, multiply, 81,21; 88,26; 89,3; 94,23; 95,7; 101,30.32.33

plêthos, multiplicity, 18,12.13; 25,15; 34,20; 42,17.27; 45,30; 46,15.23; 88,3; 90,26; 101,1.7.30; plurality, 22,9; 26,30.31; 27,27; 28,25; 29,8; 34,24; 73,16.24; 74,10; 80,31; 82,13; 84,32.33; 91,10; 93,11.12; 96,16; 99,15; 100,21bis.25; muchness, 25,22

pleura, side, 54,24-63,29 *passim*; 67,7-69,31 *passim*

poiêtikos, efficient, 3,17.26; 6,13.14; 7,4.7.14.17.20; 8,1.4.7; 10.10; 11,18.20.31; 25,27; 31,10.21; 34,14.16; 38,23.27; 39,13; productive, 5,6; poetic, 24,20

poion, quale, 72,5.9.12.16.19.23.27; 73,31; 75,10.15.17.19.27; 76,27; 77,1; 80,27; 82,9bis.22; quality, 20,7; 49,30; 73,2.23.29; 74,20; 97,18

poiotês, quality, 72,31-32; 73,31; 79,21; 82,7; 95,21; 96,6; *kata poiotêta(s)*, qualitative, 35,27; 44,7; in quality, 39,23

poioun, agent, 11,1.11.15; 25,18; efficient [cause], 26,14

polos, pole, 53,18

polugônos, polygonal, 54,21; *polugônon*, polygon, 55,6.7.8.10

polukoirania, rule of many, 87,10

polukhroniotês, long-lastingness, 10,16

poluônumos, many-named 82,21; *poluônumia*, many-namedness, 82,22

porisma, corollary, 64,28; 68,12

poson, quantity, 20,7; 49,30; 52,12; 72,29; 73,1.29; 74,20; 76,8.22; quantum, 52,11; 72,5-77,7 *passim*; 82,10.22.13.14

posotês, quantity, 39,24; 74,29; 76,22; 82,6

pragma, thing, 2,9; 3,14; 11,25; 14,31; 15,17.30; 17,19; 18,24-25; 20,3; subject, 7,29; object, 12,16; 47,26; 49,25; 50,9; 51,26; 52,5; 53,23; 89,15; reality, 73,9; 74,8bis.13; 98,1; *pragmati, pragmasin*, in reality, 72,7.8.10.16; 73,7.9

pragmateia, treatise, 2,7.20.22.30; 3,3.5.6-7.13.20; 4,13; 5,15.22.29.31; 6,4; 8,9.18; 12,12; enquiry, 48,7.28; *pragmateian poieisthai*, occupy oneself with, 26,9-10

praktikos, practical, 1,12; 4,23; 14,5

praxis, practice, 1,12; 10,4; action, 11,15; 41,5

proagein, bring forward, 7,11; 51,11; lead, 23,24; extend, 26,26; bring forth, 38,13; introduce, 88,23; make progress, 98,6

proapodeiknunai, see *apodeiknunai*

proballein, pose, 83,10; 90,4; project, 88,16; 102,15

problêma, problem, 20,30; 21,11; 46,12; 48,7.27; 49,10; 60,16; 75,2

proêgeisthai, come first, 5,28; precede, 11,6.9.28; 15,27; *proêgoumenos*, principal, 4,27; *proêgoumenôs*, primarily, 76,32

proepinoein, see *epinoein*

prographein, construct, 64,9

prohuparkhein, see *huparkhein*

prokeimenos, at hand, 3,13; 50,26; present, 12,12; present topic, 17,33

prokopê, progress, 17,14

prokheirizein, take up, 3,24; 22,4; 45,33; 50,1

prokheiros, close at hand, 8,14; 15,22; 16,10; 17,4; easy, 64,25; 84,21; obvious, 71,29; 92,25; at hand, 100,10

prolambanein, assume, 47,28

prolêpsis, conception, 93,28-29

proodos, progression, 14,23; 88,21

prooimion, introduction, 3,21; 8,32; 12,26; 17,32; 21,1

proparaskeuê, preliminary preparation, 89,4

prophanês, manifest, 8,12; 15,28; 16,18; *prophanôs*, manifestly, 80,31

prophora, utterance, 91,17

prosagein, introduce, 42,19; 92,30; 93,2

prosdialegomenos, discussant, 50,9; interlocutor, 54,6

prosekhês, proximate, 3,26; 6,13; 7,26; 8,4; 12,1bis.2.5; 36,16; *prosekhôs*, immediately, 3,2; 47,20

prosistorein, see *historein*

prostaktikos, imperative, 91,19

prosthêkê, addition, 91,15.16

protasis, premise, 9,6; 11,13; 12,19; 13,18bis; 14,15.16; 15,6.8; 49,2; 50,28; 51,9.11.15.19; enunciation, 61,10

prôtistos, the very first, 11,20; first, 39,18

prôtourgos, primarily productive, 102,12

prohupokeisthai, underlie first, 72,22

pseudein, speak a falsehood, 12,24; speak falsely, 51,8; say falsely, 54,6

pseudos, falsehood, 54,10.14; 58,8; 75,12; 91,18; *pseudês*, false, 13,11; 38,26; 39,10; 50,30; 51,14.26; 54,3; *pseudôs*, falsely, 51,5.19; 53,5

pseudographêma, diagrammatic fallacy, 54,11; 57,25; 58,2.20; 60,18; 69,10; *pseudographia*, diagrammatic fallacy, 58,24; *pseudographeisthai* or *pseudographein*, be graphically fallacious, 68,34; 69,18

psukhê, soul, 1,6.7.9; 2,2.4; 4,20.22.30; 5,3.7; 14,8; 15,19.23; 39,19; 53,20; 70,24.25; 72,12; 73,23; *peri psukhês* psychology, 1,22

psukhikos, of the soul, 5,11

psukhros, cold, 31,6; 34,23; 36,5

rhêma, word, 29,29; verb, 91,21.25.27; 93,30; 100,19

rhêton, saying, 40,17; passage, 42,12, 43,20; word, 44,16

rhusmos, rhythm, 28,18

saphêneia, clarity, 60,28

selênê, moon, 35,6.12; *hupo selênên*, sublunar 2,15; 34,6

sêma (in Parmenides), sign, 30,25; 39,3; 78,9

sêmainein, signify; 74,33; 75,13; 80,25; 97,25; 99,26; mean, 75,31; 76,21; *sêmainomenon*, meaning, 10,27; 74,31; 80,29; 82,16.21; 83,2; 86,19; 90,24; 92,29; 97,11; what something signifies, 74,3; sense, 80,22

sêmeion, point, 17,2; 47,27; 49,4; 55,1.14.17.19; 81,8; 82,17; (in Parmenides) sign, 77,34; 78,11; 79,10

skepsis, investigation, 71,15

skhêma, shape, 7,9; 10,32; 35.29.31; 36,2; 43,27-45,8 *passim*; 81,28; 100,4; figure, 17,1.11; 28,21.25; 54,31; 69,9; 82,7; form, 51,20

skhisma, schism, 29,1

skopein, examine, 46,9.10.24; 50,5; 51,31; 70,29.30; 75,30; *episkopein*, investigate, 14,1; examine, 16,28; 26,22; 43,17; 48,14

skopos, object, 1,3; 3,13.21; 4,6; 8,32; 83,29; aim, 47,25

simos, snub-nosed, 91,6; *simotês*, snubness, 76,17.18bis

sôma, body, 1,7; 2,18; 3,27.29.30.34; 4,3; 5,4; 6,21; 7,23.34; 9,9.10.18.21; 15,24; 21,8.9; 31,11; 35,24; 36,2.4.5.16; 42,30; 47,29; 81,25.29; 82,10; 87,5.6.8.18; 94,16.30.31; *hoion sôma*, quasi-bodily, 94,30

sômatikos, bodily, 2,9; 3,15; 4,30; 7,8.24; 25,21; 27,4.22; 35,31.

sophisma, sophism, 97,2

sophismatôdês, sophistical, 51,24

sophistikos, sophistical, 50,29; *Sophistikoi elenchoi*, *Sophistical Refutations*, 52,15; 70,21

sophos, wise, 98,5; *sophia*, wisdom, 37,1

sôphrosunê, temperance, 4,26.31

sôreuein, heap up, 94,16

sphaira, ball, 52,21.23.26; 89,22

sphairikos, spherical, 59,17

sphairoeidês, spherical, 23,16.18

sperma, seed, 23,25; 34,24; 35,2.13

spoudaios, important, 6,1

spoudazein, is careful, 8,14; pursue, 40,28

spoudê, attention, 95,31

stereos, solid, 81,28

stereôpa, solid, 33,11

sterêsis, privation, 6,12; 7,35; 8,1; 20,12.17

sterrotês, solidity, 82,2

stigma, punctuation, 70,12; point, 82,1.8; 97.15.18.19; 99,11

stizein, punctuate, 70,5

stoikheion, element, 2,15.23.25.26; 3,18; 4,24; 5,26; 7,10.13.22.24.26.34;

Greek–English Index

9,18.19.35; 10,9.12.14bis.18.19;
11,12.21.23.28.32.35.36; 12,5;
13,16.22bis.25.29bis.30.bis.31.33;
14,14.26; 16,14.15.33; 17,5.8.25.35.36;
18,15; 19,13; 21,2; 22,5.6.13.25;
24,9.11.12.15.17.22.23; 25,9.17.21.25;
27,22; 28,9.24; 31,7.9.20.26.30;
35,23.27.30bis; 36,8.16.18; 39,12; 41,18;
53,17; *Stoikheia*, (Euclid's) *Elements*,
55,9; 56,14; 60,29; 61,10; 62,2.9.27;
64,9; 65,2.11; 66,13; 68,13; 69,8
stoikheiôdês, elemental, 6,35; 7,12.27;
16,8-9; 17,22; 26,27; 30,20; 34,14; 36,17;
38,13
sullambanein, assist, 4,23; comprehend,
10,2; collect, 46,25
sullogismos, syllogism, 9,31; 13,17.20;
14,14.18; 15,8.25; deduction, 49,13.14;
51,3.9.17; *sullogistikos*, syllogistic,
15,14; 51,20
sullogizesthai, use a syllogism, 9,1; deduce,
15,19; 16,4; 50,27; 51,14; make
deductions, 47,26; 49,10; offer
deductions, 51,8
sumbebêkos, accident, 75,21; 76,3.4.16;
91,6.9.11.15.25; 92,14; 93,31; 95,1.3.5;
96,5-97,4 *passim*; 99,26.27.30; 101,29;
102,5.6.9; *kata sumbebêkos*, accidentally,
6,15; per accidens, 72,32; 76,27;
summarturein, see *marturein*
summixis, see *mixis*
sumpaskhein, sympathize, 44,21
sumpatheia, affinity, 5,19
sumpephorêmenôs, in a jumbled-together
way, 25,2
sumperainein, see *perainein*
sumperasma, conclusion, 9,36.37.39
sumpherein, come together, 29,5; bring
together, 50,18
sumphônein, agree, 21,14; 43,28; 44,28;
90,2; be in agreement, 75,24;
sumphônia, agreement, 20,12
sumphurein, jumble together, 78,2;
sunanaphurein, jumble together, 77,23;
79,6
sumpiptein, meet, 63,6; 64,20
sumplekein, interweave, 50,16; 91,12
sumplêrein, fill out, 17,9; complete, 31,12;
38,28; 102,9; exhaust, 92,29

sumpnoia, coordination, 35,20
sumproienai, proceed in tandem, 16,29
sunagein, bring together, 31,22; conclude,
51,15.21; 96,15; infer, 82,31; 86,7;
follow, 82,33
sunagôgê, inference, 55,12
sunairein, synthesize, 17,6;
18,2.9.10-11.13; 34,19
sunaisthanesthai, be aware, 88,13
sunaition, auxiliary cause, 3,16.17.19; 6,11;
11,31; 26,6; 36,19
sunanairein, see *anairein*
sunanakerannumai, mix together, 4,29
sunanaphurein, see *sumphurein*
sunapodeiknunai, simultaneously
demonstrate, 21,21; 42,21.24
sunaptein, connect, 73,4; touch, 81,18;
follow, 90,19; attach, 93,29
sundesmos, see *parasunaptikos*
sundiairein, see *diairein*
suneisagein, [mutually or reciprocally]
entail, 15,20; introduce together with,
37,26; 39,22-3.24; 46,15.23; 48,2
sunekheia, continuity, 83,23; 85,20.30;
87,21
sunekhês, continuous, 3,31bis.34;
6,19bis.20; 73,12; 77,31; 78,15;
81,7-86,21 *passim*; 87,18; 88,15.28;
90,25; 92,6.8.15; 96,17
sunekhizein, make continuous, 81,15;
connect, 85,4; 92,8
sunektikos, holding together, 36,10
sunergein, cooperate, 1,8.11
sunetos, comprehensible, 8,28
sunêthês, familiar, 18,5; customary, 70,20;
83,30
sungenês, akin, 5,7; 28,20; kindred, 27,13
sungramma, treatise, 4,12; 25,7; 40,12;
70,16; work, 5,27.33; 8,32; writing, 8,16
sungraphê, text, 5,24
sungraphein, write, 2,31
sunistanai, constitute, 3,2; 31,9; 93,19;
94,34; compose, 26,17; 43,10; come
together, 32,16; establish, 47,14.15;
construct, 62,10.14; 69,30.33; coexist,
92,20.21
sunkeisthai, be composed, 9,9; 16,14;
17,35; 19,28; 21,10; 36,5; 51,18; 59,33;
60,5; 65,25; 84,4; 98,22

246 *Greek–English Index*

sunkekhumenon, confused,
16,9.21-2.24.30.31; 17,15.19.21.39;
18,27; 19,14
sunkhôrein, concede, 47,10; 48,14; 85,33;
99,12; agree, 58,18; *mê ... sunkhôrein*,
refuse, 28,8
sunkrasis, blending, 32,2; 100,18
sunkrinein, combine, 25,25; mix together,
35,1; compare, 35,11.14
sunkrisis, being combined, 25,23;
combination, 27,6; 28,2.21; 41,27
sunthesis, way of being composed, 51,18;
composition, 51,20; 59,1.6.9; 84,22;
95,16; *episunthesis*, cumulative
composition, 59,10.12.13.15
sunthetos, compound, 2,11.20.21.27;
9,9bis.10.16; 11,22; 13,32.33; 15,9;
16,8.9.10.11.23.30; 17,6.22.24.34.36bis;
18,26; 19,13.4.18.28.34.36; 21,9bis;
27,1; 35,23; 51,17; composite, 37,18
sunokhê, continuity, 88,14
sunousiôsis, compresence, 35,20
sunônumos, univocal, 93,27; 95,11; 101,27
suntattein, group together with, 24,25;
rank, 25,31; line up alongside, 77,6
suntelein, make a contribution, 4,23; 14,5
suntemnein, abridge, 92,27
suntomia, concision, 22,18; 42,30
suntomos, concise, 28,30; *suntomôs*,
concisely, 48,29; 63,28; 74,19; briefly,
77,10
sunuparkhein, see *huparkhein*
suntemnein, see *temnein*
sustasis, constitution, 47,8.13
sustoikhia, pair of opposites, 26,28
sustoikhos, corresponding, 4,21
suzugia, pairing, 2,25

taxis, order, 4,12; 20,30; 24,5.20;
84,22.26.27.28; 88,10; ordering, 4,5;
5,27; 28,19; 36,3; 44,5.17; rank, 7,33;
87,20; 88,33; arrangement, 17,32; level,
tekhnê, art, 4,18; 10,29; 47,7.31bis; 48,29
tekhnêtos, artificial, 10,29
tekmêriôdês, sign-inferential, 15,24; 18,28
teleios, complete, 29,10; 30,12; 37,13; 40,8;
48,28; 74,3; perfect, 32,8; *to teleion*,
completeness, 74,14
teleiôsis, perfecting, 1,6; perfection, 4,22

teleioun, perfect 1,15; 4,21
teleôs, fully, 5,4
teleutê, finish, 10,28; conclusion, 12,32;
end, 29,23.25.26; 41,14; 42,1
telikos, final, 3,17; 6,14; 7,8.14.17-18;
11,8.31; 26,15; 43,8.11; ultimate,
71,12
telos, end, 1,13.14; 11,2.15.17.19; 14,6.7;
23,6; 26,6; 30,12; 41,5; 87,8.11.17;
completion, 29,10.11; 30,12
temnein, divide, 55,4; cut, 55,19; *dikha
temnein*, bisect, 54,24.26.32; 56,3;
64,17.27; 65,7; *apotemnein*, cut off,
62,23; 63,22; 69,29
tetartêmorion, quadrant, 56,16bis
tetragônikos, square, 59,19; 60,22; 69,31
tetragônismos, squaring, 54,12; 55,25;
58,3-61,23 *passim*; 63,19; 68,34;
69,4.13.19.20
tetragônizein, square, 56,20-21-62,12
passim; 64,4.5; 67,4-69,32 *passim*
tetragônizousa, quadratrix, 60,13
tetragônon, square, 54,13-69,17 *passim*
teuxis, attainment 1,13
thauma, wonder, 5,18.19; 33,2
thaumastos, surprising, 10,23; 43,7; 59,25;
79,22; 100,30; 101,5.11
thaumazein, wonder, 19,11; 86,19; admire,
36,31; be surprised, 52,1; 74,14; marvel,
100,14
theios, divine, 5,12.14.16; 7,17; 8,3; 29,3;
88,22
thelumna, close-packed, 33,11
theologia, theology, 4,21; *theologikos*,
theological, 1,19
theôrein, consider, 20,24.32; 28,11; 32,1;
34,5; 44,4.10; 48,5; 88,26; 94,17; 101,22;
observe, 17,14; 19,35
theôrêma, theorem, 6,8; 59,29; 60,17;
61,28; 62,2.8
theôrêtikos, theoretical, 1,14; 14,6; for
contemplating, 14,22
theôria, study, 3,25; 4,29; 5,12; 47,3.11;
88,23; contemplation, 10,5
theos, god, 5,19; 14,8; 15,21; 22,21.30.33;
25,17bis; 33,17; 39,17.18; 43,6; *Peri
theôn*, *On the Gods*, 23,16
thesis, position, 6,21; 44,18; 45,4.8; 74,16;
orientation, 28,19; 36,3.4; 43,33; 44,17;

Greek–English Index

thesis, 46,23; 50,10.12; 51,22-52,2 *passim*; 53,12.28

thorubein, disturb, 90,23; 91,3.7; 96,25

tmêma, section, 21,29; 38,10.14; 40,24.29; 46,25; 73,3; 83,4.6; (in geometry) segment, 54,27; 55,25.26.27; 56,18; 57,15; 61,7-63,32 *passim*; 65,7–69,33 passim

tomê, point of division, 54,25.28.32

topazein, guess, 75,13

topos, place, 3,2-4,4 *passim*; 6,21.22.23; 26,24; 35,10.12; 39,24; 52,19bis

trapezion, trapezium, 57,18bis; 62,15-65,15 *passim*

trigônon, triangle, 54,30; 56,11.19bis; 61,25; 62,2.6.7; 63,9; 65,7.10.12.16.18.26; 66,20; 68,14-28 *passim*

tritêmorion, third part, 61,14bis

trophimos, nourishing, 36,10

tropê, turning, 28,18

tropos, method, 3,10; way, 10,25.28.29; 16,2; 48,19; 55,7; 61,23; 72,14; 82,6; 94,9.19; 95,23; 96,22; 97,29; manner, 14,32.35-36; 15,25; 21,23; 42,1; 51,20; 60,29; 70,20; procedure, 19,28; 20,26; mode, 50,7.26; 83,11.14; 86,11.12

tukhê, luck, 6,15; chance, 94,11.28

xunistas, composer, 26,16; 43,10

zêlôtês, admirer, 25,20; ***zêlôtês genomenos***, in emulation, 80,17

zêtein, investigate, 6,35; 9,11.13.16; 10,8; 19,1.20; 20,20.29; 21,11.14.15bis.16; 28,8; 71,15; 99,25; seek, 8,4; 36,17.19; 53,21; 54,2.12; 59,22.29; 78,5; look for, 28,7.8bis.17; 35,27; 45,13-46,7 *passim*; 48,3.6.12.18.23.27; enquire, 75,8; apply a question, 93,34; 94,1; ***zêtoumenon***, question, 7,31; ***epizêtein***, investigate, 48,12.18;

zêtêma, enquiry, 3,32; problem, 95,3

zêtêsis, investigation, 6,6; 74,31; 82,29; 95,32; question, 6,25; 93,34; 94,2.4;

zêtêtikos, inclined to investigate, 48,27

zôê, life, 4,34

zôiogonos, life-generating, 24,6; 36,11

zôion, animal, 3,5.6bis.9; 16,12.15bis.19.22bis; 17,9; 19,6; 35,3; 43,22; 53,16; 74,25; 76,11; 93,7.21.22bis.23.24; 95,10.11; 102,8; living body, 4,34

zôiophuton, zoophyte, 3,6

zôtikos, vivifying, 36,11

Index of Names

Many of the names listed here are more fully discussed in Simplicius, *On Aristotle Physics 1-8*: General Introduction to the 12 Volumes of Translations.

Adrastus, 4,11; 6,5

Alexander of Aphrodisias, named at 2,5
(on *On the Soul*); at 2.17 (on *On the Heaven*); and, on the *Physics* (on the lemma that Simplicius is currently commenting on), at 10.9.13; 11,16; 12,7.15; 13,12.21.28; 14,9.21; 17,26; 19,5.8.21.29; 22,1; 23,16; 26,13; 37,12.22; 38,2.18.25; 40,16; 41,2.23.30; 42,18.26; 43,3.8; 44,9-10.20; 45,22; 46,11; 49,20; 50,1; 51,21.27; 52,2; 53,20.22; 55,13; 58,25; 59,4; 60,18; 67,7-8.9-10; 69,2.4; 70,5.17.32; 71,5; 73,4.17.25; 76,4; 77,9; 79,7.12; 80,16; 83,19.29; 84,22; 85,2.11.20; 96,21.30; 99,12.18.29. How often Simplicius is taking something from Alexander without naming him, how far a quote from Alexander extends, and whether it is a verbatim quote or a paraphrase, are questions of interpretation, discussed in the endnotes.

Alexander on the agent *nous*, 2,4-6

Alexander (contrasted with Eudemus) on Hippocrates, 55,25-57,24; 60,18-21; 67,7-10; 68,34-69,6

Alexander (following Eudemus) on what causes are elements, 10,8-24; 13,21-27

Alexander on what causes and principles Plato posited, 26,13-15

Alexander (claiming to follow Eudemus) on Plato and the 'later ancients', 99,25-31

Alexander (claiming to follow Eudemus) on Zeno, 96,21-30; 99,12-28

duplication between a passage of Simplicius speaking in his own voice and a quote from Alexander, 13,16-21; 14,13-19

Alexander the Great, 8,20-30

Ammonius, son of Hermias (6th century CE), 59,23

Anaxagoras, 7,3-6; 8,2-3; 21,19; 22,6-7; 24,23-25; 25,1-3; 25,19-20; 26,31-28,3 (citing B11 at 27,9-10 and a small part of B12 at 27,10-11); 34,18-35,21 (citing the beginning of B1 at 34,20, citing B4 at 34,21-16 and 34,29-35,9 but with the latter part of the passage first, and citing B9 at 35,14-18); 41,1; 43,26-45,12

does Anaxagoras posit two or three levels of forms? with 34,18-35,21 *see* n. 212

harmonizing Anaxagoras with Parmenides and Empedocles, 34,18-35,21

Plato's and Aristotle's criticisms of Anaxagoras for not using *nous* in explanations, 7,3-10

Theophrastean doxography of Anaxagoras, 27,2-23

Anaximander, 6,32; 22,12; 24,13-25 (DK print 24,14-15 and 24,18-20 as B1); 24,26; 27,12.23; 36,8.14; 40,30; 41,17-19

Anaximenes, 22,12; 24,26; 27,3; 36,12-13; 40,30; 41,19-21

Antiphon, 54,13; 54,14-16; 54,20-55,24

Apollonius of Perga, 60,13-15

Archimedes, 59,30; 60,12

Aristotle, *passim*

250   *Index of Names*

Categories, 69,18-23 (citing 7, 7b31-33)
division of Aristotelian philosophy,
    1,3-3,12; sequence of treatises in
    natural philosophy (after the
    Physics and *On the Heaven*),
    2,30-3,12
On the Heaven, 2,11-30 (2,22-24 citing
    3.1, 298b6-8)
On Sophistical Refutations, 52,14-15
    (loosely citing 33, 182b32-33);
    70,20-21 (citing 1, 164b22-23);
    70,22 (citing 1, 165a3-4)
On the Soul, 1,22
Physics, passim: passages beyond 1.2
    explicitly cited: 3,23-25 (citing 3.1,
    200b21-25); 9,25-27 (citing 1.9,
    192a34-b1); 36,21-23 (citing 1.5,
    188b30-33); 36,23-24 (citing 1.5,
    188b36-37); 44,16-19 (citing 1.5,
    188a22-26); object of the *Physics*,
    3,13-4,7; structure of the *Physics*,
    6,4-30
Posterior Analytics or *Apodictics*, 15,1-2
    (citing 1.1, 71a1-2); 15,12-15
    (citing 1.1, 71a1-2); 20,29-31
    (cf. 2.1-2); 76,10-15
    (cf. 1.4 73a34-b3)
Metaphysics, 8,29-30; 12,27-28 (citing
    1.1, 980a21-22); 37,2 (citing 1.5,
    986b27-28); 48,3-6 (cf. 11.1,
    1059a23-26)
Nicomachean Ethics, 14,6-9 (cf. 10.7,
    1177b26-1178a8)
spurious correspondence with
    Alexander the Great, 8,20-30
Topics, 47,22-24 (citing 1.2, 101b3-4)

Christians, 28,32-29,3

Democritus, 22,7-8; 28,15-27; 28,28;
    35,22-28; 36,1-7; 41,1; 42,10-11;
    43,26-45,12; 82,2-3
Diogenes of Apollonia, 25,1-12

Empedocles, 21,18; 22,7; 25,19-26,4 (citing
    passages from B17 at 25,29-30 and
    26,1-4); 31,18-34,17 (citing B98 at
    32,6-10, all but the first two lines of
    B35 at 32,13-33,2, all but the first

    two and last two lines of B21 at
    33,8-17, and B26 at 33,19-34,3);
    50,12-23 (Plato's *Sophist* on
    Heraclitus and Empedocles,
    continuing further on Heraclitus)
Empedocles on intelligible and sensible
    worlds and the roles of Love and
    Strife, 31,18-34,17
Eretrians, 91,28-92,11
Euclid, named 60,28-29; 61,9-10 (*Elements*
    12.2); 61,28 (3.33); 61,33 (3.def11);
    62,2 (1.47); 62,9 (2.14); 63,7-8
    (1.13); 63,9 (1.32 and cf. 1.16);
    64,29 (3.1); 65,19 (1.5); 66,13 (3.31);
    68,13 (4.15); 69,8 (3.def6). *Elements*
    but not Euclid named, but with a
    clear reference to Euclid's *Elements*,
    55,9 (2.14); 56,13-14 (12.2);
    62,26-27 (1.9); 65,1-2 (3.3), and
    65,11-12 (4.5). At 17,1-3 Simplicius
    quotes Euclid's definition of circle
    (1.def15) without naming him. At
    55,15-16 he describes what 'the
    geometer' does 'in the third book',
    and the reference is to Euclid 3.16.
    At 62,28-30 he implicitly cites
    Euclid 1.4, at 63,4-5 he quotes 1.33
    without naming the source, at
    65,5-6 he quotes 1.15 without
    naming the source, and at 76,14-15
    he quotes a definition of 'even' close
    to (but not identical with) 7.def6.
Simplicius' plan of supplementing
    Eudemus' exposition of
    Hippocrates of Chios with
    propositions from Euclid's *Elements*
    that are being implicitly applied,
    60,27-30
Eudemus, named 7,14 (7,10-19 = fr. 31
    Wehrli); 10,3.12.23 (10,3-23 =
    fr. 32); 11,17; 22,15 (22,15-16 =
    fr. 33a); 42,13 (42,13-15 = fr. 33b, a
    second citation of the same passage
    of Eudemus); 48,6.26.28 (48,3-26 =
    fr. 34); 55,23; 60,22.27.29; 63,19;
    68,33 (54,12-55,28 and 60,18-68,33,
    with omissions, = fr. 140); 69,22;
    74,18.29 (74,18-29 = fr. 35);
    83,27.28.31 (83,24-33 = fr. 36);

Index of Names

251

85,21.23; 86,5; 97,7.9;
99,10.13.17.19.21.25.29.30
(97,7-99,18 = fr. 37a). All of these
references and citations are from
Eudemus' *Physics*, except those
from 55,23 through 69,22, which
are from his *History of Geometry*.
on Hippocrates of Chios, 60,22-68,33
on what causes are elements, 7,10-14;
10,12-24; 11,16-23
on what science knows the principles,
10,3-7; 48,3-29
on Zeno and the 'later ancients',
97,11-99,6
see also sub-entries under Alexander of
Aphrodisias

Heraclitus, 23,33-24,11; 36,9; 36,11-12;
50,9-26; 51,21-31; 77,29-33;
82,23-24
Hippasus, 23,33-24,4; 24,6-11
Hippo, 23,23-29
Hippocrates of Chios, 54,10-19; 55,25-
69,34; Alexander's reconstruction of
Hippocrates' squarings, 55,25-60,21;
Eudemus' reconstruction of
Hippocrates' squarings, 60,22-68,33

Iamblichus, 60,7-18

Leucippus, 25,3; 28,4-15; 35,22-28; 36,1-7
Lycophron, 91,13-15; 93,29-30; 97,21-25

Melissus, 22,24; 29,19-28 (citing B2 at
29,22-26); 40,9-21 (citing parts of
B7 at 40,12-15 and 40,18-21);
41,12-16 (citing B2 at 41,13-14);
41,30-42,1 (citing B2 at 41,31-
42,1); 42,31; 52,8; 52,11 (quoting
Physics 1.2, 185a32-33); 70,16-17;
71,8; 75,21-26; 76,29-77,8; 80,4-14
(citing parts of B7 at 80,7-10 and
80,11-14 – the same parts that were
cited at 50,12-15 and 40,18-21);
82,11 (quoting *Physics* 1.2,
185b17-18); 87,2-7 (citing B9 at
87,6-7)
on lists of early philosophers who
taught about higher things, 29,7

'Parmenides and Melissus', 21,29-30;
22,4.12.19; 34,13; 37,22.23.32; 38,4;
45,26.33; 46,27; 51,12.24; 70,4;
71,27; 72,27; 75,24-25; 79,12; 93,4
Menedemus, *see* Eretrians

Nicolaus of Damascus, 23,14-16; 25,8-9

Parmenides, named 22,28; 25,20; 28,5.6;
34,14.27; 36,28.31; 37,2; 38,19-
20.25.29; 39,25; 41,5; 52,9.22.25;
71,7; 77,6.34; 79,10.11.30; 82,12.18;
86,20.25-26; 87,5.13; 88,12.30.31bis;
89,21; 93,26; 99,10.14; 100,22
alleged prose text, 31,3-10
on lists of early philosophers who
taught about higher things, 7,1;
21,18; 29,6
on the principle as one and finite/
limited and unmoved,
22,24-25; 29,7-18 (citing B8.38
at 29,18)
Parmenides and Empedocles
compared, 34,8-17
'Parmenides and Melissus', 21,29-30;
22,4.12.19; 34,13; 37,22.23.32; 38,4;
45,26.33; 46,27; 51,12.24; 70,4;
71,27; 72,27; 75,24-25; 79,12;
93,4
'Parmenides' One-which-is', 88,4-33
Plato's Parmenides, sometimes
compared and contrasted with the
historical one, 29,14; 87,24-88,4;
88,30-33; Plato's refutation of
Parmenides in the *Sophist*,
88,33-90,22
positing only one being, or only one
principle (which is being in the
strict sense), 45,23-46,8
Way of Doxa, account of the sensible
world, 25,15; 30,14-31,17 (citing
B8.50-52 at 30,17-19, B8.53-59
at 30,23-31,2, and B12.2-6 at
31,13-17); 38,20-39,21 (citing
B8.50-61 at 38,30-39,9, B12.1-3
at 39,14-16, and B13 at 39,18)
Way of Truth, 29,28-30,14 (citing B8.35
at 30,1-3 and B8.29-33 at 30,6-10);
39,21-40,9 (citing B8.26-28 at

Index of Names

39,27-40,1 and B8.30-33 at 40,3-6);
41,5-9 (citing B8.50-51 at 41,8-9);
52,15-53,7 (citing B8.43, from
Plato's *Sophist*, at 52,23, and
B8.43-45, from Plato's *Sophist*, at
52,26-28); 77,21-79,12 (citing
B6.8-9 at 78,3-4, B7.2 at 78,6, B8.1-3
at 78,8-10 and B8.3-14 at 78,12-23);
79,29-80,4 (citing B8.26-28 at
79,32-80,2); 86,19-87,1 (citing
B8.25 at 86,22, B8.22 at 86,24,
B6.1-2 at 86,27-28 and B8.36-38 at
86,31-87,1); 87,12-23 (citing
B8.34-36 at 87,14-16, B8.4 at 87,21,
and B8.25 at 87,23); B.8.43-45 cited
from Plato's *Sophist* at 89,22-24
Zeno's relationship to Parmenides,
99,7-18
Peripatetics, 1,6-2,6; 3,4-12; 47,21-22;
see also Theophrastus, Eudemus,
Alexander, Themistius
Plato, 5,10-14; 6,32; 7,6-19; 12,5-9;
36,25-32; 49,7-9; 87,9-12;
88,30-89,5; 97,25-98,3; 99,25-
101,24
comparison of Plato and Aristotle,
7,19-8,15; 10,32-11,3
how many kinds of causes and
principles did Plato posit, 3,18-19;
7,6-19; 26,5-25; 43,3-23
how Plato surpassed earlier
philosophers, 7,10-19
Parmenides, 29,12-14 (first
Hypothesis); 87,24-88,4 (142D9-
143A3); 88,30-33 (cf. 141E10-
142A1); 99,7-10 (128A4-E4);
100,26-101,10 (129C4-E4);
101,18-21 (cf. 129B6-C1); 101,22-
24 (cf. 129B5-6)
Phaedo, 7,3-6 (98B7-C2)
Phaedrus, 75,3-5 (237B7-C2)
Philebus, 99,32-100,1 (14D4-16A3,
cf. 53E5)
Plato on easy and hard one-many
problems, 99,25-101,24
Republic, 12,8-9 (cf. *Republic* 6,
510B4-511B2, *Republic* 7, 533B6-
5); 12,29-13,1 (*Republic* 7,
533C3-5); 13,1-3 (*Republic* 5,

476D8-9); 13,3-5 (*Republic* 5,
479D7-8)
Sophist, 50,12-23 (242D7-243A1);
52,21-53,5 (244E2-245A6);
88,33-90,22 (244B6-245E5);
100,1-15 (251A8-C6); 101,12-14
(253C6-E5); 101,16-22
Timaeus, 7,6-10; 18,29-30 (29B2-D3);
26,16-18 (29D7-E2); 26,19-25
(51E6-52B5); 31,23-28 (39E3-
40A2, cf. 51B7-C1); 35,24-36,1;
43,9-10 (29D7-E1); 43,15-19
(52A1-6); 43,19-20 (53B4-5);
43,21-23 (39E7-9); 79,1-4 (37E4-
38A2)
Theaetetus, 13,10-12 (187B2-5);
18,11-14 (*see* n. 99)
Plotinus, 14,4-5 (cf. *Enneads* 1.3.3,5-7)
Plutarch of Chaironeia (1st–2nd century
CE), 8,29-30 (*Life of Alexander* 7)
Porphyry, named 9,11 (9,10-27 = F119
Smith); 10,25, 11,6.23 (10,25-11,17
and 11,23-19 = F120); 44,1
(43,26-44,10 = F121); 70,12
(70,5-19 = F122); 73,2, 74,5-6
(71,19-73,4 and 74,5-18 =
F123); 80,24 (80,23-30 = F124);
82,31; 83,10 (83,6-19 = F125);
85,9 (85,2-11 = F126); 86,10
(86,7-11 = F127); 92,26; 95,33;
97,5 (92,26-96,4 and 96,15-20
and 97,4-8 = F129); 101,25
(101,25-102,3 = F130)
close relation (but not duplication)
between a passage of Simplicius in
his own voice and a passage cited
from Porphyry, 3,16-19; 10,32-35
long extract from Porphyry on why we
must distinguish senses of being
(185b25-186a3), 92,25-95,30, with
Simplicius' comments 95,31-96,14;
97,4-8
Porphyry on the aporia of whole and
part, and on non-continuous parts
(185b11-16), 83,6-19; 85,2-11;
85,34-86,18
Porphyry on a higher science knowing
the principles of a lower science,
9,10-22

Index of Names 253

Porphyry on the 'metaphysics of prepositions' and which kinds of causes Plato and Aristotle posited, 10,25-11,15; 11,23-29

Porphyry vs. Alexander on how to construe a passage about Democritus (184b20-22), 43,27-45,12; on how to construe a passage about the Eleatics (185a17-20), 70,3-32; on how Aristotle's division of senses of being connects with his division of senses of unity (185a20-b5), 73,2-74,18; 80, 20-30

Proclus, never explicitly cited but see discussion of parallels in the notes

Proclus' distinction between intelligible (*noêton*) and intellectual (*noeron*), n. 212, n. 610

Proclus' interpretation of the *Parmenides*, n. 618

Proclus' interpretation of the *Sophist*, n. 610

Proclus on levels within the One-which-is, n. 546

Proclus on matter and (immanent) form as 'auxiliary causes', n. 12, n. 61, n. 63

Proclus on natures as moved movers, n. 35

Proclus on three kinds of universals, n. 92

Proclus on the triangles of *Timaeus* as having depth, n. 221

Simplicius defends Aristotle's physics against Proclus, n. 36

Simplicius, *passim*

Commentary on Aristotle's *On the Heaven*, parallel passages cited in n. 8, n. 73, n. 75, n. 132, n. 134, n. 183, n. 184, n. 186, n. 202, n. 211, n. 212, n. 213, n. 214, n. 218, n. 221, n. 227, n. 232, n. 244, n. 245, n. 270, n. 417, n. 419, n. 428, n. 489, n. 542, n. 545

Commentary on Aristotle's *Physics*, *passim*

Stoics, 25,16-18; 94,13-14

Thales, 6,31-7,1; 23,21-33; 24,14; 36,8-11; 40,30

Themistius, 42,11-13 (*In Physica paraphrasis* 2,29-30); 43,28-44,1 (2,30-3,2); 70,31-32 (4,15-17)

Theophrastus, named 9,7 (9,5-10 = FHS&G fr. 144B); 18,34 (18,29-34 = fr. 142); 20,19 (20,17-26 = fr. 143); 21,10 (for 21,8-10 cf. fr. 144b); 22,28-29 (22,22-23,20 = fr. 224); 23,31 (23,21-24,12 = fr. 225); 24,13, 25,6 (24,13-25,13 = fr. 226A); 26,7 (26,5-15 = fr. 230); 27,11 (26,31-27,28 = fr. 228a); FHS&G also print 28,4-31 (where Theophrastus is not named, but which is likely to be from him) as fr. 229. All of these are from the *History of Physics* except the references to 143 and 144B, which are from the *Physics*, and fr. 142, which is also plausibly from the *Physics*. There is also a reference to Theophrastus' *On Metals* (or *On Minerals* or *On Mines*), without Theophrastus' name, 3,4-5 (*see* n. 10), compare fr. 197A–C.

Theophrastus' added syllogism on why natural things have principles, 9,7-10; 21,8-10

Theophrastus on Anaxagoras' material principle, 27,11-23

Theophrastus' doxographical division, 22,20-28,31; its inadequacy, 28,32-29,5

Theophrastus on how to grasp the principles of natural things, 20,17-27

Theophrastus on Plato, Theophrastus vs. Alexander on how many principles Plato posited, 26,7-15

Theophrastus and the Pseudo-Aristotle *On Melissus, Xenophanes, Gorgias* on Xenophanes, 22,26-23,14 (*see* nn. 128-129)

works of Theophrastus considered alongside works of Aristotle in the division of Peripatetic natural philosophy, 3,1-10 (*see* n. 10)

254   *Index of Names*

Timaeus of Locri (fictional author),
7,6-10; 7,25-27; 31,24-28;
35,22-36,1

Xenophanes, extended discussion
22,26-23,20 (citing B26 at 23,11-12
and B25 at 23,20); shorter summary
29,5-14
on lists of early philosophers who
taught about higher things or who
said that the principle was one, 7,1;
21,18; 29,6-7; 'Parmenides and
Xenophanes' 28,5-6; 36,28

Zeno of Elea (5th century BCE)
did Zeno argue only against the many,
or also against the one? 99,7-18
Eudemus on Lycophron's, Plato's, and
the correct (Aristotelian) answers
to Zeno's arguments, 97,21-99,6
(Zeno named 99,2)
Eudemus on Zeno, 97,11-21
mentioned by Alexander in the
context of the 'later ancients', 96,24
Zeno as a character in Plato's
Parmenides, in a quote from Plato,
101,10

Index of Subjects

Many of the subjects listed here are more fully discussed in Simplicius, *On Aristotle Physics 1-8*: General Introduction to the 12 Volumes of Translations.

aporiai, difficulties, problems, solutions, 46,11-13; 48,3-7; 48,26-29; 52,8-15; 71,19-26; 74,29-75,6; *see also* one-many problems, and, under 'whole and parts', aporia of whole and parts
are the Eleatics stating 'natural aporiai'? 70,3-71,16
Posterior Analytics II on the four kinds of scientific problems, 20,29-31; 21,10-13
the problem of squaring the circle, 60,7-18
atoms, indivisibles (Democritean and Timaean); 7,21-22; 22,7-8; 28,4-31; 35,22-36,7; 42,10-11; 43,27-45,12; 81,34-82,8; 85,23-24; 94,15-16; *see also* one as indivisible

categories (substance, quantity, quality, etc.), 20,5-9; 49,28-30; 72,4-73,2; 73,18-74,5; 74,18-29; 75,6-77,8; 80,25-27; 91,4-92,14; 95,19-97,29; 99,20-31; 101,25-102,15
causes, *see* principles and causes
circle-squaring, 54,12-69,34
Antiphon's, 54,12-16; 54,20-55,24
Hippocrates', 54,12-14; 54,16-19; 55,25-69,34
continuity, 3,30-4,2; 6,19-21; 73,3-13; 78,14-15; 80,19 (citing lemma 185b5-25); 81,10-82,8; 83,6-7; 83,25-26; 86,19-22; 87,18-23; 88,14-16; 88,27-29; 90,24-26; 92,1-15; 96,15-19; continuous and non-continuous parts, 83,9-14; 84,15-86,18

Demiurge, Maker, composer, 5,18; 7,17-19; 15,8; 26,16-18; 43,9-10; 88,8-11 with n. 545

elements, distinguished as those principles which are constituents of their effects, are the lowest or proximate causes, and are auxiliary causes rather than causes in the strict sense, 7,6-19; 10,7-12,5; 13,28-33; 14,18-28; Eudemus and Alexander say that only matter is an element, 10,8-24; Simplicius argues that both matter and form are elements, 11,16-23
epistasis, ephistanai, observations, remarks, objections, calling attention
see the Editors' Preface, p. 13, for the role of *epistaseis* in Simplicius' comments on each lemma,
at 12,15 Alexander remarks something, and at 43,8 Alexander fails to observe something
in the other passages, Simplicius remarks/observes or encourages his readers to remark/observe: a pair of remarks 13,28 and 14,1; a series of three observations 17,33 and 17,38 and 18,24; a remark 19,25; an observation, 21,5-6; an observation 22,9; a programme of remarks, 37,7; it is worth remarking, 59,5 and 59,18; a series of seven observations 74,29-77,8, although the word 'observe' is used only at 74,30; a command to observe, 82,25; citing from Eudemus, in order to observe more fully the things he says, 97,10; it is worth remarking, 102,3

256 *Index of Subjects*

fifth substance (of the heavens), 2,11-14

generation, coming-to-be, perishing,
2,27-3,12; 4,32-5,6; 7,12-13;
22,33-23,4; 24,6-8; 30,20-22;
36,8-14; 38,20-24; 78,24-29
genus,
being is not a genus, 94,5-13
the categories as genera, 72,15-26;
75,18-29; 76,7-10; 96,4-7
Democritus on the atoms as a single
genus, 43,27-45,12
genera and species as second in
comparison to individual substance,
102,6-12
knowing (*eidenai*) as the genus of
scientifically knowing (*epistasthai*),
12,14-25
one in genus or species, generically or
specifically one, 72,9-11; 73,9-
74,11; 80,28-81,6; 93,5-12; 95,
19-23
God, gods, divine things, 5,10-20; 7,17-19;
8,2-3; 14,5-9; 22,30-33; 23,14-16;
25,16-18; 26,7-13; 29,1-3;
31,14-17; 33,17; 34,14-16;
39,16-20; 43,4-6; 88,22-23; *see also*
Demiurge, *nous*

harmonization of earlier philosophers,
28,32-37,9
heavens, heavenly bodies, 2,11-30;
24,16-18; 41,16-19; 53,16-20

infinity, 3,32-4,2; 5,1-3; 6,19-21; 11,13-15;
19,21-22; 21,29-22,20; 22,23-24;
22,26-29; 23,4-6; 23,14-19; 24,8-9;
24,13-18; 24,26-28; 25,4; 25,14-15;
26,31-27,28; 28,7-11; 28,22-27;
29,5-30,14; 34,18-27; 41,10-43,3;
44,2-6 (and 44,23-25 and 45,3-5);
52,8-20; 70,32-71,4; 72,27-73,2;
74,27-29; 75,21-29; 76,7-77,8;
81,16-21; 82,3-6; 82,11-15; 87,2-7;
87,19-23; 88,3-4; 88,20-22; 90,24-25;
95,26-30; 97,19-21; infinite regress,
13,18-19; 14,16-17; 48,20; 49,11;
divisibility ad infinitum, 55,19-24;
69,24-28

knowledge
confused and scientific knowledge,
16,8-18,23
different kinds of knowledge and
different terms for knowledge,
12,14-13,21; 14,9-28
knowledge of principles and of things
derived from the principles,
15,4-16,8; 18,24-34; *see also*
principles as fundamental
propositions of a science

lunes, *see* circle-squaring, Hippocrates'

mathematics, 1,21-2,2; 12,29-13,1;
13,21-14,9; 48,10-17
mêpote, 'perhaps', 11,29; 12,28; 14,18; 19,12;
20,3; 21,6; 21,8; 34,8; 41,30; 42,1;
45,1.23; 46,16; 49,23; 60,17; 69,23;
77,3; 84,29
metaphysics, first philosophy, theology;
1,17-21; 4,20-22; 8,29-30; 9,19-27;
12,10-13; 20,29-21,7; 26,7-10;
47,30-31; 48,26-29,16; 'metaphysics
of prepositions', 10,25-11,15 with
n. 57; *see also* Aristotle, *Metaphysics*
motion, 3,25-31; 6,16-30; 20,9-11;
20,17-26; 40,23-28; 53,10-21;
79,12-29
Anaximander on motion and its
causes, 24,21-25; Empedocles,
25,21-26; Democritus, 28,4-23
division of principles as moved or
unmoved, 21,22-25,13; 41,27-30;
42,7-26
Parmenides and Melissus against
motion, 39,20-40,21; 79,29-80,14
self-moved and unmoved movers,
5,10-16; 8,1-9; 11,16-21;
15,15-25

nature, natural things, natural science;
better known by nature
noera diakrisis (intellectual differentiation)
vs. *noêtê henôsis* (intelligible
unification or union), 34,18-35,21
with n. 212; *see also* 100,23-16 and
101,10-24 without mention of the
noêton; *see also* 31,18-34,17 and

Index of Subjects

88,4-29 without mention of the *noeron*, but it's implied at 34,8-17

nous (Reason, intelligence, intellect)
actual and potential intellect in the Peripatetic division of philosophy, 1,6-21; the actual as well as the potential intellect is part of the soul, against Alexander, 2,2-6
nous as intellectual intuition contrasted with demonstrative science in the *Posterior Analytics*, 15,12-15
Reason as the first efficient cause in Anaxagoras, Plato and Aristotle, 7,3-8,9; in Xenophanes, 23,19-20; in Anaxagoras, 27,15-23; in Plato, 43,3-23; in Aristotle (with background in Parmenides and Plato), 87,7-18 and 88,5-11
numerically one, one in number, 72,2-15; 73,9-15; 73,30-33; 80,30-81,10; 95,19-23

one as indivisible, 73,11-13; 81,6-10; 81,34-82,19; 83,14-19; 84,1-2; 85,23-24; 86,19-87,18; 90,24-91,1; 95,5-6, *see also* atoms; one as continuous, *see* continuous; one as whole, *see* whole and parts; one in number, *see* numerically one; one in genus or species, *see* genus
One beyond being, 88,30-89,4; 100,22-23
One-which-is, 34,26-27; 38,11-13 with n. 231; 77,7-8; 86,19-88,22 with n. 546
one-many problems, 90,24-102,15; Plato on easy one-many problems, 99,25-101,6; Plato on hard one-many problems, 101,6-24

'perhaps', *see mêpote*
place, 3,28-47; 6,21-25; 39,22-25; 81,25.29
Platonic Forms; *see also* (under 'cause') paradigm, paradigmatic cause
potentiality and actuality as senses of being, 98,3-99,6
a continuous whole is one in actuality and many in potentiality, 81,10-

82,8; 92,1-25; 93,17-20; 96,15-19; 97,1-4
potential and actual intellect, *see* under *nous*
principles and causes, Simplicius (following Proclus) distinguishes six kinds, the efficient, paradigmatic (= separate formal), final, material, formal (= immanent formal) and instrumental, of which the first three are properly causes and the last three are 'auxiliary causes' (*sunaitia*); matter and form are also called 'elements', *see* 'element'
Aristotle posits four causes, Plato adds the paradigmatic (and instrumental), 3,19-20; 10,32-35; cf. 7,10-19
Aristotle seeks both higher and lower causes, 8,4-9
causes vs. auxiliary causes, both are principles, 3,16-20; 6,10-14; 11,29-12,4; 26,5-7; 36,18-19
paradigmatic and formal causes, Plato recognizes both, 26,18-25
what kinds of things have material and final causes? 13,25-14,9
principles as fundamental propositions of a science,
how do we establish them? 15,4-20,27; 47,4-19; 49,16-51,21
does it belong to a higher science to establish them? 15,29-16,2; 47,19-49,16

simple bodies (earth, water, air, fire, aether), simple things, 2,11-30; 4,35-5,1; 16,8-17; 16,25-30; 17,21-25; 26,31-33; 35,22-36,1; 53,16-17; 93,5-6
skopos, object, aim; object of the *Physics*, 1,3-5; 3,13-4,7; 8,32-34; object of *On the Heaven*, 2,11-30; object of dialectic, 47,25-26; object of Aristotle's discussion of parts and wholes, 83,28-29
soul, 1,5-14; 1,21-2,6; 3,3-6; 4,17-5,16; 14,5-9; 15,15-25; 34,29-35,4;

258   *Index of Subjects*

39,16-20; 53,16-20; 70,23-25;
102,6-15
species, *see* genus

theôria and *lexis, see* n. 115
time, 3,28-4,2; 4,32-5,3; 6,25-26; 24,4-6;
24,19-21; 78,29-79,4; 81,23-31

universals, 1,22-2,2; 3,23-25; 10,23-24;
16,17-20,2 with n. 92; 37,15-20;
53,25-26; 75,30-76,7

void, emptiness, 3,32-4,7; 6,23-25;
21,10-12, 70,32-36; the atomists
posit the void, 22,7-8; 28,11-17;
28,27-29; 44,16-17; Melissus' denial
of void and therefore of motion,
40,9-21; 80,4-14

wholes and parts, one as whole,
aporia of whole and parts, 83,6-86,18;
87,18-88,4; 90,24-26; 92,1-25;
93,17-20; 94,18-23; 96,15-97,4;
101,25-102,15
do we start by knowing the whole
or by knowing the parts? 16,7-
17,13; 17,33-18,23; 19,12-17;
37,15-20
our bodies as parts of the cosmic
whole, 4,32-5,1
Parmenides on being as a whole
(in texts by Parmenides himself
and by Plato), 29,28-30,13;
52,21-53,5; 78,11-15; 86,19-87,1;
89,19-90,17
'whole' as Proclus' second intelligible
triad, 88,11-17 with n. 546

Printed in the USA
CPSIA information can be obtained
at www.ICGtesting.com
LVHW021623300324
775854LV00001BA/131